PBY
The Catalina Flying Boat

PBY
The Catalina Flying Boat

BY ROSCOE CREED

Naval Institute Press
Annapolis, Maryland

Library of Congress Cataloging-in-Publication Data
Creed, Roscoe.
  PBY: the Catalina flying boat.
  Bibliography: p.
  Includes index.
  1. Catalina (Seaplane)   I. Title.
UG1242.R4C74   1986   358.4'183   85-21540
ISBN 0-87021-526-4

Printed in the United States of America

To the men who conceived and designed the PBYs;
to the men and women who built them;
to the men who flew them, fought on them, died on them;
to the men who kept them flying;
to the men who still fly PBYs
and to those who still keep them flying;
this book is dedicated.

Contents

Foreword

Back in 1941 following "the day that will live in infamy," there were those who said she was too old, too slow, and too vulnerable to last even a few weeks against the modern weapons she would soon face. How wrong they were! In this book, so well written and so thoroughly researched, Roscoe Creed tells the fascinating story of the PBY Catalina, which those of us who flew her in war and peace knew as "The Cat." This tough, ubiquitous aircraft, with unlimited versatility, proved she was readily adaptable to a variety of missions afloat or ashore, whether in the heat of the tropics or in the ice of the Arctic Circle. A unique and extremely interesting feature of this book is the skillful way in which the author weaves the development and technical growth of "The Cat" into the ever-changing combat requirements.

In reality this book is two books in one. It tells of the problems encountered in building, producing, and continually improving a large flying boat. At the same time, it describes in detail a multitude of combat, rescue, and special missions which "The Cat" performed so well in all oceans of the world. In fact, anyone who reads this book, particularly those of us who spent thousands of hours as pilots and crew members, is in for a nostalgic experience. To me, men and events, which in some cases had faded from memory, zoomed into sharp focus as friend and foe alike came to life as if it were only yesterday. And overlaying all of this, I found an accurate chronology of the intent and operation of the Japanese and German forces, as well as those of the Allies, as both sides tried to achieve unconditional surrender. This background lends purpose and rationale to the missions of "The Cat" and highlights the great contribution she made to victory in World War II.

My own experience with the PBY began with my assignment to VP-22 based on Ford Island in Pearl Harbor. It was quite an experience to shift from fighters aboard the *Enterprise* to a very large seaplane with a hundred-foot wing span. But I found the aircraft very easy to fly and also very tough. It had to be to withstand the damage from the block-buster landings I made at the outset. At that time our primary mission was long-range search and patrol, although we spent hours training in horizontal bombing using the Norden bombsight which was tied in with the automatic pilot. After the war started, however, experience quickly proved that high-altitude bombing was out of the question, so low-alti-tude bombing attacks were rapidly developed, primarily for night op-erations. The training of the PBY squadrons in Hawaii also included Advanced Base Operations. We anchored in the atolls of Canton, Pal-myra, Johnston, French Frigate Shoals, Midway, and Wake Islands and received support from a small tender converted from a "Bird Class" oceangoing tug. This advanced base experience proved invaluable once the war began, as Roscoe Creed describes so well.

One experience that impressed me very much occurred just a few months before Pearl Harbor. As the war clouds gathered, two of the PBY squadrons from Pearl Harbor were sent to the Philippines to form Patrol Wing Ten. Some months later B-17s were also ordered to the Philippines. Because Congress had refused funds to fortify Wake and Guam, the B-17s were forced to make the long flight through Australia. An advance team from the Army Air Corps was needed in Australia to arrange for communications as well as for large quantities of the very rare 100-octane gasoline. The question was: How can we get two lieu-tenant colonels of the Army Air Corps to Rabaul and Australia in a timely manner? Once again the versatile PBY provided the solution, and I was fortunate enough to be selected as one of the two plane com-manders to make the flight.

I loaded aboard six hundred pounds of assorted canned goods, a large number of spare parts, including one each of starters, generators, air speed meters, and so forth, plus a couple of colonels. We departed Pearl Harbor and navigating only by the sun, moon, and stars proceeded via Canton Island, Fiji Islands, Noumea, Rabaul, Port Moresby, Darwin, Townesville, and return. We maintained complete radio silence; we de-voured most of my canned goods; my crew did all of the maintenance necessary; and we returned to Pearl Harbor without incident. Shortly thereafter the B-17s arrived in the Philippines. Little did I realize that I would be retracing my steps to Australia around Christmas time.

No sooner had I returned to Pearl Harbor when my squadron, VP-22, was ordered to Midway Island to conduct long-range patrols. At that time we all became convinced that war would be upon us any minute. The question was where it would start, not whether it would start.

While at Midway, I escorted the marine fighters from the *Enterprise* to Wake Island. About the same time Kurusu, the special Japanese envoy to Washington spent the night in Midway having arrived via Pan American Clipper. We paraded as many marines as possible in full view to show him that a battle at Midway could cause the Japanese problems. On Thursday, 4 December 1941, we received an order from Wing Headquarters that I consider a classic. The message said: "Be prepared to take six or twelve planes either east or west." At least one staff officer in Hawaii understood the versatility of the PBY!

The order we finally received was to return to Pearl Harbor. We arrived later Friday, 5 December. The war began Sunday morning.

On the morning of 7 December I was at home immediately adjacent to Pearl Harbor. I heard many aircraft go overhead and also heard: "This is no drill!!!" I proceeded to the naval base, jumped in the first available boat and made it to what was left of my squadron. I arrived in the middle of the first attack, which had begun at about 7:50. The second attack, directed primarily at the battleships, followed at 8:30.

I found VP-22 in shambles: several aircraft were on fire, and all aircraft had been hit by machine guns. Men were firing at the Japanese with the guns they had removed from the aircraft—in many cases holding them until the heat of the barrel burned the flesh from their hands. They did succeed in shooting down one plane, and when it was examined we found a Japanese commander, now dead, in the rear seat with his uniform over civilian clothes. Apparently he thought that if he were forced to bail out, he could find refuge in the Japanese community.

During the day we managed to repair two aircraft suitable for flight. My orders were to take off and head for Kwajalein, fly all night well past the position the Japanese carriers could reach, and then reverse course and head for Pearl Harbor. Since we had no radar at that time, we had to rely entirely on eyesight for detection. Inasmuch as the Japanese were north rather than southwest, my mission was not productive.

A few weeks later President Roosevelt announced that reinforcements were being sent to the Philippines. These reinforcements included VP-22, now equipped with new aircraft flown from the East Coast of the United States. Since the Japanese had captured Wake Island, once again we found it necessary in VP-22 to head for Australia.

Upon arrival it was clear that the Japanese had taken control of the Philippines and consequently we were ordered to conduct patrols throughout the Dutch East Indies. In addition, I personally rescued many civilians stranded on outlying islands and returned them to Java or Australia. It was on 19 February that I took off from Darwin in search of the Japanese aircraft carriers reported in the vicinity of Ambon. The weather was hazy and visibility was not good. At about 9 o'clock I was attacked by a large number of Zero fighters, and it was at that time that my respect for "The Cat" reached its peak. The Japanese 20 millimeter explosive projectiles started large fires throughout the aircraft, which spread rapidly since we had no leakproof fuel tanks. In addition, all of the fabric on the trailing edge of the wings and most of the fabric on the ailerons and tail was consumed by fire. Nevertheless, the aircraft responded to the controls to a sufficient degree to permit a very hazardous downwind landing. My crew and I subsequently got clear of the aircraft, which soon exploded and sank.

A short time afterwards we were picked up by a Philippine ship, the *Florence D*. She was loaded, I soon learned, with ammunition and attempting to make it to Corregidor. I was certain the ship would be attacked, and I ordered my crew to take a position as far aft as possible and be prepared to jump over the side in the event of an attack. This dive bomber attack came in the afternoon, blowing the bow of the ship amid many explosions. We had jumped overboard as the aircraft released their bombs and all but one member of the crew, who had gone forward and was never seen again, escaped serious injury. After the Japanese finally withdrew, we managed to reboard the ship, release the lifeboats, and rescue all survivors. I then rigged sail and using the Southern Cross as a reference point headed for Australia, many miles away. We finally beached the lifeboats on Bathurst Island, northwest of Australia and wrote very large letters in the sand asking for water and medicine. An Australian aircraft dropped a note stating that it would be back with water and medicine. True to its word, it returned, dropping another note saying that an Australian corvette would pick all of us up at daylight the next morning. We boarded the ship and, although we were attacked enroute to Darwin, we arrived safely to find the town completely abandoned. We set up shop in the one hotel and were finally picked up and flown to our squadron headquarters in Perth, Australia.

Not enough can be said about the PBY and the great variety of operations in which this aircraft participated and the innovations introduced by the courageous crews in all kinds of situations. Fifty-five-gallon fuel drums were fitted with fuses and used as napalm fire bombs on the Japanese fleet; rods were attached to bomb fuses to produce "daisy cutters"; one-hundred-pound bombs were tossed out of the tunnel hatch; aircraft were painted black; radars were finally installed; PBY-5A was produced, making an aircraft that could land on sea or airstrips; in the Atlantic the PBY hounded the German submarines to the end, finally being most effective in closing the Gibraltar Straits.

As antisubmarine warfare officer of Airforce Atlantic Fleet, I saw the PBY equipped with searchlights, magnetic detectors, sonar buoys, and homing torpedoes. There was no end to the versatility of this great flying machine. "The Cat" will be long remembered by those who developed and manufactured her, and by the German and Japanese enemy who had to oppose her. Certainly no military units have been manned by more skillful, more courageous, and more determined men than those who maintained her, flew her, and fought on to victory.

My experience constitutes only a minuscule part of the PBY saga told in such full and accurate detail by Roscoe Creed. No aircraft in all of history has been utilized in so many places and in so many configurations or has flown on so many unusual missions. After serving us well for over half a century, "The Cat" has become a legend, but she is still a working airplane. Today she is busy fighting forest fires from the air.

THOMAS H. MOORER
Admiral, U.S. Navy (Ret.)

Acknowledgments

Many people contributed their time, writings, photos, names of personal contacts, letters, clippings, articles—any and all forms of data relating to the PBY—and because of it have made this book a far better one than it would have been. For the most part I will make no attempt to say whose contributions were the greatest. Some provided a greater volume than others, but in other instances the mere supplying of a single name had a great impact on the overall outcome of the book. This sort of help came not only from people in the United States, but from Great Britain, Canada, Australia, New Zealand, and the Netherlands. It came from authors, historians, former military and naval pilots and crewmen, former commercial pilots, former Consolidated employees, fixed base operators, and PBY enthusiasts from a variety of callings. All contributions, great and small, are much appreciated, and I express that appreciation here and now by publishing their names.

Those whom I must single out for special recognition are persons who made continuing contributions throughout the three years that have gone into the researching and writing of this book. In the order in which I met and began working with them are: William (Bill) Barker, a wartime ordnanceman with VP-11 and amateur (in the sense that he doesn't get paid for it) historian, who loaned me data and photos from his files; Captain Richard Knott, USN, author of *Black Cat Raiders of World War II* and *The American Flying Boat*, former flying boat pilot, and head of Aviation Publications and History at the Navy Historical Center in the Washington Navy Yard, who opened his official and personal data, contact, and photo files to me; Captain William E. Scarborough, USN (Ret.), a former PBY pilot, author of numerous PBY magazine articles and a book, *PBY in Action*, and the foremost authority on the PBY, who has contributed data, contacts, photographs, consulting and counseling services, and has edited the manuscript for technical and historical accuracy. Two others have been with me for the duration; my friend Homer Shanks, oracle of military and naval history, who edited the manuscript from an overall historical standpoint as well as grammar and style; my wife, JoAnne, who edited the manuscript for grammar, punctuation, and style.

Also I must recognize those who corresponded with me over a considerable length of time to make specialized contributions on particular subjects and in particular areas: B.C. "Bruce" Reynolds, archivist at the San Diego Air and Space Museum who, along with his staff, provided me with the data, photographs, and contacts with others that made up a large part of Section One; author Dwight Messimer, who provided photographs and data on Patrol Wing 10; K.M. Molson, Canadian historian and author, who contributed data, photos, counsel, and editorial services on wartime and postwar Cansos; Jim Pengelly, former water bomber pilot who provided not only data on PBY water bombers but food and lodging as well; Andrew Hendrie, a wireless operator on Catalinas with the Royal Air Force during World War II, and an author soon to publish his own book on Catalinas with the RAF, who traded data and contacts; Author David Vincent who, when I asked for guidance to obtaining data on Catalinas with the Royal Australian Air Force, sent me his book on the subject, *Catalina Chronicle*, with his permission to use what I needed, plus photographs and additional data; Nico Geldhof, historian and authority on the Royal Netherlands Air Force, who shared his RNN wartime and postwar Catalina data; Dr. Dean C. Allard, head, Operational Archives Branch, Navy Historical Center; Dr. R.L. Scheina, historian, U.S. Coast Guard; Lloyd Cornett, Presley Bickerstaff, and Judy Endicott of the Simpson Historical Research Center, Maxwell Air Force Base, Alabama.

Beyond these are persons with whom I corresponded one or more times on particular subjects and areas within the book:
United States:
Ray Wagner, author; Richard Hobbs, acquisitions editor, Naval Institute Press; Captain Murray Hanson, USN (ret.), author; Rear Admiral Albert Scoles, USN (Ret.), former PBY pilot; Captain Carl Amme, USN (Ret.), former PBY pilot and executive officer of VP–43; Con Frieze, former ordnance man; Captain H.C. "Bennie" Smathers, USN (Ret.), former PBY pilot; R.C. Blaike, deputy director, U.S. Naval Aviation Museum; Vice Admiral Malcolm Cagle, USN (Ret.), editor, Naval Aviation Museum Foundation magazine; George Poulos, former PBY pilot; Captain Jack Coley, USN (Ret.), former PBY pilot; Anne-Marie Cousteau, Sandra Bond, and Corinne Preziotti, The Cousteau Society; Gordon Jackson,

former historian, Convair; Bob McGuire, editor, Liberator News, the Liberator Club; William Wagner, author; G. Garner Green, former chief structures engineer, Consolidated Aircraft Corporation; Ken Jackman, former physical testing engineer, Consolidated; Barrett Tillman, author; Dr. Robin Higham, editor, Aerospace Historian; Lieutenant General Leigh Wade, former Consolidated test pilot; Captain A.W. (Jake) Gorton, USN (Ret.), test pilot on the XPY–1 Admiral; William Chana, aviation consultant; Dr. William J. Armstrong, historian, Naval Air Systems Command; Dr. Norman Haber M.D., former PBY pilot; Captain Jack Reid, USN (Ret.), former PBY pilot; Louis Peterson, former PBY pilot; Commander Alan Rothenberg, USN (Ret.), former PBY pilot; Commander Jess C. Barrow, USCG (Ret.), author; L.M. Myers, former sergeant, 2nd Emergency Rescue Squadron, USAF; Dr. Robert Angel Jr., historian; V. Lee Bracken, historian; Lieutenant Colonel Robert Mills, USAF, historian.

Great Britain:
Air Commodore Alan Probert, Ministry of Defense; E. Hine, department of photographs, Imperial War Museum.

Canada:
Carl Vincent, president, Canada's Wings; Jack McNulty, photographer and historian; Major F.C. Middleveen, commanding officer, Canadian Forces Photographic Unit; Bruce Powell, managing director, The Powell Corporation; R.W. Bradford, director, National Museum of Science and Technology; W.A.B. Douglas, director of history, National Museum of Science and Technology; J.A. Griffin, historian and author; Dr. William McAndrew, director of history, Department of National Defense; Larry Milberry, aviation author and publisher, Can Av Books; J. Knox Hawkshaw, vice president, Field Aviation; Joe Reed, chief pilot, Powell Corporation.

Australia:
G. Imashev, curator, photographs, Australian War Museum; J. Heaton, Curator, Military Technology, Australian War Museum.

New Zealand:
R.S. Dearing, director, Museum of Transport and Technology; Squadron Leader J.K. Barry, director, Royal New Zealand Air Force Museum.

South Africa:
Major G.E. Visser, Office of the Chief of the South African Defense Force, Military Information Bureau.

The Netherlands:
Commander F.C. van Oosten, RNN (Ret.), historian; Lieutenant Joop Steinkamp, RNN; G.J.A. Raven, director of naval history, Ministrie van Defensie.

PBY
The Catalina Flying Boat

Introduction

Few aircraft of World War II vintage have a history as distinguished as that of the Consolidated PBY Catalina flying boat. Designed in the early 1930s to serve as the long-range patrol craft of the fleet, it also had the ability to deliver a punch. But the plane was obsolescent when World War II began; the prototype of its intended successor was already flying. Even so, the Catalina was ready at the outbreak. It could be produced more quickly and in greater numbers than any other patrol plane, and it could be used in many different ways. It became the Allies' most popular flying boat, largely because of its long range, its carrying capacity, its reliability, and its ability to land where there were no airfields, on any body of calm water. Many of those same qualities account for the fifty-year-old design continuing in civilian service today.

The big patrol bomber's versatility became apparent in the desperate early days of the war. On one hand, it was an angel of mercy. As a cargo plane, it hauled medical supplies and food; as a passenger plane, it carried evacuees; as an aerial ambulance, it ferried the sick and wounded. Finally, and most significantly, as a rescue ship the flying boat had recovered by war's end thousands of downed airmen from oceans and beaches on all fronts. The only PBY pilot ever to be presented a Medal of Honor earned it by flying three times into enemy fire to rescue a total of fifteen waterlogged army fliers from the Pacific.

On the other hand, the PBY was an angel of death, but not in the way its designers had intended. In theory, the PBY was a long-range U.S. Navy patrol plane with a high-and-low altitude bombing capability. In practice in the South Pacific, it proved too slow and too lightly armed to serve as a day bomber. So the PBYs were painted black and sent out at night, when darkness provided its own defense and when the plane's low speed gave time to observe and maneuver unseen. True to the breed, these cats could see in the dark: they were among the first American planes to be equipped with airborne radar which, although primitive by today's standards, was good enough to help them find targets and, by seaman's eye, unload their 4,000 pounds of ordnance with deadly accuracy.

So equipped, the Black Cats played a crucial part in stopping the nocturnal runs by the Japanese down "The Slot" to resupply troops on Guadalcanal in the Solomon Islands. Along with U.S. Navy submarines and surface craft, they reduced the Japanese merchant fleet from big ships to little ships to barges by the end of the war—to say nothing of the damage they inflicted on the Imperial Japanese Navy.

The Catalina's versatility went far beyond being a mercy ship and a night bomber. Early in the war, the Catalina saw service as a torpedo bomber. It performed aerial reconnaissance, with and without photo equipment. It flew spy missions, depositing and picking up agents in enemy territory. It flew electronic countermeasure missions, scouting Japanese radar locations. Armed with depth bombs, the Catalina engaged in antisubmarine warfare along the North Atlantic convoy routes. Outfitted with magnetic airborne-detection gear, it became a "MAD CAT" U-boat hunter in the Mediterranean theater. Of the fifty-five submarines sunk by U.S. Navy aircraft in all theaters during World War II, twenty were sunk by PBYs.

The PBY had its faults. Slow, prone to vibrate, and heavy on the controls, it was not the most maneuverable plane in the air. It was hot when the weather was hot, cold when the weather was cold. It was noisy.

But the plane had good points, too. Its galley provided hot food and coffee, and the Catalina had a head and bunks, all of which made long patrols more bearable. It was dependable; its Pratt and Whitney engines nearly always started, no matter whether in the steaming heat of the South Pacific or the freezing damp of the Aleutians, and they kept running until their switches were cut. It was tough; the airframe could take a beating from gunfire and heavy seas and nearly always come home, unless the odds were just too great.

All things considered, the PBY was a good airplane, one whose performance in the hands of pilots and crews of the U.S. Navy, Air Force, and the allied nations made it great.

Nearly four thousand Catalinas and Cansos were built in the United States and Canada during a ten-year period, more than all other flying boats combined. The proliferation of PBYs was such that no matter where a person went during World War II, in any theater on any ocean, there was that unmistakable shape, by whatever name or national markings.

PBYs were party to many major events during World War II. A Catalina of the British Coastal Command found the *Bismarck*, and, later, after the first plane had broken off, a second Catalina shadowed the ship until the Royal Navy could catch up. The first U.S. Navy plane to play a role in sinking a Japanese submarine was a PBY, which located the enemy vessel near Pearl Harbor and, along with surface ships, saw to its dispatch. A PBY found the Japanese fleet heading for Midway Island and sent out the message that galvanized U.S. Navy carrier planes into action, enabling them to strike a blow from which the Imperial Navy never recovered.

By late 1944 many of the Catalinas had been replaced by newer, faster patrol planes: Martin Mariner flying boats, and land-based PB4Y-1 Liberators, PB4Y-2 Privateers, and PV-1 Venturas. The navy's PBYs headed for home, paint faded and peeling, airframes bullet-holed, dented, and patched. When the war ended, some served on as standby air-sea rescue and utility planes at naval stations around the world. Others were turned over to Naval Reserve units. The U.S. Coast Guard and U.S. Air Force continued to use their Catalinas until the mid 1950s. For many of those decommissioned, retirement was short. They were snatched up, overhauled, and revamped, beginning a new life with short-haul airlines, aerial survey companies, forest-fire-fighting units, and even the armed forces of other nations.

Although the PBY was unique in appearance and features, it was not a revolutionary design. The aircraft, in fact, evolved from a long series of successful land-and-sea-based aircraft bearing the "Consolidated" name, all honestly designed to be the safest, most dependable, most serviceable aircraft in the world.

To say that the Catalina lived up to its heritage would be an understatement. Its record before, during, and after World War II causes it to be ranked among the great aircraft in the history of aviation and to be considered the greatest of the flying boats. This book tells its story.

1

From Trainers to Bombers

The Catalina was the product of Consolidated Aircraft Corporation, an organization founded by Reuben Hollis Fleet. His dream when he started the company had nothing to do with making navy flying boats, but rather with building small army training planes. Fleet's dreams would expand rapidly, along with his corporation's capabilities, and within five years flying boats would be on the drawing boards.[1]

Fleet was an ambitious, aggressive, sometimes abrasive businessman, intensely patriotic, with great foresight and innate mechanical understanding. His single high standard for men and machines was spelled out simply and unmistakably 9 feet high and 480 feet long on the wall of the Consolidated plant in San Diego: "Nothing short of right is right."

He was born in the logging and lumbering town of Montesano, Washington Territory, in 1887, where he began his business career as a boy raising and selling garden vegetables and chickens. After a four-year education in Culver (Indiana) Military Academy, he returned home to become a captain in the Washington National Guard. By the age of twenty-two, he was a success in the lumber and real estate businesses.

Two events in 1914 changed the course of Reuben Fleet's life and influenced the future of aviation: He was elected a representative to the Washington State Legislature, and he took his first plane ride. Lifting off from Seattle's Lake Washington in a Curtiss seaplane, he was tremendously impressed by that initial flight. From that day on he was an avid proponent of aviation.

Fleet often flew with a friend, Al Stromer, in Stromer's home-built seaplane based at Tacoma. To demonstrate the practicality of aviation, Fleet once had Stromer fly the payroll out to his National Guard unit while it was in the field.

Because of his military education and guard affiliation, Fleet was made chairman of the legislature's military affairs committee. His experience with aviation told him that here was a giant in its infancy, one that held great potential for military as well as civilian service, and he pressed his committee for more aviation involvement by the Washington National Guard. His committeemen said that if he could fly around the capitol for thirty minutes they would support any bill he proposed. He did, with Stromer, and the committee introduced a bill for $250,000—some $25,000 more than the appropriation recommended for military aviation by the U.S. Congress. The action of Fleet's state committee caused a reexamination of the nation's needs, and the federal appropriation was boosted to $13,000,000.

Tied to the appropriation was a provision for training one National Guard officer from each state as a flier. Fleet applied for Washington's slot and won it over the objections of the state adjutant general, who thought it too dangerous an assignment for a married man with children.

Fleet closed his businesses in March 1917 and left Montesano for the Signal Corps Aviation School on North Island in San Diego. He arrived there on 5 April; the following day the United States declared war on the Central Powers.

At age thirty, Fleet was older than the other trainees at the Signal Corps school, and he got off to a slow start. He soon caught up, however, and graduated ahead of his class. He earned Junior Military Aviator Wings number seventy-four and a promotion to major. He would be "Major Fleet" the rest of his life.

Two aspects of Fleet's training would combine to be invaluable to him in the years ahead when he became an aircraft manufacturer: learning how to fly, and learning about aircraft construction and maintenance. What most struck him at this time was how frail, unreliable, and unsafe the Curtiss Jenny and Standard trainers were. Assigned to set up flight training schools for World War I aviators, he found that training fatalities in the air service were several times those of other army branches. He also noted that about two-thirds of the seventy-three men who received their wings before him had died in air crashes.

The training school assignment gave Fleet the opportunity to observe and take part in the British method of training aviators. The standard British training plane was the Avro 504, built by A.V. Roe & Company, a biplane powered by a 110-horsepower Gnome Monsoupape rotary engine. It was an extremely reliable and rugged aircraft, with a ski-like runner under the landing gear to prevent nose-overs, and wing tip skids to prevent damage from ground loops.

The Avros were fully aerobatic, with forward-stagger wings that aided in spin recovery. The dihedral angle of the wings made for improved stability. The trainers also featured the Gosport tube, a simple device that allowed the instructor to speak directly to the student, a great improvement over a kick in the back and hand signals. A plane like the Avro seemed to be the answer to the air service's training problems. Now Major Fleet had a goal: He would be the man to build such a plane in the United States.

When the Great War ended, Major Fleet stayed in the army when others were getting out. He was told to cut his own orders, and he assigned himself to the Air Service Engineering Division at McCook Field, near Dayton, Ohio. Here, in the midst of the air service's procurement, design, and test facilities, he was sure he could produce his safe training plane.

It was not to be. The shift to peacetime status had left McCook Field in turmoil. As contracting officer, Major Fleet first straightened out the books and paid the overdue bills, then found all his time taken up with obtaining the material and services needed to design, build, and test army aircraft.

Although he added to his store of aviation-related business and mechanical knowledge, it was a frustrating period. At the end of four years he was no closer to building his safe trainer than he was at the beginning. In November 1922 Major Fleet resigned his commission.

Fleet was immediately offered executive positions with Boeing and Curtiss. He accepted neither, instead taking a third offer, this to become vice president and general manager of Gallaudet Aircraft Corporation in East Greenwich, Rhode Island, a firm well known for the engineering innovations of its founder, Edson Gallaudet, and for its experiments with all-metal aircraft.

Fleet had hoped the Gallaudet engineers could produce an outstanding training plane, but he soon found that the company was in deep financial trouble, and the aircraft designs on its drawing boards showed little promise. He began to look elsewhere.

He found the aircraft features he sought in the TA-3 and TW-3 biplanes of the Dayton Wright Company in Ohio. The two versions were the same airplane but for the engines. The TA-3 had either an 80- or 110-horsepower LeRhone air-cooled rotary engine; the TW-3 a 180-horsepower liquid-cooled Wright E model, the American version of the French Hispano-Suiza V-8 engine.

The designs featured wings with forward stagger and dihedral. Rather than wood, steel tubing was used in landing gear and wing struts and in fuselage and tail surface framing. Only the wings were of all-wood construction. For ease of maintenance, as well as for reduced costs, the upper and lower wings were interchangeable. So too were the control surfaces for the rudder and elevators. Fleet's interest undoubtedly increased when he learned that the U.S. Army had already bought two TW-3s and thirteen TA-3s.

In the spring of 1923 he acted. He leased the Gallaudet factory, contracted with Dayton Wright for the trainer designs, and incorporated a new aircraft company. After toying with several names, he settled on one that would wear well over the long run under any circumstances. It would come to rank among the best known and most respected names in military and civil aviation circles around the world during the next twenty-five years: Consolidated Aircraft Corporation.

A short time later Consolidated got its first order from the air service for twenty TW-3 trainers. The corporation was in business. A year after its founding, an improved version of the TW-3, the PT-1 Trusty, won Consolidated an army contract for fifty trainers over five competitors, among them such big names as Fokker and Vought.

The PT-1 didn't win because of its looks. Put kindly, its lines were functional. They were, in fact, almost square, from the big uncowled Hisso engine through fin and rudder. But it was square in its performance, too: rugged, thanks to the use of steel tubing; forgiving, thanks to its forward stagger wings which would enable a recovery from a spin even if the pilot did nothing; and safe. During the first year the PT-1 was in service at Brooks Field in San Antonio, Texas, 531 aviators re-

Consolidated staff members assemble in front of their first aircraft, the PT-1 Trusty. The firm's founder, Major Reuben Fleet, stands in the center, his hand on a flying wire. (Convair via San Diego Aero-Space Museum)

ceived their wings without a single serious injury or fatality. Reuben Fleet had reached his goal.

So began a long relationship. Consolidated PT-1s and later versions would be the army's standard trainers during the 1920s and 1930s.

In considering orders in hand for trainers and prospects of more to come, Fleet saw a need for increased production facilities and a larger labor force. Both were available in Buffalo, New York. Consolidated leased a plant formerly used by Curtiss for World War I aircraft production and moved there in the fall of 1924.

Next Consolidated set its sights on supplying the navy's training-plane needs. Basing its bid on the PT-1, the company won a contract for sixteen trainers, underbidding fourteen competitors. The trainers, designated NY-1, were to be powered by 200-horsepower nine-cylinder Wright J-4 air-cooled radial engines, in place of the Hisso V-8s. They were easily converted from wheels to floats. For better control on the water, the vertical fins were made larger. This, in addition to the radial engines, vastly improved the planes' appearance. The name "Husky" was applied to the NY-1 and to all succeeding radial engine versions for both branches of service, the army's version being designated PT-3.

In 1930 Consolidated delivered the last of its trainers based on the original PT-1 design, making a total of 865 planes. Although the company introduced an updated trainer model, the PT-11, the following

The NY-2A, the navy's version of the army's PT-1, had a radial engine and redesigned vertical fin and rudder. The plane could be fitted with either floats or wheels. (U.S. Navy)

year, its military-trainer phase had largely run its course. Three years earlier, encouraged by successes in contract dealings, aircraft design, volume materials buys, and assembly line production, the always-enthusiastic Reuben Fleet had begun to alter the corporation's course more toward the burgeoning markets in civil aviation and multiengine military aircraft.

Consolidated's experience in the civil aviation market seemed to indicate that the company was destined to be primarily a supplier of military aircraft. Three planes were designed expressly for civilian use. The Model 10, a five-place high-wing monoplane, featured a fuselage triangular in cross section, as well as an overhead control stick. These proved too innovative to attract buyers, however, and the design ended with the prototype. Models 14 and 17 were financially successful, each displaying a technical excellence that caught the attention of the military.

Fleet Aircraft, a Consolidated subsidiary in Fort Erie, Canada, built the Model 14, the prototype of which was built in the United States and introduced in November 1928 as the Husky Junior. The craft was marketed, however, under the name "Fleet." It was a scaled-down version of the PT-3 and NY-2 Husky military trainers, these having wingspans of 36 feet 6 inches compared with the Model 14's 28 feet. The little biplane was designed around a 110-horsepower Warner Scarab air-cooled radial engine, but later versions were equipped with a variety of engines from a half-dozen manufacturers which ranged in horsepower from 90 to 170. Fully aerobatic, the Fleet was the hit of airshows across the nation. Famed stunt pilot Paul Mantz once set a world record of forty-six consecutive outside loops in a Fleet. Such exposure made it one of the most popular sport and training planes in the world and, in various configurations, it sold in twenty-four countries. The Fleet was as rugged and dependable as its military antecedents. In fact, it had been designed to meet military standards. The army bought sixteen, designating them PT-6s. The navy versions, N2Y-1s, were equipped with skyhooks and used to test aircraft launch-and-retrieval systems aboard the airships Akron and Macon.

Consolidated's Model 17 Fleetster first flew in October 1929. Clean and sleek, it was a high-wing monoplane that could cruise with seven passengers and pilot at a respectable 150 miles per hour behind a 575-horsepower Pratt and Whitney Hornet engine. Several of the Model 17's features were firsts for Consolidated: its single wing was fully cantilevered; its air-cooled engine was shrouded in a new NACA cowling which added 15 miles per hour to its cruising speed; its fuselage was of all-metal construction, providing strength while reducing weight. In the leading edges of the wings were the first successful integral fuel tanks,

an innovation that would be a part of Consolidated's and other manufacturer's designs from that day forward.

The Model 20 was the mail plane version of the Fleetster, with a
parasol wing a foot above the fuselage, and the pilot's cockpit behind
the passenger compartment.

Consolidated built almost two dozen of Models 17 and 20, which were
bought mostly by airlines for short-haul and airmail work. Three Model
17s were bought by the army for fast command transports.

The navy, however, saw another possibility in the Fleetster. Consolidated's Model 18—the navy's XBY-1—was an experimental carrier-based
bomber. Built in 1932, it was basically a Model 17 with bomb bay doors
and with all-metal wings, the navy's first with stressed skin construction.
(The civilian version featured a wood-framed wing covered with ply-
wood.) For whatever reason, the project was abandoned and only the
prototype Model 18 was built.

When Reuben Fleet decided to take Consolidated into the multiengine
area in 1927, he did it with the same all-out effort and planning that
went into all his activities. He first set up a heavy aircraft division and
then placed a carefully selected man in charge—Isaac Machlin Laddon,
who had headed the army's heavy aircraft design team at McCook Field.

Mac Laddon had joined the Army Air Service Engineering Division
when it was housed in the Smithsonian Institution in Washington, coming there from a job as experimental engineer with the Cadillac Motor
Car Company. He remained with the division when it moved to McCook,
where he designed, among other aircraft, the first all-metal plane in the

The XBY-1 was the navy version of Consolidated's Fleetster. Built in 1928, it
featured all-metal construction, an internal bomb bay, and integral leading-edge
fuel tanks. (U.S. Navy)

United States. The prototype would be built by the Gallaudet Aircraft Corporation as the army's CO-1 observation plane.

Laddon and Fleet met at McCook Field, and they developed a mutual respect for each other's capabilities. Although sparks sometimes flew between the two, the chemistry between Laddon's cool head and Fleet's enthusiastic nature produced great airplanes. Together they led Consolidated to a position of dominance in flying boats in the 1930s and put the company in a position to be a major supplier of multiengine aircraft in World War II.

Consolidated's first attempt to enter the multiengine military market was a cooperative one: Consolidated's production facilities and a Sikorsky design.

When the army announced a design competition for a heavy night bomber in early 1927, Fleet set Laddon and his heavy aircraft engineers to work on the Model 11. Shortly afterward Fleet was approached by Igor Sikorsky who, up to that point, had been a competitor. Sikorsky had been designing successful multiengine aircraft since 1912 and had fled his native Russia during the 1917 revolution. He explained to Fleet that his company, housed in an old hanger at Roosevelt Field on Long Island, New York, could build only the prototype of the design he proposed. If his firm and Fleet's could team up and win the competition, he would turn over future production orders for the plane to Consolidated. The two reached an agreement whereby Sikorsky would design and produce the prototype; Consolidated would furnish engines and instruments and would be responsible for armament installations and stress analysis.

Sikorsky's proposed bomber was a refinement of his S-37, which in turn was a refinement of his S-35. Both planes were built in attempts to win the $25,000 prize offered in 1919 by New York hotel owner Raymond Orteig to the first aviator to fly nonstop between New York and Paris. In the rush to be first, the S-35, a tri-motored sesquiplane, was not tested with a full load of fuel and under the overload it crashed and burned while taking off on its transatlantic try in 1926. The S-37, with two motors rather than three, had been thoroughly tested and was ready to go when Charles Lindbergh and his *Spirit of St. Louis* flight ended the competition. The S-37 saw out its days as an airliner in Argentina.[2]

The military version of the S-37 was the Consolidated–Sikorsky Model 11 Guardian, military designation XP-496. It was a boxey, open cockpit sesquiplane with a 100-foot-plus wingspan. Its most outstanding features were elongated nacelles behind twin Pratt and Whitney 525-horsepower Hornet air-cooled radial engines. These nacelles contained the fuel tanks.

Showing extreme faith in their product, Sikorsky, six of his men, and

Consolidated's first venture into multiengine aircraft: the XP-496 Guardian. A cooperative venture between Consolidated and Sikorsky, the plane was too slow to garner a military contract. (National Archives)

Laddon climbed aboard the Guardian for its first flight. At the controls was Leigh Wade, who had flown one of the Douglas World Cruisers on the army's round-the-world flight in 1924 and was now Consolidated's test pilot. After a stop to reverse the rudder cables—Sikorsky's mechanics had hooked them up Russian style so when left rudder was pushed the plane turned right and vice versa—the Guardian took off. According to Laddon, the flight was successful, but the plane was extremely slow.

Lack of speed was only the beginning of the Guardian's problems. Others showed up in stress analysis. The Guardian was the first plane to use large aluminum tubes as structural members. Consolidated engineers found that some were twice as strong as necessary, while others were only half as strong as army specifications called for.

With little hope of receiving a contract, Wade and Reuben Fleet flew the Guardian to Washington for the army's assessment. It finished third of four competing designs, the contract going to Curtiss with its B-2 Condor bomber.

The Guardian was one of Consolidated's few failures. The lessons learned, however, were soon put to good use.

2

The Early Flying Boats

While the army was evaluating entries in its 1927 bomber competition, the navy called for bids to design a new long-range flying boat and build a prototype. This opportunity for Consolidated and its competitors was an inadvertent result of General Billy Mitchell's campaign, begun in 1919, to combine army and navy air arms into a single U.S. Air Force. The army saw this as a fine idea; the navy did not. By 1924 Mitchell's continual attacks and proposals had made the merger a distinct possibility. The navy took the position that the nation's naval air defense could best be handled by aircraft designed for fleet use and manned by fleet-trained crews. This point needed to be made quickly and with as much public attention as possible. In April 1924, Admiral William Moffett, chief of the navy's Bureau of Aeronautics, announced a plan for the first nonstop West Coast–Hawaii flight by navy flying boats.[1]

The only flaw in the plan was that at the time the navy had no planes capable of making the flight. Fleet aircraft consisted mainly of aging F-5L and H-16 flying boats left over from World War I, supplemented by an assortment of updated look-alikes that had been added in ones and twos. Most fell one thousand to fifteen hundred miles short of the needed range.

The aircraft that came closest to being able to make the flight was the Naval Aircraft Factory's PN-9 flying boat, a typical twin-engine, open cockpit biplane. It was the latest version of the PN-7, having been fitted with new, lighter 425-horsepower Packard 1A-1500 liquid-cooled engines and reduction gearboxes for improved propeller efficiency. On 1–2 May 1925 a PN-9 set an endurance record of 28 hours, 35 minutes, 27 seconds. If this sort of fuel efficiency could be maintained, and if the usual 20-knot easterly tradewinds were blowing, then the PN-9 could fly the twenty-one hundred miles from San Francisco to Maui, the closest of the Hawaiian Islands, and arrive with something more than damp fuel tanks.

The navy had an ace in the hole, but it was still on the drawing boards: the Boeing PB-1 was being designed specifically for long-range trans-pacific flights. At the navy's urging, Boeing compressed eighteen months of production and testing into eight. The plane arrived in San Francisco in time for the flight, but it was beset by so many problems that the craft was scrubbed from the mission on the eve of takeoff.

Under the command of Commander John Rodgers, two fuel-heavy PN-9s struggled off San Francisco Bay on 31 August 1925. A hundred miles out an oil line broke on the number-two plane. It landed safely in the Pacific and was towed back to the starting point by a destroyer.

Rodger's plane droned on, but without the anticipated tailwinds and with decreasing fuel efficiency. When the engines finally chugged to a stop, the PN-9 set down intact, adrift in the Pacific four hundred fifty miles short of its goal.

A massive search was carried out, but in the wrong places because of errors in position reports from guard ships along the route. The PN-9's radio receiver kept Rodgers apprised of the situation, so he and his four-man crew rigged sails made of fabric torn from the lower wings and a leeboard from floorboards and sailed the plane backwards for nine days, living on rain water and a one-day supply of sandwiches. Finally, starving and dehydrated, in sight of the island of Kauai, they were found by a submarine and towed to harbor.

The navy's goal of publicity was achieved, even if the plane did not achieve its destination. The daily banner-headline coverage in the news-papers, followed by the heroes' welcome accorded the survivors—who had been given up for lost—focused the attention of the public, the Congress, and the president on the need for improvements in American aviation, civil as well as military.

Shortly after the flight President Calvin Coolidge appointed a board, headed by Dwight Morrow, to study U.S. aviation. The board recommended that General Mitchell's single-air-force concept not be implemented, but rather offices of Secretary of Aeronautics be established for both the army and navy. The commission saw a solid aviation industry, at first supported by military contracts, then becoming self-supporting through development of civil aviation, and eventually returning the military's investment through reduced costs.

Legislation passed by Congress in June 1926 put most of the commission's recommendations into effect, among them a five-year program to increase the navy's air strength to one thousand planes. With its new appropriations in hand, the navy moved to complete designs and issue contracts to Douglas, Martin, Keystone, and Hall Aluminum for the planes it could get the quickest—mostly updated versions of the PN-9. Although these planes used more and more metal in their construction, and although lighter air-cooled radials replaced heavy, liquid-cooled V-model engines, navy planners knew that the open cockpit biplanes they were ordering were merely variations on an old theme. A design break-through was needed. In 1927 a call went out for bids on a monoplane flying boat, all metal except for fabric-covered wings, with radial engines, a 100-foot wingspan, a 110 mile-per-hour cruising speed, and a range of 2,000 miles.

Undoubtedly other factors prompted the desire for a larger, longer-range flying boat than merely a natural tendency to improve the breed. Among military and governmental leaders was a growing belief—one which originated a few years after Japan's successful surprise naval attack on the Russian fleet in 1908—that a confrontation between the United States and Japan over control of the Pacific was inevitable.[2] If so, the longer-ranging the patrol planes, the more warning the Philippines, Hawaii, and Alaska would receive and the more time they would have to take action.

Even though Consolidated had never before bid on a flying boat, it had the advantage of the experience of its heavy-aircraft design chief, Mac Laddon. Not only had he designed large aircraft, he had designed all-metal aircraft and, while still at McCook Field, had moonlighted on the hull design of the Boeing PB-1, the flying boat that was to have accompanied the PN-9s on their flight to Hawaii two years earlier.[3]

Armed with specifications supplied by the Navy's Bureau of Aero-nautics, Laddon and a thirty-man team set to work on Consolidated's first flying boat design. It was good work. The corporation was awarded a $150,000 contract for its design and a prototype flying boat in February 1928.

The navy designation for the plane was XPY-1—"X" for experimental, "P" for patrol, "Y" for Consolidated, first rights to "C" having gone to Curtiss years before—but Reuben Fleet called it the "Admiral," in honor of his and aviation's friend, Admiral William Moffett.

The XPY-1 had the 100-foot wingspan called for in the specifications. Fourteen feet on either side of the 62-foot-long hull were pontoons supported by struts from the hull and wing. Strut-mounted between the parasol wing and the hull were twin 450-horsepower Pratt and Whitney R-1340-38 Wasp radial engines. Twin vertical fins were set atop a 21-foot horizontal stabilizer.

The plane was to have a five-man crew: a pilot and copilot in an open cockpit; a navigator-bombardier in an open hatch in the nose, a radioman in the hull, and a mechanic who doubled as gunner, firing a .30-caliber machine gun from an open hatch in the hull midway between wing and tail.

Construction of the prototype commenced in March, and Consolidated's people soon found the project fraught with "learning opportunities." Many of the problems they solved arose because of the sheer size of the plane, the largest they had worked on. More than half of the design shop floor was covered with full-scale layouts of the wing and hull. In the metal shop, workmen perfected new techniques in forming outsized pieces of aluminum alloy, in large-scale riveting, and in heat-treating metal.

Although the original specifications called for a cruising speed of only 110 miles per hour, Edward Warner, assistant secretary of the navy for air, later added a stipulation that the XPY-1 must have a top speed of 135 miles per hour before he would accept it. As a result, Laddon added mounts atop the wing center section for a third engine in case it was needed.

On a trip to inspect final assembly at Consolidated's Buffalo plant in November 1928, Warner heartened the corporation's executives by saying that if the XPY-1 performed as expected, the navy would buy thirty-two production models for use in Hawaii. Late the next month the big flying boat was ready for its first flight, but now the location of the plant became a drawback. The Niagara River and Lake Erie, valuable adjuncts to testing flying boats in summer, were frozen solid in the dead of winter. Reuben Fleet, ever impatient, wouldn't wait for the spring thaw. The XPY-1 was disassembled and shipped in three huge sections on railroad cars, by a roundabout route, avoiding low bridges and tunnels, to Washington, D.C., where it arrived the day after Christmas. From there the subassemblies were taken by barge to the Naval Air Station across the Anacostia River for reassembly.

Early on 10 January 1929 the XPY-1 was ready. Since none of Consolidated's test pilots had flying boat experience, the navy made available Lieutenant A. W. (Jake) Gorton to lift the big boat off the river for the first time. His observer was Mac Laddon, who was following his practice of riding along on the first flights of planes he designed.

The flight was an unqualified success. Further tests showed that the XPY-1's big wing allowed it to land five miles per hour slower than its operational biplane counterparts, that it had a service ceiling of 15,000 feet, and that at maximum it could exceed the 2,000-mile range requirement by 620 miles.

It also delivered the 110 mile-per-hour cruising speed with two engines as promised, but its top speed was only 118 miles per hour. Secretary Warner continued to insist on a top speed of 135 miles per hour, so the third engine was set atop the wing on the mounts Laddon had

Consolidated's first flying boat, the XPY-1 Admiral, about to touch down on the Anacostia River in Washington, D.C., after its maiden flight. It pleased the navy in all respects except top speed, but the production contract went to Martin. (U.S. Navy)

provided. It served only to make hangaring and servicing difficult, with no significant increase in performance. Warner, pleased with the XPY-1 in all other respects, said no more about the 135 mile-per-hour top speed, and the third engine was removed.

Since his days at McCook Field Reuben Fleet had been irritated by the military's practice of letting a contract to one manufacturer for an aircraft design and prototype, then contracting with another for production. The consequent competitive bidding kept the military's costs to a minimum, but the low bidder didn't have the benefit of the experience gained by the prototype manufacturer, and along with low price the military often got poor quality. Fleet would never allow Consolidated to bid on another manufacturer's designs. In the case of the XPY-1, the dual contracting procedure brought more than irritation to Fleet and his organization; it almost brought financial disaster.

During Consolidated's trainer production heyday, Fleet had used volume materials buying and assembly line techniques to hold down costs, and as a result always underbid his competitors for the right to build his own corporation's designs. Confident he could repeat this performance with the XPY-1, he allowed development costs to exceed the $150,000 contract by $500,000, with the intention of making up the overruns on the production models—the thirty-two that Secretary Warner had said would be forthcoming. In addition, he had made large-volume buys of raw materials in anticipation of that first order. The order never came.

The navy, true to its time-honored mission to trim costs, put the XPY-1 production contract up for bids, and the Glenn L. Martin Company, with no development cost overruns to recoup, submitted the lowest bid. The navy issued an order for nine planes. Three would be built as P3M-1s, and six, with larger engines and enclosed cockpits, would be built as P3M-2s. Insult was added to injury when Martin was awarded a second contract, this for an updated prototype of the Consolidated design, the XP2M-1.

Fleet's recovery was swift, as usual. He simply shifted Consolidated's flying boat emphasis from the military to the civilian market. He was well aware of the value of a trade-off between military and civilian aviation, as cited in the Morrow Board's report of 1926, and he had had the XPY-1 Admiral designed so that with relatively few changes it could become the Model 16 Commodore.

With dimensions identical to the XPY-1, the Commodore would be the largest, longest-range flying boat in civil aviation use. The demand for such a plane was at hand, Fleet felt, since airmail routes were being opened, and others considered, to Central and South America. He heightened that demand in January 1929 by becoming a major stockholder in the New York, Rio, and Buenos Aires Airline (NYRBA), a new venture headed by Ralph O'Neill, a World War I fighter pilot and engineer. The airline route O'Neill had arranged was the world's longest, 7,000 miles, from Miami down the east coast of South America to Argentina's capital city. The NYRBA would be the world's biggest—and only—user of Commodore flying boats.

The Commodores were the luxury airliners of their day. Fleet hired a decorator to give the planes' interiors style and comfort beyond anything in the air. Each passenger compartment was paneled in its own shade of pastel fabric and had its own set of windows. Seats were upholstered, rather than covered with the imitation leather then in vogue, and floors were carpeted. A lavatory was provided. The planes themselves were eye-catchers, with coral-colored wings and cream-colored hulls. They were painted black below the waterline.

The first Model 16s were configured to carry twenty-two passengers, eight in each of two compartments, three in each of two drawing rooms. Later models, designated 16-1s, had seating for twenty-five, and the final two—16-2s—could seat thirty-three. In actual operation, a gross weight of 17,600 pounds determined the number of passengers. With a full fuel load of 650 gallons and a 600-pound cargo, only ten passengers could be carried. So laden, the Commodores had a range of 1,000 miles at 108 miles per hour. All Commodores were powered by two 575-horsepower Pratt and Whitney engines with three-bladed propellers.

A pilot, copilot, and radio operator-steward constituted the crew. The

The Commodore airliner was the civilian version of the XPY-1. Fourteen of the luxury seaplanes were sold to the New York, Rio, and Buenos Aires Airline in 1929. (National Archives)

first Commodore off the assembly line had an open cockpit like the XPY-1's, but pilot fatigue from wind, weather, and noise was taken into consideration and the cockpit was later enclosed, as were the cockpits of all succeeding models.

In making delivery of Commodores to the NYRBA, Consolidated set something of a record, producing fourteen flying boats in fifteen months. It was able to do this because of the experience gained through the design and production of the XPY-1 and because Fleet had stockpiled raw materials for the anticipated military order. Consolidated far outstripped Martin, which, lacking prototype experience and detailed drawings, took twenty-seven months to turn out its nine-plane order. Reuben Fleet undoubtedly felt grim satisfaction in the fact that the navy soon changed its contracting procedures: The XPY-1 was the last navy aircraft to be designed by one manufacturer and produced by another until World War II.

The Commodores had teething problems. Hull seams opened in rough water landings; an engine broke loose on one plane and the propeller cut into the cabin; another landed safely with an engine on fire; still another lost power in both engines over Cuba and landed deadstick, sliding down the rows of a cane field on its keel with little damage and no injuries. But in all, the planes compiled an enviable service record. In five years the Commodores covered five million passenger miles without an injury. Nine years after delivery thirteen of the fourteen were still in service, one having been destroyed in a hangar fire. Twenty years later, one was still carrying passengers for Bahama Airways, Ltd.

The NYRBA lasted slightly more than one-and-one-half years, merging in August 1930 with Pan American Airways, but through it Reuben Fleet did more than just recoup Consolidated's losses on the XPY-1. The sale of the fourteen Commodores, along with ten Fleetster mail planes and ten Fleet trainers, not only made up the corporation's half-million-dollar deficit; it turned a quarter-million-dollar profit.

After losing the XPY-1 production contract to Martin, Reuben Fleet was determined not to lose his next opportunity to build flying boats for the navy. He set his engineers to work improving the XPY-1 design, and on 26 May 1931 the navy awarded Consolidated a contract to implement the improvements in the prototype XP2Y-1 flying boat.

The XP2Y-1 Ranger had the same 100-foot parasol wing and 62-foot hull of the XPY-1 but beyond that were major differences. Most noticeable, it was a sesquiplane: short, shoulder-height wings were mounted on the hull, replacing the struts that supported the XPY-1's outrigger floats. The Ranger's floats were tucked under the short wings, along with provisions for carrying up to 2,000 pounds of ordnance.

The Ranger's appearance was sleeker than the XPY-1's. The cockpit was enclosed—a feature borrowed from the Commodore—and the sturdy sesquiplane wings made it possible to remove many of the flying wires and struts that braced the XPY-1. The engines, 575-horsepower R-1820-E Wright Cyclones, remained strut-mounted between wing and hull but were fitted with NACA cowl rings and three-bladed, variable-pitch propellers. The navy liked what it saw on paper early in the design stages, and in July 1931 ordered twenty-three production aircraft.

The Ranger prototype was assembled outdoors at the Consolidated plant in unusually good weather for Buffalo in March 1932. The first flight was made 26 March, taking off from the Niagara River, but it was cut short because ice moved into the landing area. Two weeks later, with ice continuing to be a problem, Consolidated decided to fly the plane to Washington to continue flight tests.

The navy didn't give up easily on its theory that three engines were better than two, and on request the prototype Ranger was built with a third engine atop the wing. But, as with the XPY-1, the advantages in speed and performance were outweighed by the disadvantages in maintenance and fuel consumption, and the engine was removed. With two engines, the Ranger had a top speed of 126 miles per hour.

While the first order of P2Y-1s was in production, Mac Laddon continued to improve on the design, and the last plane in the twenty-three-plane order was fitted with fully cowled 750-horsepower Wright Cyclone engines mounted on nacelles faired into the leading edge of the wing. The overall effect was a 10-mile-per-hour increase in cruising speed with a corresponding increase in range, and the navy ordered twenty-three more of the new model, designated P2Y-3. In time, the P2Y-1s were converted to the -3 configuration and redesignated P2Y-2.

First deliveries of the Rangers were made on 1 February 1933. By September the navy was ready to prove the planes' long-range capabilities. Pilots and crews from VP-5 in San Diego were sent to Norfolk, Virginia, to ferry six P2Y-1s to VP-10 at Coco Solo Naval Air Station in the Panama Canal Zone.

Under the command of Lieutenant Commander Donald Carpenter, the Rangers took off at 1700 on 7 September 1933, and landed in Coco Solo 25 hours, 19 minutes later, 2,059 miles away from their starting point. It was a new record for mass long-distance flight, breaking the one set by Italian General Italo Balbo with his flight of twelve Savoia-Marchetti flying boats from Africa to Brazil in 1931.

In October six P2Y-1s of VP-10 were flown from Panama by way of Acapulco to San Diego, and in January on to San Francisco. They left there on the 10th for a new station at Pearl Harbor in what the navy modestly called a routine transfer of aircraft. It was far from routine; it was the first time naval aircraft were flown to Hawaii, rather than traveling disassembled and crated aboard ship.

Commanded by Lieutenant Commander Knefler McGinnis, the flight began at 1204 when the first two of the gasoline-laden Rangers became airborne. But the remaining four planes couldn't break loose from the calm waters of San Francisco Bay until "blown off" by other flying boats taxiing at high speed ahead of them to break up the surface. The two lead planes circled for two hours before all six joined up and headed west over the Golden Gate.

Flying at altitudes from 500 to 5,000 feet, depending on cloud height, the six planes averaged 98.4 miles per hour, and covered the 2,408-mile distance in 24 hours, 35 minutes, setting another long distance record for mass flight.

For "a routine transfer of aircraft," the flight garnered a remarkable amount of national and international attention. A crowd of fifteen hundred greeted pilots and crews, whose comments were broadcast coast-to-coast on mainland radio.

Admiral Ernest King, who became chief of the navy's Bureau of Aeronautics following the death of Admiral Moffett in the Akron airship disaster in April 1933, sent a message to McGinnis saying: "The Chief and Officers of the Bureau of Aeronautics heartily congratulate Commander VP-Squadron Ten and his officers and men on the successful

P2Y Ranger was the first Consolidated flying boat to receive a navy production contract. Rangers set long-distance records to Panama and Hawaii in the early 1930s and remained in service as trainers into the 1940s. (U.S. Navy)

and workmanlike accomplishment of the nonstop flight from San Francisco to Honolulu, which is the longest formation flight in the history of aviation."

President Franklin Roosevelt also sent congratulations for "successful completion of the greatest undertaking of its kind in the history of aviation, the formation flight from San Francisco to Honolulu, Hawaii, a magnificent accomplishment."

And a spokesman for the Japanese navy commented somewhat ominously: "It shows what increased powers this development has placed at the disposition of mankind. It remains to be seen whether these powers will be used beneficently or destructively."

On station, the Rangers acquired a reputation for being the most dependable flying boats the U.S. Navy had. They did their part in promoting Consolidated's reputation for longevity of product. They remained in front-line service for six years, then were relegated to training duty at Pensacola Naval Air Station, where they served well into the 1940s.

The early 1930s were busy years for the VP squadrons. They took part in fleet exercises at Guantanamo Bay, Cuba. They conducted mass flights to the Galapagos Islands, 1,200 miles southwest of the Canal Zone; to French Frigate Shoals, 780 miles northwest of Oahu; to Alaska and Dutch Harbor in the Aleutians. On 1 May 1935, planes from Pearl Harbor deployed to Midway Island, extending patrol capabilities even closer to Japan.

The concern over Japan's grand design for the Pacific was becoming more widespread and well-founded. In 1931 Japan added Manchuria to Korea, Formosa, and various Pacific islands in its area of control. By 1934 it was evident that Japan had broken the arms limitation treaties signed after World War I and was actively building a formidable, modern navy.

Admiral King, like Admiral Moffett, was a firm believer in the value of naval aviation and saw the need for a patrol bomber more advanced than the ones then in service. He would get what he was looking for in the third generation of Consolidated flying boats, the plane destined to be the most famous of them all: the PBY Catalina.

PBY Design and Development

Mac Laddon apparently had the PBY design—by whatever designation—in mind long before 13 June 1933, the date on which the navy agreed by contract to pay Consolidated $25,000 for drawings of a new flying boat. Pratt and Whitney's *Engineering Daily Report* of 5 March 1932 contained a note reading: "Laddon is quite interested in 1830 for use in a projected flying boat design." This was even before the first 14-cylinder R-1830 Twin Wasp was delivered to Grumman to be used as the power plant for the XJF-1 Duck.[1] That the drawings were due only seven days after the date of the contract—on 20 June 1933—indicates that a great deal of preliminary thinking and activity had taken place, as indeed was the case.[2]

As early as 23 March 1933, R. N. Whitman, Consolidated's construction vice president, wrote a letter to the inspector of naval aircraft at the plant requesting a long list of specifications needed for preliminary design work on a new flying boat. Consolidated forged ahead, using whatever information it had and with the encouragement and aid of the navy Bureau of Aeronautics, toward the construction of a full scale mock-up of the new flying boat. On 12 May Whitman asked the inspector of naval aircraft for sixty-eight items to be used in the mock-up, ranging from engines to navigation lights, bilge pump, life raft, batteries, radios, guns, ammunition magazines—even a boat hook.

On 20 May a memo signed by Lieutenant Commander D. Royce was sent to the chief of Materials Division recommending contracts for engines for "XP3Y-1 and XP3D-1" (the Douglas entry in the flying boat competition). These were to be Pratt and Whitney GR-1830-54 models. Consolidated's pair were to be used in the mock-up. On the 24th, a request was sent to the supply officer at Anacostia Naval Air Station for a three-blade propeller, 11 feet 6 inches in diameter, also for the mock-up.

Isaac Machlin Laddon, whose design genius was behind all of the great planes
that bore the Consolidated name. (San Diego Aero-Space Museum)

The engines still had not arrived at Consolidated by the time the
navy's Mock-up Inspection Board was to do its work in early August
1933, and the board's members were directed to disregard a complete
mock-up of engine nacelles. The engine mock-up "would be forwarded."

The Mock-up Inspection Board saw a wooden frame covered with
thin cloth, with as many of the actual aircraft components in place as
feasible. The report of the board's inspection, dated 8 August 1933,
contained a reference to a retractable nose turret which, when raised,
interfered with the field of view of both pilots, as did a fairing behind
the turret that extended back to the windscreens. The board said a
decision would be reached later regarding the turret, but if it was retained, the pilots' cockpit would have to be moved forward to improve
visibility.

The board lauded Consolidated for development of a new waterproof
anchor box built into the nose, but recommended that sliding, rather
than hinged, hatches be used above the pilots and an engine crank be
kept near the anchor gear for emergency use on the retractable wing
tip floats or the engine starters. Normal operation of the floats was by

electric motor, and the engines were equipped with electric inertia starters.

Memos flew back and forth for the next few months between the navy and Consolidated, discussing details that would improve the XP3Y-1's serviceability and performance. One memo said the hull design was too strong and the anchor was too heavy (a davit was required to handle it), both of which would result in unnecessary weight. The anchor was reduced from 125 pounds to 95. Whether the hull was redesigned is unknown but, if it was, it may have led to near disaster later on. Other memos covered the type of fuel filters, electrical system components, locations of switches, and placement of bomb-sight mounts.

Apparently the memos produced results satisfactory to both parties, as a contract for the PBY prototype was let by the navy to Consolidated Aircraft Corporation in Buffalo 28 October 1933. Item three of the contract, Navy Schedule 900.6678 Aeronautics, called for an airplane, Model XP3Y-1, at a cost of $162,000, to be set up, serviced, and ready for flight at Anacostia Naval Air Station within 270 days of the contract's acceptance. The intent, the contract said, was to "procure design data, drawings, and engineering information for a long range patrol airplane constructed in accordance with Bureau of Aeronautics Specifications SD-205 dated 1 February 1933." A major consideration in that intent was a flying boat with at least a 3,000-mile range.

The XP3Y-1—Model 28 in Consolidated's records—was the cleanest flying boat ever designed. It was the culmination of all that Reuben Fleet, Mac Laddon, the people of Consolidated, and the navy had gained from their experience with earlier flying boats.

Laddon once said of the XP3Y-1 in an interview: "I'd taken advantage of all the mistakes I'd made on the previous ones." His design went somewhat beyond the correction of mistakes, however. On the patent application dated 26 September 1933 it was described as "a new, original, and ornamental design." On paper and in the mock-up it was obvious that the XP3Y-1 was a unique airplane.

Most obvious was the method of mounting the wing. Where its predecessors had parasol wings held above the hull by a multitude of struts, the XP3Y-1's parasol wing was set cleanly on a single pylon, and braced to the hull with only one pair of struts per side.

Just how and when Laddon came up with the pylon idea no one knows, but it was an excellent compromise between basic flying-boat needs: The hull must have a cross-section small enough to present minimum drag, yet have a beam wide enough to be hydrodynamically efficient and provide enough height for crew head room and cargo storage. The wing must be mounted directly behind the engines for maximum

The XP3Y-1, the culmination of all the experience the navy and Consolidated had gained from previous flying boats. Here it rests at Anacostia Naval Air Station ready for test flights in March 1935. (National Archives)

efficiency, yet the engines and propellers must be raised high enough to prevent water damage.

Laddon's choices were to use struts to mount the wing as before, or resort to a deep hull and a shoulder-mounted wing, or a less-deep hull with a gull wing, or set the wing on a pylon. His choice is history. Installing the flight engineer's compartment in the pylon, where he was out of the way of other members of the crew and where he could observe the operation of his engines, was stroke of genius.

Also obvious was the absence of struts on the full-cantilever tail section, a bonus made possible by the greater strength inherent in a horizontal stabilizer and vertical fin covered with metal rather than fabric. Less obvious, but evident under study, were the retractable floats that Laddon visualized. When retracted, the support structure folded into recesses in the lower wing surface, and the floats became a part of the wing tip. The intent was to add lift while reducing drag, but in actuality retraction or extension of the floats made no difference in the plane's speed.

Not obvious at all were the integral fuel tanks, hidden in the wing center section. Consolidated's Fleetster had been fitted with aluminum alloy tanks mounted in the leading edges of the wings, as close as any aircraft manufacturer had come to an integral fuel tank up to that time, and they had worked well. The XBY-1, the navy's version of the Fleetster, also contributed to the XP3Y-1 design. The XBY-1 was the first to employ a plate-and-stringer type of wing construction, which left cavities within the wing. By using sealants and gaskets, Consolidated's people turned the cavities in the XP3Y-1's wing into the fuel tanks themselves. The saving in weight was calculated at a half-pound per gallon of fuel capacity, which added substantially to the plane's payload and range.

With a fuel capacity of 1,750 gallons, this would mean a weight saving of 875 pounds.

The XP3Y-1 was considered an all-metal airplane, even though the wing sections aft of the rear spar were fabric-covered, as were the control surfaces. It was the first to use extruded aluminum wing stiffeners and bulkhead borders.[3]

The hull was the best yet. The bow turret and cockpit were totally enclosed. Two sliding hatches covered the gun positions amidships. Bulkheads divided it into seven watertight compartments, which contained accommodations for an eight-man crew: a bombardier who doubled as a bow gunner, a pilot and copilot, a navigator, a radioman, a flight engineer, and two waist gunners. For crew comfort on long flights, the center compartment contained bunks and a galley, and a toilet was located in the aft compartment. A window was fitted in the bow for the Norden bomb sight, with a sectioned cover that could be rolled up or down in front of the window for protection.

Armament consisted of a .30-caliber machine gun in the nose turret and two more machine guns in the waist hatches, which could be either .30-caliber or .50-caliber.

Even with Consolidated's experience in building flying boats, construction of the XP3Y-1 was not a smooth process, for once the construction contract was signed, the design modifications began. They ranged from details as small as the size and type of rivets to considerations of the number and type of engines. Both Consolidated and the navy initiated changes.[4]

On 6 March 1934, for example, the navy requested that the wing be strengthened to accommodate an 1850-pound torpedo which could be carried as an alternative to the originally planned bomb load of up to 4,000 pounds. Controllable pitch propellers also were requested. This resulted in some heated discussions between Consolidated and the inspector of naval aircraft. The navy specified Hamilton Standard controllable pitch propellers, but Consolidated wanted to use Curtiss Electric models. It became a moot point, however, for the Curtiss propellers weren't approved by the time they were needed and, with the exception of fourteen PBY-2s delivered with Electrics, Hamilton Standard propellers indeed became standard for Model 28s from then on.

On 22 August an amendment called for the installation of cowl rings with "controllable trailing edges"—cowl flaps—with controls extending into the mechanic's cockpit. The flare chute was modified to one similar to the P2Y's, and the direction of rotation of the hand crank for the starter of the port engine was reversed.

In general the modifications made to the XP3Y-1 affected details but not its basic design. Modifications were discussed that would have drastically changed the configuration, however.

Apparently to cover previous discussions, Mac Laddon wrote a letter to Lieutenant Commander Walter Diehl in the Bureau of Aeronautics on 26 October 1934, detailing an XP3Y-A variant to be powered by Allison liquid-cooled engines rated at 1,100 horsepower at 2,700 revolutions per minute at 10,000 feet, and fitted with pusher propellers. Laddon estimated the top speed of the plane to be 203 miles per hour at 10,000 feet, with a cruising range of 4,000 miles at 159 miles per hour. No further action was taken on the idea.

In a memo written 12 November 1934, Commander Diehl suggested that split flaps be considered for the XP3Y-1. Consolidated was lukewarm to the idea at first, saying that flaps would add only minimal lift. But in a letter written 4 December 1934, Consolidated Vice President Lawrence Bell told the chief of the Bureau of Aeronautics that wing flaps would make a considerable improvement in the XP3Y-1's performance, specifically a five to seven mile-per-hour reduction in landing speed and a three mile-per-hour reduction in takeoff speed. The installation cost would be $23,000. Bell encouraged a quick decision, so that delivery time for the plane would not be lengthened.

In a note penciled on the back of a memo dated 14 January 1934, the inspector of naval aircraft told the chief of the bureau he felt flaps should be considered in the future but not on the prototype. He went on to say it sounded to him as though Consolidated couldn't meet the performance guarantees based on the original design of the XP3Y-1 and wanted to improve its chances by installing flaps. And he didn't like the price: Consolidated "could not now or at any future time proceed on a price basis so out of line as quoted."

Another major modification was considered as late as 5 April 1935. Lawrence Bell's letter to the chief of the Bureau of Aeronautics on that date contained a proposal to convert the XP3Y-1 to a four-engine aircraft, designated XP3Y-2. Top speed of the plane was estimated at 226 mph, with a range of 3,000 miles. Cost of the conversion was to be $76,560. The proposal was not mentioned again, but it is likely that the eventual result was the development of the PB2Y Coronado, Consolidated's first four-engine flying boat.

Despite the lack of major modifications, the minor ones—plus delays caused by unavailability of parts from other suppliers—were enough to cause the XP3Y-1 to miss its target delivery date of 15 November 1934, and it was rescheduled for delivery on 15 February 1935. Also contributing to the need to reschedule was, as R. N. Whitman put it, ". . . the magnitude of designing, constructing and testing a flying boat of such size."

In the interim, static testing was conducted in the Buffalo plant. While most testing was done on small sections, the XP3Y-1's wing was tested full scale, using the time-honored method of loading it with shot bags until it broke. Thousands of man hours went into planning and setting up the test, which included building a 23-foot-high structure to hold the wing, and scaffolds and platforms to hold the 20,000 pounds of shot bags that were hand-stacked on the wing. Eight hours were needed to load the wing's center section to failure, a point sufficiently above the design load specification to ensure safety and maximum use of structural material.[5]

Anticipating the plane's delivery on 15 February, Secretary of the Navy Claude Swanson requested on 5 February 1935 that the Navy Department's Board of Inspection and Survey conduct service acceptance trials at Anacostia Naval Air Station on that date or as soon as possible thereafter. The Bureau of Aeronautics responded, but included approval of a request from Consolidated to change the flight test location to Norfolk Naval Air Station.

But Consolidated missed the 15 February delivery date, too. On the 25th, Consolidated wrote the inspector of naval aircraft, saying the XP3Y-1 would be ready for shipment "by the end of the week."

And it was. At that time the Niagara River was frozen solid, so, like its predecessors, the plane's major components were loaded on four special railroad cars and shipped to the test site for assembly by a Consolidated crew.

Instructions for the first demonstration flight of the XP3Y-1 were issued on 15 March 1935: Three takeoffs and landings, horizontal flight, turns, spirals, sideslips, and maneuvers on water, all with useful payload. Wing tip floats were to be operated electrically and manually.

The XP3Y-1 took off on its first flight around noon on an unseasonably warm, 85-degree Thursday, 21 March, from Hampton Roads. Bill Wheatley, Consolidated's chief test pilot, was at the controls and, as always with his new designs, Mac Laddon was aboard as a passenger.

Later that day, at the Consolidated plant in Buffalo, Lawrence Bell made this announcement to employees: "Just received preliminary reports of the first flight of the XP3Y-1 at Norfolk this afternoon.

"Wheatley, Laddon, and crew flew the boat for an hour and report that in the preliminary tests everything functioned satisfactorily. The entire structure was without vibration and is rigid in all respects. The floats were operated in the air electrically and by hand several times with complete success. Wheatley reports ship has excellent flying characteristics.

"From these first reports the XP3Y-1 looks very good, but additional tests will be necessary to prove all features."[6]

The public was informed the plane had flown but got no details. A story published in a Norfolk newspaper 22 March was headlined: "Secrecy Shrouds Flight of Plane At Air Station Here." The story said, "Another 'mystery plane' took to the air yesterday . . . and flew over both the land and the water . . . . Officials at the Norfolk Naval Air Station declined to give out any information about the flight. It was learned on reliable authority that the pilot was a representative of the Consolidated Aircraft Corporation, of Buffalo, the builders of the plane . . . . The craft is a rival of the 'mystery plane' that has attracted so much attention on the West Coast."[7]

The cloak of secrecy was to last, at least in part, until 1936: Jane's *All the World's Aircraft* for that year carried a photo of the "P3Y-1" and said that it was equipped with retractable wing tip floats and two "Wright Cyclone engines. No further details have been released by the manufacturers."

The navy's report, a telegram sent 25 March from Norfolk to the inspector of naval aircraft, was not quite so glowing as Lawrence Bell's announcement to Consolidated employees. It said performance demonstrations of the XP3Y-1 had been completed, but difficulty had been experienced in port engine oil cooling, with the engine electrical generators and the auxiliary generator. The contractor was sure the problems could be solved in time for the final demonstration on the 26th, however. A telegram sent the next day seemed to bear this out: "Completed all XP3Y-1 tests satisfactorily. Will be transferred to Anacostia tomorrow."

In May the XP3Y-1 was back at Norfolk for accelerated service tests and rough water trials. These brought out the inevitable imperfections, which were to be expected in a plane that large and complex: wing-tip floats failed to operate electrically at times, a problem traced to a faulty switch; sheet metal and bracket breakage was encountered in engine and cowl mountings; the hull "washboarded" next to the chine after nine hours; and the chine separated from the hull in three places.

One problem that came to light, however, was to plague the plane for months. In fact, it would not be fully solved until the introduction of the high-tail PBN Nomad in February 1943. This problem was a lack of directional stability. It was first described in a memo written 10 May by the commanding officer at Anacostia to the chief of the Bureau of Aeronautics recommending discontinuation of overload tests "because of tail buffeting with engines throttled back and within 15–20 knots of landing speed."

A solution to the problem was attempted by changing the rudder configuration to a triangular shape, thus adding surface area, but another telegram on 25 May told the chief that the modifications had increased the yaw "to a dangerous extent" and said that the plane was considered unsatisfactory for bombing and flight tests. This undoubtedly did not sit well with the Bureau of Aeronautics, as the chief had requested the Bureau of Ordnance to conduct horizontal bombing tests on the XP3Y-1 at the Dahlgren Naval Proving Ground on 7 May.

The final report of the Service Acceptance Trials was sent 21 June 1935 to the chief of the Bureau of Aeronautics, under a cover letter signed by Claude Swanson, secretary of the navy. It contained 18 pages of needed corrections and suggested improvements in the XP3Y-1. These ranged from the forward gun turret not revolving freely to screw slots in the navigator's table damaging maps when course lines were drawn.

The report compared the manufacturer's guarantees at the time of contract with the actual performance of the aircraft.

	Guarantee	*Actual*
Weight empty	13,179.02 pounds	12,567 pounds
Stall speed	60 miles per hour	50 miles per hour
Top speed	159 miles per hour	171.3 miles per hour
Service ceiling	15,000 feet	15,000 feet
Takeoff time	60 seconds	15 seconds (with 6-knot wind)
Altitude of level flight on one engine	200 feet	3,200 feet

The report continued:

> The demonstration flights clearly indicate that the subject plane has exceeded contract performance requirements.
>
> The various experimental features of this plane functioned satisfactorily. There appeared to be no tail vibration and the retractable wing tip floats were operated in the air a number of times without difficulty. The integrally built gas tanks in the center section have given no evidence of any leaks.
>
> The engines functioned smoothly at all speeds.
>
> In conclusion, the Inspector considers subject plane an excellent flying boat. Its quick takeoff, high speed, and smooth handling in the air and on the water are to be noted.
>
> Attention is invited to the fact that the contractor has in most major items more than met contract requirements. There are a number of items, however, as noted in the foregoing report, that could be improved, but in the main do not detract from the plane for the purposes for which it was designed and constructed.

Secretary Swanson's cover letter said: "The Model XP3Y-1 airplane having fulfilled satisfactorily all the performance guarantees, the Secretary of the Navy hereby authorizes as recommended by the Trial Board and concurred by the Bureau of Aeronautics acceptance of said airplane as a service type."[8]

Consolidated was in. Eight days later—29 June 1935—the U.S. Government awarded the corporation the largest aircraft contract since World War I: $6,000,000 for sixty airplanes, now designated PBY-1.[9]

Douglas's XP3D-1, a sleek, shoulder-wing monoplane with twin engines mounted on wide, faired struts above the wing, had passed the performance tests six weeks ahead of the XP3Y-1 but was eliminated in the final accounting because of Consolidated's lower cost per plane, $90,000 as opposed to Douglas's $110,000.[10]

Acceptance of the XP3Y-1 did not mean an end to testing. "Debugging" continued. The 100-Hour Accelerated Service Report of 10 July said that an oil leak had developed in the port engine but had been repaired. The cowling of the same engine had burned through because it was too close to the discharge pipe of the collector ring. The electric tachometer had failed on the starboard engine. The electric wing tip float retracting mechanism broke down after ninety hours. Cylinder head baffles had collapsed at various times. Most important, further changes in the rudder design had only added to its operating forces without resolving the yaw problem.

All of the problems nearly came to an early end 27 July during the XP3Y-1's first rough-water landing test. The single full-stall landing in four-to-five-foot seas carried away the bombardier's window and the forward hatch cover, cracked the copilot's windshield, wrinkled the hull on the right side and even more on the left, and damaged all propeller blades. The watertight bulkheads held, however, and the plane was towed to shore for repairs. A lesser plane might have sunk.

Consolidated employees repaired the hull and added stiffeners to guard against future damage. Even so, the plane was not ready for more tests a month later. A memo sent 20 August 1935 from Norfolk Naval Air Station to the chief of the Bureau of Aeronautics said that because of hull failure in the rough-water test the guns had not been fired, the plane had not flown at night, engines had not been serviced on water, and rough-water tests and anchor-holding tests had not been made.

Norfolk's memo of 30 October 1935 said, however, that new rough-water tests conducted earlier in the month on the XP3Y-1 had proven "satisfactory."

Following these final tests the XP3Y-1, which had been outfitted with an automatic pilot in September, was flown to the new 247,000 square-foot Consolidated plant at Lindbergh Field in San Diego, to which the corporation had moved earlier that year to escape the cold Buffalo winters.

The XP3Y-1 did not take the most direct route, however. With Lieutenant Commander Knefler McGinnis, who had commanded the massed P2Y flight to Hawaii the year before, at the controls, the XP3Y-1 left Norfolk to prove its sought-after 3,000-mile range. The plane arrived in Cristobal Harbor, Coco Solo Naval Air Station, Panama Canal Zone, 17 hours, 33 minutes later. McGinnis had hoped to fly from there non-stop to Seattle, but the rudder problem put an end to the idea: When the plane was fully loaded with fuel, the rudder dipped into the water, resulting in a lack of control when an attempt was made to bring it up on step.

With a lighter fuel load, McGinnis had to settle for San Francisco, where he arrived on 15 October, 33 hours, 45 minutes and 3,443 miles away from Coco Solo, setting a new world distance record for Class C seaplanes.

The following day McGinnis flew the XP3Y-1 to San Diego, where it was displayed as part of the dedication ceremonies for the new plant on 5 October 1935. Following the dedication, the plane spent the next six months in the factory while many of the navy's suggested improvements were incorporated. Among them was installation of a "tunnel" hatch and .30-caliber machine gun in the bottom of the hull past the step for protection from fighter attack from underneath. It was also re-engined with new 850-horsepower Pratt and Whitney R-1830-64s, which increased top speed to 184 miles per hour at 8,000 feet. Still another modification was made to the rudder. This one worked: The hull was extended beneath the rudder, and the problem of lateral control when fully loaded on the water was ended. The plane was redelivered to the navy in May 1936 as the XPBY-1.[11]

Navy PBYs
in the Prewar Years

Consolidated's move from Buffalo to San Diego was made with little down time. Production halted in mid-August 1935 in Buffalo, the same month the PBY order was received, and part of the factory was running again in San Diego a few weeks later. The move was made in 157 freight cars, with the machinery that would be needed for the start-up packed to arrive first. In San Diego Consolidated faced a dual challenge: building fifty PB-2A two-place pursuit planes for the army even while beginning production of sixty PBY-1s for the navy.

Both challenges were met, with the first PBY-1 rolling out in September 1936, eleven months after the new plant was dedicated. The plane was towed on its beaching gear across Lindbergh field and launched in San Diego Bay. On 5 October 1936 old VP-11 became the first navy patrol squadron to receive a PBY.

Once the PB-2A order was out of the way, Consolidated began work on a second order of PBYs, one for fifty planes of an improved version, the PBY-2. This order was placed on 25 July 1936, even before the first plane in the sixty-plane PBY-1 order had been delivered. The two orders would continue to overlap: The first PBY-2 was delivered in May 1937; the last PBY-1 was delivered in June.[1]

The PBY-1 was identical to the XPBY-1 except that it was 1,500 pounds heavier with full equipment. Both had Pratt and Whitney Twin Wasp R-1830-64 engines, but the PBY-1 delivered a slightly lower top speed—177 miles per hour compared with 184—and had a lower service ceiling—20,900 feet compared with 24,000. Its range was 1,210 miles with a ton of bombs and 500 gallons of fuel, and 4,042 miles if it carried no bombs and a full fuel load of 1,750 gallons.

Armament of the PBY-1 consisted of a .30-caliber machine gun in the bow turret, usually stowed behind the turret on the right side; one .30-caliber gun for each waist position; and one in the tunnel position in the bottom of the hull. Each gun was provided with 1,000 rounds of ammunition, except for the tunnel gun which had 800, all in 100-round boxes. With adapters, .50-caliber machine guns could be mounted in the waist positions, each with 800 rounds of ammunition in 50-round boxes.[2]

The PBY-1 had two bomb racks fitted internally on either side under the wing center section, each able to carry up to a 1,000-pound bomb or depth charge. Twelve 100-pound bombs could be carried on auxiliary external racks hung from the internal ones, each rack carrying three bombs each. Top secret at the time was the inclusion of Stabilized Bombing Approach Equipment (SBAE), a navy-developed automatic pilot coupled to the Norden MK 15 gyrostabilized bombsight, which allowed the bombardier to control the plane during bomb runs. All navy PBYs would be so equipped.

The PBY-1 also could carry a 1,435-pound Mark XIII torpedo under each wing, or a torpedo under one wing and an equal weight of bombs or depth charges under the other. This not only balanced the load but it also permitted dual-purpose missions.[3]

Only minor changes differentiated the PBY-2s from the -1s. Reinforcing plates were attached to the hull in line with the propeller arc to prevent damage when ice flew off the blades. A cutout was made in the rudder to accommodate the horizontal stabilizer on the PBY-2, rather than the -1's cutout in the stabilizer for a solid rudder.[4]

As more and more PBYs became operational, the navy set up a school on North Island in San Diego to train pilots and crews in handling the sophisticated new flying boat. There was much to learn. Starting and takeoff procedures on the water, for instance, involved close coordination, using intercom and signal lights, between the pilot in the cockpit and the plane captain in the pylon. The plane captain would build up fuel pressure with a hand pump, then prime the engines, while the pilot positioned throttles and set propeller pitch.

On the pilot's signal, the plane captain switched on the inertia starter and, when the flywheel had whined up to speed, called "Contact!" over the intercom to the pilot and flipped the "engage" switch. The pilot turned on the ignition switch, and the engine chunked over a few cylinders, usually barking into life. As soon as the number one engine was started, number two was fired up as quickly as possible. This was a must in order to maintain control on the water and to avoid overrunning the buoy if tied up to one.

The engines warmed up while the PBY taxied, and when oil and head temperatures reached normal, magneto checks were made, running each engine at 2,000 revolutions per minute while the pilot held the plane in a tight circle. Good judgment was needed to keep cylinder heads from overheating and spark plugs from fouling, which could happen if the engines were idled too long. When the pilot and copilot completed the takeoff checklist, the pilot turned the plane into the wind, and the crew took takeoff positions.

At full power—2,700 revolutions per minute and 48 inches of manifold pressure—the PBY-1 was off the water in about twenty seconds with a light load and a good breeze. It took a full minute with a full load on a calm day.

A sense of timing was needed to get full power and nose-up elevator coordinated with the rise and fall of the swells so that the PBY's bow would ride up and over the crest and the hull would rise onto the step. Anything less could result in porpoising, which, if not quickly corrected, could bring on progressively worse bounces and finally a crash. Once the plane was on step, the elevator was neutralized and the plane allowed to accelerate to takeoff speed of 65 knots. Back pressure on the yoke lifted the plane off the water. With the pilot holding it straight and level just above the surface, the plane increased speed to 80–85 knots, the minimum for control if an engine quit. The wing tip floats were raised and climb power was set for 600–800 feet per minute.

In the air, the PBY showed few quirks. Stalls were gentle, with plenty of notice given through buffeting, poor response to the rudder, and a dropping nose. Once stalled, the plane would sink with wings level but would recover quickly when the nose was pushed over and the throttles opened.

A new pilot quickly discovered a widespread pilot's complaint: many said the PBY was heavy on the controls, particularly with regard to the elevators. Old timers who had flown the open-cockpit, biplane F-5L, PN, PM, PH, and PD boats disagreed, saying it was a dream to fly. Both groups concurred, however, that the automatic pilot was indispensable on long flights. New pilots and crews were equally quick to lodge two other complaints. With no insulation, the PBY was uncomfortable in temperature extremes, and it was extremely noisy. Of course the PBY was not alone in these problems; they were also true of the earlier flying boats.

Power-on landing approaches were the rule. The downwind leg was made at 85–90 knots; on final approach, speed was reduced to about 75 knots, the PBY trimmed for best landing attitude, and the plane flown onto the surface if it were relatively calm. As soon as the hull touched water, the throttles were eased off and the plane settled in like any other boat. If touchdown was far from the ramp or buoy, the plane could taxi at high speed on the step until near enough to cut the throttles.

Open-sea landings called for a full-stall landing technique. The approach was made power-on until the plane was about 50 feet off the water, then the pilot eased off the throttles and pulled the nose up. If all conditions—altitude, airspeed, and wave-top timing—were met, the PBY would stall just above the surface and settle in with little forward speed. If not at a full stall, however, the plane would bounce when it hit the surface, sometimes quite high, and the next touchdown was usually jarring enough to pop rivets and open hull seams. Crew members learned how to plug rivet holes with the navigator's pencils; pilots learned that a quick takeoff or beaching was the only defense against open seams.[5]

The first class at the navy's PBY school was made up of seven pilots and twenty-four mechanics, all experienced in handling the older flying boats, from VP-6 at Pearl Harbor, and commanded by Lieutenant Commander William McDade. They were to take part in the first of four mass formation flights of PBYs to U.S. outposts in 1937. Each flight was made without mishap, and demonstrated to the world—particularly to the Japanese—the long-range capabilities of the navy's new patrol planes.[6]

As with the P2Ys in 1934, VP-6's flight from San Diego to Hawaii on 28 January 1937 was referred to by the navy as "a routine transfer of men and equipment." The news media of the day placed far greater importance on it, however. When the twelve new PBY-1s took off from San Diego Bay and climbed to 10,000 feet, they found a camera plane waiting to take newsreel footage of their formation departure.

Bill Wheatley, Consolidated's chief test pilot, was aboard for the flight. "The first three or four hours we bucked a 40-knot headwind," he wrote in his report.

> I marvelled at the clarity and confidence Lt. Harvey displayed in computing our position after making an observation. Neither he nor his radioman left their posts during the entire flight. One of the mechanics acted as mess boy; coffee, bacon, and eggs were prepared on the electric hot plate.
>
> All hands were fitted out in fur boots and flying suits, but we all suffered keenly from the cold. It was just above freezing most of the time, both inside and outside the plane.
>
> About halfway across we began to pick up a slight tailwind. During darkness it was colder and pitch black until the moon came up. It was beautiful above the clouds as we passed over the Navy ships spotted along our route.
>
> Three hundred miles from the Hawaiian Islands we flew through some clouds and rough air. About an hour before reaching Pearl Harbor we all reduced power and got into closer formation.
>
> Twenty-one hours and 48 minutes out of San Diego the lead plane, with a tired, bewhiskered, but happy Commander McDade at the controls, landed off the Naval Air Station.[7]

Admiral King in San Diego received a terse, "routine" message: "Patrol Squadron Six arrived in excellent condition, reported for duty, ready for service."[8]

Wheatley had high praise for his company's flying boat. He was enthusiastic over the practicability of a big flying boat that offered enough space for pilots and crew to rest while off duty on long flights. He was equally enthusiastic over the benefits of the automatic pilot, which . . . "holds the plane so much steadier than the human pilot can that navigation is better and blind flight safer." His only complaint was the universal one: "Even between mild San Diego and milder Pearl Harbor it is so damn cold at 10,000 feet that a heating system should be given serious consideration!" It was not, until late in World War II.

The second mass formation flight began 12 April 1937 when twelve planes of VP-11, commanded by Lieutenant Commander L. A. Pope, left San Diego for Pearl Harbor. Benefiting from VP-6's experience, Pope's planes were off the bay in 35 minutes—half the time it took McDade's—and the PBYs landed in Hawaii 21 hours, 21 minutes later.

The final mass formation flights in 1937 went to the Panama Canal Zone. On 21 June, twelve PBY-1s commanded by Lieutenant Robert Morse set a new record of 27 hours, 58 minutes for the longest formation flight: 3,292 miles over Mexico and Central America to Coco Solo Naval Air Station. The weather along the route gave the planes the first of many in-flight structural tests.[9]

Charles Kinney, a Consolidated employee, made the flight with the navy crew and wrote back to Bill Wheatley:

> Just a line to let you know that I am still around after having experienced the soupiest flying weather that the Navy personnel and our boats will see for a long time.
>
> It looked as though the flight would be made under ideal conditions, but about ten o'clock we saw thunderheads ahead of us and then we started flying blind. This condition existed the entire night, and with the approach of dawn . . . the planes began to ride the thunderheads, and believe you me the planes were given a good test.
>
> After passing the lower coast of Mexico, the storm ceased and gave us our first glimpse of land since Monday afternoon.

Kinney, too, had high praise for navy navigation and the Sperry autopilot.[10]

Lieutenant Morse's record lasted only six months. On 8 December fourteen PBY-2s under Lieutenant Commander B. E. Grow flew the same route to Coco Solo in 22 hours, 20 minutes. Better weather conditions undoubtedly had something to do with it.[11]

Early in the year Bill Wheatley set a record of his own in a PBY. The plane had been designed to fly on only one engine, but whether it could

"Routine transfers of men and equipment" to the Canal Zone and Hawaii by
U.S. Navy PBYs became the norm in the late 1930s, with each formation flight
almost consistently breaking the long-distance record set by the previous one.
(National Archives)

take off on one was open to speculation. Wheatley ended the guessing
game by putting on a demonstration in which he not only took off using
a single engine but did so carrying enough fuel in the tanks to fly on
for 1,300 miles.[12]

As 1937 ended, the navy had just taken delivery of the first of sixty-
six PBY-3s ordered the year before, a further improved model with R-
1830-66 engines that developed 1,000 horsepower on takeoff. On 18
December Consolidated received an order for thirty-two PBY-4s, these
with R-1830-72s producing 1,050 takeoff horsepower, a top speed of
197 miles per hour at 12,000 feet, and 176 miles per hour at sea level.

The first twenty-eight planes in the order would look similar to earlier
PBYs, with rudders having a rounded trailing edge and sliding hatches

over the waist gun positions. The last four, however, delivered in June 1939, were the first to have what would become a PBY trademark: transparent blisters over the waist guns. Also they had the first rudders with straight trailing edges. All PBY-4s were characterized by spinners on the propellers, the only PBY variant to be fitted with them.[13]

The mass formation flights of PBYs to naval air stations overseas, now no longer front page news, continued in 1938. Eighteen PBYs left San Diego 18 January in two nine-plane sections, one commanded by Lieutenant Commander Spencer Warner, the other by Lieutenant Commander W. G. Tomlinson, and flew to Pearl Harbor in 20 hours, 30 minutes. This latest flight put forty-two PBYs at Pearl Harbor, where they played a major part that spring in a large-scale war game involving the defense of the Hawaiian Islands.

At the conclusion of the exercise, Consolidated's Reuben Fleet and Mac Laddon were invited to attend the official critique. They were chagrined to find that in one squadron of eleven PBYs the hulls of ten had been damaged in open-sea takeoffs from French Frigate Shoals 600 miles west of Pearl Harbor. The minor damage, mostly wrinkled skin and lost rivets, resulted from the planes rocking back on their tails beyond the rear step in takeoffs in heavy seas. Consolidated reinforced the hulls, adding about 25 percent more strength but only seventeen pounds more weight.[14]

For the most part, PBY operations during 1938 and in the remaining prewar years were devoted to training of all sorts. Flights were made day and night to improve navigation, gunnery, bombing, and torpedo-launching skills. Aerial photography assignments were also carried out, such as recording the effect of surface craft gunnery on target sleds. The squadrons also trained in advanced-base operations from seaplane tenders.[15] The year ended quietly for the navy's air arm, with fourteen PBYs flown to the Canal Zone on 2 September, and seventeen flown to Pearl Harbor on the eighth. The Pearl Harbor flight was another record setter. The PBY-4s, commanded by Lieutenant Commander Aaron Storrs III, covered the 2,500-mile distance in 17 hours, 17 minutes.[16]

Another major achievement marked the beginning of 1939. Forty-eight PBYs and 336 men of Captain Marc Mitscher's Patrol Wing 1 constituting four squadrons—VP-7, VP-9, VP-11, and VP-12—left San Diego on 19 January and flew to the Canal Zone, setting a record for the largest mass formation flight. Forty-five PBYs made it nonstop; three others made one intermediate stop to refuel.

Twelve days later the forty-eight PBYs flew to Puerto Rico to take part in fleet exercises and then on to Norfolk, from where they participated in an exercise off the New England coast. When this was com-

pleted, two squadrons remained on the East Coast, while the other two
returned to San Diego by way of Guantanamo Bay and the Canal Zone.[17]

The navy's "in-service test program" continued to prove the toughness
of the PBY in open-sea landings and flights through severe weather.
One unique "test" was made unintentionally in March, when planes of
VP-12 were ducking under rain squalls while enroute from San Juan to
Norfolk. One of the PBYs, flown by Lieutenant Albert Scoles, was con-
fronted by a water spout upon emerging from a squall. With no time to
turn, the plane plunged into the towering column. For a few terrifying
seconds pilots and crew were blinded by tons of water and bombarded
by pots and pans from the galley and anything else not tied down. Then
suddenly, with engines still running, the PBY emerged from the spout
a thousand feet higher than when it entered and on a course 135 degrees
off its original flight path. After being upbraided on radio by the squadron commander for "horsing around," Scoles brought the PBY back in
line. A wing tip float was hanging at a 45-degree angle and a large
number of rivets was missing, but nonetheless he brought the plane in
for a safe landing at Norfolk.[18]

The most important modification in the PBY's long production life
began 7 April 1939 when the navy ordered its first amphibian from
Consolidated. A contract was let which allowed the last PBY-4 in a previous order to be modified into the XPBY-5A.

Reuben Fleet had long said that flying boats should carry their own
beaching gear so they could taxi up a ramp under their own power
anywhere after landing on the water. In addition, the gear should be
strong enough for landings on hard-surface runways. His own engineers
fought the idea, however, because they disliked giving up crew and cargo
space in the hull to make room for wheel wells and retracting machinery,
nor did they like the deleterious effect the extra weight would have on
range and performance.[19]

As usual, Fleet won out, and his corporation set another record: Consolidated produced the world's largest amphibian. The XPBY-5A made
its first flight 22 November 1939.[20] Said Mac Laddon:

> We had not designed landing gears since the Buffalo days, and the task
> of providing a fully retractable tricycle type for a fourteen-ton flying boat
> with its necessarily high center of gravity was not an easy one. It was our
> first whole-hearted venture into the field of hydraulic controls, and as a
> matter of fact, we had more difficulty with these than with the landing
> gear.
>
> Fortunately these troubles were of the pre-flight variety, and the air-
> plane went through its demonstration and acceptance trials with a clean
> slate. The partially exposed main wheels did not have a detrimental effect

The XPBY-5A, the last PBY-4 on a navy order, extends its on-board beaching gear on an in-flight test. The gear was intended for hard-surface landings in emergencies only. (U.S. Navy)

upon speed, and the functioning of the tricycle gear, including its ground handling qualities, came up to our expectations.[21]

The navy found the on-board beaching gear to be of great benefit. The speed of the aircraft had not been reduced and on the water there were no adverse effects. In fact, the opposite was true; when the wheels were lowered in the water as the PBY taxied, handling improved. The lowered gear acted as a sort of sea anchor, helping control drift in crosswinds while approaching a buoy or ramp. More engine power could be applied for short turns without acceleration and with less skidding. The wheels also prevented hull damage from contact with a ramp. The sea anchor effect was equally valuable in rough, open-sea operations.[22]

The PBY-5, in flying boat and amphibian configuration, was the greatest of all the PBYs. It was the most powerful, with 1,200-horsepower R-1830-82 engines, the first to use 100 octane fuel; the fastest, delivering 200 miles per hour at 5,700 feet; and the heaviest, at 17,400 pounds.[23] It would be produced in larger numbers than any other flying boat. Of the thousands of -5s that would be ordered in succeeding years, about half would be amphibians.

A little less than a month after the contract was signed for the XPBY-5A, the Model 31 amphibian, the prototype for the next generation of Consolidated flying boats and the would-be successor to the celebrated PBY, made its appearance at the San Diego plant. By 1939, two hundred PBYs had been delivered to the navy, and no new orders for the plane were in sight. Consolidated was at work on its new four-engine flying boat, the Model 29, which first flew 17 December 1937 as the XP2Y-1

PBY-5As under construction at the Consolidated plant in San Diego. This model was produced in larger numbers than any other flying boat. (Smithsonian Institution)

and was destined to become the PB2Y Coronado of World War II. The Model 32 bomber, the B-24 Liberator, was also on the drawing boards. But the company was not so busy that it couldn't take on a new project. Strictly on its own, with no input from the navy, Consolidated management forged ahead with plans for the Model 31 flying boat.

The Model 31 had none of the graceful lines of its predecessor. When it waddled out of the plant on its integral tricycle beaching gear, its 22-foot-deep, 73-foot-long hull immediately earned it the title "pregnant guppy." Its incredibly thin, shoulder-mounted, 110-foot wing seemed incapable of lifting its 55,000 pounds.

The Model 31's performance belied its appearance, however. It rose from San Diego Bay the next day, 5 May 1939, after a takeoff run no longer than a land plane of similar size would need, and it handled like a pursuit plane, according to test pilot Bill Wheatley. Flight test results showed the plane exceeded the performance of comparable aircraft by 20 percent. Top speed was reported to be 250 miles per hour, and range was projected at 3,500 miles, compared with the PBY-4's 197 miles per hour and 2,070-mile range.

Much of the credit for the Model 31's performance was given to its radical wing. The high-aspect-ratio design was the brainchild of David

Davis, whose name the wing would come to bear. The plane was well under way when the test results of the Davis wing were released. They were so promising that a conventional wing design was discarded in its favor.

No small share of the Model 31's performance credit belonged to its twin engines. They were 2,000-horsepower Curtiss Wright 3350s, swinging 16-foot Hamilton Standard propellers.

But the navy was lukewarm toward the Model 31 from the start, and when its patrol plane needs became urgent, it threw its weight behind the proven PBY. It was not until January 1943 that a contract was let for the Model 31—navy designation P4Y-1 Corregidor—and a government plant formerly used by Sikorsky at Lake Ponchartrain, near New Orleans, assigned to Consolidated for its construction. But the 3350 engines so vital to its performance were also vital for the army air force's high-priority B-29 Superfortresses, and not enough of the big engines were available for both planes. The PBY was handling the patrol bomber job quite well, so the P4Y contract was canceled, and the New Orleans plant was outfitted for more PBY production. Thus, the Model 31's greatest contribution to aviation turned out to be as a test bed for the Davis wing, which so enhanced the range and speed of the B-24.[24]

By the end of 1939, the United States had become an island of peace in a world obsessed with war. In the Far East, Japan continued to test its new army and navy aircraft and give its pilots combat experience in

Consolidated's Model 31, dubbed "Pregnant Guppy" by employees, was the heir-apparent to the PBY, but lost out because its engines were needed for B-29 production. The "Guppy" pioneered the narrow Davis wing and the twin fins that distinguished the B-24 Liberator bomber. (San Diego Aero-Space Museum)

a war that had been raging with China since 1937. In Europe, the three-year Spanish Civil War, only recently ended, had provided a testing ground for Russian, Italian, and German aircraft as well as a training arena for pilots of many more nations. But on 1 September, Hitler, who up to that time had achieved his expansionist goals without firing a shot, sent his Stukas against Poland, dragging the nations with whom it had mutual defense pacts into World War II.

On 5 September 1939 the role of the PBYs expanded to fit the new circumstances. President Roosevelt proclaimed the neutrality of the United States in the European war and directed that the navy organize a Neutrality Patrol to enforce it. The chief of naval operations immediately ordered the commander of the Atlantic Squadron to set up combined sea-and-air reconnaissance of the sea approaches to the United States and West Indies to report and track belligerent air, surface, or underwater units.[25]

The redeployment of PBY patrol squadrons that would serve in the Neutrality Patrol began six days later, when on 11 September VP-33 was transferred from the Canal Zone to Guantanamo Bay for operations in the Caribbean. On the 13th the PBYs of VP-51 arrived in San Juan, Puerto Rico, from Norfolk Naval Air Station to patrol the southern approaches of the Caribbean through the Lesser Antilles.[26]

Regular long-range patrols were flown over specified areas in search of foreign vessels, with each ship positively identified and reported. PBYs carried no bombs on Neutrality Patrol missions, but guns were armed in case a belligerent ship lived up to its name during the identification process.

In addition to regular patrols, each squadron kept a "ready plane" and crew on duty twenty-four hours a day to follow up on reports of suspicious activity, as well as to act as an aerial ambulance for ships at sea and to look for missing aircraft and boats.[27]

In a move to protect U.S. interests in the Pacific, fourteen PBY-4s of VP-21 took off 21 September from Pearl Harbor bound for the Philippines via Midway, Wake, and Guam. Upon arrival, the squadron became the first patrol unit with the Asiatic Fleet since 1932 and the first squadron of what would become Patrol Wing 10.[28]

On 20 December the navy issued contracts to Consolidated for 167 PBY-5 flying boats and 33 PBY-5A amphibians. These would replace aging, less capable PBY-1s and -2s and equip additional squadrons needed to bolster the Neutrality Patrol. Totaling $20,000,000, the order was the navy's largest for aircraft since World War I. To meet delivery dates, Consolidated doubled the size of its plant.[29]

Events in 1940 moved the United States closer and closer to war, and its patrol squadrons became better and better prepared for its onset.

On 15 February the commander in chief, U.S. Fleet, noting that reports on air operations in the European war stressed the need for reducing aircraft vulnerability, recommended that naval aircraft be equipped with self-sealing or leak-proof fuel tanks and with armor for pilots and observers. The Bureau of Aeronautics and the Bureau of Ordnance had been studying such protection for two years, and this formal statement gave impetus to procurement and installation. On 28 October the chief of naval operations reported that aircraft with some form of armor and fuel protection were beginning to enter service, and within a year all fleet aircraft would be so equipped.[30]

Late-model PBY-5s were the first to have armor on the pilot's seats and armor shields on the waists guns, the tunnel gun, and the fuel sumps under the wing center section. In addition, they were fitted with self-sealing fuel tanks, as well as with dump valves to unload unwanted fuel quickly.[31] Idenfication of Neutrality Patrol planes was improved when, on 19 March, squadrons received authorization to apply national star insignia on the sides of the fuselage or hull.

By mid-year the European war was no longer "phony." The Finns had been defeated by the Russians; the Germans had overrun Denmark and had beaten the Allies in Norway. On 10 May Hitler sent his victorious Wehrmacht, Panzers, and Luftwaffe slashing into France and the Low Countries. On 14 June, the day the German army marched in triumph down the Champs-Elysees in Paris, the U.S. Congress acted to bolster the navy's air arm by passing the Naval Expansion Act, which authorized an increase in aircraft strength to 4,500 "useful" planes. The following day Congress amended the act and increased the authorization to 10,000 aircraft. A month later the act was amended again, this time to 15,000 planes.[32]

Rear Admiral John H. Towers, chief of the Bureau of Aeronautics and commander of the Curtiss NC flying boats in 1919 on the navy's first transatlantic crossing, spoke of the importance of the naval expansion program and its effect on the patrol plane:

> An equally important and equally urgent feature of the Naval Expansion Program is the early increase in the number of patrol type planes for the Fleet and for local defense purposes.
>
> It is particularly in the field of the flying boat that the Consolidated Aircraft Corporation has made contributions of great value to the national defense. The non-stop, long-distance flights of this type of plane carried out by the Navy have become almost synonymous in recent years with the designation "PBY."
>
> The Naval specifications for patrol planes are more encompassing every year. The efforts of the Navy and those of aviation manufacturers have

lifted the patrol planes from the purely defensive category and placed them high on the list of offensive weapons.

They are capable of long-range scouting [which] relieves us from building vast numbers of surface vessels for the purpose. They can be used effectively also for bombing or torpedoing hostile vessels. Their advent has had an enormous effect on naval strategy and tactics. Their long range and high speed [has] in effect greatly reduced the sea areas in which enemy surface vessels can operate without fear of detection and destruction from shore-based aircraft.

They can operate not only from established shore bases, but also from any fairly sheltered waters where tenders with fuel can base. They can shift quickly from one area of operations to another. If [planes] are needed on our East Coast, those on the West Coast can be flown overland without a stop, and in a matter of not many hours.

The value of the flying boat to the Navy has, over a period of years, been conclusively demonstrated.[33]

It was not until November, however, that additional PBYs were ordered by the navy: 134 more PBY-5A amphibians, two of which went to the army air corps, which was watching with developing interest the air-sea rescue operations of the British and Germans during the Battle of Britain.

Great Britain placed its first order for thirty PBYs that month. It was this order of planes that first bore the name Catalina, after the island off southern California.

Technological advances in 1940, both general and specific to the planes, improved the efficiency of PBYs. On 29 August the first exchange of information concerning radar began at a conference attended by members of the British Tizard Commission and representatives of the U.S. Army and Navy. The primary topic was how the British were able to detect German bombers and identify friendly aircraft, but in later meetings British shipboard and airborne radar were discussed. Of particular importance to airborne radar was the development of the cavity magnetron, a tube capable of generating high-power radio waves of a few centimeters in length.

On 3 October the chief of naval operations requested that the naval attache in London obtain samples of a variety of British "radio echo equipment" including aircraft installations for interception (AI), surface vessel detection (ASV), and aircraft identification (IFF). On 22 October Rear Admiral Harold Bowen, technical aide to the secretary of the navy, proposed a program that formed the basis for the navy's development of "radio ranging equipment," both shipboard and airborne. So began RADAR, which would provide patrol planes with the invaluable ability to "see" through clouds and in the dark.[34]

While Consolidated employees worked to produce the PBY-5, their counterparts at the Naval Aircraft Factory in Philadelphia worked to improve it. During 1940 NAF engineers developed several worthwhile hydrodynamic and aerodynamic modifications for the plane, but these couldn't be incorporated without stopping Consolidated's production lines and slowing much-needed deliveries of the current model. So the navy took a different tack: On 16 July 1941 an order for 156 modified PBY-5s went to the Naval Aircraft Factory itself.

The NAF version, designated PBN-1 and named "Nomad," featured a longer hull—64 feet 8 inches—a sharper bow, a 20 percent taper step amidships, and a shallow breaker step just forward of the tail. Wing tip floats were redesigned for more lift and improved planing. More fuel tanks were added in the wing center section. Wings were strengthened to carry 38,000 pounds gross weight. A new electrical system was installed. The most noticeable change, however, was the two feet in height added to the vertical fin. The armament was unchanged with one exception: a .50-caliber machine gun in a hydraulically powered turret replaced the .30-caliber gun in the bow.

The first Nomad didn't come off the NAF assembly line until February 1943, and even then the navy got little use from the design. Of the 156 PBN-1s produced, 138 went to the U.S.S.R. under Lend-Lease.[35]

A modified Nomad design was produced by Consolidated late in World War II as the PBY-6A amphibian—the first was delivered in January 1945. It differed from the PBN-1 boats in having a 63-foot hull, a radome above the cockpit, and a rotating ball turret on the bow fitted with twin .30-caliber machine guns. This turret was also used on late-model PBY-5As.[36] (By the end of 1939, .50-caliber machine guns had become standard in PBY waist positions. Power-fed ammunition from central magazines at each position became standard in mid-war.)

The area covered by Neutrality Patrol ships and planes guarding the strategically important sea approaches to the East Coast and Panama Canal expanded greatly through a trade with Britain on 2 September 1940: In exchange for fifty old four-stack destroyers, the United States received what amounted to a 99-year lease on bases in the Bahamas, Jamaica, St. Lucia, Trinidad, Antigua, and British Guiana. Similar rights were granted for bases in Bermuda and Newfoundland. On 15 November the PBYs of VP-54 began operations out of Bermuda, based on the tender USS *George E. Badger,* and that same month Neutrality Patrol protection was extended to Newfoundland and Iceland.

The era of the silver-and-chrome-yellow navy planes ended on 30 December, when the Bureau of Aeronautics directed that fleet aircraft be painted in nonspecular (matte) colors. Shipboard planes were to be

The PBY-6A produced by Consolidated late in World War II featured the high tail of the Naval Aircraft Factory's PBN Nomad, an "eyeball" bow turret fitted with twin .30-caliber machine guns and improved radar. (Convair via San Diego Aero-Space Museum)

light gray overall; patrol planes were to be light gray except for surfaces seen from above, which were to be blue-gray. With war only eleven months away, the navy's air arm took on a warlike look.

On 26 February 1941 aircraft markings were changed: National star insignia were applied to both sides of the fuselage or hull, and those on the upper left and lower right wing surfaces were eliminated. Fuselage bands, wing chevrons, and cowl markings were discontinued. All colored tail markings were removed. The colors of all markings other than national insignia were changed to ones of least contrast to the background color.

In October the Bureau of Aeronautics made an additional change in aircraft colors: To further lessen the possibility of being seen from above, *all* planes were to wear the light gray and blue-gray of the patrol planes. Only trainers were excepted.

Technological advances continued during 1941. In May, work began at the engineering experiment station at Annapolis to develop a liquid-fueled, assisted-takeoff unit for patrol planes; JATO (Jet Assisted Take Off) was born. Of more immediate importance was the installation on 18 July of the first British-type ASV radar in one PBY-5 each of VP-71, VP-72, VP-73, and two PBM-1s of VP-74. IFF equipment was installed about the same time. By the end of October a number of patrol bombers in Patrol Wing 7 were equipped with radar, the navy's first wing to so operate. In October the new technology began to demonstrate its uses, when a PBY from Quonset Point located the submarine S-48 while testing a Magnetic Anomaly Detector (MAD gear) for the National Defense Research Committee.[37]

The United States was feeling the heat from the fires of war in Europe and Asia. Hitler had lost the Battle of Britain and, having given up his plan to invade England, pounded its cities unmercifully with an aerial blitz. On 22 June he unleashed 120 divisions in a "lightning war" against Russia, while General Erwin Rommel's armor battered the British in North Africa. In the Atlantic, Hitler's U-boats wreaked havoc on convoys attempting to make the crossing. In the Far East the Japanese Imperial Army and Navy had occupied French Indochina with the forced consent of the French and had obvious designs on the Philippines and the Dutch East Indies.

In his 29 December 1940 fireside chat, President Roosevelt called the Axis powers a threat to America and urged Americans to turn their country into an "arsenal of democracy." A week later, in his annual message to Congress, he asked for legislation approving Lend-Lease aid to anti-Axis nations; in March he got it, mainly to furnish much-needed help to the stalwart British.

In April the United States took on the defense of Greenland in return for the right to set up bases there, and on 11 April the president extended the Neutrality Patrol zone to Longitude 26 degrees, declaring it the United States's new "sea frontier." The build-up of planes for the patrol squadrons continued in 1941, with thirty PBY-5As ordered in June, and twenty-two more in October. Ninety PBY-5s were ordered in September.[38]

VP-52's PBYs became the first planes to fly patrols over the North Atlantic convoy routes, based on the USS *Albemarle* anchored at Argentia, Newfoundland. The squadron designation was changed to VP-72 in mid-year, and its PBYs roved farther afield. They were based from 4 July until 17 July on the tender USS *Goldsborough* in the harbor at Reykjavik, Iceland, flying patrols to cover the arrival of Marine Corps units from the States. A month later the PBYs of VP-73 began flying regular North Atlantic convoy route patrols from Reykjavik.[39]

In an attempt to stop Japanese aggression in the Far East, the United States had placed an embargo on scrap iron and steel in 1940. The Japanese said it was "an unfriendly act" and otherwise ignored it. The pressure was stepped up on 26 July 1941 when all trade with Japan was halted, Japanese assets in the U.S. frozen, and Filipino forces nationalized under General Douglas MacArthur. This time the embargo could not be ignored, for it included oil. Great Britain and the Netherlands East Indies joined in, and Japan's oil supply was completely cut off. Japan had no oil of its own and only enough was on hand to last a few

The distinctive lines of the PBY caught the eyes of movie makers in the prewar years. Here flying boats of at least four patrol squadrons at North Island in San Diego form a backdrop for the 1938 Warner Brothers film, "Wings of the Navy," which starred Olivia De Havilland and George Brent. (R. V. Harris collection)

months. The route to the oil fields in the Dutch East Indies had to be reopened, and without the interference of the U.S. Fleet, now based at Pearl Harbor. The Japanese high command began making war plans in earnest.

On 26 November the U.S. government offered to renew trade with the Japanese, but only if Japan agreed to leave China and Indochina. The terms were not accepted: This was one day after a Japanese strike force, which included six carriers, was ordered to sail from the Kurile Islands, bound for Pearl Harbor.

On 6 December, President Roosevelt sent a personal message to Emperor Hirohito, urging him to use his authority to keep the peace in the Pacific. But four days earlier, the strike force had been sent a coded radio message: "Climb Mount Niitaka." Decoded, it said, "Attack Pearl Harbor."

On the eve of "a day that would live in infamy," the navy had 247 PBYs in twenty-five patrol squadrons in eight patrol wings based at strategic locations around the world. In the Pacific, Patrol Wing 1 had been moved from San Diego to a newly constructed base at Kaneohe, Hawaii, with thirty-six PBY-5s of VP-11, VP-12, and VP-14. On Ford Island in Pearl Harbor, Patrol Wing 2 had twenty-seven PBY-3s of VP-21 and VP-22, and twenty-eight PBY-5s of VP-23 and VP-24.

In the Philippines the twenty-eight PBY-4s of VP-101 and VP-102 constituted Patrol Wing 10, based at Cavite. Patrol Wing 4's Alaskan

Command was equipped with twenty-four PBY-5s: VP-41 was stationed at Sitka; VP-42 and VP-43 were based at Seattle, Washington.

In the Atlantic, Patrol Wing 3 covered the Canal Zone with thirteen PBY-3s of VP-32 and eleven PBY-5s of VP-33. Patrol Wing 5 in Norfolk had twenty-six PBY-5s in VP-51 and VP-52; Patrol Wing 7 had thirty-six PBYs in VP-71, VP-72, and VP-73, plus thirteen PBM-1s in VP-74.

New Patrol Wing 8 had eight PBY-5s in VP-81 and ten PBY-5As in VP-83.[40]

At 0752 hours on Sunday, 7 December, planes of the Japanese Imperial Navy struck Kaneohe Naval Air Station, and five minutes later attacked Pearl Harbor, destroying or heavily damaging eight American battleships, many smaller vessels, more than three hundred planes—among them most of the PBYs—and killing nearly 2,400 Americans.

The following day the U.S. Congress declared war on Japan. The "Arsenal of Democracy" was now irrevocably at war.

5

Commercial PBYs
in the Prewar Years

As early as 1936, Consolidated had begun to extoll the virtues of the now-tested-and-proven PBY for the commercial market, undoubtedly aiming for a repeat of the success of the Commodore flying boats of 1929, most of which were still flying. The corporation's first commercial sale was not to an airline, however. It was to an individual, a man who would bring Consolidated a windfall of excellent publicity that must have exceeded even Reuben Fleet's fondest dreams, publicity that would continue for the next two years.

On 27 January 1937 the U.S. Navy granted permission for Richard Archbold, a research associate at the American Museum of Natural History, to buy a Model 28-1—a PBY-1 specially equipped for all-weather flying and without armament—for use on an expedition he would lead in Dutch New Guinea. The navy's only stipulation was that, in the interest of national security, the plane not be allowed to leave the United States until September, one year after the first PBY-1 was delivered for patrol duty.[1]

Archbold had been in New Guinea in 1933 and 1936 on expeditions similar to the one now proposed, observing birds, beasts, plant life, and native tribes. On the first, he realized that an airplane would be invaluable in transporting food and supplies in the jungle, and when he returned to the island three years later he took along a single-engine Fairchild amphibian. He flew the plane just long enough to verify his judgment before it was destroyed in a windstorm.

The Model 28, named "Guba" by Archbold, a word meaning "sudden storm" in New Guinea's Motu dialect, was ready for flight at midyear. From that point, the plane began to make its name and Consolidated's known. It set a record—the first of many—merely by rolling out of the factory: It became the largest privately owned aircraft in the world.

On 18 June, with Archbold, his pilot, Russell Rogers, and Consolidated's Bill Wheatley on board, Guba became the first seaplane to land on Lake Mead as they practiced lake-surface landings and takeoffs. On 24 June 1937 Archbold, Rogers, Wheatley, and a crew of three took off from San Diego on a nonstop, coast-to-coast overland flight, the largest plane and the only flying boat ever to do so. Archbold, with only a private pilot's license, landed the plane off North Beach Airport in Queens, New York, 17 hours, 3 minutes later. After the 2,700-mile flight, the PBY still had enough fuel remaining to fly on to Bermuda and back to New York.

Archbold had planned to leave for New Guinea in November, but altered his plans when he was asked to aid in a mission of mercy. Sigismund Levanevsky, the "Lindbergh" of Russia, and his crew of five were reported missing 13 August shortly after crossing over the North Pole in a four-engine bomber on a 4,000-mile flight to Fairbanks. Working through Reuben Fleet, Soviet government officials asked Archbold to sell Guba to them for use in the search for the downed fliers. He agreed to the sale and the plane was flown to Coppermine, in Canada's Northwest Territory, where it arrived 18 August to begin its work.

The Russians hired Australian polar explorer and aviator Sir Hubert Wilkins to head the air operation. Wilkins made search flights for over a month, but to no avail: Levanevsky and his crew were never found, and the search was called off when landing areas began to freeze over.

Wilkins wrote a letter to Fleet, saying he had flown 19,000 miles ". . . under the most adverse weather conditions, flying over rough and uncharted terrain, and for the most part heavily loaded with fuel, supplies, and equipment. It is my privilege to congratulate you and your associates, and all those who had a part in the fabrication of this airplane, and in no uncertain terms. Without this magnificent airplane, we could not have attempted our difficult task."

Guba, now designated L-2, was flown to New York, dismantled, and shipped by steamer to Russia in late 1937, where it was used to fly cargo. It was reported to have been destroyed by shellfire from a German submarine at Moller Bay on Novaya Zemblya Island in 1942.

Richard Archbold's plans for the New Guinea expedition were set back only slightly. When Guba was sold, he contracted for another plane, a Model 28-3 which bore the same registration number, NC 777, that had been assigned to its predecessor. It was ready in November, and on 3 December 1937 he, Rogers, and Wheatley took off from San Diego for a shakedown flight to Miami. Guba II arrived there in 14 hours, 10 minutes. In March a similar flight was made, but this time the plane continued on to St. Thomas in the Virgin Islands.

Guba II, like the first Guba, was equipped for all-weather flying and was fitted with four reinforced platforms inside the hull to accommodate

"Guba," a Model 28-3, was flown by Richard Archbold on a research expedition to Dutch New Guinea for the American Museum of Natural History in 1938 and continued on around the world, the first seaplane to do so. (Convair via San Diego Aero-Space Museum)

five tons of cargo. Since it would also be used to transport members of the 200-man expedition, seats were installed for ten passengers. Looking ahead to times when Guba II would land and maneuver on unknown lakes, Archbold had a nine-horsepower outboard motor installed in the rear tunnel hatch. This gave the big plane the ability to slowly approach the shoreline with its Pratt & Whitneys switched off, to turn on a dime, and even to back up, a facility that captured the attention of old-time flying boat pilots when it was demonstrated in San Diego Bay.

Over a six-month period Archbold and his crew put Guba II thorough fifty-three flight tests to check out the plane and its equipment. Since the plane would be used daily to fly men and supplies from the expedition's seacoast base at Hollandia to the advanced camp at 11,500-foot-high Lake Hebema—a trip that took three months on foot and two hours by air—numerous takeoffs were made from 6,000-foot-high Lake Tahoe, using only the takeoff power that would be available at the higher elevation. Loads were built up in the plane until, at 23,700 pounds gross weight, it was barely able to stagger off the water.

With engines overhauled, Guba II took off 2 June 1938 for New Guinea, 6,000 miles across the Pacific. After stops at Pearl Harbor and Wake Island, the plane landed at Hollandia 10 June.

The expedition remained in the field for eleven months, collecting birds, mammals, and plants. Said Archbold: "In addition to the biological specimens we brought home, we discovered a 'new' tribe of 60,000 natives in an unexplored valley of the Balim River. We made 168 flights in and around New Guinea from 15 June 1938 to 10 May 1939, carrying 568,000 pounds of food and equipment over jungle impassable on foot. Guba enabled us to do in ten minutes work which could not have been done in two years, had we used the available means of land transportation."

Guba II's saga didn't end there, however. It had a record of its own to set. The Australian and British governments had asked Archbold if on his way home he would survey a new air route west from Australia across the Indian Ocean to Kenya in Africa. It was believed the proposed route from Port Hedland to Mombasa, by way of the Cocos, Chagos, and Seychelles Islands, would provide a valuable alternative to the existing England–Australia route via Singapore and Java should war break out.

With new engines installed, Guba II took off 12 May for Sydney, where the plane was outfitted and provisioned for the flight, and Captain P. G. Taylor, who had flown with Sir Charles Kingsford-Smith in the record-setting Fokker, Southern Cross, was taken aboard. The flight from Sydney was made nonstop across Australia to Port Hedland, where the survey flight began 3 June 1939.

After an uneventful flight Guba landed in Kenya on 21 June, ending the survey and "creating considerable interest," Archbold said modestly. From there the plane flew across Africa and the South Atlantic, making Guba the first seaplane to fly around the world. In addition it marked the first time any airplane had circled the earth at its largest diameter.

After crossing the Atlantic, Guba II stopped at the New York World's Fair for an "official" welcome home. On 6 July the plane set down in San Diego Bay after thirteen months of flying. The zigzag course from Hollandia back to San Diego had covered 24,080 miles.

On 28 February 1937, a month after Richard Archbold ordered his PBY, Consolidated made its second commercial sale: Through its purchasing agency, Amtorg, the U.S.S.R. ordered three Model 28-2 cargo-mail flying boats. One plane was assembled and test flown before delivery. The other two were shipped unassembled so they could be used for training in assembly operations after delivery to Russia. Three Russian engineers spent several months at the Consolidated plant in San Diego studying PBY construction methods.

Negotiations began about that time among the United States, the U.S.S.R., and Consolidated to license a Russian PBY plant and send personnel to help them get into production. Agreement was reached, and eighteen Consolidated engineers were sent over in 1938.

The Russians' only complaint about the GST—their designation for the PBY—was that the engines ran too cool. Consolidated sent drawings showing how to cowl the engines tighter and hold in their heat. Apparently it worked, for there were no more complaints.

GSTs were first powered by M-62 engines, the Russian designation for 840-horsepower R-1820-G3 Wright Cyclone engines built there under license. Later these were replaced with 950-horsepower M-87 engines, which the Russians claimed raised the GST's top speed to 204 miles per hour. The planes were fitted with Russian-made bow turrets. An estimated 150 GSTs were built at the plant in Taganrog on the Sea of Azov before the German army overran the area in 1941.[2]

Meanwhile Consolidated continued its efforts to reestablish itself as a supplier of commercial seaplanes for transoceanic flights to Europe and the Orient. But Pan American Airways had a near monopoly on overseas flights. Also it was the only airline that could meet the requirements of the U.S. Post Office for flying mail overseas. Aside from Consolidated's aging Commodores, Pan American's planes were four-engine Clippers built by Sikorsky, Martin, and Boeing, and its interests seemed to lie in more of the same.

In late 1937 Reuben Fleet announced that Consolidated had spent $150,000 designing a new four-engine, three-deck flying boat that could carry 100 passengers and a ton of mail at 190 miles per hour across the Atlantic, making the crossing in twelve hours, With only 50 passengers, its range would be 5,000 miles.

On the heels of this announcement, Pan Am invited Consolidated and seven other manufacturers to submit plans for a long-range, ocean-service aircraft that would carry 100 passengers in staterooms nonstop for 5,000 miles at not less than 200 miles per hour. Despite the Consolidated design being so close to the specifications, no more was heard of the bid, and no orders came to the company from Pan Am.

A second ray of hope for overseas airline sales beamed in February 1938 when American Export Lines, whose ships plied the seas between ports on the East Coast and the Mediterranean, announced it would enter the transoceanic airline business. In September American Export Airlines ordered a Model 28-4 that could cruise 4,000 miles with a crew of six and a one-ton payload. It would be used to survey overseas routes for the new airline.

After flight testing in San Diego, the Model 28 was flown to New York, where, on 20 June 1939, it was christened the "Transatlantic." Doing the honors was Mrs. Anne Towers, wife of Rear Admiral John Towers. Under the command of Chief Boatswain P. J. Byrne, a multiengine seaplane pilot since World War I and on loan from the navy, the Transatlantic lived up to its name. From 9 July 1939 and until 4

A Model 28-4 (PBY-4), the "Transatlantic," was used by American Export Lines in 1938 to survey airline routes to Europe. Here it demonstrates the ease with which a PBY could fly on one engine. (San Diego Aero-Space Museum)

August, it flew 24,935 miles while surveying routes between New York, Horta in the Azores, Biscarrose—France's new transatlantic air base southwest of Paris—and on to Marseilles.

Although the Transatlantic turned in an apparently flawless performance, no more PBYs were bought by American Export Airlines. The airline began regular service in 1942 with four four-engine Sikorsky VS-44 flying boats, which were larger and faster than the PBY.[3] The Transatlantic was impressed by the navy shortly after the start of World War II, redesignated a PBY-4, and served as a transport until stricken from the rolls in November 1944.[4]

During 1938 Consolidated kept the pressure on other commercial market possibilities for the PBY in the United States. Not only did the marketing department attack the obvious ones along the seacoasts, but it attempted to create a market among inland carriers as well. A survey showed that more than four hundred lakes, rivers, and harbors in the United States south of the 38th parallel were large enough for flying boats to land and take off. It also showed that many of the largest inland cities in the United States had harbors on lakes and rivers. It would be difficult, Consolidated said, to pick a route across the nation that didn't have potential seaplane ports every 60 or 100 miles; consequently flying boats of the PBY type, capable of flying on one engine, would be able to negotiate cross-country routes with safety equal to or greater than land planes. The company also pointed out that the cost of building a ramp for seaplanes was much less than the cost of runways for land planes.

Finally, Consolidated said, flying boats have a greater load-carrying capacity than a land plane because flying boats weigh less without landing gear and usually have unlimited room to get up to flying speed, whatever the load, while land planes are limited by the length of the runway.[5]

In July Consolidated published information on four commercial versions of the Model 28 that it would build to order. An exploration and survey version similar to the one used by Richard Archbold was available, along with an "air yacht" that provided luxurious accommodations for the sportsman or executive. The air yacht was designed to sleep ten, with a master compartment for two, a guest room for four, and crew quarters for four.

A cargo-mail version offered a main cargo compartment in the hull directly under the wing and auxiliary compartments in the bow and aft of the wing. Consolidated felt it was an ideal aircraft for carrying a ton of mail and express from New York to Southampton, England, over the "Great Circle" route. Flying at 130 miles per hour with a crew of five, range was estimated at 4,100 miles.

Consolidated devoted the most space in its literature to the Model 28 passenger transport version, which weighed in at 28,000 pounds. With a crew of four it could carry forty passengers for 600 miles, or twelve for 2,500, at a cruising speed of 150 miles per hour. Consolidated recommended it especially for feeder, coastal, and scenic airlines. According to Consolidated, a flying boat would eliminate a common complaint among airline passengers: that of having their downward vision obstructed by the low wing. The Model 28's high wing solved the problem.

An even greater boon to airlines would be the amphibian version of the Model 28. The ability to set down on a lake or river and taxi up on land using its own self-contained beaching gear was seen as an important sales point. But, while the tricycle landing gear was strong enough for the plane to operate from hard-surfaced runways, Consolidated saw it done only in emergencies; the PBY was still essentially a flying boat in the minds of management. (The PBY-5A was still almost a year away.)

In all versions considerable emphasis was placed on strength and safety. Consolidated said that transport flying boats were safer than land planes because more good water-landing areas were available than were airfields, and a forced landing in a seaplane on land was less dangerous and costly than the same landing in a land plane. This was because the seaplane had a reinforced hull, especially the bottom, and its engines and propellers were up out of harm's way.

The Model 28's strength and safety would be demonstrated in January 1941 by a navy PBY-5. Enroute from San Diego to Pensacola, the plane became lost after battling a storm for hours and, low on fuel, landed at night on what was thought to be a lake in west Texas. The pilot, Lieu-

14-P-11 sits high, but not quite dry, on the step after landing in six-inch-deep water on a mud flat in south Texas. Undamaged, the plane took off the following day. It continued active service until it was destroyed in a hangar during the bombing of Midway, 4 June 1942. (Captain Murray Hanson)

tenant (jg) Murray Hanson, found out in the morning that the "lake," a dry mud flat most of the year, had been flooded by winter rains to a depth of only six inches. The PBY had slid to a stop in slick mud, high but not quite dry, perfectly balanced on the step. When Hansen reported in, he was told not to attempt a takeoff. He was to taxi close to solid ground and unload preparatory to dismantling. Next day, with engines roaring and with the help of a rancher, his tractor, and ropes, Hansen broke the suction under the plane, but when it began to slip forward faster and faster through the ooze, the opportunity was too great to resist: He took off, and the next landing was in the harbor of Corpus Christi. A check of the hull showed that except for scratched paint it was none the worse for wear. After refueling, the plane flew on to Pensacola.[6]

Consolidated concluded its marketing pitch for commercial PBYs by saying: "All bugs have been eliminated in the course of construction of 182 boats. Since PBY flying boats are now in large production, Consolidated is in a wonderful position to produce and deliver these boats in a much shorter time [than would be needed to produce a comparable new design from the beginning]." This large production "also reduces the selling price to a minimum."

But the benefits of the PBY as a commercial aircraft fell for the most part on deaf ears. Consolidated sold only one more "commercial" PBY, this in July 1939 to the British Air Ministry, which wanted to evaluate the plane for its own needs. The Model 28-5 (PBY-4), licensed N P9630, was painted in Royal Air Force colors and carried British roundels. It

Consolidated's final "civilian" sale was to the British Air Ministry. N P9630 made history by making the first military ferry flight to Europe prior to World War II for evaluation at Felixstowe.

was flown by the former crew of Guba II from San Diego to New York and then nonstop to the Marine Aircraft Experimental Station at Felixstowe, England.

The flight resulted in still another record for Consolidated: N P9630 had made the first World War II ferry flight of an essentially military aircraft to Europe.[7] Successful completion of the RAF evaluation at Felixstowe led to large orders for Catalinas for Coastal Command and Commonwealth air forces. After an extensive tour as a trainer in Coastal Command squadrons, N P9630 was lost in wartime service 10 February 1940.[8]

Later the British bought Guba II, registered it as G-AGBJ, and turned it over to British Overseas Airways, with which it provided shuttle service to West Africa until early 1944. It was scrapped after sinking in a storm during mooring tests at Carnavon, North Wales.[9]

By November 1939, 198 Consolidated Model 28s had flown 662,182 miles carrying 1,260 men, a record resulting from the navy's mass formation flights, the Wilkins polar search, the Guba around-the-world flight, and the American Export Airlines survey work.[10]

Despite the PBY's excellent record in terms of miles flown and air safety, and in the face of the favorable publicity, Consolidated simply was unable to interest the major commercial markets in the PBY. The DC-3 was sweeping the transcontinental market in the United States, and the overseas carriers were interested in bigger, faster, longer-range, four-engine flying boats with greater passenger carrying capacity. The PBY had been designed as a superb navy patrol bomber, which it was, and apparently that was the light in which it was seen by commercial customers.

Consolidated's activity in the commercial market faded away during 1939, partly due to lack of sales to commercial customers, but most likely because of increased sales to its number one military customer, the U.S. Navy. Its largest PBY orders ever—totalling 200 aircraft—were placed in December, and Consolidated once again devoted its full attention to its prime calling as a supplier of military aircraft.[11] The corporation would realize its dream of seeing large numbers of PBYs in commercial service, but only after they were sold as surplus, stout hearted warriors returned home with honors from the greatest war the world had seen.

Pearl Harbor

At 0745 Sunday morning, 7 December 1941, on the Hawaiian island of Oahu, the officers and enlisted men of Patrol Wing 2 at Ford Island in Pearl Harbor looked forward to a well-earned day of rest. They were tired from months of conducting a rigorous training program for new PBY crews, some of which, as fast as they were trained, were shipped out to the new squadrons in the rapidly expanding patrol wings. The day began like any other Sunday. On Ford Island and aboard the ships of the United States Pacific Fleet moored in Pearl Harbor and at the shore installations, men were dressed in whites, ready for early church services or a day on the town. At duty stations the watch was about to change. It promised to be another beautiful day; the forecast was good, and the morning clouds were clearing.

There had been talk of war with Japan, and most believed it was imminent. But not today. Today was another idyllic day in Hawaii. Japan was 3,000 miles away in another world. Besides, the consensus was that when war came Japan would strike first at the closest U.S. outpost, the Philippines, which would allow ample warning for the ships in Pearl Harbor to prepare and put to sea.

Nonetheless Admiral Husband Kimmel, commander of the Pacific Fleet, had seen fit to order his eight battleships and a complement of cruisers and destroyers into port that morning. He had good reason: Earlier he had sent the aircraft carriers USS *Enterprise* and USS *Lexington*, along with their task forces, to Midway and Wake Islands, respectively, to deliver marine fighters and dive bombers to the stations there. This had left the battle fleet without air cover, and the admiral felt it best for the ships to be in port, under the protection of the army fighters on Oahu.[1]

General Walter Short, the army commander on the island, also had taken precautions. The intelligence he had received said he was to be mainly concerned with preventing sabotage, and accordingly he had parked his fighters and bombers wing tip to wing tip in the center of the hardstands at Wheeler, Bellows, and Hickam Fields so they could be easily protected by walking guards.[2]

On Ford Island in the harbor, most of the PBYs under Rear Admiral Patrick Bellinger, commander of Patrol Wing 2 and Task Force 9—the latter placing him in overall charge of the naval air defense of the island—were aligned neatly on the ramp: forty-one PBY-3s and PBY-5s assigned to VP-22, VP-23, and VP-24. VP-21 was also under his command but was on detached service, flying patrols out of Midway, in the direction most likely for an attack to come.[3]

Four planes from VP-24 were in the air. These had taken off at 0600 hours with the squadron's commanding officer, Lieutenant Commander John Fitzsimmons, riding as a passenger aboard 24-P-1 for a flight to Lahaina Roads, an open-sea area between Molokai and Kuai. There they were to practice landing and refueling and rearming from a submarine. It had not been done before; if it proved successful, the plan was to extend PBY patrol areas far to the north in search of potential danger to the base.[4]

Across Oahu on the north shore at Kaneohe Bay Naval Air Station— so new that buildings were still under construction and roads were still being paved—were the thirty-six PBYs of Patrol Wing 1. The wing, under Commander Knefler McGinnis, was composed of VP-11, VP-12, and VP-14 and was also a part of Admiral Bellinger's island defense force. Thirty PBY-5s were aligned on the ramp or were being serviced in the hangars. Three more were moored at buoys in the bay. Three planes, all from VP-14, were airborne that morning, having taken off early on surveillance patrol.

Like Admiral Kimmel, Admiral Bellinger was wary, and had ordered all planes in both patrol wings armed with guns and ammunition. The surveillance planes also carried depth charges. All planes and crews were in some state of readiness. Six planes and crews from VPs 12, 14, and 24 were ready for flight on thirty minutes notice. All of the planes in VPs 11, 22, and 23 were in "Condition Affirm," ready for flight in four hours. Seven of VP-21's planes at Midway were in the air, flying 450-mile searches, and four more were on the water, armed with machine guns, ammunition, and 500-pound bombs, ready for flight on ten minutes notice. In total, seventy-two PBYs were either in the air or could be ready for flight in four hours or less. Only nine planes were out of service, these undergoing maintenance.[5]

In the number-one hangar at Kaneohe a VP-11 work crew was installing self-sealing fuel cells in a PBY. Because of the deterioration of relations with Japan, the squadron was due to deploy with its new PBY-

5s to Wake Island later that week—an advance party had already gone to there to make preparations for the squadron's arrival—and the crew had worked the graveyard shift to get the plane ready for the flight. They were about to be relieved by the Sunday crew when nine planes, which some said looked like army air corps trainers, were seen approaching from the north in a shallow dive, heading straight for the base. But as the planes rapidly closed, their cowlings and wings suddenly lit up with bright orange flashes, accompanied by the popping of machine guns and the thump of cannon. As the gray-painted raiders zoomed overhead, the men could see the rising suns of Japan painted on their wings and fuselages. The time was 0752.

Within seconds pandemonium reigned on the once-orderly ramp. The Catalinas of VP-11 were the closest to the attackers and were the first hit, with the fire of the attacking planes raking on through the remaining squadrons. Men dashed for cover as bullets rattled and ricochetted off the concrete; fireballs erupted from PBYs as gas tanks exploded. Men fell; some dead, some wounded. Ensign Rodney Foss of VP-11 had eight minutes to go as duty officer when he was struck and killed by a 20-millimeter cannon shell at his station in the hangar.[6] Somehow the hangar's sprinkler system was touched off; it would run until it drained the station's reservoir.[7]

The attackers roared in for two more strafing runs, then wheeled out to sea and headed north in the direction from which they had come. The relative quiet that followed was broken by the crackle of flames and the shouts of men fighting fires, attending wounded, and moving planes away from those already ablaze. Not a single plane had been left untouched.[8] The three moored in the bay were destroyed, as were many

Officers and enlisted men at Kaneohe Bay Naval Air Station, Oahu, haul a PBY hit by Zeros in the first attack on 7 December 1941 into a position where firefighters can extinguish the blaze. (National Archives)

on the ramp. All others were holed by gunfire to a greater or lesser extent. Only two were considered flyable.[9] And not a shot had been fired except by the Japanese.

Few people at Pearl Harbor paid much attention to the low-flying planes sweeping in from the south. Officers and men aboard the ships in the harbor thought, like their compatriots at Kaneohe, they were seeing U.S. Army planes, flown by stunting pilots. Passengers on an incoming liner were pleased to witness what they believed were remarkably realistic training exercises for defense of the base.[10]

But their opinions were altered moments later. Above Ford Island Val dive bombers nosed over—the first of 173 planes to attack—and at 0757 a bomb exploded on Ramp No. 4, VP-22's parking area.[11] One minute later Commander Logan Ramsey, Admiral Bellinger's operations officer, rushed to the radio room and ordered the message broadcast that echoed all the way from the Philippines to Washington, D.C.: "Air raid Pearl Harbor. This is no drill."[12]

Bombs were raining down all over the seaplane base now. The air was filled with bomb fragments, machine gun bullets, flying debris, and smoke as hangars and PBYs and Vought Kingfisher float planes were hit, torn apart, and set afire. A large "flying missile" severed a wing spar in VP-24's ready plane, then it was strafed, hit in the center section, and set ablaze. The ground crews were quick to recover from the initial shock, however. The fire in the ready plane was extinguished.[13] Other ground crewmen sprinted through the hail of flying metal to the machine guns in the turrets and blisters of the undamaged PBYs and began arcing tracers up at the diving Vals. At VP-22 three machine guns were manned.[14] At VP-24 five spare machine guns were pulled from the armory and mounted on Kingfishers parked near the hangar. Rifles and pistols were distributed among the crews. The combined fire caused the attacking planes to fly higher, which lessened the effectiveness of their strafing. At least one enemy plane was hit; it crashed into the harbor near the seaplane tender *Curtiss*. Other sailors, weaponless, pulled aircraft from the burning VP-24 hanger.[15] In each squadron area, sailors aided the wounded, manned hoses and doused fires, and towed the least damaged planes away from burning planes and hangars despite being continually under fire.

Pandemonium was not solely the province of Kaneohe and Ford Island. Almost at the same time the bomb hit VP-22's ramp, Kate torpedo bombers slammed two missiles against the side of the USS *Oklahoma* in the harbor. Moments later the USS *California* was struck by two torpedoes and began settling to the bottom. The USS *Nevada*, her bow blown open by a torpedo, made a try for the open sea but was hit several times by enemy dive bombers and beached at Waipio Point.

The *Arizona* already had been blasted by several torpedoes and bombs when a bomb pierced her deck and exploded in a forward magazine. The concussion from the mammoth explosion that followed was felt for hundreds of yards, even by enemy bombers 2,500 feet above. Fiery chunks of the *Arizona* crashed down on surrounding ships; flames roared nearly 500 feet in the air. Then three more bombs hit the ship and she sank quickly, taking one thousand men with her.

A magazine aboard the destroyer *Shaw* let go with a spectacular blast; the destroyers *Cassin* and *Downes* were hit and sunk, as was the target ship *Utah*. The *Curtiss* was set afire when a dive bomber crashed into her deck. No ship in the harbor escaped damage. About ten minutes before the attack ended, the *Oklahoma* capsized, rolling over so slowly that some of the men on her deck were able to walk across her sides and up on her bottom.[16]

On the army airfields, General Short's precautions against sabotage worked in favor of the attacking Zeros. Unopposed, they strafed the closely grouped fighters on Wheeler and Bellows Fields, then the seventy

Sailors on Ford Island pause in their attempts to salvage damaged seaplanes to watch a fireball rise from the stricken destroyer *Shaw* in Pearl Harbor. (National Archives)

neatly aligned bombers on Hickam, their accuracy attested to by billowing clouds of smoke rising from planes burning in their own gasoline. Admiral Kimmel's last hope of fighter protection for his ships died when all but one of the forty-eight Marine Corps fighters were destroyed at Ewa, ten miles west of Pearl Harbor.

As with the ground crews on Ford Island, crewmen aboard the ships in the harbor were immobilized by the first explosions that morning, but they quickly galvanized into action. Canvas awnings, rigged to shade church services on the decks, were slashed to reveal a field of fire. On some ships ammunition lockers were opened immediately, the guns armed, and firing commenced. On others, the lockers were locked, and no one knew who had the keys. Some sailors fired rifles and pistols at the attackers. One, totally frustrated, was seen throwing wrenches at planes that passed nearby.[17] Despite the foul-ups, more and more guns began to respond, and soon the air above Pearl Harbor was dotted with the black puffs of exploding shells.

Other air defenses began to make themselves felt. Five army air corps pilots managed to get in the air in P-40s and P-36s from Haleiwa, a small training field in northwestern Oahu. One pilot claimed four Japanese planes shot down. But not all danger was from the enemy: One P-36, landing for the third time to refuel and rearm, was shot down and the pilot killed by "friendly" ground fire.[18]

About five minutes after the attack began a new sound was added to the cacaphony created by more than a hundred-fifty roaring, diving, climbing planes, the thunder of bombs and torpedos, the thump of antiaircraft guns, and the pop of machine gun and small arms fire: the drone of a dozen new B-17s arriving from the mainland. Set upon at once by Zeros, the Flying Fortresses were unable to live up to their name: They had been stripped of armor and ammunition for the fourteen-hour flight from the West Coast, and all machine guns were packed in Cosmoline. The Hickam Field tower calmly radioed landing instructions to the bombers, adding almost as an afterthought that the field was under attack. One bomber was hit by enemy fire and destroyed as it rolled to a halt. Surprisingly it was the only B-17 lost, even though others were damaged in landings on fighter strips and other fields, one on a golf course.

A final element of confusion was added to the melee when the Dauntless dive bombers of VS-6, scouting ahead of the Enterprise, came in to land on Ford Island. They arrived over the island minutes after the attack began and were immediately pounced on by Zeros. The Dauntlesses fought back, but they were no match for the swift enemy fighters: Seven Dauntlesses were shot down or crash landed, with the loss of three pilots and five gunners.[19]

Then suddenly, at 0830, the enemy was gone. On Ford Island the guns fell silent, and the business of aiding the wounded and fire fighting continued unmolested. But the possibility of a second attack was uppermost in many minds. Admiral Bellinger was no doubt stunned to find that of the sixty-one PBYs he had at his disposal on Oahu that morning he now had ten: the seven in the air, two at Kaneohe, and one at Ford Island. He ordered Lieutenant Commander Massie Hughes, commanding officer of VP-23, to get the lone Ford Island plane in the air and seek out the Japanese carriers from which the attackers must have come. He sent similar orders for the two planes at Kaneohe. The task fell to the two at Kaneohe, however. Hughes's PBY could not be launched; it was hemmed in by burning aircraft and debris.

Word of the attack and search orders were flashed to the seven PBYs already in the air at 0800.[20] All planes carried instructions for sector searches if enemy submarine activity was reported, and they set a course to fly those sectors.

Ensign Fred Meyer, pilot of 14-P-2, had taken off that morning with a crew of seven on what he thought would be a routine four-hour antisubmarine patrol. When the word of the attack came he swung the Catalina around and headed for his sector to the north of the island, still thinking in terms of submarines, not aircraft. He had flown about forty miles north when he changed his thinking. He saw eight or ten planes approaching and, on the chance that they might be hostile, he pushed the nose over and took the PBY down to about 25 feet above the wave tops to prevent an attack from underneath. The planes circled behind the Catalina, too far away for identification, but nonetheless Meyer gave his gunners instructions to keep a sharp eye. Seconds afterward Meyer saw splashes in the water below and ahead of the plane, and an instant later he heard his gunners open up. He could hear the pop of enemy rounds breaking the PBY's aluminum skin somewhere behind him, but the plane kept flying. The Japanese planes, part of the second wave of Pearl Harbor attackers, flashed past, heading for their primary target. One spiraled down, smoking, but Meyer wasn't sure it was because of hits by his gunners. The PBY was holed, but apparently without major damage, so Meyer continued his patrol, flying out to maximum range without catching sight of the Japanese strike force.[21]

The four airborne PBYs of VP-24 were almost ready to land at Lahaina Roads when the news of the attack and orders to search for the carriers came. In 24-P-1 the first reaction of Commander Fitzsimmons was to get back to headquarters at Pearl Harbor as fast as possible, but his pilot, Chief Aviation Pilot H. C. "Bennie" Smathers, talked him out of it, saying that if they went back they would be shot down. Fitzsimmons saw the merit in the statement. Smathers continued on his search course, and in doing so flew beneath the second wave of attacking Japanese planes. They were too far away to see the PBY, however, and no Zeros dived to the attack.[22]

Lieutenant Tatom, VP-24's executive officer, and his crew on 24-P-4 sighted an unidentified submarine ten miles south of Barber's Point near the cruiser USS *Indianapolis* and four destroyers, which were part of the returning *Enterprise*'s support group. When the submarine crash-dived, Tatom marked the location with a float light and, with no depth charges or bombs to drop, called in the ships to take over the job.[23] The submarine may or may not have escaped; one of several large Japanese submarines attached to the strike force failed to return after the attack.

American aircraft were suspicious of each other, but thankfully they still refused to operate under the "shoot first and ask questions later" rule. Later in the day Tatom and Smathers saw each other from a distance and moved to investigate. Two planes from the *Enterprise* saw the pair and tracked them for a short time, then made identification and broke off.[24]

At 0854 the 143 planes of the Japanese second wave began their runs on Pearl Harbor. This time the attackers paid a higher price, although it was partly their own doing: With the primary targets obscured by smoke, the dive bombers selected targets of opportunity, many aiming for the ships in the harbor that were throwing up the most antiaircraft fire, apparently thinking they were the least damaged.[25] The supporting Zeros also selected targets of opportunity, hosing military and naval hangars and barracks—as well as civilians, homes, autos—with indiscriminate machine gun and cannon fire.

On Ford Island more antiaircraft positions had been added during the twenty-four minute respite. Defenders manning machine guns in the planes were joined by others at machine guns stripped from destroyed aircraft and set up in the open, their swivels clamped in bench vises and attached to other makeshift but suitable mounts. Two planes were claimed shot down by VP-22 gunners off the southern end of the island[26]; one was claimed by a VP-24 gunner.[27] Despite the increased firepower, however, Japanese planes managed to knock out the base's telephone, teletype, and radio; communications personnel worked frantically through the height of the attack and repaired the radio tower.[28]

At 0930 a second wave of Japanese planes struck the station at Kaneohe Bay in a loosely coordinated attack. The defenders had had a little more than an hour to prepare, driving steel pipes into the ground and mounting machine guns from stricken planes on them. Revetments were formed by dragging cars and trucks damaged and destroyed in the first attack into circles around the guns.

The machine guns were useless during the first part of the attack, however, for the two nine-plane formations of level bombers crossed over the base at 1,500 feet or more, well above their range. The gunners watched helplessly as the bombs fell, exploding among the PBYs on the ramp and in the number-one hangar, setting it afire and killing a number of men inside, among them VP-11's second duty officer, Ensign Joe Smartt.

When the bombers had passed, a flight of nine Zero fighters swooped in and made three strafing runs on naval and civilian targets. The machine gunners in their scrap-iron emplacements and in the PBYs not yet ablaze opened up, supplemented by men firing rifles and pistols from behind buildings and trees or out in the open. Some of the fighters pulled away smoking and others trailed streamers of gasoline, but none caught fire or fell.

Then, as the main body moved away, a solitary Zero streaked in from the sea, its guns blasting at the fire fighters. Again the machine gunners opened up, all concentrating on the single target. Chief Petty Officer John Finn would receive a Medal of Honor for continuing to man his .50-caliber machine gun, even though he was squarely in the path of the oncoming plane. Ensign George Poulos, who had already emptied his .45-caliber automatic at the first nine planes, saw the fire rip the plane's canopy apart and the bullets ricochet off its engine as it flashed by no more than ten yards away. An instant later the engine sputtered and stopped, and the plane nosed down and slammed into the road below the married officers' quarters.[29]

Ensign Norris Johnson fired the seven rounds from his pistol at the Zero as it approached, its projectiles kicking up dust all around him. The Zero's crash ended the attack, and in the moments that followed he walked over to the crash site. On the ground Johnson found the pilot's navigation chart crumpled into a ball. When he straightened it, he saw three pencil-marked circles about three hundred miles northwest, north, and northeast of Kahuki Point, Oahu. He was sure they were rendezvous points and commandeered a car to take him to Patrol Wing 1 headquarters, where he turned the chart over to an intelligence officer.[30]

No one knows what happened to the chart, but apparently it was never delivered to Admiral Bellinger, who would have been elated to get it. The second wave broke off at Pearl Harbor about the same time as the one at Kaneohe—0945—and he was trying harder than ever to find the enemy carriers. He attempted to enlist the army's aid in tracking the retreating planes with radar. His only radar, aboard the *Curtiss*, had been knocked out by the crashing dive bomber. When telephone communications were restored across the island, he found he would get no more help from Kaneohe: The two unscathed PBYs that remained after the first attack had been eliminated in the second.[31]

The Admiral's one bright spot came when Commander Hughes, with a way finally cleared through the destruction, got his PBY into the water and into the air. But so far that morning most of the planes seen by the gunners aboard ship and ashore were Japanese, and he immediately found his plane the target of friendly antiaircraft fire. The gunners' aim was not good, however, and Hughes's PBY, still undamaged and obviously bearing a charmed life, quickly cleared the area.[32] But it was all for naught. He returned that night having seen only empty ocean.

After completing their sector searches, the four VP-24 Catalinas were guided back to Pearl Harbor by the towering columns of black smoke rising from the still-burning oil of destroyed and damaged ships. CAP Smathers and Commander Fitzsimmons returned at 1500 after nine hours in the air. Smathers landed without being fired on; his greatest concern at that moment lay in picking a proper course through the debris in the harbor as he taxied to the ramp.[33]

The army was quick to set up perimeter defenses around the island. At Kaneohe Bay the station's commanding officer, Commander Harold "Beauty" Martin, was placed in charge of defenses for the entire Mokapu Peninsula, which included armed troops, two batteries of 155-millimeter guns and two antiaircraft batteries. The base itself was judged undefendable, and a strongpoint was made by digging positions on nearby Hawaiiloa Hill.[34]

Rumors of Japanese invaders arriving by ship and by air ran rife over the island. Commander Martin received word that enemy paratroopers were landing and were wearing dungarees. Martin immediately ordered his dungaree-clad sailors into whites to differentiate them from the enemy, but this seemed to increase their chances of becoming a target.[35] Then an ingenious soul came up with a solution to the problem: The whites were dipped in coffee, and each man had a ready-made set of khakis.[36]

The number-one hangar at Kaneohe continued to burn after darkness fell. It served as a beacon to Ensign Fred Meyer as he set his punctured PBY down on the bay and tied up to a buoy by firelight.

Commander Martin had seen fit to render the landing mat unusable to enemy planes by parking cars, trucks, and maintenance machinery on it, but two Dauntlesses from the Enterprise touched down in the darkness, careened between the vehicles, and braked to a safe stop.[37] The night was a fitful one for Kaneohe's defenders, who were harassed by false alarms and pelted by rain as they tried to sleep rolled up in blankets in the mud.[38]

On Ford Island, other planes from the *Enterprise* were not so lucky. Six Wildcats, low on fuel from searching for the Japanese carriers, cleared with the tower and attempted to land. They approached with gear down and landing lights on, but a shore-based machine gun opened up and was quickly joined by others. Three Wildcats were shot down, one pilot was killed, and two others died later of injuries. The remaining three headed out to sea. Two finally managed to land, but the third lost its engine and the pilot was forced to parachute into the sea.[39]

In the smoke-hazed morning of 8 December Admiral Bellinger again took stock of his patrol planes. The count did not take long. He had eight that would fly: Hughes's, plus the seven that were in the air when the attack began. Commander Martin reported thirty-three planes destroyed at Kaneohe; in the final accounting twenty-seven were total losses and six were repaired by using spare and cannibalized parts. Of the three squadrons at Ford Island, VP-24 had fared the best. It had only six planes assigned; the four in the air at the time of the attack were untouched, and the two on the ground were repairable.[40] The remaining thirty-four in VPs 22 and 23 were either destroyed or damaged to the point that considerable work would be needed to get them into the air again. VP-22 reported six PBY-3s destroyed by fire, one PBY-1 damaged beyond repair, and the remaining five out of commission for one to ten days.[41]

With the number of flyable PBYs so small, Admiral Bellinger thought

Aftermath: The burned-out hull of a VP-12 PBY-5 lies in a graveyard of Patrol Wing 1 aircraft following the 7 December attack on Kaneohe Bay Naval Air Station. (National Archives)

it best to consolidate all search efforts at Ford Island, and the planes and crews of VP-14, along with relief crews from Patrol Wing 1, were sent over and placed under control of Commander Ramsey.

As the VP-14 PBYs landed in Pearl Harbor, Lieutenant Murray Hanson, a squadron division leader, was appalled at the destruction:

> As I lost altitude over the harbor entrance, approaching a landing in East Loch, I saw below me the crippled battleship *Nevada*, deliberately run aground on Waipio Peninsula so as not to sink in the middle of the channel and bottle up other ships trying to sortie that day. Just before touchdown, as I held the control yoke back in my lap, I glanced past my port wing tip to scan the huge belly of the *Oklahoma*, resting upside down on the bottom with some 400 sailors still on board. It seemed to narrow our landing area by half.

The PBY crews lived, ate, and slept in one big hangar under difficult conditions for a month and worked the surviving PBYs to the maximum. Hanson logged 220 hours of flying during the period, averaging seven hours a day.[42] His activity was typical of the pilots and crews searching for the Japanese strike force.

But the enemy was gone, having sailed jubilantly away after the second wave returned. Only the weather and the obstinancy of Admiral Chuichi Nagumo saved Pearl Harbor from a third wave. Commander Mitsuo Fuchida, flight leader of the attack, had requested a third wave because of strategic targets as yet untouched. He was prepared to take off even though the carriers were pitching so badly that some of the second wave planes had been heavily damaged on landing and were pushed over the side. But the weather was a moot point: Admiral Nagumo had quashed the request by saying simply that the strike force's objectives had been achieved.[43]

Fuchida had to be content with reviewing the success of the mission. Code named Operation Z, it had gone like clockwork from the time rehearsals began six months earlier until the planes swooped down on Pearl Harbor. They had carried off a favorite Japanese tactic, the surprise attack, and wreaked great destruction on the U.S. Pacific Fleet. Their newest weapons, a 1,760-pound armor-piercing bomb and a shallow-running torpedo, had worked to perfection.[44]

The cost had been relatively light: they lost only twenty-nine planes out of 353 that had taken part, plus five midget submarines and one large one. Not a single surface ship was so much as scratched. Sixty-four of their men were known dead, plus an unknown number on the large submarine.[45]

The American tally was appalling. The PBYs constituted the majority of the 92 navy planes destroyed that morning. Thirty-one more planes were damaged. The army fared even worse, with 96 planes destroyed and 128 damaged.

In the harbor eighteen ships had been sunk or damaged. Of the eight battleships, the *Oklahoma* and the *Arizona* were lost, but the other six were repairable. The *Pennsylvania* and *Maryland* would be out of service for only a matter of weeks; the *California, West Virginia,* and *Tennessee* would be out for months. Also lost were the destroyers *Downes* and *Cassin* and the target ship *Utah.* The cruisers *Helena, Honolulu,* and *Raleigh* could be repaired, as could the destroyer *Shaw,* despite its spectacular magazine explosion, and the seaplane tender *Curtiss.*

The navy had lost 2,008 men killed—half of them on the *Arizona*—and 710 wounded. One-hundred-nine marines were killed; 69 wounded. Army losses were 218 killed; 364 wounded. Sixty-eight civilians were killed; 35 wounded.[46]

As the search patrols and the damage surveys continued and the possibility of another attack lessened, the survivors mulled over the events of 7 December and asked, "How could this have happened? How could we have been caught with our pants down?"

The answer was simply that no one thought it could happen. Pearl Harbor had been too serene; it lulled its defenders into a false sense of security. Although moderate precautions were taken, no one really believed the Japanese could possibly sail undetected across 3,000 miles of ocean or that they be so bold as to launch an air attack against the air and sea power massed at Pearl Harbor. An attack on U.S. territory east of the Philippines was unthinkable. If the Japanese attempted an attack, its task force would certainly be discovered by patrol planes, submarines, or surface ships long before it sailed within range. So years and months and days and minutes of indications, detections, and warnings were rationalized away, misread, or ignored almost to the moment the first bomb dropped.

The first inkling that the United States might someday be forced to fight Japan for domination of the Pacific came in 1908 when Admiral Heihachiro Togo surprised and defeated the Russian fleet at Port Arthur.[47] Some U.S. Navy personnel felt that war was imminent at that time, among them Ensign Chester Nimitz, commanding officer of a destroyer based at Manila, who said so in a letter to his father.[48] During the 1920s, military tacticians and strategists wrote books on the subject, some of them outlining the route that Japan would follow in its conquest of east Asia, the islands of the Pacific, and even the attack on Pearl Harbor. These speculations were not lost on the Japanese Imperial Navy, or on the U.S. Navy, either.[49]

In 1932 the commander of the Pacific Fleet, Admiral Frank Schofield, decided to find out whether a surprise air attack could be successfully carried out against Pearl Harbor. Up to that point it was felt that the thirty-eight planes stationed there were sufficient for its defense. But the new carriers *Lexington* and *Saratoga* sailed across the Pacific and launched 150 planes sixty miles from Pearl Harbor before dawn on a misty morning in heavy seas—almost as the Japanese would do nine years later. Undetected and unchallenged, the planes dived through the clouds and made mock attacks on the ships in the harbor. The attack was judged successful.[50] Similar war games carried out in 1936 and again in 1938 suggested that an attacking force would come out the winner.

Relations between United States and Japan worsened over the years, beginning with the U.S. government's condemnation of Japan's conquest of Manchuria in 1931, stiffening with U.S. protests over conquests in Korea, China, and Indo-China, and culminating with the oil embargo of July 1941. In retrospect, some military strategists said the greatest surprise concerning the Pearl Harbor attack was that the Japanese waited so long to carry it out.[51]

As early as March 1941 Admiral Bellinger and Brigadier General Frederick Martin, who was in charge of the army air corps, Hawaiian Command, issued a joint statement concerning air defense. "It appears that the most likely form of attack on Oahu would be an air attack," they prophesied. "It is believed that at present such an attack would most likely be launched from one or more carriers, which would probably approach inside of 300 miles." They encouraged daily patrols as far as possible to seaward through 360 degrees but said such an effort could be carried out with present personnel and equipment for only a short period, and should not be undertaken "unless intelligence indicates a surface raid is probable within narrow limits."[52]

There were three reasons for the hedge. First, total protection would require patrols out 360 degrees to 700 miles; there weren't enough planes on the island to do that. Second, most of Martin's B-17s, the army aircraft best suited for long-range patrol work, had been sent to the Philippines. Third, Bellinger's PBYs were tied up in training exercises, and the planes were wearing out rapidly under the heavy schedule. Replacement parts were in short supply, and the crews were overworked from long hours in the air.

The Japanese diplomatic "Purple" code had been broken for a year prior to 7 December; American authorities in Washington knew the content of all messages sent to the Japanese embassies in Washington and Honolulu as soon as the Japanese did.[53] One message to the Honolulu embassy, dated 24 September 1941, showed increased interest in Pearl Harbor. It asked for a map of the harbor divided into sectors and weekly reports showing the names and exact positions of ships.

Hardly any information extracted from the decoded "Purple" messages was forwarded to Admiral Kimmel and General Short, however.[54] The strongest hint of an impending attack was sent to Kimmel on 27 November by Admiral Harold Stark, chief of naval operations. It was a "war warning," saying that "an aggressive move by the Japanese could be expected within the next few days," but the message speculated that the attack would probably be made on the Philippines or southeast Asia. No mention was made of Hawaii. Other than antisabotage measures, no defensive action was taken.[55] In late November, Admiral Kimmel found out that naval intelligence had heard no radio transmissions from the big Japanese carriers since 11 November and had no idea of their whereabouts. His terse comment was to the effect that they could be steaming around Diamond Head at any moment and he wouldn't know about it.

Also he had been advised to rig torpedo nets to protect the battleships in Pearl Harbor, but he rejected the idea, saying that the nets would restrict the flow of traffic in the channel. Besides, there were no known torpedoes that could operate in such shallow water.[56] The harbor's sole protection from torpedo attack was a single antisubmarine boom across the entrance.

The island was to have three more warnings. Had they been acted upon, disaster might have been averted. The first was sounded on 29 November when the radio operator aboard the SS *Lurline*, a luxury liner sailing from San Francisco to Honolulu, picked up unidentifiable low-frequency signals, in actuality messages being transmitted between ships in the Japanese strike force. The operator and the ship's captain suspected their origin and notified naval authorities as soon as they reached port, but no action was taken.[57]

The second warning came early on the morning of 7 December. Shortly before 0700 a small submarine was sunk about a mile outside Pearl Harbor. Its periscope had been spotted by the watch officer of a patrolling minesweeper, the USS *Condor*, at 0345. U.S. Navy submarines were under orders not to run submerged in that area, so the officer sent a call to the destroyer USS *Ward*, which also was patrolling the area. The *Ward* responded but failed to locate the sub. Then at 0630 Ensigns William Tanner and Clark Greevy, pilot and copilot of 14-P-1, one of the surveillance PBYs out of Kaneohe, saw the sub and dropped float lights to mark its position. This time the *Ward* closed to within 100 yards and opened fire with its deck guns, then followed up with depth charges. Tanner dropped his own depth charges. The submarine disappeared. Both Tanner and the commanding officer of the *Ward* were concerned that they might have sunk a navy submarine, and said so in their reports of the incident. Positions of navy subs were still being checked when the first bomb fell on Ford Island.[58]

There was a final warning. The U.S. Army had five mobile radar units operating on Oahu, and a radar information center had been set up at Fort Shafter. Under orders from General Short, the units operated only for a few hours each morning, for he felt that if an attack came it would be during that time. Usually the units operated until 1100; on Sundays they closed down at 0700.

On 7 December a unit was working overtime at Opana, on the northern tip of Oahu. Two men were on duty, one with some experience in operating the new device, the other a trainee. At 0702, two minutes after they were to shut down the unit, they saw a huge blip on the screen. They reported it to Fort Shafter with some degree of excitement but were told by a young officer there not to worry about it; the blip had to be either a squadron of navy planes coming in ahead of the *Enterprise* or a flight of new army B-17s due in from the West Coast. Then the blip separated into two blips, one going down each side of the island, and disappeared from the screen. The men turned off the unit and headed for breakfast. The time was 0752.[59]

For the Japanese, the Pearl Harbor attack was only partially successful from a military standpoint. They had crippled the U.S. Pacific Fleet and Pearl Harbor's air defenses by hitting most of their primary targets. But in their elation they forgot for the moment about the targets they failed to hit. They had hoped to find and destroy the Pacific Fleet's four carriers at Pearl Harbor; they had found none, an oversight they would soon live to regret. The fleet's oil storage tanks were left untouched; without them the remaining ships would have had to sail to the West Coast in order to refuel. Neither had the repair facilities been destroyed; because of this, the damaged ships were back in action more rapidly than they otherwise would have been and, in the case of the older battleships, much better equipped than they were before the attack.[60]

In Tokyo, Admiral Isoroku Yamamoto, commander of the Combined Fleet, realized the importance of the missed targets, especially the carriers. A strong proponent of air power for many years, Admiral Yamamoto had insisted on using the Imperial Navy's air arm against Pearl Harbor, an idea so brash that he had to threaten to resign before it was approved.[61] The attack was intended to end interference from the United States in Japan's aggressive quest for natural resources and to allow time for defenses to be strengthened. Yamamoto knew they must succeed the first time. There would be no second opportunity. Having served as military attache in Washington, he was well acquainted with the United

States and its resources and could foresee the outcome when its industrial might was turned into a war machine.

From the point of view of the psychological effect on the American people, the Pearl Harbor raid was a disaster for the Japanese. One of Admiral Nagumo's greatest worries had become a reality without him knowing it: His planes had struck before the declaration of war was delivered to the State Department in Washington, because of a delay in decoding the message. As a result, the carefully planned surprise attack became a sneak attack in the eyes of U.S. citizens. This united them solidly behind President Roosevelt and made them one in their determination to fight alongside the Allies in bringing the Axis nations to unconditional surrender. Yamamoto said he feared that the most Japan accomplished at Pearl Harbor was to awaken a sleeping giant. Even so, it was Japan's greatest victory in World War II. The Rising Sun would ride high for a few more months, and then an ever-darkening cloud of American planes, ships, and men would begin its eclipse.

The serenity was gone from Pearl Harbor now. As the army and navy began the cleanup and repair of their shattered equipment and facilities, Japan's home islands seemed much closer. Gone, too, was the cartoonlike impression of little yellow, near-sighted, spectacle-wearing pilots flying planes made largely from old beer cans, launched from carriers heavily ballasted to keep them from capsizing. On 7 December the Americans had seen excellent airmanship in aircraft well suited to their purpose and used in a mission that they had to admit was superbly executed.[62]

On Monday, 8 December, the dead were buried at Kaneohe Bay—the Americans as well as the lone Japanese flier. On the U.S. mainland the recruiting offices were swamped with volunteers eager to sign up for any branch of service. In San Diego, Consolidated workers cut metal and hammered rivets with grim determination. There were a lot of PBYs to replace.

From the Philippines to Australia

Word of the Pearl Harbor attack was quick to reach the U.S. Asiatic Fleet headquarters at Cavite Naval Base a few miles south of Manila on the island of Luzon. Admiral Thomas Hart, the fleet commander, learned about it early that morning, 8 December on that side of the international date line. The only surprise to him was that the attack had been made on Hawaii; he had expected one for years, but had thought the blow would be struck there, in the Philippines. He was so sure of it that he had sent the fleet dependents home a year earlier.

Admiral Hart had had Catalinas flying Neutrality Patrol missions since VP-21 arrived in the Philippines over two years before. The planes were watching developments in the South China Sea. He was able to increase surveillance when the squadron was replaced by Patrol Wing 10, commanded by Captain Frank Wagner. The wing was made up of two squadrons: VP-101, under Lieutenant Commander John Peterson, and VP-102, under Lieutenant Commander Edgar Neale. There were twenty-eight PBY-4s in all. In recent months the PBY crews had reported a buildup of Japanese combat and transport shipping on the Indochina mainland. As they reconnoitered they were in turn reconnoitered, with American and Japanese planes passing within shooting distance and fully prepared to fire if necessary.

Captain Wagner was as concerned over a possible attack as Admiral Hart and had dispersed his planes to various locations some time before 8 December to prevent them all being caught in the same place at the same time in a surprise attack. Seven had been sent to Sangley Point up the peninsula from Cavite in Manila Bay. Others were stationed at Los Banos near the southern shore of Laguna de Bay, a large lake southeast of Manila. Seven more operated from Olongapo on Subic Bay, across the Bataan Peninsula from Manila. Another group was based on the seaplane tender *Childs* near Manila. Three were 500 miles to the south

The officers and men of VP-101 strike a traditional pose on and in front of a squadron PBY. (Dwight Messimer)

with the tender *William B. Preston,* anchored in Malalag Bay on Mindanao, and were engaged in patrolling the island's Davao Gulf and southwest over the Celebes Sea. Fuel and supplies had also been cached at strategic locations for emergency use.

Patrol Wing 10's pilots were awakened at 0400 on 8 December and briefed on the situation while their planes were fueled, armed, and made ready to search for the enemy. The enemy found them first, however. At Malalag Bay, the least likely place for attack, Japanese dive bombers caught two PBYs on the water, strafing and sinking them. Luckily the third had taken off before dawn on patrol. The *Preston* was not damaged, and its gunners shot down one of the attacking planes.[1]

At noon Japanese bombers caught Major General Lewis Brereton's army air corps fighters and bombers on the ground at Clark Field near Manila. Early that morning, as soon as he had heard of the Pearl Harbor attack, General Brereton had ordered his planes loaded with bombs and into the air for a strike against the Japanese air fields on Formosa. But permission from General MacArthur's headquarters to launch the strike was hours in being issued, and the planes were forced to land and refuel before starting their mission. While refueling was in progress, the crews had lunch. At that moment the Japanese bombers passed across the field at 22,000 feet. Eighteen B-17s, fifty-three P-40s, and many other aircraft—almost half of MacArthur's air arm—were destroyed in the bombing and strafing that followed. The damage would have been greater had not General Brereton, under orders from MacArthur, taken precautions similar to Captain Wagner's and dispersed some of his planes to other fields.[2]

The tenth of December was an eventful day. In Europe Hitler and

Mussolini declared war on the United States. Off the coast of Malaya Japanese torpedo planes found the British battle cruiser HMS *Repulse* and the battleship HMS *Prince of Wales* steaming without air cover and sank them both.[3] On Guam, after a five-hour assault by Japanese invasion forces, the 427-man garrison of marines and sailors surrendered the tiny Pan American Airways Clipper stop, the last remaining piece of American territory between Wake Island and the Philippines.[4] In the Philippines Japanese planes hammered the remaining air corps fields to rubble, softening up the islands for the invasion that would soon begin.[5]

Early that morning a PBY flown by Lieutenant Clarence Keller, Jr., located the invasion fleet about 250 miles west of the island. He reported his find and continued to shadow the fleet, flying in and out of clouds to avoid the float plane fighters sent up to dispatch him. Captain Wagner sent out five PBYs from Los Banos under command of Lieutenant Commander Peterson, each plane carrying four 500-pound bombs. They made a high-altitude level bombing run through antiaircraft fire and released all twenty bombs on the convoy. The ships, however, had begun to zigzag. Only one hit was observed, this on the fantail of what they believed to be the battleship *Haruna* (it was not; most likely it was a cruiser), which began to circle, apparently with damaged steering. One PBY was hit by antiaircraft fire and lightly damaged; the others were unharmed.[6]

Four PBYs at Sangley Point were armed with torpedoes for an attack on the fleet. They were running engine checks, circling on the water, when Japanese Zero fighters, part of a force on its way to attack Cavite, dropped down and strafed them. Two planes, one commanded by Lieutenant Harmon Utter, the other by Ensign James McConnell, made takeoff runs and became airborne, but were badly shot up.[7] Utter was forced down at sea some twelve miles from the base, and McConnell circled inland to land on Laguna de Bay. The two others took off, got away without damage, and continued their mission. They were unable to find the convoy, however, and flew back to base. In the meantime Utter taxied his Catalina in for repairs. McConnell's plane never flew again. It was scrapped at Laguna de Bay.[8]

Cavite Naval Base was left in shambles by the attacking planes. As the base radio was among the casualties, Captain Wagner moved Patrol Wing 10 headquarters aboard the *Childs*.

When word that Japanese troops were coming ashore on Luzon was received on 12 December, the seven PBYs at Olongapo took off to search for other possible invasion forces farther down the coast of the island but found nothing. They returned to their base and tied up to the buoys. As the sound of their engines died away, it was replaced by the sound of other engines: those of Japanese aircraft roaring down at them. All seven planes were destroyed.[9]

The next day brought the only good news that had been heard for forty-eight hours, and one of the few bits of good news that would be heard for several months: At Wake Island, another Clipper stop, 447 marines and seventy-five army and navy men had repulsed a Japanese invasion fleet consisting of three light cruisers, six destroyers, two patrol boats, and three transports. With shells from 5-inch guns and bombs from four Wildcat fighters, they sank two destroyers and damaged three others, as well as damaging two cruisers and a troop transport. The Japanese lost 500 men, the marines 1. The fleet sailed away, but only to return a week later, this time overwhelming the defenders of the tiny atoll.[10]

Aboard the *Childs*, Captain Wagner evaluated his situation. He was up against an enemy that was better trained than he had thought, an enemy with excellent aircraft and the intelligence to use them to best advantage. Three days of bombing and strafing by the Japanese had completed the destruction of army air corps planes on Luzon, which meant his PBYs would fly alone with no fighter cover. Of the twenty-eight planes under his command on the morning of the eighth, seventeen remained, and only eleven were flyable. On 15 December his problem was solved for the moment. The flyable planes were ordered to the Dutch East Indies, along with Admiral Hart's small Asiatic fleet of one heavy cruiser, two light ones, four elderly destroyers, several auxiliary vessels, and a few submarines.

The Catalinas made a refueling stop at Lake Lanao on Mindanao before the long flight south, losing one when it sank after striking a rock. The tenders *Childs* and *William B. Preston*—along with the *Heron*, which had been covering the entrance to the Celebes Sea with small float planes—headed south to rendezvous at Surabaja on the island of Java by Christmas. The *Childs* was attacked by a Japanese flying boat at Manado on Celebes Island but was not damaged.

Patrol Wing 10 was now down to ten Catalinas that could still fly. On 23 December VP-102 was decommissioned and the remaining aircraft and crews transferred to VP-101 under Lieutenant Commander Peterson. The unit began operating out of a Dutch base on Ambon, a tiny island between Celebes Island and New Guinea.

Back on Luzon four of the six nonflying PBYs were repaired and made airworthy, then flown to Laguna de Bay where they were kept heavily camouflaged during the day. At night they flew to Cavite for repair parts and supplies.[11]

When the time came to move south, the planes returned to Cavite

Patrol Wing 10 PBYs make a pass over their tender, the USS *Langley*, as they take off on patrol during prewar operations in the Philippines. (Dwight Messimer)

after dark to evacuate personnel there, and Lieutenant Utter suddenly found himself host to a VIP: General Brereton came aboard, along with members of his staff, in a transfer of army air corps headquarters to the Dutch East Indies. They got more of a ride than they bargained for. Utter was making his takeoff run without lights across the blackness of the bay, already on the step, when he saw the silhouette of a motor launch, also without lights, running on a collision course. Utter slammed the throttles closed and stood on right rudder. The PBY careened to starboard and a major catastrophe was avoided, but a wing tip float was badly damaged. Utter was able to taxi back to the ramp, where his shaken passengers were transferred to another PBY for their flight south.

The Catalina was beached in the open and repairs were begun on the damaged float. Working furiously by hooded flashlight, the men completed in five hours a job that normally would have taken eighteen. The plane was flown back to Laguna de Bay just at dawn and hidden beside another PBY. The camouflage job was so good that the crew was without food for three days: The chow boat was unable to find them. Early on Christmas Day a Japanese reconnaissance plane flew over the area, apparently taking pictures with infrared film, for just before noon planes bombed and strafed the exact position where the PBYs were hidden. Utter's plane was destroyed, and the other so riddled with bullets that it sank. The attack came just before the chow boat arrived, bearing a Christmas turkey dinner for the crews.

Lieutenant Harold Swenson and his crew, whose PBY had been sunk, weren't through yet. They repaired and pumped out the sunken plane, and at sundown took off for Cavite. They no sooner became airborne, however, than one engine lost oil pressure, and Swenson shut it down. They landed at Cavite on the remaining engine and, going ashore, were surprised to find the base deserted. Almost too late they learned that the base had been evacuated, and charges had been set to blow up whatever installations the Japanese had not already destroyed. They got away safely, but without their plane and their personal possessions.

Now without aircraft, the remaining personnel of VP-101 became a guerrilla force, but remained in contact with the authorities. They were ordered to Bataan, and after a time some boarded the submarine Sea Wolf and were taken to Surabaja to rejoin Patrol Wing 10.[12] One-hundred-fifty-four, however, remained behind on Luzon.

The first retaliatory air strike against the Japanese was launched from Ambon on 27 December by VP-101's PBYs, the only planes with enough range to make the trip. It was known that the Japanese had established a base on Jolo, an island about halfway between Borneo and Mindanao, from where they could command the passage between the Sulu and Celebes Seas. The mission plan called for PBYs to make the 800-mile flight in darkness, surprise the enemy at dawn, drop their bombs, and run for home. At midnight the day after Christmas six PBYs, each carrying three 500-pound bombs and enough fuel for a sixteen-hour flight, took off and formed two three-plane sections. The first section was commanded by the strike leader, Lieutenant Burden Hastings, the second by Lieutenant John Hyland. Hastings's plane could make only about eighty knots and held his section back. Hyland's planes were faster, and as a result the two sections became separated as they droned on through the black night.

Hyland's section arrived over Jolo just at dawn. No other planes were in sight, and targets in Jolo City on the island below were still invisible in the darkness, so Hyland circled to the east to await more light. At 0625 he could wait no longer and began his bombing run. But by now their arrival was no surprise. The Japanese defenses were ready for them, and antiaircraft fire from the shore and from three cruisers and

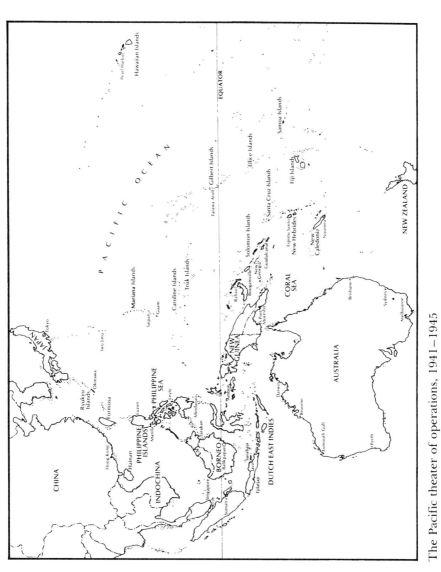

The Pacific theater of operations, 1941–1945

two transports in the anchorage was intense. Hyland's bombardier didn't like the approach and called for a turn to get better position. As the three planes maneuvered, eight enemy fighters pounced on them. The Catalinas headed for cloud cover, but Ensign Leroy Deede's plane was so badly hit that he was forced to make an open-sea landing.

At that moment Hastings's section arrived on the scene and began a bomb run through a sky full of fighter planes and extremely accurate antiaircraft fire. Ensign Earl Christman, pilot of a PBY in Hastings's section, realized his plane was under attack when he heard the waist guns open up and saw a fighter fall away in a fatal spin. Other fighters dropped their belly tanks and moved in. It became obvious that a mass level-bombing attack was suicide, so the planes broke formation and made individual dive-bombing attacks on the ships below. Hastings's PBY was last seen diving toward the ships.

Christman nosed his Catalina over to sixty degrees and dived at two hundred knots, dropping his three bombs on a cruiser. He pulled the plane out at 5,000 feet and headed west along the Sulu Archipelago, taking along a single fighter that harrassed the plane for twenty minutes. Christman turned the PBY into some of the fighter's passes, throwing off the pilot's aim, but finally a 20-millimeter cannon shell pierced the PBY's fuel tank. Gasoline flooded down through the pylon and into the radio compartment. On the next pass another cannon shell exploded in the fume-filled center compartment, and the PBY burst into flames.

Christman was letting down for an open-sea landing when two crewmen in the rear elected to bail out at 300 feet. Despite the low altitude, they hit the water without injury. Christman brought the PBY down safely and escaped from the blazing plane with the three remaining members of his crew. The plane sank in about five minutes. His copilot, Ensign William Gough, swam away to a nearby island to get help. The other three stayed together, buoyed up by their inflated life jackets, and were picked up by natives twenty-nine hours later. Christman's badly burned radioman, R. L. Pettit, died during the night. Gough, in the meantime, had also been retrieved by natives and taken to a village where he was cared for by a Filipino schoolteacher. Later he was brought to another island where he met one of the two crewmen who had bailed out; the other had drowned during the long swim.[13]

The third PBY in Hastings's section was flown by Ensign Jack Dawley. The plane was hit immediately by antiaircraft fire after starting its bombing run but kept on target. Then fighters swept in and killed both of his waist gunners. First Mechanic Evren McLawhorn took over both guns, switching from side to side as the fighters came in. Although hit seven times in the arms, legs, and one eye, he kept shooting. Like Christman, Dawley dived on a cruiser and dropped his bombs by seaman's eye. As he moved out to sea, fighters shot the PBY to junk. Fuel tanks were punctured, the rudder cables cut, and the starboard engine knocked out. Using ailerons, elevators, and the port engine, he set the plane down a few hundred yards off a beach near a native village. The PBY caught fire just as it touched down, and the crew went over the side. A strafing fighter finished it off.

Armed natives paddled out to meet the flyers, but they were friendly, and took them to the Philippine constabulary in Siasi on the island of Tapul, where they were reunited with Christman and his crew. The natives took the sunburned and fire-burned crewmen to Tawau on North Borneo and then south to Tarakan. From there a Dutch flying boat took them to Balikpapan, where Dawley and McLawhorn took a commercial airliner to Surabaja, arriving on 10 January. Christman and crew arrived two days later by steamer. Only two Catalinas, these in the second section, made it back to base. The crew of the third plane in the second section, the one flown by Ensign Deede, was rescued by a PBY on 28 December.

Natives who saw the attack said that some damage had been inflicted and one transport possibly sunk, but there was never any confirmation.[14]

In the performance and recommendations portion of his action report for the mission, Christman said that the firepower of the PBY-4 was totally inadequate and that armor protection should be provided for gunners and fuel tanks. "It is impossible to outrun fighters with a PBY-4," he concluded. "Under no circumstances should PBYs be allowed to come in contact with enemy fighters unless protected by fighter convoy."[15]

A submarine deposited Admiral Hart at Surabaja 1 January 1942, where he set up headquarters for the U.S. Asiatic Fleet. On the fifteenth a combined force called the American, British, Dutch, and Australian Command (ABDACOM) was announced, headed by British Field Marshall Sir Archibald Wavell. It was not a close-knit organization, for each element had its own defense concerns: the British with Singapore; the Dutch with the East Indies; the Australians with their homeland. The Americans took over the defense of what was left: the area on the eastern flank of the command, east from Borneo to New Guinea and north to the Celebes Sea. Aside from an occasional glimpse of an army air corps plane, everything else the pilots and crewmen of Patrol Wing 10 saw in the air over the broad expanse of the island-dotted sea was Japanese. They named the area "Cold Turkey Alley."[16]

Morale was raised several points on 11 January when VP-22 arrived at Ambon with a dozen PBY-5s to strengthen Patrol Wing 10s shrinking complement of aircraft.[17] The morale boost was sorely needed. The news since the wing had left the Philippines had not been good. On 23 December General MacArthur began to pull his American and Filipino troops back into the Bataan Peninsula where he could establish a defense line. That same day Wake Island fell. On the twenty-eighth Japanese planes bombed Manila, now an open city, and inflicted severe casualties on the civilian population. The only bright spots in December came in the form of two announcements. One said Admiral Chester Nimitz had been named commander of the Pacific Fleet, replacing Admiral Kimmel, who, along with General Short, had been relieved of his command and charged with dereliction of duty following an investigation into the Pearl Harbor attack. The second said that Admiral Ernest King had been made commander in chief of the U.S. Navy.

On 2 January the Japanese army entered Manila, now defenseless with all of MacArthur's troops on Bataan. On 11 January, while Japanese troops on the Asian mainland were dogging the heels of British troops retreating headlong toward Singapore, Japanese invasion forces landed on Tarakan Island, off the Borneo coast, and at Manado on Celebes Island. These moves would give them eventual command of Makassar Strait and access to the Dutch East Indies, as well as control of the Molucca Sea and an open road to New Guinea.[18]

Seven army B-17s sortied from Malang Field on Java to bomb the invasion force at Tarakan. Four turned back because of bad weather. The remaining three continued on and bombed through an overcast from 30,000 feet, doing no damage whatsoever.

Patrol Wing 10's PBYs did no better. Along with other ABDACOM long-range planes, four Catalinas left Ambon to attack the Japanese invasion force at Manado. Again they were out-gunned. The invaders were backed by two carriers and three heavy cruisers whose float plane fighters engaged the PBYs before they could reach the target. Ensign Jack Grayson saw them coming and banked his PBY toward cloud cover. At that point his worn, high-time port engine gave out. Coming out of the cloud he found himself left with a load of bombs, one engine, and two enemy float plane fighters for escort, which quickly knocked out the remaining engine. He jettisoned the bombs and made a dead stick open-sea landing. The crew went over the side as the fighters strafed the downed plane. The plane refused to sink and finally the fighters gave up, leaving the survivors alone in the water. The crew swam back to the PBY and tried to get out a radio message. They failed but unloaded life rafts, food, and water just as the plane went under. After three days under blistering sun and one violent rainstorm they came ashore on Mangole Island, where natives took them to Dutch officials who radioed for a pick-up by a VP-22 Catalina.[19]

The news of Japanese victories continued as the Imperial Army and

Navy carried out their Far East version of lightning war. On the twenty-seventh Japanese troops took Rabaul from the small Australian garrison on the island of New Britain, a stronghold they would maintain until the end of the war. The same day they took Kieta on Bougainville.[20] Shortly afterward they increased their hold on Borneo, moving down the coast to land troops at the Dutch oil port of Balikpapan, tracked all the way by Patrol Wing 10 PBYs. Dutch aircraft harassed the invasion force with little effect. On the night of 24 January the four-stack destroyers of the U.S. Asiatic Fleet attacked the invaders, sinking four troop transports and a patrol boat, but the landing continued without further interruption.[21]

Now the Japanese were close enough to mount air attacks against the PBY haven at Ambon. Lieutenant Doyle Donaho, executive officer of VP-22, arrived there on 15 January with two PBYs and flew headlong into a flight of Zeros. They opened fire and Donaho's plane began to blaze along the starboard wing. The second PBY also was set ablaze, but both were able to land and taxi in to the beach. Donaho's plane suffered damage only to the fabric on the starboard wing, but the second plane was destroyed. The only injury was to a crewman on the second plane.[22]

Further operations from Ambon were out of the question, and the detachment joined the remainder of the squadron at Surabaja. From there Patrol Wing 10 PBYs covered the Makassar Strait, while the tenders *Childs, Heron,* and *Preston* slipped from anchorage to anchorage in the islands to the north from where rotating detachments of PBYs could cover the Molucca Sea.[23]

Cheering news was heard by Patrol Wing 10 pilots and crews on 1 February: The U.S. Navy had struck back. Carrier planes from Task Force Eight under Admiral William Halsey and Task Force Seventeen under Admiral Frank Jack Fletcher had bombed and strafed Japanese installations in the Gilbert and Marshall Islands. To prepare the way for the advance of the two task forces, on 16 January the PBYs of VP-23 began daily searches of the waters between their temporary base at Canton Island and Suva in the Fijis.[24] It was the only cheering news they would hear that month.

On 3 February Japanese planes attacked Surabaja, setting fire to several Dutch seaplanes and damaging a Patrol Wing 10 Catalina. Two PBYs on patrol were attacked by Zeros, but they returned with a score of PBYs one, Zeros nothing.

On 5 February Japanese planes bombed and strafed Surabaja for an hour. Two Dutch Catalinas and one Patrol Wing 10 PBY were destroyed at their moorings; another was demolished in a hangar when two 500-pound bombs exploded from the heat of a fire. That afternoon a PBY on patrol was shot down and lost. By 11 February Patrol Wing 10 had twelve planes left out of forty-five that had been on its records—twenty-eight originally in VP-101 and VP-102, twelve in VP-22, and five that had been turned over to the wing by the Dutch. Six were at Surabaja, six at Darwin, Australia. Only five were flyable, however, and these had many hours on the engines.[25]

Even Darwin, on Australia's northern coast, was no longer immune from enemy attack. On 19 February a Japanese attack force with carriers and battleships sailed into the Timor Sea and launched its planes, these joined by land-based bombers from Kendari on Celebes Island. Darwin had no air raid warning system; the attackers were first seen as they began their bombing runs. An ammunition ship took a direct hit and exploded, sinking a nearby troopship. The destroyer *Peary* was bombed and sunk. In all a dozen ships—tankers, transports, cargo vessels, and small ships—were destroyed. Others were damaged, some saved by beaching. Dock facilities and the airfield were demolished, and the city was left in flames. The tender *William B. Preston* was hit and set afire, her steering knocked out and ten of her crew killed, but she stayed afloat. Three of her PBYs were destroyed at their moorings.[26]

One PBY was out on patrol. Lieutenant Thomas Moorer had taken off that morning to reconnoiter toward Ambon. Near Melville Island he circled to check the identity of a freighter below. As he did so nine Zeros swooped out of the sun and opened fire on his Catalina. The Zeros made one pass, holing the fuel tanks, knocking out the port engine, and setting the plane on fire. The wing tip lowering mechanism was also jammed, and Lieutenant Moorer made a bouncing downwind landing with no tip floats. As the plane burned on the water, Moorer and crew climbed into the one serviceable life raft. The attacking planes, part of a flight of seventy-two, flew on to Darwin.

After a few hours at sea, Moorer and his crew were picked up by the freighter they had intended to check out. She was the SS *Florence D.*, under contract to the U.S. Navy to run supplies to Corregidor. Their wounds were treated, they were fed and given a change of clothing. Their time of comfort was short, however, for at 1500 Japanese dive bombers found the ship and hit it with two bombs. The *Florence D.* began to sink, and Moorer ordered his men over the side. When the attack ended, two life boats were still serviceable, and the survivors—including all but one of Moorer's men—climbed aboard. The ship's captain had been badly wounded in the attack, so Moorer, the senior officer, took charge. With himself in one boat and his copilot, Ensign Walter Mosely, in the other, they rigged sails and shortly after dark landed on Bathurst Island. Almost two weeks went by before they attracted the attention of a Royal Australian Air Force plane, which sent in a subchaser the next day to take them to Darwin.[27]

On 15 February the British stronghold of Singapore fell. On 31 January all British forces had been pulled back onto the island, the causeway to the mainland blown up, and all guns aimed out to sea in anticipation of the coming invastion. But the Japanese, almost unopposed, repaired the causeway and poured onto the island from the mainland side. Some 70,000 prisoners were taken, the worst defeat ever to be suffered by a European power in Asia.[28]

That same day Sumatra was invaded by Japanese forces, which headed inland for the city of Palembang, a Dutch oil trade center. A force also moved to the south coast of Borneo, taking Bandjarmasin, less than 300 miles across the Java Sea from Surabaja. On the eighteenth invaders took over the island of Bali, at the eastern end of Java and only 150 miles from Surabaja, from where they proceeded to bomb the PBY base there into ruins.

The air belonged to the Japanese. The PBYs remaining at Surabaja took off at dawn and returned after dark to avoid being caught on the water. It was only a matter of time until Java fell, and three PBYs were sent to Broome, Australia, to prepare for the evacuation.

On 24 February another PBY was lost. Lieutenant (j.g.) John Robertson, the pilot, radioed that he had found a large invasion fleet near the city of Makassar on Celebes Island. Ordered to attack the transports, he reported a near miss, following which he was attacked by fighters. There were no more radio messages.

The constant attrition showed its ultimate effect on the detachment when, on 26 February, the commander reported no aircraft available for patrol. He had three planes, the report read, but one would not be ready for patrol until the following day. A second was flyable, but had no radio and would be used to evacuate personnel to Broome. The third plane had a radio but could only receive, and its wing tip floats would not operate. Two of the three needed new engines badly.

As promised, next morning a PBY left on patrol, and a second, with Lieutenant John Hyland at the controls, headed for Broome. He made it only as far as Tjilatjap on the far side of Java, however, where the starboard engine quit, and the plane had to be abandoned.[29]

On 27 February the seaplane tender *Langley*, headed for Java with thirty-two P-40s for the Dutch, was sunk by Japanese planes.[30] That same day ABDACOM warships squadron under Dutch admiral Karel Doorman was all but put out of action in the Battle of the Java Sea. On 1 March, when remnants of the squadron made a last-ditch effort to forestall invasion of the island, the last of the U.S. Asiatic Fleet's cruisers and destroyers was sunk.[31]

The PBYs from Surabaja retreated across the island to Tjilatjap, the only deep-water port remaining open, and on 2 March Captain Wagner and Patrol Wing 10 departed in the last Catalina out of Java. The seaplane tender *Childs* was waiting in Broome for their arrival, but even though it was 700 miles to the southwest of Java, it was no sanctuary. Two days later Japanese planes attacked and destroyed two Patrol Wing 10 PBYs and several Dutch seaplanes on the water.

Patrol Wing 10 had reached its lowest ebb: Its aircraft complement consisted of three planes. But it was still flying, and on 7 March the decimated wing moved to Perth, on Australia's southwest coast, to begin patrols there.[32]

By 9 March the Japanese had completed their conquest of the East Indies, taking 100,000 prisoners and ending four centuries of Dutch rule.[33]

Fifteen-hundred miles to the north on Bataan the "Battling Bastards" had made General Homma's troops pay for every inch of land they gained in February, so dearly that Homma pulled his men back for a two-month rest while they waited for reinforcements to arrive.[34] The Americans' food, ammunition, and supplies were almost gone, however. Morale was low among the gaunt defenders, and dropped lower still when General MacArthur was ordered out of his headquarters on Corregidor to assume command of the forces that were to assemble in Australia for the coming counteroffensive.[35] Morale reached zero when Pres-

21-P-10 begins a descent to investigate a coastal freighter as part of Neutrality Patrol activity in the Far East in 1940. (Dwight Messimer)

ident Roosevelt said in a radio message that no reinforcements would be forthcoming from the United States.[36]

Fighting renewed on Bataan on 3 April, Good Friday. About 2,000 persons, including 104 nurses, escaped to Corregidor. On 9 April, U.S. forces on Bataan—some 76,000 starving and battle-weary men—surrendered.[37]

For a month afterward the island fortress of Corregidor held out, the 13,000 Americans and Filipinos in its tunnels bombarded by a thousand rounds a day from a hundred Japanese guns. One by one the fifty-six heavy guns and mortars on the island were silenced. The walls of the bombproof tunnels cracked; dust and dirt filtered down on the living, the dying, and the dead.[38] It was during this period that PBYs from Patrol Wing 10 flew one of the most heroic missions ever to be carried out.

By mid-April the only outside contact with the defenders on Corregidor was by submarine. The airfield there was too small for army B-17s to land, and if a plane could get in past the Japanese air defenses the likelihood of getting out again was even more remote. The end for Corregidor would soon come, and the army command in Melbourne requested a navy seaplane to evacuate high-ranking officers and nurses. The seaplane was to leave Perth, pick up a cargo of medical supplies, antiaircraft shell nose fuses, and radio parts, and deliver them to Corregidor. A fuel stop was to be made at Lake Lanao on Mindanao, with the army supplying the fuel and the refueling detail.

Rather than sending one seaplane as requested, the navy responded with two. One was flown by Lieutentant (j.g.) Thomas Pollack, with Naval Aviation Pilot D. W. Bounds as copilot and Lieutenant Commander Edgar Neal aboard as mission commander. The other was flown by Lieutenant (j.g.) Leroy Deede, with Lieutenant (j.g.) William Gough as copilot, and Naval Aviation Pilot W. D. Eddy as third pilot. The operation, code-named Flight Gridiron, began at 1000 on 27 April when the two PBYs took off from Perth for Sharks Bay, 400 miles north, and on to Darwin, where they caused an air raid alert. The mission could have ended there: The pilots didn't know the latest identification procedures and, with the city being bombed twice daily by the Japanese, the antiaircraft gunners were understandably trigger-happy.

At Darwin the supplies for Corregidor were loaded aboard, and at 1630 hours the planes took off, heading north on what they hoped would be a 3,900-mile round trip. It hardly seemed likely. For most of the next week they would be over or in enemy-held territory; they would land at night on Manila Bay within range of Japanese artillery, unload cargo, take on passengers, and then take off and fly the same course back to Darwin.

Pollack, in the lead PBY, did the navigating. The planes droned over islands that sent up swarms of fighters during the day, but which, thankfully, took no notice of them that night. Off the port beam they saw the Japanese-held city of Manado on Celebes Island, arrogantly "lit up like a Christmas tree," Pollack said in his report, totally unconcerned about enemy aircraft. Although the PBYs progressed unnoticed through the clear night sky, the pilots breathed easier when cloud cover moved in to hide them later on.

The PBYs arrived over Lake Lanao on Mindanao at 0430. They made safe power-on landings in the predawn blackness, later finding that one plane had landed downwind, the other crosswind. The planes were towed to shore and camouflaged under trees, where pilots and crews tried to sleep until darkness returned.

At 1845 the Catalinas took off on the last leg of the flight. Pollack and Deede had no trouble in finding Corregidor; a blazing fuel tank served as a beacon, and smoke from the fire gave them wind direction. The two planes became separated on the final approach; when Pollack eased off his throttles, Deede no longer had any exhaust flames to follow.

The planes landed safely on Manila Bay with their heavy cargoes and waited "an eternity—all of five minutes" until they were met by small boats near Cabalo Island. The cargo was quickly off-loaded, but the passenger loading seemed slow. "Let's get those old women aboard and get outta here," Pollack said into the intercom. "There's Jap artillery on both sides that can make us very unhappy." Second Pilot Bounds came forward and said, "You were right about the women; we have fourteen aboard." Pollack asked how many passengers in total were aboard the plane. Bounds answered, "I can't be sure, but there must be about thirty; you can't walk from one end to the other." Aside from the nurses, the rest of the passengers were army officers, among them a finance officer with $2,000,000 in Philippine bills stuffed in his shirt. Deede's plane had almost the same passenger count.

Pollack moved his passengers as far forward as possible and Bounds opened the throttles. The heavily loaded PBY mushed forward, straining to get up on the step, spray covering the windshield and putting Pollack on instruments for a few moments, then she was up, bounding across the swells, finally lifting and slowly climbing away from the bay.

In clouds and darkness the two planes became separated. Pollack found Lake Lanao again and made another power-on landing. Deede was not so lucky, however, and spent the night in a sheltered cove on the Mindanao shore. He landed his PBY on the lake the next morning just after daybreak, much to Pollack's relief.

The planes were towed ashore and camouflaged again. The passengers were taken to hotels to rest throughout the day while the planes were refueled and made ready for the long flight to Darwin. During the day they heard Japanese planes overhead, but they weren't searching for PBYs; they appeared to be on final approach for landing at an airfield about seven miles away.

The Catalinas were refueled, loaded, and ready for takeoff at 1830, but when the time came to shove off from shore, Pollack's heavily loaded plane couldn't be moved. It was finally towed off by motorized canoe, but after a short distance a wind came up and caused the plane to drift onto a submerged rock. The hull was holed in several places.

Water poured in, but the passengers put blankets over the holes and stood on them, staunching the flow. Pollack started the engines and turned into the wind, but word came that the plane was taking on water too fast to attempt a takeoff run, so he taxied back to shore and beached the plane. He used a signal light to tell Deede, who was waiting with engines running, to take off without him.

Pollack's PBY was sinking fast. The passengers were unloaded, and all removable gear was taken off, including the radio. Watertight bulkheads were closed, but the plane continued to sink. They watched the waterline rise on the plexiglas gun blisters. The water was four feet deep in two compartments; the navigator's table was underwater.

The plane's bow and port wing were resting on shore, but the tail and starboard wing were in deep water. Empty fuel drums were lashed together and pushed in place to keep them from sinking further. An army man kept diving and running his hands under the hull until he found all the damage. He located holes in two compartments, one of which was about two feet square. Muslin was pasted over the smaller holes with marine glue, and bailing was begun, using a small engine-driven pump furnished by the army fueling detail.

All the other leaks were now stopped, and the plane was no longer sinking, but nothing could be found to patch the large hole. The breakthrough came when a blanket was worked under the hull, and as bailing progressed, water pressure pressed it into the hole, stopping the leak. Two hours later enough water had been pumped out so the men could work. The blanket was left in place, and a wooden tray was wedged between the stringers to cover the hole and reinforce the hull.

It was now 1600 hours; Pollack and his helpers had worked through the night and all the following day. The PBY was as ready to go as it would ever be. Pollack was sure, however, that he could not take off with a full load of passengers, so half were left behind to be picked up later by an army B-17. The others were loaded on board and the plane was towed out into the lake as brush camouflaging the wings was pushed off. The engines were started, and as the plane began to move, the blanket lost its pressure, and water started pouring in again. It was now or never. With the passengers bailing furiously, Pollack opened the throttles on the still-cold engines and charged ahead, with the plane heading straight for a mountain. It was the longest takeoff run of his life, he said, but gradually the plane rose on the step. As the shore neared, he pulled the plane off and it staggered into the air, gradually picking up speed. Banking away from the mountain, he found the plane was very unstable because of the several hundred pounds of water in the hull, but the condition remedied itself as the water drained out. Japanese planes were flying in the area, but the PBY escaped unseen and headed south.

Pollack followed the same flight path back to Darwin, arriving there the next morning. The PBY bounced three times on landing, "the worst landing of my life," Pollack said, but the patch held and, with continuous bailing, the plane stayed afloat while it was refueled and the crew ate a hot breakfast, the first in six days. With servicing complete, Pollack took off for Perth, landing there at 0130 on 3 May and beaching the PBY. Deede had arrived the day before. For their efforts Pollack, Deede, and crews were awarded the Silver Star for one of the longest rescue missions ever recorded—7,300 miles from Perth to Corregidor and return.[39] The only sad note in an otherwise joyful mission was the failure of the B-17 to arrive and pick up the passengers left behind at Lake Lanao. They were eventually taken prisoner and held for the remainder of the war.[40]

On the day Pollack arrived back in Darwin, the last big gun emplacement on Corregidor took a direct hit. Three nights later General Homma's troops landed on the island with tanks and artillery and zeroed in on the last line of defense, which was manned in part by 400 sailors, including those left behind from Patrol Wing 10, who were fighting as infantrymen.

On 6 May, General Jonathan Wainwright, who had been left in command after MacArthur's departure, surrendered the island and all of the Philippine defense forces, rather than have Corregidor's tunnels turned into slaughter houses for the nurses, wounded, and civilians sheltered there. The fighting units on the main islands were ordered by radio to surrender. They did so reluctantly, but not before thousands escaped into the hills to fight on as guerrillas.[41]

The surrender of Corregidor sent morale to rock bottom for the Americans, who had been pushed all the way back to Australia. Now the Pacific belonged to Japan from the Kuriles in the north to the East Indies on the south, and from deep in mainland China on the west to Wake Island on the east. The Japanese had the oil and the resources they had sought. Now they would strengthen their defenses. They would destroy what remained of the U.S. Pacific Fleet. They would take New Caledonia and surrounding islands, cutting off supplies to Australia and eliminating it as a potential staging area for a reconquest of the South Pacific by the Allies. They would squelch any possibility of a northern invasion by the United States by taking the Aleutians. They would complete the transformation of the Pacific into a Japanese lake by taking Johnson, Palmyra, and Canton Islands, possibly even the Hawaiian Islands—and of course Midway.

8

Midway

The idea of attacking Midway was not readily accepted by decision makers in Japan. Like Operation Z, the Pearl Harbor attack plan, Operation MI was the proposal of Admiral Isoroku Yamamoto, commander in chief of Japan's Combined Fleet, and again like Operation Z, was approved by the simple expedient of his presenting its logic to his peers and superiors and then threatening to resign if it was rejected.

Yamamoto had written dual objectives into Operation MI: the capture of Midway for use as a staging area for conquest of the Hawaiian Islands; and the final destruction of the U.S. Pacific Fleet, which had been badly eroded at Pearl Harbor and in actions during the Japanese advance through the Philippines and the South Pacific. Many members of the Imperial Navy hierarchy disagreed with one or the other or both aims. Some felt that Midway atoll's two small islands were not large enough to accommodate the military might needed to take Hawaii, and they doubted that the United States would risk the last of its Pacific seapower to defend such an insignificant outpost, which had been mainly another Pan American Clipper refueling stop.

Counterproposals were made. One would have the army drive deeper into mainland China and capture Chungking. Another would have the navy steam into the Indian Ocean and capture Ceylon. Still others would offset the threat of American counterattacks. As a sop to all opponents, Yamamoto wrote into his plan a diversionary attack on the Aleutians and promised that after the successful completion of the Midway campaign the Combined Fleet would move south, conquering the mid- and South Pacific islands to isolate Australia.

The arguments began shortly after Pearl Harbor and continued until early April, when Yamamoto tendered his resignation. From then on it was a matter of working out details and fine-tuning the mammoth undertaking.[1] Doubts remained among some of Yamamoto's senior and junior officers as to the wisdom of the Midway plan. Some had specific but private objections to an attack with two objectives, neither of which complemented the other. Others were concerned about the division of forces into three major groups. One would provide the feint in the Aleutians. The remaining two would hit Midway, one as the invasion force, the other as the strike force. Finally, critics were opposed to Yamamoto's holding the battleships in reserve, leaving the carriers in the van with only a screen of cruisers and destroyers.

With all of its flaws, however, not a single officer from Yamamoto on down doubted that the Midway campaign would be anything other than a rousing success. The unbroken chain of conquests had brought on what was called the "victory disease." The Japanese high command was confident that the Combined Fleet could attain any military objective it desired, anywhere, anytime.[2]

Yamamoto saw Lieutenant Colonel James Doolittle's carrier-launched strike against Japan on 18 April as prime evidence of the need to complete the destruction of the U.S. Pacific Fleet and to establish an island picket line as close as possible to the West Coast of the United States. The strike showed that the Americans still had a will to fight and were capable of carrying the fight to the sacred Japanese homeland. Such an attack was not unanticipated, but the staff of the Combined Fleet had expected it to come from carrier-based aircraft no more than 300 miles off the coast, not from army B-25 bombers taking off from a carrier 700 miles out, dropping their bombs on Japan, and flying on to land in China. The B-25s further surprised the Japanese defenses by flying at wavetop height, evading the army fighters.[3]

The draw between the Japanese and the Americans in the Battle of the Coral Sea 4–8 May and the turning back of the invasion fleet which was to take Port Moresby was not considered a setback of any consequence, partially because it was reported as a great victory. The Japanese felt that the loss of one small carrier, the *Shoho*, was a fair trade for the *Lexington*, which they mistook for the *Saratoga*, and the capture of Port Moresby could be attempted again at a later date. Neither was the loss of the services of the big carriers *Shokaku* and *Zuikaku* considered important to the success of the Midway plan. American Dauntless dive bombers had inflicted serious damage on the *Shokaku*, and the *Zuikaku* had lost many of its men and planes, but the Japanese had evened the score by damaging the *Yorktown*. They were confident that the remaining four big carriers would be enough to carry out the Midway attack, and repairing and restocking the veterans of the Coral Sea was carried out at a leisurely pace.

The attitude of the staff of the Combined Fleet might have been different if they had known what was going on in the basement of a building near the Pearl Harbor docks. Commander Joseph Rochefort, chief of the Combat Intelligence Office, and his team of cryptanalysts had been working diligenty to crack the Japanese navy's operational code, JN25, and by March 1942 were able to read much of its coded transmissions. Because of this, patrolling PBYs of Patrol Wing 1 (VP-23 began operations from Canton Island and Suva in the Fiji Islands on 16 January, and VP-14 began operating off the *Curtiss* at Noumea, New Caledonia on 21 February) were able to locate the Japanese fleet steaming south toward Port Moresby and guide Admiral Frank Jack Fletcher's Task Force 17 into position for the Coral Sea battle.

By the time this battle ended, Commander Rochefort was positive from the transmissions his team was decoding that the Japanese were preparing a strike for Midway. He was sure that the letters "AF" meant Midway, and proved it to his satisfaction by having Midway radio transmit a phony message to Pearl Harbor saying the water was in short supply. A few hours later Rochefort's men intercepted a Japanese message saying that "AF" was short of water.[4]

Even in the face of this, a belief persisted among the American military that the attack would be made on Pearl Harbor, or perhaps even on the West Coast. But Rochefort had one staunch supporter, and his was the vote that counted: Admiral Nimitz, who on 3 April had been given overall command of forces in the Central Pacific, balancing MacArthur's command of the Southwest Pacific.

On 2 May the admiral made an inspection tour of Midway and later informed Commander Cyril Simard, the naval air station commander, of an impending attack on Midway, which, by best intelligence estimates, would be launched on 28 May.[5] From that time up until 4 June, Admiral Nimitz began to pack Midway's Sand and Eastern Islands with all the defensive force they could support.

Before 21 May, the atoll's air defenses consisted of the twenty-one Brewster Buffalo fighters and twenty-one Vought Vindicator dive bombers of Marine Air Group 22.[6] The following day the buildup began: the first six of twelve PBY-5As of VP-44 under Lieutenant Commander R. C. Brixner arrived from Pearl Harbor to provide long-range patrol capabilities.[7] Small groups continued to wing in, a hodge-podge of PBYs on temporary duty from VP-14, VP-23, VP-24, VP-51, VP-72, and VP-91. The seaplanes operated from Sand Island, and the amphibians from the runways on Eastern Island, these under Lieutenant Commander John Fitzsimmons, commanding officer of VP-24, who had flown out with the first of the squadron's planes on 30 April to take charge of the detachment.[8]

Beginning 18 May, groups of Boeing B-17 Flying Fortresses arrived almost daily, providing heavy bombardment capability and doubling as

What the fight was all about on 4 June 1942: tiny Midway atoll. PBY-5As operated from Eastern Island's runways; PBY-5 seaplanes from a base on Sand Island. (National Archives)

additional long-range patrol planes.[9] Nineteen Douglas Dauntless dive bombers and seven Grumman Wildcat fighters, along with pilots and crews, were unloaded 26 May by the USS *Kitty Hawk* to beef up MAG 22's strength.[10] On the twenty-ninth, four Martin B-26 Marauder medium bombers landed.[11] At the end of May, Midway's beaches and runways were lined with planes: six new Grumman TBF Avenger torpedo bombers, twenty-seven dive bombers, an equal number of fighters, thirty-two scout planes, and twenty-three medium and heavy bombers.

Overall charge of the combined army-navy-marine air defense effort at Midway was given to Commander Logan Ramsey, operations officer under Rear Admiral Patrick Bellinger at Pearl Harbor.[12] On 30 May he ordered a coordinated air-search program, with sector patrols flown by the PBYs beginning at 0415 each morning.[13] Fifteen minutes later the B-17s followed, and finally, after the long-range planes were 400 miles out, the shorter range scouts were sent up.

Ramsey was concerned not only with finding the Japanese attack force, but in staving off a possible long-range bombing attack from Wake Island. The possibility became more realistic that morning when two patrolling PBYs were attacked and badly shot up by multiengine aircraft that could have come only from Wake. Two days later, on 1 June, the performance was repeated, this time with only one of the PBYs hit but with three men wounded.[14]

Ramsey's air searches were begun not a minute too soon, for Japan's Midway forces were beginning to move. The invasion fleet—troop ships carrying a 5,000-man force, cargo vessels, and auxiliary vessels, forty ships in all— left Yokosuka and Kure on 20 May for Saipan, from where they would sortie for Midway on 27 May. That same day the strike force left Japan.[15] In command of the impressive array of carriers, battleships, cruisers, destroyers, and miscellaneous servicing ships was Admiral Chuichi Nagumo, who had been in charge of the Pearl Harbor operation. Since that time his First Air Fleet had conducted successful operations throughout the Pacific and in the Indian Ocean, sinking a carrier, two cruisers, five battleships, seven destroyers, and numerous smaller craft, all without the loss of a single ship. Although the training of pilots and crews for the Midway operation had not been as thorough or as rewarding as he would have liked, he and his officers, like Yamamoto and the others in the Combined Fleet, basked in the confidence that Operation MI's joint goals could be attained: destruction of the U.S. fleet and the capture of Midway.[16]

Two days later, on 29 May, Yamamoto's main body left to follow Nagumo's strike force at a distance of 300 miles. From the flagship, the giant battleship *Yamato*, Yamamoto intended to direct and coordinate the entire operation across 3,000 miles of sea from the Aleutians to Saipan. The main focus would be on Midway, where the attack would begin on 4 June Midway time. On the morning of 3 June, his ships had sailed within a few hundred miles of the atoll undetected, thanks to fog and radio silence.

Yamamoto's plan had worked almost to perfection. Only two segments had failed to fall into place. One was Operation K, in which two Emily flying boats were to provide up-to-date intelligence on the position of the U.S. fleet by flying a reconnaissance mission over Pearl Harbor. To do so they were to refuel from submarines at French Frigate Shoals, but when the refueling submarines arrived there on 30 May, they found the islands being used by the U.S. Navy as a seaplane base, and Operation K was abandoned.[17] The second failure was not recognized as such at the time. A screen of submarines was to be in position between Midway and Hawaii by 2 June to report movements of the U.S. Fleet. They were too late; by that date Task Force 16 and Task Force 17 had already passed their location and were well on their way to ambush the Japanese task force.

Admiral Nimitz had counted on Vice Admiral William Halsey to head the U.S. Navy strike force, but when Halsey's Task Force 16 dropped anchor in Pearl Harbor on 26 May, he was hospitalized with dermatitis, brought on by nervous tension and too much tropical sun. Nimitz asked him to pick his own replacement, and he immediately named Rear Admiral Raymond Spruance. Spruance was briefed on the impending Midway attack and was instructed to move Task Force 16 out on 28 May.[18]

Almost as soon as the Coral Sea engagement ended, Task Force 17 had been called back to Pearl Harbor. It anchored there on 27 May. Admiral Fletcher was surprised to find himself facing an immediate turnaround: he and his ships were being sent to Midway as soon as the damage from three bomb hits on the *Yorktown* could be repaired. Around-the-clock effort achieved the goal of both task forces. Spruance's Task Force 16 sailed as scheduled on 28 May. Task Force 17 sailed two days later, on 30 May, with a not-perfect-but-adequate *Yorktown* serving once again as Fletcher's flagship. The two task forces rendezvoused 325 miles northeast of Midway at a location Nimitz called "Point Luck," and the two task forces steamed ahead. On 3 June they were nearing the point 200 miles north of Midway from which to launch their planes against the Japanese strike force once it was sighted. The scales were heavily weighted toward the Japanese, whose ships outnumbered the Americans' eighty-six to twenty-seven, with four carriers to three.[19] But fate entered on the side of the Americans and would tip the balance in their favor.

On Midway the pilots and crews of the PBYs got little rest. They flew 700-mile sector searches for eleven hours almost every day, with additional time taken up for briefing and debriefing. The briefings gave their primary objective as spotting a Japanese fleet approaching Midway and reporting it without being seen themselves. There was never a mention of two fleets. The days were hot and dry, with few clouds and little rain. Pilots spent their first days in the BOQ, but then moved into dugouts, where comforts were few and sleep was at a premium.

On 3 June Ensign Jewell (Jack) Reid and his crew in a VP-44 PBY-5A were excited. Reid was sure that on that day they would sight the Japanese fleet. "Our patrol was uneventful the first 700 miles," he said. "Our radio man, Chief Musser, was guarding the Midway radio frequency on one receiver and listening to Japanese traffic on another. He told my navigator, Ensign Swan, the Japanese ships were using the low, short-range frequency and we were very close to their position." Reid and his copilot, Ensign Hardeman, got their heads together with Swan and Musser and decided to fly another thirty miles farther out.

"We were flying 270 degrees at 1,000 feet," Reid said, "At the end of 730 miles, just before I was to turn on a north heading, I spotted what at first appeared to be specks on the horizon or dirty spots on the windshield. After a second look, I shouted, 'Enemy ships thirty miles dead ahead!' Hardeman snatched the binoculars and, after looking, shouted, 'You're damned right, they're enemy ships!'"

The time was 0900. Reid immediately dived the PBY until it was skimming the white caps and turned on his north heading. He made no attempt to count ships at that point, but could see three columns steaming east. A message was encoded to Midway: "Sighted main enemy fleet, course 90 degrees, range 730 miles." His greatest concern at the moment was to remain unseen. "There was talk around the squadron that to spot the Japanese fleet would be suicide. The Emperor's little men would

The men who found the Japanese invasion fleet on 3 June 1942. Back row: R. J. Derouin, Francis Musser, Ensign Hardeman, Ensign Jewell (Jack) Reid, Ensign R. A. Swan. Front row: J. F. Grammell, J. Goovers, P. A. Fitzpatrick. (National Archives)

send up everything they had to shoot you down, so the plane couldn't return to base and give a comprehensive report," he said.

Reid's tactics worked. He maneuvered until the PBY was on the same heading as the fleet, then from a distance of twenty-five miles or less he and his crew fed data on numbers and types of ships back to Midway for the next two hours with no hint of being seen by the Japanese. They counted seventeen, identifying them as battleships, cruisers, destroyers, transports, fuel tankers, and supply ships.

Finally, with minimum fuel remaining, Reid broke off and headed for Midway. He was told to land on the lagoon, as B-17s and B-26s from Pearl Harbor had taken up all of the parking spaces along Eastern's runways. Just after touching down one engine died of fuel starvation, and as they made the buoy the other quit. They had been in the air for 14.3 hours.[20]

With no carriers reported by Reid, Commander Ramsey was unconvinced that the fleet coming in from the east was the strike force. Neither did Admiral Nimitz believe it. He radioed Admiral Fletcher that the PBYs had found the invasion force, not the strike force, and to expect the strike force the next day. Whatever its mission, the enemy fleet could not be allowed to continue on unmolested, however, and at noon nine B-17s were dispatched from Midway to bomb it. The bombers found the ships and began their run at about 10,000 feet. Apparently aware for some time that they had been discovered, the Japanese ships were quick to send up a thunderous cloud of antiaircraft fire. The B-17s rained down their bombs. But when each side checked for damage, none was found.[21]

Darkness fell, but the defenders of Midway saw no reason to cease harassing the Japanese fleet. That afternoon two PBYs had arrived, each carrying two torpedoes, and Commander Ramsey quickly conceived a plan for a night torpedo attack, the first ever for PBYs.

Ensign Alan Rothenberg had also flown in that day. He was awakened at 0200 that morning and told he was going to Midway. "Mid-way to what?" he asked; he had never heard of the place. He was on his way there at 0700, however. He was on the ground about an hour and had just dropped off his gear in a dugout when word came that all PBY people were reporting to the operations office. "I went there," he said, "and Commander Ramsey was saying that the Japanese fleet had been discovered about 600 miles out, and he was sending out four volunteer PBY crews to launch a torpedo attack. He said, 'Red Richards will lead the attack in Lieutenant Hibberd's plane, and the volunteers are Propst, Davis, and that little ensign back there,' and he pointed at me. After he finished, I walked out and sure enough they were hanging a torpedo on my plane."[22]

It was a motley crew. Rothenberg was from VP-51, Lieutenant (j.g.) Charles Hibberd from VP-24, and Lieutenant Doug Davis from VP-23. Ensign Gaylord Propst would be copilot on the fourth PBY, which was commanded by Chief Aviation Pilot H. C. Smathers of VP-24. Smathers was the only one of the four experienced in launching a torpedo. He went through flight training in 1930, and was a pilot in VT-2 on the *Saratoga* in 1934, dropping torpedoes from Great Lakes biplanes. His plane was one of those that had ferried in torpedoes that morning. He had had no idea that he would be using one of them himself.[23]

The torpedoes, 2,200-pound Mark XIII's, were designed for air launch but were erratic weapons of dubious value. Ideally they were dropped from no more than sixty feet altitude at a relatively low speed. Once in the water they might deviate from their intended course in any direction, up or down, port or starboard, and if by chance they reached the target there was no guarantee they would explode.

Three of the four PBYs took off from Eastern Island at 2115. Rothenberg was delayed by a mounting ladder that the crew could not detach. "Finally I told them to take an axe and chop it off," he said. "So that's what they did."[24] The planes were to operate without lights and observe radio silence, so when their leader, Lieutenant William Richards, executive officer of VP-44, had Hibberd climb through an overcast at 2,000 feet, only Davis managed to locate him again in the dark.[25] Smathers and Rothenberg continued on toward the target on their own.

At 0115 Hibberd's radar showed a group of ships about ten miles off to port. They were quickly spotted visually, aligned in two columns as reported in the pilots' briefing. Richards directed his two-plane group down-moon of the fleet. The ships seemed unaware of any danger and steamed placidly ahead. Richards selected the largest ship in the port column as a target and Hibberd moved in on it at 100 knots. At 800 yards he dropped the Mark XIII, and the PBY roared up and over the ship, now identified as a transport. One of the gunners yelled that he saw a bright flash, but Hibberd, aware of the torpedo's reputation, wondered if what the gunner had seen was the muzzle blast of an antiaircraft gun at close range.[26]

Davis began a run on a ship at the same time as Hibberd but, aware that he had only one shot at it and unhappy with the angle of attack, circled for a better one. This time the ship turned and presented its stern, but he elected to drop anyway. He moved in to 200 yards, probably too close for the warhead to arm, and released his torpedo, then opened the throttles and pulled up over the ship's stern. As he did so the ship's antiaircraft guns and those of every ship nearby opened up on him. His port waist gunner let fly with his .50-caliber machine gun as he went past, but his were apparently the only missiles from the PBY to strike the ship: there was no explosion.[27]

At 0130 Smathers found himself over the Japanese fleet at 1,000 feet. "I immediately went down-moon at a low level and dropped the torpedo," he said, aiming at a large ship at the end of a column. Experience paid off: the torpedo ran true and a crewman reported a flash followed by flame.[28] Smathers had hit a tanker, the *Akebono Maru*. It was the only hit of the evening.[29]

Rothenberg, flying in clouds, never found a target, although he was fired on by shipboard antiaircraft guns twice, and an unidentified aircraft made several runs on his plane.

The damage was not great on either side. Smathers's PBY had one bullet hole in it. Davis's, however, had a number of small caliber holes in the wings, tail, and bow, and the bombsight was damaged.[30] The hit on the *Akebono Maru* killed or injured twenty-three men, but the ship was only slightly damaged and was soon back in formation.

At sunrise the four PBYs, now flying independently, approached Midway. Rothenberg was close enough to see the Japanese air armada heading for the atoll. "We saw them flying overhead about an hour out and sent a message, 'Many planes,' " he said. Before he and the others arrived they learned by radio that the air attack had begun. They diverted to Lisianski Island, 250 miles down the Hawaiian chain, but bad weather forced them to fly 100 miles farther to Laysan Island, where a converted tuna boat waited to refuel them. Three of the four planes landed with a few cupfuls of fuel remaining and spent nearly all day refilling their tanks by can, five gallons at a time.[31] Smather's PBY ran out of gasoline not far from Lisianski. He and his crew spent three days on the water before being picked up by Ensign Richard Humphrey piloting a VP-44 Catalina. According to Smathers, Humphrey's plane was in poor shape for rescue work. "He had been over the Japanese islands to the south and the plane was pretty badly shot up. It was full of holes and leaking, so we had to get off in a hurry after he picked us up."[32]

The forced landing had damaged Smathers's PBY, which was later sunk by gunfire.[33]

An uneasy quiet prevailed at Midway throughout the night of 3-4 June, broken only by the whine of inertia starters and the blast of exhausts as the PBYs fired up for an 0415 takeoff on the morning patrols. For most, the day was uneventful. Jack Reid and crew found the invasion fleet again, still steaming relentlessly ahead and full of fight after the night's harassment. The escorting cruisers opened up on the PBY, and

PBYs could carry one 2,200-pound Mark XIII torpedo under each wing. The same rack was used for torpedoes and 1,000-pound bombs. Here a practice torpedo is winched into place. (National Archives)

Reid withdrew out of range from where he tracked the fleet until time to return to Midway.[34]

But the news the admirals had been waiting for began to break an hour and five minutes after the PBYs took off from Midway. At 0520 a radio message was received from Lieutenant Howard Ady of VP-23, saying he had sighted an unidentified plane. A short time later he reported two carriers, three battleships, four cruisers, and six to eight destroyers. No carrier planes were in the air at that time, and he continued to shadow the enemy force, finally breaking off to rendezvous with surface ships at Pearl and Hermes Reef for refueling.[35]

The calm at Midway was coming to an end. Ground crews began

warming up aircraft engines while pilots and plane crews were rounded up by truck. Antiaircraft gunners armed their weapons under orders to shoot anything not identified as friendly.

A second PBY apparently found the strike force about the same time as Ady. Lieutenant (j.g.) August Barthes radioed that he had sighted a large carrier and what he thought were two battleships, two heavy cruisers, and six destroyers. Barthes was sure his plane had not been sighted, but he began to exercise caution when the carrier turned into the wind and began to launch aircraft. He continued to shadow the fleet from up-sun, using "clouds, clouds, and clouds," he said in his report, as cover.[36]

At 0545 Lieutenant (j.g.) William Chase, flying his PBY through cumulus clouds and scattered showers, sighted the enemy aircraft after they had formed up. Not waiting to encode the message, he also reported "many planes"—fifty, he said afterward—heading for Midway. Twelve minutes later he reported two carriers and screening ships and gave their course and speed. At the same time Chase's plane was spotted by the Japanese, but he managed to evade opposition by dodging in and out of the cloud cover.[37]

The radar at Midway picked up the incoming enemy planes at 0553, and twenty-five Brewster Buffalos and Wildcats of MAG-22 took off to intercept them. What followed was an unequal battle in terms of numbers and equipment. In exchange for a half-dozen enemy bombers and fighters, the marines lost all but ten of their fighters, and only two of those that returned were capable of another sortie.[38]

The raid was destructive enough but missed putting Midway's defenses completely out by a considerable margin. The power plant was knocked out on Eastern Island, as well as the mess hall and post exchange. On Sand Island the seaplane hangar was set afire, as were gasoline storage tanks. The dispensary was hit, and one antiaircraft emplacement was put out of action. In all, twenty men were killed on the ground. The runways on Eastern Island were scarcely damaged, however, causing some defenders to suspect that the Japanese were thinking of saving them for their own use later.[39]

The enemy found few flyable planes to destroy on the ground at Midway. All of the PBYs were out, and, as usual, fifteen minutes after they left the B-17s took off. The six new Grumman TBFs were airborne with torpedoes shortly after 0600. Hard on their heels were the four Martin B-26s, also armed with torpedoes. At 0610 sixteen Dauntless dive bombers took off, only minutes before the Japanese bombers began unloading on the atoll.

The TBFs reached the strike force at 0710, at the same time the B-26s did. The TBFs were the first to attack, drawing so many Zeros that they got in each other's way. One by one the TBFs fell. Only one returned to Midway, so badly shot up that it never flew again.[40] Among the crewmen who never returned were two navigators who had been borrowed from VP-24 to guide the TBFs on the flight out from Pearl Harbor.[41]

The B-26s, on their first mission as torpedo bombers, began their runs on the strike force's carriers just after the TBFs started theirs. Two B-26s were shot down; the remaining two returned to Midway but needed considerable work before they would return to the air. No torpedo hits were scored by either group.[42]

A little more than a half hour later Midway's Dauntlesses found the strike force, and at the same time the Zeros of the combat air patrols found them. Most of the Dauntless pilots were green and had never practiced dive bombing attacks, so they resorted to glide bombing. Harried by the fighters, they angled downward toward the ships, rear gunners firing until all ammunition was gone. But the best they could do was splash water on the carriers with near misses, and at a cost of half the force. Like their predecessors, the eight dive bombers that returned to Midway were so badly damaged that many were no longer flyable.

Just before 0800, about the time the Dauntlesses were beginning their glide attacks, nine of Midway's B-17s made a bombing run over the strike force. Their bombs were dropped from 10,000 feet and, like the Dauntlesses, scored only near misses at best. Unlike the other attackers from Midway, however, the Zeros had little to do with the big bombers, possibly being held in check by the name, "Flying Fortress." One B-17 had an engine knocked out and a gunner wounded in the hand; no damage or injuries were reported aboard the other planes.

One final attack from Midway was launched on the strike force at 0820 when the twelve old and slow SB2U Vindicator dive bombers began their attack on a cruiser, which was mistaken for the battleship *Haruna*. Towering columns of water enveloped the ship, but it did not receive a scratch. The defending Zero pilots seemed not up to form for this attack, for despite the Vindicators' deficiencies only two were shot down. Two others, both damaged, ran out of fuel and ditched on the way back to the field.[43]

By 0830 Midway's air defense force could hardly be called that. Its fighters and torpedo planes were either destroyed or damaged beyond airworthiness. Its dive bomber force was reduced by more than 50 percent for the same reasons. Only the antiaircraft batteries remained, weapons the Japanese fliers had totally ignored.

Since there was no communication between the atoll and Task Forces 16 and 17, the Midway defenders could not know that Ady's and Chase's reports had been heard aboard the flagships and that the offensive had been taken over by the planes of the *Yorktown, Hornet,* and *Enterprise.*

The *Hornet* began launching planes at 0700 and the *Enterprise* six minutes later, in all a force of 116 fighters, dive bombers, and torpedo planes. The *Yorktown*, with scout planes to recover, launched at 0838.

The coordinated attack visualized by Spruance never materialized. The American planes had been launched two hours sooner and many miles farther away from the Japanese strike force than originally planned, creating a fuel shortage. In the air the fighters, dive bombers, and torpedo planes became separated, causing them to arrive at different times over the target, if at all. As a result, the dive bombers and torpedo planes had no fighter cover. To make the operation even more difficult, the Japanese strike force made an unreported course change and was not at the expected point of interception when the U.S. task force planes arrived. The *Hornet*'s dive bombers failed to find the Japanese ships at all, most ending up on Midway and some down at sea from lack of fuel. One of the downed crews was picked up later by a PBY. All of the ten Wildcat fighters flying cover from the *Enterprise* ran out of fuel and ditched.

The fifteen torpedo bombers of VT-8 from the *Hornet* were the first to find the Japanese and moved to attack at 0918. With no fighter cover, the slow, obsolescent Douglas Devastators were quickly knocked into the ocean by the Zeros of the combat air patrol. Of the fifteen planes, none survived; of the thirty pilots and gunners, only Ensign George Gay lived; of fifteen torpedoes, there were no hits.

A half hour later fourteen Devastators of VT-6 from the *Enterprise* headed for the Japanese carriers. The mission was almost a duplicate of VT-8's: Ten of the fourteen planes were shot down; no hits were scored. Only four planes returned to the *Enterprise*, one so badly damaged that it was pushed over the side.

At 1015 the *Yorktown*'s VT-3 began its runs on the strike force carriers, achieving no more success than the two previous units. In all, forty-one Devastators had sortied against the Japanese strike force; only the four from the *Enterprise* returned. The enemy ships sailed on, unscathed by either land-based or carrier-based planes, its officers and men expressing admiration for the unexpected bravery of the Americans who had flown in the face of death.[44]

The planes of the four Japanese carriers were rearming for a second strike on Midway prior to the torpedo attacks, then a decision was reached to rearm the level bombers with torpedoes and go after the American carriers.[45] But luck had run out for the Japanese. A few minutes later— about 1025—the Dauntless dive bombers from the *Yorktown* and *Enterprise* dropped out of the sky, intent on laying their 500- and 1,000-pound bombs on the busy carrier decks below. Within five minutes three of the four Japanese carriers—the *Akagi*, *Kaga*, and *Soryu*—were ablaze, dying at the hands of the Dauntlesses and their own bombs, torpedoes, and fuel hoses which had been left scattered about the decks during the hasty exchange of ordnance.[46]

The fourth carrier, *Hiryu*, was far enough away from the other three to escape the interest of the dive bombers for the moment. It launched its planes for a strike against the U.S. carriers. The *Yorktown* bore the brunt of their fury, receiving three bombs in the noontime onslaught. The bombs brought her to a halt but within an hour she was repaired and under way again. At 1443 a second strike moved in at considerable loss through the fighter screen and heavy antiaircraft fire, again singling out the *Yorktown* and hitting her with two torpedoes. This time the damage appeared fatal, and her captain ordered her abandoned.

One minute after the torpedo attack began, a scout plane from VS-5 radioed back the location of *Hiryu* to the American carriers. The remaining airworthy Dauntlesses were immediately launched. A few minutes after 1700 the dive bombers nosed over above the *Hiryu* and placed four bombs on her foredeck. In a short time the last of the Japanese carriers was blazing from bow to stern, still under way, the wind fanning the fires to even greater heights.[47]

When Yamamoto and his staff aboard the *Yamato* 300 miles away learned of the loss of the carriers, the shock was profound. Never had a report of such disastrous magnitude been received in Combined Fleet Headquarters. Yamamoto's first action was to assign the unfinished job of softening up Midway for the invasion to four heavy cruisers and two destroyers, which were to bombard the atoll at dawn on 5 June. But the ships, too far away to meet the timetable, could not be on station until broad daylight. This, coupled with an overstated estimate of Midway's defense capabilities, caused Yamamoto to call off the bombardment. When the ships received the order, they began a turn away from their course to the island in 0200 darkness, and the cruiser *Mikuma* crashed into her sister ship, *Mogami*. The *Mikuma* began to trail oil, and the *Mogami,* the more seriously damaged, could only make twelve knots.

As the day wore on, the Americans on Midway, unable to tell from the volume of conflicting reports whether all the carriers of the Japanese strike force had been put out of action, also overestimated their opponent's capabilities. Commander Ramsey feared for the B-17s parked along the runway; if the Japanese planes returned, they would easily be destroyed. He was equally concerned over the safety of the PBYs and decided to fly out all those not absolutely essential to operations.[48]

At sunset the crew of a PBY circling in the distance out of range of the guns of the *Soryu*'s escort ships watched the big carrier burn. At 1900 a thunderous explosion shot flames high into the sky, and a few moments later the *Soryu* slid beneath the sea. Twenty-five minutes later the *Kaga,* wracked by two explosions, settled out of sight. At 0500 the next morning the *Akagi* was scuttled, and ten minutes later the *Hiryu* was torpedoed by a Japanese destroyer to hasten her sinking.[49]

Darkness had brought little peace to Midway. Throughout the night repairs proceeded on planes, defenses, and facilities, with only a few minutes' interruption when the Japanese submarine I-168 ineffectively shelled the atoll. The attack ended when the submarine was ordered away to seek out and sink the damaged *Yorktown.*[50]

The PBYs were out on their regular sector patrols before dawn on 5 June. At 0630 Lieutenant (j.g.) N. K. Brady picked up an oil slick and followed it to a neighboring sector. "Ten minutes later sighted two large capital ships in same direction of oil slick. Plane in that sector reported it ahead of us, so sent in an amplifying report," his commentary on the action read. The PBY in that sector had radioed back a report of "two battleships," damaged and leaking oil, and gave the position. MAG-22 sent up its remaining Dauntlesses and Vindicators, and found rather than battleships the damaged *Mikuma* and *Mogami.* Brady watched from "a reasonable distance," flying at low altitude to keep the ships below the horizon and occasionally pulling up to observe the action. Despite numerous hits from the dive bombers and near misses from a flight of Army B-17s, the two cruisers continued under way, although their superstructures were reduced to scrap heaps.[51]

That same morning Ensign T. S. Thueson of VP-23, searching for the Japanese invasion force, came upon two groups of ships. He radioed that in the larger group three carriers and one other large ship were burning. Cruisers and destroyers were circling the burning ships, apparently picking up survivors. High-altitude bombers were attacking the second group. He observed one hit on a battleship or cruiser, but dived and made steep turns to get away from a lone Japanese plane that suddenly appeared and made two passes at him. His gunners made hits on the attacker but apparently caused no serious damage.[52]

Ensign Jack Reid also reported sighting a Japanese force of two battleships, four heavy cruisers, four destroyers, and a burning carrier. His plane was fired on by the battleships.[53]

Through the remainder of the day reports of large concentrations of ships and burning carriers were received at Midway and aboard the ships of Task Forces 16 and 17. They were checked out, but no engagements of consequence resulted. The *Yorktown* continued to float and was reboarded by a damage control crew, then taken in tow for the long haul back to Pearl Harbor.[54] In the meantime Yamamoto attempted to regroup his shattered, scattered forces and save face to whatever extent possible. Shortly before 0300 he called off the invasion of Midway, but he had far from given up his second major goal, that of delivering a final, fatal blow to the U.S. Pacific Fleet.[55] All day long the float plane scouts of the Japanese cruisers and battleships attempted to find the Americans, but Yamamoto had no better luck locating them than Spruance's scouts had in locating him.[56]

The morning of 6 June started off with a bang: the sound of 500-pound bombs delivered by the *Enterprise*'s and *Hornet*'s Dauntlesses exploding on and around the battered *Mikuma* and *Mogami* and another cruiser, the *Asashio*. This time the *Mikuma*, ravaged by fire and explosion, succumbed and sank late that night. The *Mogami* and *Asashio* received additional damage, but made good their escape.[57] Twenty-six B-17s were sent out from Midway to finish the job but, instead of attacking a cruiser, bombed the USS *Grayling*, which, undamaged, submerged with some haste.

In the early afternoon the Japanese submarine I-168 found the *Yorktown* in tow. Four torpedoes were fired at her mammoth bulk; one missed, one tore the destroyer *Hammann* almost in half, and the other two blew a huge hole in the side of the carrier. The *Yorktown* stayed afloat throughout the night, and finally subsided beneath the waves near dawn on the seventh. With the sinking of the *Yorktown*, Task Force 17 disbanded, with some of the ships heading for Pearl Harbor that morning and others joining Task Force 16.[58]

Yamamoto ordered one more effort to locate and attack the American fleet, but his strike force's short-range search planes turned up nothing. Finally, he called his remaining ships together for the long run home to Japan.[59]

Spruance, feeling that the U.S. task forces had done their job in protecting Midway, followed Nimitz's directive not to risk the carriers any more than necessary and turned the ships of Task Force 16 toward Pearl Harbor.[60]

From 7 June until the twenty-sixth the Midway-based PBY search patrols turned into air-sea rescue missions. The best publicized of these occurred two days earlier, however, when Lieutenant (j.g.) S. O. "Pappy" Cole and crew took ensign George Gay aboard their VP-44 PBY. Gay, the sole survivor of the *Hornet*'s VT-8 and wounded in one arm, had bobbed in the water for nearly thirty hours. When pulled aboard the PBY, he found that Cole had taken a vote among his crew as to whether to land and pick him up and risk being caught on the water by a Zero, or to report his position for later pickup by a PT boat. The vote was unanimous to pick him up. Hospitalized at Pearl Harbor the following day, Gay was visited by Admiral Nimitz, who wanted to hear Gay's account of the battle from his vantage point under a floating cushion at ringside.[61] Gay received the Navy Cross and the accolades of a hero throughout the United States. He was headlined in newspapers, featured in magazines, and interviewed on radio, telling the Midway story and building much-needed morale for a nation that, aside from the Doolittle raid, had heard little but six months of bad news.

On the eighth a VP-72 PBY picked up three survivors of VF-8 from the *Hornet*, hungry, sunburned, and frightened by a shark. The Wildcat pilots had ditched during the battle on the fourth.[62]

On 10 June Ensign Thomas Ramsey and his gunner from one of the *Enterprise*'s ditched Dauntlesses were picked up by a PBY. To Ramsey's surprise, he found he had been rescued by Lieutenant (j.g.) August Barthes, a friend from high school days in Biloxi, Mississippi.[63]

On the eighteenth a VP-11 PBY (the only VP-11 representative at Midway, having ferried out bombs from Pearl Harbor on the fifth) piloted by Lieutenant Don "Speedball" Camp spotted a lifeboat with about thirty-five men in it and flying a Japanese flag. When the waist guns were swung out the flag was quickly dropped and surrender was indicated. Camp called in the tender USS *Ballard* to pick up the men. The *Ballard* did so, boat and all. Upon questioning, the men were found to be the chief engineer, several engine room crewmen, and others from the *Hiryu*. Trapped when the carrier was bombed, the engine room crew had chiseled through a steel bulkhead to reach topside. They had launched the *Hiryu*'s cutter, rigged a sail, and were heading for Wake when Camp found them.[64]

The period was not without gunfire. Patrol planes were still alert for a return engagement by the Japanese, and as a result on 19 June a PBY fired on an "enemy bomber," which turned out to be an army B-17 seventy-five miles out of its sector. The PBY gunners gave a good account of themselves. Numerous hits were made and "material casualties" were inflicted but thankfully the B-17 crew was uninjured.

A search by Lieutenant (j.g.) J. E. White in PBY 24-P-10 on 21 June turned up "much wreckage" from 325 to 025 degrees 400 miles from Midway, apparently drifting debris from the battle on the fourth. On the way back White found a rubber raft with two men in it, the survivors of a TBD from the *Enterprise* shot down in the Japanese carrier attack on 4 June. They, too, had fought off sharks and had almost been picked up by a Japanese submarine that circled them, decided they were not worth shooting or saving, and sailed away. For weeks afterward, life rafts and lifeboats were found in that area, but there were no more survivors.[65]

On 26 June most of the PBYs returned to their regular units at Pearl Harbor and Kaneohe Bay. Six planes from VP-24 stayed on at Midway for routine patrol work. Task Force 16 returned to Pearl Harbor sadder over the loss of comrades and ships but wiser concerning carrier warfare, and with the grim satisfaction that comes from a hard-fought, hard-won victory.

On 15 June Admiral Nimitz presented the Silver Star to Lieutenant Commander Richards and the Distinguished Flying Cross to Chief Aviation Pilot Smathers for their torpedo attack on the Midway invasion fleet. Smathers received a simultaneous promotion to ensign, which resulted in a forty-dollar-per-month cut in pay. Other PBY pilots and crewmen received awards that day: Ensign Richard Humphrey, Air Medal; Lieutenant Donald Gumz, Distinguished Flying Cross; Aviation Ordnance Man First Class Phillip Fulghum, Navy Cross; Lieutenant William Chase, Air Medal; Ensign Theodore Thuesen, Distinguished Flying Cross; Lieutenant (j.g.) John White, Air Medal; Chief Aviation Pilot J. I. Foster, Distinguished Flying Cross.[66]

Arriving in Japan, the strike force slipped quietly into main island harbors where its officers and crews were interned to suppress news of the disaster. Japanese citizens were informed of great losses inflicted on the United States.[67] Actually U.S. losses amounted to 307 men, one carrier, one destroyer, and 147 aircraft. Japan lost 2,500 men—including a hundred or more of their best pilots—four carriers, one heavy cruiser, and 332 aircraft.[68] Yamamoto was forced to salve the wounds of a major defeat with the balm of a minor victory: the invasion of the Aleutians.

The Aleutians

Admiral Yamamoto included the invasion of the Aleutians in Operation MI only as a means of getting his Midway attack plan approved. The move pacified opponents of the plan who viewed the Aleutians as an American springboard from which invasion forces could bound into the Kurile Islands and from there directly into the heart of the empire. After the Doolittle raid in April they applied even more pressure to establish defense bases in the Aleutians. Many of them were sure the army B-25s had come from there, and they feared that if Russia came into the war against Japan, long-range U.S. Air Force bombers would shuttle from Dutch Harbor to Vladivostok. They knew enough about the miserable weather in the Aleutians to realize that operations from—and resupply to—bases there would be no easy task. But neither would it be simple for the Americans to mount a counterattack.

So Yamamoto siphoned off two carriers, six cruisers, and twelve destroyers from the Combined Fleet to support the effort. This support would include air attacks on the U.S. defenses as well as air cover for the Imperial Army invasion forces. And if the U.S. Navy took the bait and sortied out of Pearl Harbor after his strike force, he would be assured of his dual goals: destruction of the U.S. Fleet, and the capture of Midway.[1]

The Japanese forged ahead with their plans, unaware that the Americans were monitoring all of their radio messages through the broken JN25 code and were taking steps to counter their actions. The Americans could not tolerate a Japanese invasion of the Aleutians or Alaska. If the Japanese took Hawaii, they still would be 2,400 miles from the U.S. mainland. But if they took Alaska, they would be only three hours from the Bremerton Navy Yard and the Boeing plant in Seattle.[2]

On 21 May 1942 Admiral Nimitz, with the blessing of the Joint Chiefs of Staff, placed Rear Admiral Robert Theobald in overall command of the navy and army Alaskan defenses. He was to stave off the Japanese threat with a small fleet of two heavy cruisers, two light cruisers, four destroyers, six submarines, three tankers, a fleet of "Yippee" boats— converted fishing boats used for patrol work—three seaplane tenders, and the twelve PBY-5As of VP-42, one of two operational squadrons in Patrol Wing 4 and the only navy aircraft in the theatre.[3] He also controlled forty-seven U.S. Army Air Force bombers and several squadrons of P-40s at fields from Anchorage, Alaska, to Fort Glenn on Umnak Island in the Aleutians.[4]

Theobald could think of no reason for the Japanese to have designs on the barren, windswept, fog-shrouded islands of the western Aleutians. If they were to attack in the Alaskan defense sector, he reasoned, surely the target would be something of importance, which could only mean an attack on the Alaskan mainland. So he stationed his diminutive armada in the waters around Kodiak, where it could forestall an enemy fleet heading for Anchorage.

He saw fit, however, to prevent carrier-based planes from reaching the military and naval installations at Dutch Harbor on Unalaska Island in the middle of the Aleutian chain. He sent twenty-one P-40s and fourteen bombers to Cold Bay, 180 miles east of Dutch Harbor, and twelve P-40s to Otter Point on Umnak, 40 miles to the west.[5] The existence of the two fields was unknown to the Japanese. By any standards, the airfields were crude, with runways of metal Marston mat laid out across the mushy, constantly shifting muskeg. The mat made the runways us-

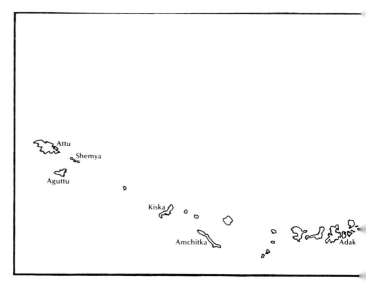

Aleutian Islands

able, but they were constantly muddy and messy, and spongy enough to create a sensation similar to landing on a mattress, some pilots said.[6]

On 28 May Theobald ordered Brigadier General William Butler, commanding officer of the army air forces, and Captain Leslie Gehres, commander of Patrol Wing 4, to institute long-range sector patrols up to 700 miles out to sea from Kodiak to search for the enemy fleet CinCPac was tracking through decoded JN25 messages. Night searches were included, with PBYs taking off at 2000 hours.

Only three days earlier Gehres had moved his headquarters from Seattle to Kodiak, the first step in moving the entire wing into the Alaskan area of operations. Gehres had taken command of the wing on 17 November 1941. He began his career as an enlisted battleship sailor in World War I. He was later commissioned, joining a select group of ex-enlisted officers known as "mustangs." After flight training he became a carrier-based fighter pilot with ability sufficient to lead the navy aerobatic team at the National Air Races.[7] But he rode from Seattle to Kodiak in a Catalina piloted by Lieutenant Commander James Russell, skipper of VP-42, partly because he had never checked out in a PBY.[8] It may have been a lack of familiarity as to what a big patrol bomber could and could not do that would cause him to ask so much of it in the days just ahead.

Before moving to Kodiak, Patrol Wing 4 had flown dawn-to-dusk patrols out of Sand Point Naval Air Station, near Seattle, Washington, these ranging from the mouth of the Columbia River northward to

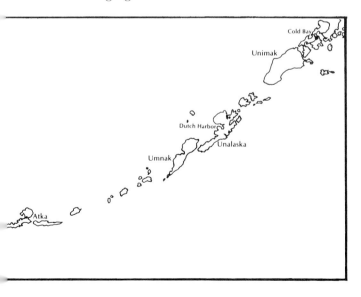

Vancouver Island. The patrols were begun in November 1941 after a message from the chief of naval operations warned Gehres's predecessor that U.S. negotiations with Japan were breaking down.[9]

On 7 December 1941 the wing's patrol area stretched for nearly 3,000 miles: along the northern Pacific coast of the United States, the Alaskan coast, and out to the tip of the Aleutians. The seaplane tender USS *Gillis* and the six PBY-5s of VP-41 were stationed at Kodiak; VP-42 operated out of Sand Point; the third squadron of the wing, VP-43, was still in San Diego, not yet having moved on station. VP-41 and VP-42 stood three-month duty tours, rotating between Sand Point and stations in Alaska and the Aleutians.

After the Pearl Harbor raid the wing's first priority was the protection of the Bremerton Navy Yard from carrier-based planes, but it was soon obvious that the greatest danger was from Japan's giant I-class submarines, which were roving unchecked between Hawaii and the U.S. mainland. Antisubmarine patrols became a joint venture between the wing's Catalinas and army bombers. An army B-26 reported sinking a sub 50 miles off the mouth of the Columbia River on 24 December. The PBYs sank no subs but could take credit for keeping them underwater during the day. No ships in convoy were sunk while being escorted by patrol planes.

At the end of January the first PBY-5As were delivered to VP-42, and in the next few weeks VP-41 was also equipped with amphibians. On 15 March, technicians began installing radar and completed the job in all planes just before June 1942.

By 28 May the Catalinas of VP-42 in the Alaskan sector were reinforced by most of the wing's twenty planes. Twelve were stationed with the *Gillis* at Dutch Harbor; four were at Cold Bay, serviced by the tender *Casco*; four remained at Sand Point, serviced by the *Williamson*. Planes were kept fueled and armed at all times and the crews alerted, ready for immediate action. In addition to the regular 400-mile sector patrols, the PBYs also escorted shipping through Unimak Pass to Dutch Harbor and flew weather observation missions. Night patrols made use of the newly installed radar equipment.

In the days that followed, the PBYs proved their value as flying boats. Basing on the tenders, they covered wide areas well beyond the reach of the few forward airfields. Their radar found enemy ships through clouds and fog and allowed the planes to take off, navigate, and land in all sorts of weather. There were no other navigational aids in the Aleutians. The PBYs' slow speed was an asset that allowed them to find and maneuver around mountains in poor visibility and to locate their bases with greater ease, but it was a liability when they were fired on by enemy planes or antiaircraft guns.[10]

Aviation's greatest enemy in the Aleutians was the weather. It would exact a price in lives and aircraft far beyond the number felled by Japanese guns. On rare days the skies were blue and visibility was unrestricted; on most visibility was limited by rain and fog. Ceilings were sometimes 3,000 feet, but more often were 2,500 feet, or 500 feet—or zero. Icing was prevalent in carburetors, but not on wing and tail surfaces; usually the PBYs flew low to stay out of the clouds and away from freezing temperatures.[11] Some said they flew so low that their hulls were actually below the wave crests.[12]

Wind was omnipresent, blowing from 10 to 25 miles per hour on slow days and increasing to 100 miles per hour and beyond during storms. Called "williwaws" by the Indians, the storms were powerful enough to fly PBYs on their mooring lines, and sometimes flip them on their backs. In the air, shifting gusty winds created severe turbulence that loosened rivets and engine mounts, bent airframes, and generated electrical interference that made instruments unreliable and created earsplitting static on radios. Aircraft were quickly blown off course; getting lost was common, especially when visibility was poor. On one such windy mission, a drift sight taken from the bow of a Catalina showed an angle of forty-five degrees. The mission was aborted.[13] The winds also caused strange flying times: The outbound leg of a patrol might require two hours, but eight hours would be needed for the return.

In winter instant frostbite could result from touching bare fingers to aircraft metal. Grease turned to stone on control cables, hydraulic fluid would not flow, and guns and bomb racks would not function. Engine oil was best drained at the end of a mission and kept by a stove until the next. Engine heaters were run for hours before pistons would move.[14]

The Aleutian weather's only redeeming feature was that it treated friend and foe alike. On the morning of 3 June 1942 fog was so thick around the Japanese strike force that Rear Admiral Kakuji Kakuta could not see the carrier *Junyo* from his flagship, the carrier *Ryujo*. Aircraft launching was delayed for a time, but at 0243, just minutes before sunrise on the long arctic day, the fog lifted and the fighters and bombers took off from both carriers and headed for Dutch Harbor.

In the fog the *Junyo*'s planes never found the target, but the *Ryujo*'s fourteen bombers and three fighters pushed on through ragged patches of broken cloud and fog, and just over Dutch Harbor the clouds opened up. For the next twenty minutes they blasted away, setting fire to gasoline storage tanks, strafing the radio station, bombing an army barracks and killing twenty-five men, and strafing PBYs on the water. Then they regrouped and felt their way back to the *Ryujo*, again in the fog.[15]

At debriefing following the raid, Admiral Kakuta was amazed to hear how quickly the Americans had swung into action. Their antiaircraft

Why land-based PBYs became popular in the Alaskan sector: A PBY-5A is about to be beached on ice-filled Woman's Bay at Kodiak following a sea landing 12 December 1942. (U.S. Navy)

began firing almost immediately. He had lost two bombers; two others and a fighter were damaged. It was almost as if they were waiting for him.[16]

They were. On 2 June Kakuta's force had seen a patrol plane, but his spotters weren't sure whether it was a PBY or a GST, the Russian-built version of a PBY. The plane had indeed been a PBY, one of VP-42's out of Cold Bay, and it had radioed the fleet's position to Dutch Harbor. The message served to increase tensions, but it came as no surprise: CinCPac had tracked the fleet to within 250 miles of the base and had kept its commanders informed.[17]

The seaplane tender *Gillis* was steaming out of Dutch Harbor at 0540 on 3 June when it picked up a large number of blips on its radar. Word was radioed ashore, and antiaircraft guns were manned there and on the six ships in the harbor. The message was relayed to the fighters at Cold Bay and Umnak. At Cold Bay they scrambled but were too far away to arrive in time to drive off the attackers. Weather prevented the message from being received at nearby Umnak, and the planes stayed on the ground, their pilots unaware that the war was about to heat up.[18]

Ensign Marshall Freerks of VP-42 had landed just before dawn at Dutch Harbor after an all-night patrol. In the darkness he had come close to the ships of the Japanese strike force, but never saw them because of clouds and rain. He had just finished tying up his PBY when the strike force planes hit.[19]

In the harbor Lieutenant Jack Litsey of VP-41 was beginning a takeoff run in his PBY on a mail delivery flight with two passengers on board. The plane was on the step when two Zeros pounced on it, their tracers setting it on fire and killing a passenger and a crewman. Litsey beached the burning plane and, along with the remaining crew members, ran for his life, reaching cover just as the PBY exploded. There might have been greater loss of life if the Gillis's antiaircraft guns had not driven off the fighters. The ship's gunners brought down a bomber later in the assault.

Ensign Hildebrand of VP-41 had just gotten his PBY airborne from a nearby cove when the Zeros saw it. His waist gunners opened fire, and as a fighter zoomed overhead the .50-caliber slugs found their mark. Hit almost simultaneously by antiaircraft fire from the ground, the Zero spun into the harbor. Hildebrand banked the PBY into a mountain cut and escaped into the clouds.

Two VP-41 PBYs returning from patrol also encountered the Zeros: Lieutenant (j.g.) Kirmse ducked into clouds without receiving any hits; Ensign Doerr's Catalina also came away unharmed.[20]

Aboard the Ryujo, Admiral Kakuta was less than pleased with the results of the morning's mission. His planes had done considerable damage for a small force, but no American shipping had been destroyed in the harbor, and no capital ships of the U.S. fleet had been drawn out to do battle. Neither had any American aircraft other than patrol planes been encountered. This lack of resistance made a second strike tempting, but the weather had closed in again; some of the planes from the earlier strike had found their carriers by flying at wavetop height.

One returning pilot reported seeing five destroyers anchored in Makushin Bay on Unalaska Island, and Kakuta seized on this. He ordered all available aircraft, even the four catapult float planes from the cruisers, out to hit the American ships. The weather came to the destroyers' rescue. Kakuta's planes never found the ships in the fog and, to make matters worse, P-40s out of Umnak found the float planes. Two were shot down, and the remaining two were so badly damaged that they were scrapped.

In the meantime U.S. Army and Navy patrol planes were scouring the area for the Japanese fleet. At 1030 an army bomber reported finding it, but the plane was never heard from again. Eight hours later, at 1700, a VP-42 PBY flown by Lieutenant (j.g.) Lucias Campbell spotted the force. He was set upon at once by the Zeros of the carriers' combat air patrol. The fleet's antiaircraft batteries landed a few good hits as well. With his wing tanks streaming fuel, Campbell banked his sieved Catalina away into the clouds and radioed in a detailed position report. He then continued to shadow the fleet while waiting for army bombers to appear. After two hours no bombers had made contact, so with fuel dangerously low he headed for home. The engines sputtered to a halt while he was still well out to sea. Fighting the battle-damaged controls, Campbell glided dead-stick through the clouds, breaking out at 300 feet. After a superb landing in mountainous seas, his crewmen frantically plugged holes and bailed to keep the Catalina afloat while his radioman sent an SOS and repeated the earlier contact report on the fleet's position. The Coast Guard cutter USS *Nemaha* heard Campbell's SOS and picked him and his crew up the next day. Once aboard, he learned that his hard-won contact reports had been garbled by static and no action had been taken.[21]

Throughout the night of 3 June the Catalinas continued the search. One failed to come home. The PBY piloted by Lieutenant (j.g.) Jean Cusick of VP-41 disappeared without a trace. It would not be learned until after the war that his plane had been shot down by the Japanese combat air patrol. Cusick and four crewmen died, but the three surviving members of the crew were taken aboard an enemy cruiser and held prisoner in Japan until the war's end.[22]

At 0641 the morning of the fourth contact was finally made. Ensign Marshall Freerks of VP-42 was on his way home from an all-night patrol when his radar operator reported six pips on the screen 240 miles southwest of Umnak. Freerks reported position and direction and circled for more than an hour. At 0710 he reported seeing an enemy carrier, then was ordered to return home before his fuel ran out. As a parting shot he made a bombing run on the fleet and for his trouble got an engine shot out. The remaining engine took him back to Cold Bay.[23]

Lieutenant Commander Charles Perkins of VP-42, ferrying a torpedo from Dutch Harbor to Umnak, heard Freerks' contact report. He homed in on it, then continued to track the fleet for two hours. Low on fuel, he decided to unleash the torpedo and a pair of 500-pound bombs before heading home. The Japanese gunners gave him the same sort of welcome they had given Freerks. They knocked out an engine, forcing him to jettison his ordnance and limp back to base to explain why he had not delivered the torpedo as ordered.[24] A third PBY arrived to track the Japanese force and guide in a flight of army B-26s. Flown by Lieutenant (j.g.) Eugene Stockstill of VP-42, the plane was attacked by Zeros from the *Ryujo*. It went down in flames with all hands lost.[25]

Without the radar eyes of the Catalinas to direct them, five of the torpedo-carrying B-26s merely bored holes in the fog. The pilot of the sixth, Captain George Thornborough, found the fleet on his own. Under heavy fire, he made two torpedo runs on the *Ryujo* and one diving attack, aborting each time because of bad position. On the third run he released the torpedo, only to have the *Ryujo*'s bow drop into a wave trough. The torpedo slithered across its foredeck and splashed into the sea on the far side. Thornborough returned to his base, saying he had dropped his torpedo on the flight deck of a carrier. Then he reloaded his B-26 with 500-pound bombs, and flew off into the fog and eternity: He was never heard from again.

Later in the day two elderly B-17s located the fleet and made low-altitude bombing runs. There were no bomb hits, and one bomber was blown to shreds by a direct hit from the fleet's antiaircraft guns. Three more B-26s tried torpedo runs with no success. The Japanese carriers and screening ships had yet to be touched.[26]

At 1500 hours Admiral Kakuta ordered planes launched for another attack on Dutch Harbor. They began their bombing and strafing runs at 1755 hours.[27] A PBY piloted by Ensign Mitchell of VP-42 was just becoming airborne at the harbor entrance and was shot down in flames. Crew members who survived the crash were machine gunned in the water. All were killed.[28] The grounded barracks ship *Northwestern* was hit and set afire by bombs; the hospital, a warehouse, and a gun emplacement were hit. Eighteen men were killed, twenty-five wounded. The fuel storage tanks were hit again, one exploding with such thunderous violence that the P-40 pilots on Umnak were alerted, and for the first time they tangled with Zeros. When the encounter ended, the score was tied: two Zeros and two P-40s.[29] Zeros found the tender *Williamson* in Umnak Pass and strafed it, but damage was slight.[30]

PBYs continued to hunt for the Japanese fleet through the night of 4 June and all day and into the night of the fifth. That night another plane disappeared with all hands, the Catalina flown by Ensign Hildebrand of VP-42, whose gunners had helped bring down a Zero in the first Dutch Harbor attack. It was the fourth PBY to be lost in two days with complete crews.

On the morning of 6 June Lieutenant (j.g.) Powers, returning from overnight patrol, made a radar contact. He radioed "many ships," but that was the extent of the message. The Japanese combat air patrol jumped his Catalina, and for the next several minutes all his attention was required in keeping himself and his crew alive. It was not until 1400 that he was able to report that he had sighted carriers.

Other search planes were sent out, and two were fired on by Japanese fighters. But no more contact was made with the enemy fleet, which by this time was retiring to the west to support the invasion force. One of the searching PBYs tangled with a submarine, dropping a 500-pound bomb with no apparent results and losing an engine to the sub's gunners. Like the others, it came home on the remaining one. The *Gillis* did better. She was credited with sinking a submarine southwest of Egg Island.[31]

The Japanese attacks on Dutch Harbor demolished some installations, destroyed some patrol planes, and took a number of lives. They did not, however, seriously damage the United States's defense capability. The Japanese lost a few submarines and a few planes which, on the face of it, appeared to be of no great consequence. Yet the loss of one particular aircraft changed the conduct of the war.

During the second strike a Zero from the *Ryujo* was hit. Its pilot, Petty Officer Tadayoshi Koga, realized he could not reach the carrier and attempted a wheels-down emergency landing on Unalaska Island. But what looked like a smooth field was actually a bog. When the wheels touched, they dug in and the plane flipped forward on its back, breaking Koga's neck. Six weeks later a patrolling PBY sighted the plane and a salvage team recovered it. Damaged but repairable, the captured Zero gave the United States its first close-hand look at the renowned and much-feared fighter. Static and flight testing revealed its strengths and weaknesses, leading to the development of combat tactics and aircraft— expressly the Grumman F6F Hellcat—that ended the Zero's reputation for invincibility and its dominance of the skies.[32]

Kakuta learned of the disaster at Midway when Yamamoto ordered him to bring his carrier force to Midway post haste to try to salvage the operation. But before the ships could change course, the order was canceled and another given to proceed with the Aleutian invasion. Vice Admiral Boshiro Hosogaya, commanding the Northern Force of transports and screening cruisers and destroyers, decided against invading Adak Island, as called for in the original plan, because it was only 350 miles from the U.S. air base at Umnak. He opted instead for Attu and Kiska at the western tip of the Aleutian chain, another 150 miles away from American planes, and 500 miles closer to his supply bases in the Kuriles.[33]

At dawn Sunday, 7 June, Japanese troops stormed ashore on the treeless, cheerless volcanic islands of Attu and Kiska. On Attu an American teacher tried to resist and was killed, the only fatality in the operation. His wife and about forty Aleut Indians surrendered. On Kiska the meteorologists at the navy weather station were taken prisoner. The Japanese troops began at once to prepare their defenses.[34]

On the eighth and ninth, Patrol Wing 4 was reinforced by the arrival of VP-43 and its twelve PBY-5As. They had little to do until the tenth, however, when the fog finally lifted enough for the navy to find out why its weather station on Kiska had ceased transmitting. Two PBYs were sent out, one piloted by Lieutenant (j.g.) Dahl of VP-43, the other by Lieutenant (j.g.) James Bowers of VP-41. They reported ships in the harbors at Kiska and Attu, the first indication that the enemy had landed.[35]

On 11 June a message was received from CinCPac: Bomb the enemy out of Kiska.[36] Five newly arrived air force B-24 bombers took up the challenge, but the Japanese antiaircraft gunners were ready and quickly got the range, shooting down one B-24 and peppering the other four before they could do any damage in Kiska harbor. A squadron of B-17s was next to try, returning unmarred but with no better bombing results than the B-24s.[37]

Captain Gehres wanted a piece of the action. With his zeal and his patrol wing bolstered by the arrival of VP-51's nine PBYs, he asked for and received permission from CinCPac to mount a bombing offensive using twenty PBYs. He was sure of himself: The day before he had sent the *Gillis* to Atka Island, where it anchored in Nazan Bay to serve as the PBY's forward base. Twenty planes were double the number normally serviced by the tender; auxiliary mess and hospital facilities were set up on the island to accommodate the overflow. Late that afternoon Gehres, after ordering the PBYs loaded with bombs, told his pilots to be ready for a mission early the following morning. They were to bomb Kiska around the clock until the Japanese withdrew or all ordnance was expended. The pilots greeted the order with mixed emotions: The new ones welcomed it as an opportunity to strike back; the experienced ones knew the PBY was too vulnerable to antiaircraft and fighters to be used as a daylight attack bomber.

On the morning of 11 June the navy's "Kiska Blitz" began. The PBYs arrived over Kiska harbor on the heels of the army's B-24s. They dived on the ships below, released their 500-pounders by seaman's eye, and headed out to sea. The Japanese could not believe what they saw; they reported an attack by giant dive bombers that looked like patrol planes. They recovered from their surprise quickly, however. Defending antiaircraft guns had been aimed at the high-flying Liberators but some were able to puncture the PBYs. One was hit with two flak bursts; an engine was set afire and two crewmen were killed in the blisters, but the plane returned to the *Gillis*. Another, badly holed, beached near the tender to keep from sinking. The results of the raid were hardly worth the cost. They had damaged an enemy destroyer with a near-miss.

For the next three days PBYs sortied, returned, and sortied again as soon as the *Gillis's* crews could refuel and rearm them. At night, when it was too dark to make a safe landing in the bay, the planes landed in the open sea and taxied in to the tender. The pilots of VP-43 and VP-51 had never seen combat. Several, in fact, had left San Diego just four days before the blitz began. They gained experience rapidly. Some perfected their dive-bombing technique, dropping through the fog at 250 knots, releasing their bombs by seaman's eye, and then pulling up into the overcast again.[38] Others oriented themselves with Kiska's volcano above the overcast and dropped their bombs on the harbor by radar.

Japanese antiaircraft gunners also perfected their techniques. They aimed their guns at holes in the overcast and waited for the PBYs to drop through. Their fire became extremely accurate. Most of the Catalinas took hits but, amazingly, only one was shot down. Ensign Leland Davis of VP-43 returned from an early mission in a Catalina so badly holed that it sank beside the *Gillis*. He transferred his crew to another plane and took off again, but this time his plane was hit and went down in flames in Kiska harbor. There were no survivors.

The blitz ended when the *Gillis* ran out of bombs and fuel. Some enemy ships and shore installations had been damaged and three Mavis patrol bombers had been burned at anchor, but the Japanese had not been bombed out of Kiska. The cost to Patrol Wing 4 was one entire crew lost, several crewmen killed on various planes, and ten of the twenty PBYs either destroyed or damaged. There would be no more blitz for the PBYs.

The *Gillis* weighed anchor on 14 June. Fearing reprisals if the Japanese took the island, most of Atka's natives were taken aboard and transported to a safer location. PBYs and the tender USS *Holbert* picked up the remaining natives the next day. Their village was burned. A PBY flown by Lieutenant Theis of VP-41 airlifted the five-man weather team off Tanaga Island during the same period and the weather station was also burned in the continuing "scorched-earth campaign."[39]

But the Japanese army moved no farther east, and its troops tunneled more and more deeply into Kiska's mountainsides to escape the cold and continued bombings by the army air force. For the next eleven months the war in the Aleutians would be stalemated. A 400-mile no-man's-land of islands, sea, and sky existed between Umnak and Kiska, criss-crossed by American bombers and patrol planes and by the Imperial Navy, which for a time continued to search for Admiral Theobald's small fleet.

During the period Patrol Wing 4 operated with a threefold mission: (1) carry out long range patrols; (2) attack enemy shipping and land installations as practicable; (3) provide air-sea rescue service.[40] Patrols were flown to the west and northwest. It was on one such patrol on 20 June that two PBYs reported a large number of unidentified ships in the Bering Sea, giving rise to speculation that a Japanese invasion force was moving toward Nome on Alaska's north coast.

Major General Simon Bolivar Buckner, who commanded U.S. Army forces in the Alaskan sector, instituted a monumental one-day airlift of 2,500 troops and supplies to Nome using every available plane: military aircraft, commercial airliners, Ford Trimotors, even bush planes. PBYs moved into the area and continued their patrols in search of the enemy fleet but found nothing. On 12 July, they went back to their bases. The original contact had been an honest one: The two PBYs had located Admiral Kakuta's strike force, which was still hoping to achieve its second goal, that of finding and destroying the U.S. fleet. The PBYs lost contact shortly afterward when Kakuta gave up and turned his ships toward Japan.[41]

In late June Admiral Nimitz made Patrol Wing 4 a part of General Butler's 11th Air Force. By doing so the admiral hoped to corral Captain Gehres, who had operated somewhat independently under Admiral Theobald and had earned a reputation for being a maverick. Despite orders to the contrary from his new commander, Captain Gehres continued PBY patrols over Kiska. As a result Lieutenant Jack Litsey's Catalina was the first to encounter a Rufe, the new float plane version of the Zero, with the loss of one crewman and damage to his plane. In the next six weeks Gehres lost four PBYs to Rufes over Kiska.

The weather continued to be as great an enemy as the Japanese, with williwaws and high seas taking their toll of PBYs at anchor. From May to late August there were eighteen hours of daylight each day, but visibility was often only a few hundred feet because of the ever-present fog. Ensign Freerks said it was possible to land on the Umnak airstrip without the tower even knowing he was there.[42]

The volume of air-sea rescue missions increased for the Catalinas after the Japanese occupation of Attu and Kiska. Heavy and accurate flak and the ever-present Rufes kept the patrol squadrons busy picking up air force bomber crews and fighter pilots who could not make it back to their fields. Most rescue missions were successful but not all.

One unsuccessful mission cost Patrol Wing 4 a PBY and left the crew to walk partway home. Lieutenant (j.g.) Lucias Campbell and crew took off at 1045 on 19 June in 42-P-4 to search a beach area north of Port Moller on the Alaskan Peninsula for the crew of a downed B-26. A parachute was sighted on the beach near Cape Senivan, so Campbell set the plane down beyond the breakers and sent two crewmen ashore in a rubber boat to investigate. Paddling in was easy; the heavy surf helped.

A PBY-5A splashes down on a mud-covered Marston mat runway in the Aleutians, throwing spray on a P-40 whose propeller shows evidence of a hard landing. (U.S. Navy)

But coming back was impossible, and at 1300 the two men were still ashore. Campbell took off and dropped food to his men, who indicated they would walk toward Port Moller.

About twelve miles away Campbell, seeing a large, hard-packed sand beach, decided to pick up his hiking crewmen. He landed and taxied the PBY-5A up on shore to wait for them. When they were on board he attempted a takeoff down the beach, but the sand was softer than it appeared and the nose wheel dug in. It had to be a water takeoff or nothing. By putting driftwood under the nose wheel, the crew edged the plane down the beach ten feet at a time until it was once again afloat. Campbell taxied out, but about fifty yards from shore a huge wave broke over the plane, and the bow refused to come up. Another giant breaker was bearing down, so Campbell opened the throttles wide to try to force the bow up. With engines roaring, the PBY slammed into a solid wall of water.

The impact tore both propellers off the engines. Taking on water, the PBY was backed into the shallows by the surf. Campbell and crew spent the night huddled around a fire. "At 0400 20 June I could see water flowing in one waist blister and out the other," he wrote. "The hull was solid full of water." Reduced to pedestrians, Campbell and crew started the long walk to Port Moller.[43]

Since the aerial bombardment of Kiska had failed to blast the Japanese invaders off the island, CinCPac ordered shelling by Theobald's cruisers and destroyers. Although they were in position on 22 July, fog made bombardment impossible. They tried again on 27 July, but Fire Control still couldn't see where to shoot. When four of his destroyers collided in the fog, Theobald withdrew. Both attempts at shelling had been timed to coincide with bombings by PBYs. The first PBY support mission was aborted; on the 27th the PBYs bombed anyway.

Naval bombardment was next attempted by Rear Admiral William Smith, whose ships had the good fortune to arrive off Kiska on a clear day, 7 August. The covering PBYs and air force heavy bombers were called in for air strikes, and four Curtiss Seagull float planes were catapulted from the cruisers to act as forward fire controllers for the bombardment. But the Seagulls were met by Rufes, which quickly shot down two and chased the other two into the clouds. The Rufes then reversed the procedure and started calling the ships' coordinates back to the Japanese shore batteries, which promptly opened up. Smith ordered blind shelling to begin from five miles out. Damage ashore was light. A freighter in the harbor was hit; it was sunk by a PBY later in the evening.[44]

The Japanese and Americans traded shots several times during August. On the third, three Japanese seaplanes attacked the seaplane tender USS *Casco* but to no avail. On the fifth and sixth PBYs and enemy seaplanes fired on each other but scored no hits. On the eighth six PBYs carried the fight into Kiska harbor, three striking at ships, three at shore installations. Dropping 500-pound and 1,000-pound bombs, the PBYs laid two on a medium-sized transport and one on a second and started fires on shore. Four Rufes punched holes in the PBYs as they left the harbor, but the blister gunners returned the fire and sent two Rufes spinning into the fog. One PBY, piloted by Ensign Herrin of VP-41, was forced down out of fuel near Umnak; he and his crew were picked up later. The PBY piloted by Lieutenant (j.g.) Raven, also of VP-41, failed to return.

Two submarines were bombed by Catalinas during the period. A third, caught on the surface while shelling a Russian freighter, crash-dived when a PBY roared down on it.

Accidents, weather, and the enemy continued to erode the supply of men and PBYs. On 20 July a PBY flown by Lieutenant Roy Green of VP-43 crashed on takeoff, killing all on board. On the thirtieth, Lieutenant (j.g.) D. A. Brough of VP-42 crashed on landing; three crewmen survived. On 8 August Ensign Kelly of VP-62 flew his PBY into a mountain; no one survived. Williwaws and high seas destroyed several PBYs at anchor and ashore. Rufe float plane fighters were a hazard on rescue missions and shipping searches.

Neither were the tenders immune to damage and accidents. The *Avocet* was holed when it struck a reef. The *Williamson* was heavily damaged when the depth charges detonated on a PBY it was towing; three members of the plane crew were killed, as was one member of the ship's crew.

Still, there were fortunate occasions. On 20 July three four-engine seaplanes bombed the *Gillis*. All of the bombs missed but one, and it was a dud. On 3 August the *Casco* was bombed by seaplanes, but it also escaped unharmed.[45]

In August 1942 approval was given to General Buckner's request to close the distance between U.S. forces and the enemy. The army occupied Adak, in the Andreanof Islands about 250 miles east of Kiska, on the thirtieth. Once the island was secure, Captain Gehres escorted Colonel Benjamin Talley, who was in charge of building the airstrip on Adak, out to the island in a PBY, but the surf was too high to put the colonel ashore. They flew to the *Casco*, which was anchored in Nazan Bay, and Colonel Talley transferred to the destroyer USS *Reid* for the trip to the island.

The *Reid* had hardly gotten out of sight when a submarine that had been lying in wait fired two torpedoes at the *Casco*. One ran up on the beach, but the other hit in the forward engine room, killing five men, wounding three others, and destroying the diesel engine. Captain Gehres, jarred off a chair in the captain's office, was scratched and bruised. The *Casco* was beached for temporary repairs, refloated on 13 September, and eventually returned to full service.[46]

Justice was swift: The day after the attack on the *Casco* three PBYs on patrol near Nazan Bay spotted a submerged submarine. One of these was a VP-43 Catalina flown by the squadron executive officer, Lieutenant Carl Amme. "Our crew had developed a technique that called for flying over a sub at 500 feet, pulling back on the throttles and allowing the plane to nose over momentarily in order to direct the aim of the depth charges, then releasing them manually. We lost only 200 feet in altitude," he said. The VP-43 Catalina used this technique on the Japanese sub. A moving oil slick told them it was damaged but not sunk. Amme flew out about twenty miles and by Aldis lamp alerted a destroyer—the *Reid*, returning from Atka.

> When the DD arrived on the scene, we indicated where the sub was by dropping smoke lights just ahead of the developing oil slick. The *Reid* could detect nothing on its sonar, apparently, since it did not drop any depth charges. Repeated smoke lights showing the position of the sub as indicated by the oil slick still elicited no action. Finally I used my Aldis lamp to send a message: "This will be my last smoke signal. Drop depth charges where I indicate. Acknowledge." The *Reid's* captain acknowledged and dropped a pattern of cans. He then secured from General Quarters.

Fortunately a crew member was still at his post at the 20-millimeter gun on the fantail when the sub surfaced. He raked the decks as the sub's crew came out to man the deck gun. The *Reid* finally sunk the sub.[47]

Five prisoners were taken. When questioned, they told their interrogators that they had torpedoed the *Casco* the day before.[48]

Colonel Talley and his engineers could find only one area on Adak that looked remotely like an airfield. On this tidal flat the engineers threw up a levee to keep the sea out and laid down a runway of hard-packed sand. Ten days after the occupation, the first plane landed.[49] On Sunday, 13 September, Commander James Russell, the commanding officer of VP-42, set up his headquarters tent on Adak. From the new base his PBYs were able to range farther toward Japan and intercept more enemy ships attempting to slip into the harbors at Attu and Kiska. The improved interception was partly due to a change on 1 August in the method of conducting searches. Rather than flying the same pattern on the same timetable, patterns and times were varied, which confused the Japanese ship captains who had been delaying their arrivals to follow the planes in on their return leg.

Mark 37 depth bombs are readied for loading at an Aleutian airfield in 1942. (U.S. Navy)

As a result, enemy supplies were reduced to a trickle. The bases on Attu and Kiska not only were unable to expand their operations but were barely able to survive, Japanese troops existing on the most meager rations. Defensive aircraft were flown in from seaplane carriers offshore and left to their own devices. Most were destroyed on the water by hit-and-run raids carried out by PBYs and air force bombers and fighters. Using hand tools, the Japanese attempted to build an airstrip on Kiska, only to have their work cratered almost daily by the raiding planes.[50]

Most of Patrol Wing 4's efforts were directed at finding, attacking, and reporting submarines. A number were sighted, but none were sunk. On most patrols no contact was made with enemy planes, but on 2 October a PBY was attacked by three float planes over Kiska. One fighter was shot down and another damaged; the PBY made it home.[51]

On 1 November Patrol Wing 4 became Fleet Air Wing 4, part of a major reorganization of all of the navy's patrol wings. The wings were restructured on the task force principle, doing away with set numbers of squadrons per wing and allowing assignment of whatever type of aircraft was needed for a wing to perform its mission in a particular area.[52]

In January 1943 the Americans took another giant step and established a base only 50 miles from Kiska on Amchitka Island. Catalinas were ordered to fly daylight antisubmarine patrols to cover the landing forces. The nearly decimated fleet of Rufes on Kiska could do little to impede either the landings or construction of the airfield on Amchitka. On 21 February the first PBY-5A touched down on the runway, but it was not until 4 May that the first regular patrols were flown from there. Until that time all space on the field had been taken up by army P-40s and P-38s engaged in raiding Kiska. In the meantime Captain Gehres's PBYs based themselves on the tender *Avocet*, which was anchored in Constantine Harbor. The new base moved search operations so far west that the PBY bases at Cold Bay and Sand Point were closed and the Dutch Harbor operation cut back. What was more, the Kurile Islands, just north of Hokkaido, one of Japan's four main islands, were now within striking distance.[53]

Late winter and early spring in the Aleutians saw the Catalina squadrons continuing their antishipping and antisubmarine patrols, sometimes carrying out their own damaging attacks, sometimes asking for help from the army. On 25 January, for instance, a PBY vectored in B-25s, which sank an armed Japanese freighter.

On 4 January Admiral Theobald was replaced in the Alaskan sector by Rear Admiral Thomas Kincaid.[54] It was Kincaid who had ordered the occupation of Amchitka before the enemy could move in. Japanese interest in the island had increased in recent months, along with their fears of an invasion of the home islands, now that American troops were moving down the Aleutian chain.[55]

Kincaid placed the six warships that Theobald had been holding in Alaskan waters under the command of Rear Admiral Charles McMorris and sent them out to cruise beyond Attu and Kiska to head off enemy supply convoys. After one Japanese merchantman was sunk by gunfire from the blockaders and two others turned back rather than risk a similar fate, Admiral Hosogaya mounted an all-out effort to get supplies through. He set out from the big base at Paramushiro in the Kuriles with three cargo ships and an escort of four destroyers and four heavy cruisers.

Early on the morning of 26 March Fleet Air Wing 4's PBYs found the Japanese convoy, but could do nothing other than report position and direction, as they were armed with depth charges.[56] McMorris's blockade ships were within striking distance, however, and turned to do battle. The action that followed became known as the Battle of the Kommandorskis, named for the Russian-held islands a hundred miles to the northwest. For the next three and one half hours the cruiser USS *Salt Lake City* exchanged fire with Hosogaya's flagship, the cruiser *Nachi*, in the longest continuous naval battle in modern history.

The battle ended when the Japanese suddenly retired. The *Salt Lake City* had begun firing high-explosive shells after she ran out of the armor-piercing variety, and Hosogaya had mistaken them for bombs dropped from American planes. Because he had no air cover, he ran for home rather than expose his ships to air attack. Despite the time and the amount of ordnance expended, only seven Americans and fourteen Japanese were killed, and no ships were sunk. The U.S. bombardment was enough to intimidate the Japanese, however. Never again did they try to resupply Attu and Kiska.[57]

In January 1943 Admiral Kincaid submitted a plan to the Joint Chiefs of Staff for the retaking of Attu and Kiska, with a target date in early May. The plan was approved, and on 11 May ten thousand troops went ashore on Attu in the first large-scale army amphibious landing. The conquest of the island was estimated at three days; it took three weeks. GIs fought five times the expected number of Japanese defenders, as well as freezing temperatures, rain, snow, ice, bottomless muskeg, gale-force winds, and the eternal fog. Continuous air support was provided by PBYs and air force bombers and fighters, plus navy Wildcat fighters from the new escort carrier USS *Nassau*. At sea, supporting firepower came from the battleships *Pennsylvania*, *Idaho*, and *Nevada*—now repaired and looking for revenge after being damaged at Pearl Harbor—along with six cruisers and nineteen destroyers.[58]

Four patrol squadrons contributed PBYs for the Attu operation: VP-43, VP-45, VP-61, and VP-62. The PBYs were augmented by two squadrons of recently arrived Lockheed PV-1 Venturas. All squadrons had a primary mission of protecting the ships from Japanese submarines. The day after the landings a PBY spotted a torpedo wake heading for the *Pennsylvania*. The plane radioed a warning to the ship, and either evasive action or good luck caused the torpedo to miss. The PBY then guided destroyers to the submarine's position, and they sank it.

By the evening of 12 May Attu's shoreline was safe enough for the *Casco* to set up shop in Massacre Bay, servicing any patrolling Catalina that dropped by. Two days later VP-45 was stationed on the *Casco* and began flying sorely needed antisubmarine patrols, for the increase in U.S. Navy ships had attracted an inordinate number of Japanese submarines. Although several were spotted and attacked, none were sunk. The heavy schedule rapidly fatigued pilots, crewmen, and servicing crews. One PBY dropped depth charges on an enemy submarine, but they failed to explode because a worn-out crewman had forgotten to arm them.

Air attacks were expected, and on 23 May a PBY's radar picked up incoming planes. Then the pilot saw them, a flight of bombers, through a break in the cloud cover. He radioed for army fighters, which shot down five of the would-be raiders. The remainder jettisoned their bombs and torpedoes and aborted the mission.[59]

On 29 May the last of the Japanese defenders on Attu made a suicide attack, and the fighting ended. All of the 2,500 Japanese troops were dead, either killed in combat or dying by their own hands; 549 Americans had died, 1,148 were wounded.[60]

Control of Attu and its neighboring islands of Shemya and Agattu now gave the United States air bases from which strikes by long-range bombers could be mounted on Northern Japan, plus a staging point for an invasion of the home islands. Admiral Kincaid and General Buckner began to make plans along those lines, with D-day slated for the spring of 1944.[61]

The Russians, our allies in Europe, were neutral in the Kommandorskis to the point of exasperation. True, there were incidents in which Russian freighters were mistaken for Japanese supply ships and received more than their share of attention from U.S. guns before the error was realized. Fly-overs of Russian soil by U.S. planes were not uncommon. The Russians responded with gunfire, internment of aircrews, impounding of planes, and diplomatic protests. They had cause for all four responses as a result of an incident in August 1943 involving two PBYs from VP-43.

A PBY-5 of VP-45 bears evidence of damage from a willawaw's high winds on its rudder, aileron, and wing trailing edge. (David Lucabaugh Collection)

A Catalina patrolling near the Kommandorskis developed engine trouble and headed for the one port in the islands with a sheltered bay. The Russians' antiaircraft batteries opened up, however, and finished off the PBY's troubled engine. With one still-functioning engine, the plane landed inland on a lake. Lieutenant Carl Amme was on duty at VP-43 headquarters at the time. When he received a radio message giving the plane's location, he sent another PBY to pick up the crew, remove the confidential publications and other gear, and sink the plane. He ordered the pilot of the second plane, Lieutenant Roy Evans, to maintain radio silence and ignore any countermanding orders from the wing. Evans was to communicate with the base only if he were in trouble or after the rescue was effected. Then Amme stayed in the radio shack to see that no one used the transmitter. All messages, including Fleet Air Wing 4 orders to recall the pilot, were received but not acknowledged, much to the discomforture of some of the radio operators on duty.

Evans landed on the lake, picked up the crew, and sank the plane as ordered. He then took off just as the Russians were paddling out from the lakeshore. Once in the air he sent a message saying the operation was successful.

"At that time," said Amme, "our radio transmitter fortuitously was put back into commission and wing headquarters was informed of the successful rescue. My neck was out a mile on this one, and I knew it. But I was damned if I would have one of our flight crews interned by the Russians. My strategy resulted from reading the story of Nelson at the Battle of Copenhagen when he put his blind eye to the telescope so that he could not read the fleet commander's signal to withdraw. Instead, he attacked and won a victory."[62]

Preparations for the taking of Kiska dwarfed the Attu operation. The garrison on Kiska was thought to be two or three times the size of the one that had been on Attu. Beginning in early August the island was softened up with eight separate bombardments by navy warships and continuous bombing attacks by air force and navy planes. PBYs flew only a few daylight bombing missions over Kiska, limiting their activity mostly to nighttime harassment. Taking part in the operation were the fourteen Catalinas of VP-45 from Attu and fifteen from VP-61 on Amchitka, each squadron with a mission similar to the one for the Attu landings: conduct searches, carry out antisubmarine patrols, and support air strike units as ordered.

On 15 August thirty-four thousand U.S. Army troops and a Canadian brigade stormed ashore on Kiska, supported by more than a hundred ships. All they found to shoot at was each other, which they did, killing twenty-four men in the fog. The Japanese had pulled out. The entire force of five thousand had been evacuated from the island 28 July in a single afternoon by a fleet of fifteen ships that had slipped past U.S. patrols in the fog.

With the occupation of Kiska the Aleutian campaign ended for the army and air force and most of the navy surface fleet. Thereafter, only a small defense force would remain. There were no more Japanese left in the islands; the threat of invasion to Alaska and the United States mainland had ended. The threat was now, in fact, to Japan's home islands. More than fourteen months had been required to turn the tables.[63]

The PBYs of Fleet Air Wing 4, however, had one more series of missions to perform. Commodore Gehres (he was promoted in July) could see no reason why he should not carry the war a little nearer home for the Japanese. He ordered his PBYs to carry out night bombing attacks on the enemy naval base and airfields at Paramushiro in the Kuriles. Since little was known about the area, reconnaissance photos were also to be taken.

It would not be the first time night bombing was tried. Plans for such missions were completed before Kiska was captured. They were to be carried out entirely by PBYs, but when the first attack was launched on 10 July, its complement was four PBYs and eight air force B-25s. The

B-25s reached the target; the PBYs were forced back because of the weather. A similar attempt on the eighteenth was also aborted. The first all-air-force effort was made in September by eight B-24s and twelve B-25s. The Japanese were still on the alert from two months before. Zeros and antiaircraft fire brought down two B-24s and six B-25s.

In contrast to the air force missions, Gehres's PBYs were to fly in the relative safety of darkness. On 6 December preparations began. Two PBYs from VP-43 took off from Umnak to test an experimental photo setup in which K-19 aerial cameras were mounted in the tunnel hatches and 52-pound Mark 26 photoflash bombs were hung from the wing racks. They flew to Agattu, dropped the photoflash bombs and returned to Umnak.[64]

The photographs were good enough to warrant mounting a full-scale raid on Paramushiro. The first raid was flown on 20 December by four Catalinas of VP-43. The planes were piloted by Lieutenant J. P. Weibler, Lieutenant M. J. Noe, Lieutenant (j.g.) A. Openshaw, and Lieutenant (j.g.) D. P. Norton. Each plane carried two 500-pound bombs and twenty 20-pound antipersonnel bombs, the latter to be tossed out of the blisters over the target. Six photoflash bombs were also carried and aerial cameras were in place to record results and obtain intelligence photos.

The PBYs took off and flew through a seven-tenths cloud cover, encountering icing and turbulence, and climbed to 8,000 feet. Three of the planes reached Paramushiro; Noe turned back when his fuel ran low. Over the target they tried to release their photoflash bombs, but the releases were frozen. Searchlights came on and flak bursts thumped around them, but no hits were made. One plane reported seeing a burst of tracer, apparently fired by a Japanese night fighter. As the PBYs' windshields were iced inside and out, a final run was made on radar and the 500-pounders and antipersonnel bombs were dropped. One picture was obtained accidentally when the release thawed out on a photoflash bomb and it dropped of its own accord.

On 19 January 1944 another four-plane mission was flown, but the planes became separated on the way. Only two found the target. One dropped all of its photoflash bombs, but this time the cameras didn't work. Crew members saw about a hundred widely scattered antiaircraft shell bursts, some close enough to jolt the planes. Lieutenant (j.g.) L. W. Black reported his Catalina was fired on by a plane that "looked like an SNJ." It made about eight passes, firing each time, but Black's gunners did not return the fire. Rather, on each pass Black closed the throttles to kill the exhaust flame, then dived and pulled up to throw off the enemy's aim. His plane took no hits. The exhaust continually gave away his position until he reached cloud cover.

Missions were flown on the next three nights, with results no better than from the first two missions. The only damage to any of the planes was a broken navigator's window, caused by ice thrown off a propeller blade.

Following the four-night blitz, Gehres sent a dispatch to the VP-43 pilots in January, saying: "You have done yourselves and the Wing proud, and the Japs probably don't love you. Congratulations and well done." And ComNorPac wrote Gehres: "Express my gratification to all hands assisting in the Paramushiro flights during the past four nights. The determination to carry the fight to the enemy and the work of all concerned merits highest praise." The message was signed Davenport Johnson, Major General, USA.

The January flights all but ended the Catalina missions to the Kuriles. Only two missions were flown in February by PBYs, then the missions were turned over to the Venturas.[65] Later the air force took up sporadic daylight attacks once more.[66] It was clear that the PBYs were not well suited for the work. Most missions needed to be flown at 9,000 feet for the photoflash bombs to operate properly. The PBYs could barely maintain that altitude. Speeds were often less than ninety knots, which meant a flight of twelve to fourteen hours. Icing on the external bomb racks caused erratic releases or none at all and also coated windshields and windows.

The PBYs had taken few if any usable pictures and had not caused any great damage with their bombs. But the planes' effect on Japanese morale was considerable. Coupled with the Ventura and air force bombing attacks that followed, the raids caused the enemy to tie up hundreds of aircraft and thousands of troops in anticipation of the dreaded American invasion through the Aleutians.

But it would never come. The war in the Aleutians lapsed into a battle in which the weather was the only enemy, an opponent that no army commander wanted to fight again with large numbers of troops and supplies. Most of the combat troops and aircraft were rotated for the mainland.

The navy did likewise with its ships and planes. VP-51 left at the end of August 1942. VP-41 and VP-42 followed in early 1943, with VP-45 leaving in mid-October. VP-62 said goodbye to the Aleutians at the end of October 1944, as did VP-61 in December.[67] Only the PBYs of VP-43, under now-Lieutenant Marshall Freerks, remained to carry on a long series of uneventful patrols and a few air-sea rescue missions throughout the final months of the war.[68]

The South Pacific

Before the Japanese sought to establish northern defenses in the Aleutians, other Rising Sun forces had raced south to cut the supply lines from the United States to Australia. Two days after the Pearl Harbor attack Japanese troops landed in the Gilbert Islands to the northeast of Australia. On 23 January 1942 they conquered Kieta on Bougainville in the Solomons. That same day they took the Australian base at Rabaul on New Britain and two days later landed on New Ireland, both islands in the Bismarck Archipelago. On 8 March they landed at Lae and Salamaua on the northeast coast of New Guinea. On 3 May they took Tulagi and Gavutu in the Solomons.[1] When the islands to the east of Australia—New Caledonia, Samoa, and the Fijis—were taken, the circle around the Coral Sea would be complete, rendering it useless as a supply channel to the island continent. Any supplies reaching Australia from the United States would have to take a route much farther south, by way of New Zealand.[2]

Despite the importance of the islands to the east of Australia, the first priority in the Japanese plan was given to the capture of Port Moresby on the south coast of New Guinea. But rather than try again to take it by sea, the Japanese would now climb over the Owen Stanley mountains from their new bases in Lae and Salamaua. For the moment, the Japanese forces at the newly built seaplane base at Tulagi would merely maintain a watch for American activity.[3] Tulagi was only about thirty miles across the Sealark Channel from Guadalcanal, to which the Japanese had crossed and where they were building an airfield. The airfield would be important in the future, for from it Japanese planes could provide air cover for the Imperial Army whenever it was ready to take New Caledonia, Samoa, and the Fijis.[4]

This fact was equally obvious to the American high command. The time had come to stop the Japanese encroachment to the south. The

Allies must push north, and the Solomons were the place to start. General MacArthur, in whose area of control the Solomons lay, wanted, characteristically, to move directly to the heart of the matter. He proposed attacking the now-heavily fortified Japanese base at Rabaul. The idea did not set well with Admiral Nimitz, however, who felt that U.S. forces should first practice on something smaller. The difference of opinion stalemated any move. The question was resolved only when the Joint Chiefs of Staff moved the demarcation line between MacArthur's and Nimitz's areas of control to the west, so that the Solomons were in Nimitz's area.

A plan was then formulated to assemble U.S. forces at a staging area in Wellington, New Zealand. From there they would take the Santa Cruz Islands just south of the Solomons, then Tulagi and Guadalcanal, and finally the rest of the Solomons. An attack on Rabaul would be the coup de grace. Once Rabaul fell, Australia would be safe from Japanese attack from the northeast.

Operation Watchtower was the official name given the operation, but with Europe and the upcoming invasion of North Africa getting the bulk of men and matériel, the meagerly manned and supplied operation was unofficially dubbed Operation Shoestring.[5]

To counter Japanese opposition to the landings, PBYs were sent into forward areas to begin surveillance. PBYs of Patrol Wing 1 had begun moving into the islands east of Australia early in the year; VP-14 and VP-71 flew into Noumea, New Caledonia, in June; VP-11 arrived in three-plane detachments at Suva in the Fijis in early July.[6] On 12 July three VP-11 planes and crews were deployed to Noumea to be based on the tender USS *Mackinac,* from where they began flying patrols to the northwest. The remainder of the squadron was based at Nandi in the Fijis.[7]

On 1 August, nine Catalinas from VP-23 and the *Mackinac* slipped into the estuary between Malaita and Maramasike Islands only seventy-five miles from Tulagi. On the fifth a five-plane detachment of PBYs from VP-11 and VP-14 was ordered to Ndeni in the Santa Cruz Islands to operate from the USS *McFarland.*[8] The fourteen planes, plus the remainder of VP-11, which was now based on the tender *Curtiss* at Espiritu Santo, began twelve-hour sector searches 600 to 700 miles long and 80 miles wide at the far end.[9] The planes flew to the east and north of Guadalcanal to prevent any Japanese surprise attack on the invasion fleet when it headed for the Solomons. They found little other than a few scouting float planes, however.[10]

On 7 August U.S. Marines charged ashore on Tulagi and Guadalcanal. Thirty-one hours later, after heavy fighting, Tulagi was secure, at a cost of 199 marines and 800 Japanese dead. The landing on Guadalcanal was unopposed. The next morning the marines surrounded the airfield, and navy Seabee construction battalions went to work immediately to complete it, using materials and equipment the Japanese laborers left behind when they ran for the jungle. Completed within two weeks, Henderson Field was named in honor of Major Lofton Henderson, a dive bomber squadron leader who died in the Battle of Midway. A PBY-5A landed on the unfinished strip on 12 August; the first Dauntlesses and Wildcats of the "Cactus Air Force"—"Cactus" was the code name for Guadalcanal—would not land until the twentieth.[11]

The Japanese, momentarily taken aback by the American wrench thrown into their smoothly operating war machinery, were quick to retaliate. The Japanese navy responded first. On the day of the American landings, Vice Admiral Gunichi Mikawa steamed from Rabaul, forming a flotilla of seven cruisers and a destroyer on the way south. Shortly after midnight on 9 August they engaged the U.S. Navy in what would be called the Battle of Savo Island. The Americans, lacking the experience of the Japanese in night fighting, lost three cruisers and more than a thousand lives—more men than would die on Guadalcanal. The Japanese ships retired scarcely damaged, but in fear of greater damage if caught in daylight by American planes.

A week and a half later the Japanese army tried its hand at retaliation, but they had underestimated the number of marines on Guadalcanal. There were ten thousand; the Japanese had thought there were no more than two thousand. On the night of 18 August enemy destroyers slipped in under cover of darkness and quietly landed a thousand crack troops bent on throwing the Americans into the sea. In the confrontation at

A PBY-5A bearing Admiral J. S. McCain was the first Allied aircraft to land on former enemy-held territory: Guadalcanal, 12 August 1942.

0300 on the twentieth over 800 Imperial Army troops died, cut to pieces by gunfire from marine rifles, machine guns, cannon, and tanks.

These Japanese were part of a regiment, the remainder of which was to arrive a few days later. It never got there, despite the best efforts of Admiral Yamamoto. Still smarting from the beating at Midway only two months before, he sought revenge in the South Pacific, and sent three carriers, two battleships, eleven cruisers, and nineteen destroyers to escort the troop ships and destroy the American fleet.[12]

PBYs on patrol from the *Mackinac* at Ndeni found the Japanese armada on the morning of 23 August, but the five PBYs that took off that night armed for an attack on the force were unable to locate it. The following morning a patrolling VP-14 PBY piloted by Lieutenant (j.g.) R. B. Clark pinpointed the position of a carrier, a battleship, and several smaller ships. In order to make positive identification, Clark headed directly for the fleet, but banked for the clouds when he saw the carrier launching planes. Three fighters were waiting for him when he came out of the cloud bank, and in a scissoring attack they punctured both of the PBY's fuel tanks, shot away rudder and elevator cables, and killed his radioman. Clark reached more clouds, but this time when he emerged eight fighters were waiting. The PBY took more hits and his plane captain in the tower was wounded, but the blister gunners sent two of the attackers plunging into the ocean. Clark headed for home with both engines streaming oil. When the port engine ran dry, the crew lightened the plane as much as possible, and they continued on the remaining engine, which was also nearly out of oil and frequently caught fire. When almost all fuel and oil were gone, Clark set the plane down near Ontong, Java, where friendly natives cared for him and his crew. A week later they were rescued by a VP-11 PBY.[13]

Clark's sighting marked the start of a two-day encounter called the Battle of the Eastern Solomons. Planes from the *Saratoga* sank the carrier *Ryujo* and a destroyer and seriously damaged several other ships. The *Enterprise* was damaged in return, with a loss of twenty planes. As soon as the capital ships broke off, the Japanese troopships and their escorts were located and attacked by planes from Henderson Field, which sank a transport, damaged a cruiser, and sent the remaining ships packing for Rabaul.[14]

Resupply and reinforcement by sea was all important in determining the outcome of the Guadalcanal campaign for both the Americans and the Japanese. Air power played a significant role. During daylight hours the planes of the Cactus Air Force and ships of the U.S. Navy kept Japanese aircraft and surface ships at bay, making resupply of the marines on the island relatively easy. The night, however, belonged to the

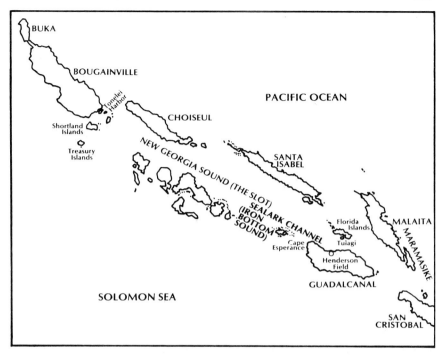

The Solomon Islands

Japanese. Their ships moved down New Georgia Sound—"The Slot"—on a schedule so regular that it came to be called "The Tokyo Express." The ships would unload reinforcements and supplies in the darkness, sometimes blasting the marine positions ashore with heavy gunfire from cruisers and battleships, then race for Rabaul to be back under their own air cover by sunrise.[15]

The Cactus Air Force was such a thorn in the side of the Japanese that on the night of 11–12 October Admiral Mikawa attempted to destroy Henderson Field by naval bombardment, but his ships ran head-on into a U.S. Navy cruiser force. In the Battle of Cape Esperance a Japanese cruiser and a destroyer were sunk and another cruiser was severely damaged by shell fire. The Americans lost a destroyer, and two cruisers retired for repairs. In the early morning hours of 14 October Mikawa tried again, and the marines on Guadalcanal awoke to the thunder of Japanese naval guns hurling 14-inch projectiles onto Henderson Field. Half of the fighters and bombers on the field were destroyed, and the Marston mat runway was put out of action. The next night a Japanese cruiser force came back to finish the job and nearly succeeded. The reason for the increased attention became apparent the following morning when six Japanese transports were located only ten miles away, un-loading some forty-five hundred men and supplies.[16]

As soon as a few Dauntless dive bombers could be patched up and fueled with gasoline drained from wrecked planes, the marine com-mander, Major General Roy Geiger, sent them out against the enemy. Even his personal plane, a PBY-5A named "The Blue Goose," joined in the fray. The general's pilot, Major Jack Cram, located the ships, took the Goose in under the Japanese fighter cover and down to the wave tops, then aimed its two torpedoes at a transport. One blew a huge hole in the ship's side as Cram headed the PBY for Henderson Field. A cloud of Zeros followed him, blazing away until he banked into his final ap-proach. Antiaircraft fire picked off two of the enemy planes; a marine Wildcat accounted for a third. When Cram landed, General Geiger looked at the bullet holes in his plane, frowned, and threatened him with a court-martial. The frown turned to a smile, however; the general was joking. Cram was later awarded the Navy Cross.[17]

Other PBYs did not get off as easily during the battle. A Catalina flown by Lieutenant (j.g.) Melvin Butler and operating off the *Mackinac* at Vanikoro Island found a Japanese task force on the night of 14 October. He radioed its position, said his plane had been hit, and was not heard from again. At dawn four other *Mackinac*-based Catalinas relocated the force. Intense antiaircraft fire brought two of them down almost at once; Lieutenant (j.g.) David Walkinshaw sent out a position, speed, and course report from his PBY, then escaped along with the remaining plane.[18]

While the Americans and Japanese were establishing daylight–dark-ness operational patterns for reinforcement and resupply, the PBY squadrons were developing tactics for night search and attack missions, tactics that would be followed, corrected, and enlarged upon until the end of the war. What evolved would eventually become known as "Black Cat" operations, but in the fall of 1942 the name had not been coined. Up until that time the navy had, for the most part, considered its patrol bombers only as scouts, to be operated in daylight, carrying bombs and depth charges to drop on targets of opportunity, and these no bigger than submarines. Anything larger was to be reported for dispatch by aircraft better equipped for the job, or by surface ships. The number of patrol bombers was too few and their value too great to risk them in attacks on larger targets unless the payoffs were very high. Such was now the case,[19] so another dimension was added to the PBY's mission. They would fly by night and, rather than simply report any ship they found, they would attack it with bombs and torpedoes.

One of the pilots in the early days of the as-yet-unnamed Black Cat operations was Lieutenant (j.g.) Alan Rothenberg. He had been sent as pilot of a one-plane detachment from VP-51 to join the PBYs of VP-11 and VP-14 at Espiritu Santo in early August. Finding and hitting targets was not easy. "Some of the planes had radar," he said,

> but we never counted on it. The screen showed a single line that went up and down like grass. When the grass started to grow and flicker you assumed that maybe you had something. On a good moonlit night you could see the silhouettes of ships, but if there was a good breeze you couldn't tell a wake from the whitecaps. About the only way you really knew if something was coming down The Slot was to get the word from a coast watcher—and the fact that they showed up almost every night anyway. We had been briefed that there were no Allied ships beyond Point Cruz, and anything west that was floating was fair game.
>
> There weren't any specific tactics that you learned in flight training for attacking ships; we were the first ones to do it, and everybody just made them up as they went along. Nobody had ever dropped a torpedo in combat until Midway. The reason we went down low was to escape detection, and also if you dropped the torpedo from any higher it would probably break up when it hit the water.[20]

Rothenberg got a chance to improve his tactics on the night of 16 October. At 0200 the detachment commander, Lieutenant J. O. Cobb, located a flotilla of enemy ships and launched his torpedo toward a large target. It didn't explode. Then he called in Rothenberg, who was also patrolling in the area that night.

Homing in on Cobb's M-O radio signals, Rothenberg dropped to 50 feet and headed toward a column of ships on radar. Suddenly out of the darkness the silhouette of an enemy cruiser filled the windshield. A collision was imminent. He hauled back on the yoke and lifted the big plane up and over the cruiser, missing it by only a few feet. All talk of a PBY being heavy on the controls was forgotten. "It's surprising how strong you are when you're scared into a state of panic," he said.

Undaunted, he banked the PBY around in a 180-degree turn, headed back for the cruiser, and found himself looking at another column of ships sailing parallel to the first. They opened up with antiaircraft guns, but the firing stopped as he dropped down to fifty feet again: Rothenberg was now between the two columns, and they could not fire without hitting each other. He found the big silhouette once more, this time a little farther away. He released his torpedo. As the PBY passed over the ship a second time there came a bright flash and a jolt. The torpedo had struck home.[21]

It was during this period that night harassment was added to the PBYs regular diet of search and attack missions. For some time the troops on Guadalcanal had lost sleep to "washing machine charlie," a lone Japanese plane that flew over in the wee hours with its engines deliberately unsynchronized to make them sound unpleasant and easily recognizable and dropped a few scattered bombs. On 18 October, in a "what's sauce for the goose is sauce for the gander" maneuver, Lieutenant Jack Coley of VP-11 was given the first assignment to keep the Japanese awake.

Coley's Catalina was loaded with two 500-pound bombs under the wings, a dozen 100-pound bombs on the bunks, and an equal number of parachute flares. The plan was to drop the flares over the Japanese lines to locate targets, then drop the high explosives while strafing.

"The first two flares illuminated only the tops of the trees," said Coley,

> but our ordnance man suggested setting the flare ignition for maximum delay and dropping them from 1,000 feet instead of 3,000, so they would drop to the ground and light up the area around them. We tried it and it worked beautifully. We located a fuel dump and set it afire and generally played havoc for two hours. The crew would screw the fuse into a 100-pound bomb and then on signal from the cockpit would drop it out the tunnel hatch; unorthodox but effective. The 500-pounders we saved till last and then dropped them on a supply area.
>
> When we circled to make a run the area below looked like a field of fireflies with all the small arms being fired at us. But when we dived and opened up with the bow and waist guns the fireflies would disappear as the Japs took cover. Even with all the guns aimed at us we took only two hits, these aft of the tunnel hatch, and both were spent rounds that barely broke the skin.[22]

On later missions empty beer and soda bottles were added to the list of harassment ordnance, keeping many a Japanese face buried in the sand for an interminable period, waiting for the explosion of the missile that had whistled down through the darkness. On such a mission Lieutenant J. O. Cobb may have coined the name by which the PBYs would become known throughout the Pacific. In an effort to hold down friendly fire, he radioed General Geiger on Guadalcanal as he took off from Espiritu Santo that he would be in the air over the island. The message said: "The Black Cat flies tonight."[23]

The Catalinas now were indeed black. Crews from VP-11, operating from the *Curtiss* at Espiritu Santo, had smeared their blue-gray aircraft with a dull mixture of soap and lamp black.[24] They were not pretty to look at by day, but by night they became invisible to both surface ships and aircraft.

In the weeks and months ahead it grew apparent that the absence speed, maneuverability, and service ceiling which made the Catalina a sitting duck in daytime was an advantage for masthead-high attacks at night. Flame dampers were installed on the exhausts, and matte black paint replaced the lamp black. Radar was common on most aircraft. A new addition, the radio altimeter, made it possible to fly at wave top height at night with absolute accuracy and safety.[25] The payload of the Cats was stretched to the limit. A rule of thumb for determining whether a Cat could take off with the load imposed was to see if it would float after launching. If it floated, it could take off.[26] Because they did not need a landing field, their value was increased. With a tender for fuel, food, and quarters—or even a prepositioned mooring buoy with a 500-gallon rubber fuel storage tank and a "handy-billy" pump—the PBYs could operate from any reasonably protected body of water.[27]

Black Cat tactics evolved for defense as well as offense. If a Black Cat met an enemy fighter that somehow managed to maintain contact, the PBY pilot simply dropped down near the surface of the sea. The fighter could not get beneath him, and if he tried an attack from above, he was likely to dive into the ocean, his depth perception thrown off by the darkness.

Flares were dropped to illuminate targets prior to a bomb run, but they blinded the Cat pilots and also illuminated the plane for the Japanese gunners, so this idea was soon discarded. The most effective attack was made in the dark, first finding the target on radar, then visually, and then flying a quartering course across it, dropping four 500-pound bombs by seaman's eye about 40 feet apart from altitudes of 50 to 150 feet. It was advantageous to carry a load of parafrag bombs—small fragmentation bombs attached to parachutes for a delayed reaction—which were tossed out of the blisters and tunnel hatches to give the shipboard gunners pause. A flare dropped over the ship just as the plane passed over on its bombing run could also blind enemy gunners momentarily.

At first the Japanese ships made no attempt to maneuver, thinking they were hidden in the darkness, either not knowing or not concerned that on a calm night the PBY pilots could see their wakes. Later they resorted to maneuvering, or in some cases stopped dead in the water to kill their wake. Neither tactic worked well. If the ship maneuvered, the helmsman was never sure which way to turn, and if it stopped dead in the water, it simply became an easier target. The ships also held their antiaircraft fire at first, apparently thinking that to fire would give away their position, but when it became obvious that the Cat pilots already knew their position, they began firing blindly into the darkness. The Cats held their strafing fire and remained hidden until they had released their bombs, then the waist gunners blazed away on retreat to keep enemy heads down.[28]

The torpedo was doomed as a Black Cat weapon because it was erratic in performance, offered only a one-shot capability, and was difficult and dangerous to launch at a moving target. In the right hands, however, the torpedo was effective against a stationary target, as was demonstrated late in October by three crews from VP-11.

Intelligence had reported a buildup of Japanese ships in Tonelei Harbor at the south end of Bougainville, in preparation for another large-scale offensive against Allied land, sea, and air forces to the south. On the night of 22 October 1942, the three VP-11 PBYs, each with a torpedo under one wing and two 500-pound bombs under the other, headed north to do their best to upset the Japanese timetable. The lead plane was flown by Lieutenant Jack Coley, accompanied by Lieutenants George Poulos and Charles "Whiskey" Willis. The plan was to fly as a group to Tonelei Harbor, carry out their attacks, then fly back independently to Tulagi where they could refuel if needed before heading back to Espiritu Santo. The outgoing leg was uneventful, with the three planes flying at 50 feet for the last 100 miles to escape radar detection. Said Coley,

> We caught the Japs by surprise. We pulled up over the picket destroyer guarding the south entrance to the anchorage and then split to carry out independent attacks. I cruised over the harbor for several minutes looking for the carrier [a coast watcher had advised them one was there] and passed up several juicy targets in the hope of finding the big one. By this time the alarm had been given and time was running out. I picked out the biggest target ahead of me and lined up for the torpedo drop. The torpedo was released just as a searchlight caught us in its beam. I turned left, dropped the two 500-pound bombs against what appeared to be a large transport, and then was fully occupied with evasive action.

Coley's torpedo struck the transport, but he and his crew were too busy to watch for results from the 500-pound bombs. Poulos's torpedo and bombs were dropped on a cruiser, and his crew reported direct hits. Willis scored a hit on a cruiser with his torpedo, and his two bombs blew a destroyer in half.

Coley continued:

> We were caught in several searchlights at once, and every ship in the anchorage was firing at us. It looked like a tremendous Fourth of July fireworks display with us in the center. I turned that PBY every way but inside out evading the gunfire. Long chains of tracers would come sweeping up and it seemed that the gunner had taken the correct lead angle, but as I would turn and change altitude the tracers would miraculously curve and pass astern of us. With streams of tracers coming from all sides it was necessary to constantly change course and altitude.

Finally he was able to duck behind an island, out of harm's way. No one was injured in Coley's plane but the plane itself took several hits, one leaving a hole as big as two fists in the right wing. This wing had a self-sealing fuel tank but the hole was too large and most of the fuel was lost. "The left tank and the fuel buoy at Tulagi got us home," said Coley.[29]

Poulos and Willis also arrived safely at Tulagi, and the trip from there to Espiritu Santo was uneventful.[30]

On 20 September 1942 Rear Admiral Aubrey Fitch was placed in charge of naval air activity in the South Pacific, replacing Vice Admiral John McCain. Fitch, aware of the potential of the Catalina in night attacks, took up the development of Black Cat operations where McCain had left off. The Cats were needed, for the Japanese had made it clear they were clinging tenaciously to their idea of retaking Guadalcanal. Transports and cargo ships of the Tokyo Express continued to disgorge troops and supplies on the northern beaches of Guadalcanal in the darkness.[31]

Admiral Yamamoto was willing to commit large numbers of warships to cover the effort. Two major naval battles were fought, the Battle of Santa Cruz in October, the Battle of Guadalcanal in November.

On 26 October four enemy carriers, four battleships, and a large number of cruisers and destroyers engaged a U.S. Navy task force off the Santa Cruz Islands, and a carrier battle erupted in which the *Hornet*

VP-52 Black Cats in daylight: Usual departure time for operations was dusk, as daylight flights drew enemy fighters and night operations drew friendly anti-aircraft fire. (U.S. Navy)

was lost and the battleship *South Dakota* was seriously damaged. On the Japanese side the carriers *Shokaku* and *Zuiho* were knocked out of action.[32]

Black Cats played a part in the battle, first locating the fleet and then making sporadic and mostly unsuccessful attempts to torpedo and bomb the big ships. Lieutenant M. K. Atwell of VP-91 had one of the successes. From 1,400 feet he pushed the nose of his PBY down in a seventy-degree dive toward a cruiser. He leveled off at about 650 feet and released two bombs when the nose of the plane was pointing at the stern of the ship. Both bombs hit just aft of the stacks. The concussion lifted the PBY to 800 feet, crushed two radio tubes, knocked out the lights, blew away the radio antenna, and threw the plane out of control for a few seconds. Concerned over leaking fuel tanks, Atwell set a course for his tender, and about twenty minutes later his crew reported two large orange flashes where the cruiser had been.[33]

In the Battle of Guadalcanal on 12–15 November a Japanese task force managed to land two thousand troops on the island, but at the cost of ten transports, two battleships, and a number of other ships and aircraft at the hands of American surface ships, carrier planes, and aircraft from Henderson Field.[34]

The Japanese then began to resupply their garrison with submarines and destroyers, these dumping lashed-together drums of food and ammunition overboard without slowing, then racing back up The Slot. On the night of 30 November a U.S. Navy squadron accosted eight destroyers on one such supply mission. The Japanese once again proved their expertise in night engagements: in exchange for a single destroyer, they sank the cruiser USS *Northhampton* and seriously damaged three others in the Battle of Tassafaronga.[35] "Iron Bottom Sound," the nickname for Sealark Channel, took on more and more meaning.

Although every PBY squadron in the the South Pacific from the time of the invasion of Guadalcanal flew Black Cat missions, Admiral Fitch saw fit for reasons unknown to designate one patrol squadron as the original Black Cat unit. Chosen for the honor was VP-12, then based at Nandi in the Fiji Islands.[36] All planes were painted flat black, and all were equipped with radar and radio altimeters. Aircraft and unit markings were painted out. The squadron, headed by Commander Clarence Taff, was divided into two detachments, one operating out of Espiritu Santo, the other out of Henderson Field, with the detachments rotating on a monthly basis. Their charter was the same as for all Black Cat units: Derail the Tokyo Express with night searches and attacks.

The first planes arrived at Henderson Field on 15 December, where the crews found that living conditions left something to be desired.

Frequent rain, simply adding to the humidity and doing nothing to relieve the heat, turned the ground into a quagmire. Over the foul-smelling black mud, Marston matting was laid out and tents were erected. Although the matting was designed to support airplanes under wet and muddy conditions, it nevertheless sank out of sight under the constant tramping of human feet. Of even greater hazard than the Japanese were the omnipresent malaria-carrying mosquitoes. Squadron Executive Officer Ron Stultz estimated that 85 percent of his squadron contracted malaria. But they flew anyway, even though they had fever, chills, and diarrhea, because there was no one to take their place.

VP-12's tour began calmly enough. An air-sea rescue mission and a night harassment mission were flown on the sixteenth. On the night of Christmas day the unit flew its first torpedo mission. Ron Stultz rode as copilot with Lieutenant Norm Pedersen, as neither Pedersen nor the other plane commander, Lieutenant William Pack, had any experience in launching the missiles. The two PBYs took off at dusk, both carrying a torpedo under each wing, and headed for Tonelei Harbor on Bougainville, where the targets were plentiful. Their black camouflage worked well. The planes even lost each other in the darkness, but they found the island on their own.

After practicing torpedo runs on a small island, Pedersen and Stultz then flew over the outer harbor of Bougainville, where a new moon silhouetted a vessel in the water. Pedersen turned and set up a long, low run, releasing a torpedo at 1,000 yards. As he pulled up over the un-suspecting target, Stultz dropped a flare, and the PBY crew reported they had just attacked a giant I-class submarine. They saw no flash to indicate the torpedo had found its mark, but when they circled the area, nothing was visible but foaming water and some debris.

They flew over the inner harbor and picked another target, launching the torpedo by the book. Again Stultz dropped a flare as they passed over the ship—it was a destroyer. Suddenly, the air was filled with an-tiaircraft fire. The destroyer evaded the torpedo, then escaped at high speed, as did Pedersen and crew.

Pack's PBY arrived on the scene shortly after Pedersen. Pack selected a group of destroyers anchored off Fauro Island in Bougainville Strait as his targets. Pack's inexperienced copilot began a descending turn to set up the run but misjudged his altitude. Before Pack realized what was happening, the plane slammed into the crest of a wave, tearing a huge hole in the hull. With water pouring in, Pack opened the throttles and struggled to get the Cat, two torpedoes, and a load of seawater into the air. His efforts paid off, but now the destroyers were firing at him. With the opportunity for a surprise attack gone, he jettisoned the torpedoes and headed for home. About to land at Henderson Field, he found that the nose wheel had been jammed when the plane struck the water. He set the PBY down nose high on the main gear, then plowed to a stop on the keel.

On the night of 4 January Pedersen and Lieutenant Hadley Lewis received orders to scout ahead of three cruisers and two destroyers that were to bombard the airfield at Munda Point. The PBYs were to act as aerial spotters for the gunfire. Finding no Japanese warships in the area, they circled the airfield at 10,000 feet. At 0100 the cruisers and destroyers commenced firing. Fire-control spotters aboard the planes radioed directions down to the ships, and the field erupted with exploding projectiles in a reverse treatment of the pounding Henderson Field had taken a few weeks before. The procedure was repeated on 23–24 January when shelling from two cruisers and four destroyers shattered an airfield under construction on Kolombangara Island northwest of Munda.

Soon after they arrived on Guadalcanal, VP-12 pilots began flying a pattern known as "Mike Search," a pentagonal three-hour course that would locate any enemy ship attempting a journey down The Slot or through Indispensable Strait between Santa Isabel and Malaita Islands. Mike Search, considered one of the squadron's most important functions, was flown every night regardless of the weather. Pilots flew three circuits on a single night patrol.

On one such Mike Search on the night of 14 January, Commander Taff was leading Lieutenants Cyrenus Gillette and Hadley Lewis through bad weather, when radar picked up several ships heading south. Dropping down, they saw the wakes of a number of destroyers and began bomb runs on the ships. Whether any hits were made was unknown, but the destroyers made a 180-degree turn and headed north.[37]

At the end of January 1943 the Japanese came to the conclusion that recapture of Guadalcanal was hopeless and decided to withdraw. Nearly twenty destroyers sortied down The Slot on the night of 1–2 February, harassed by American dive bombers and torpedo planes from Henderson Field. One Japanese destroyer was damaged by the planes, another struck a mine and sank, but the remainder were able to evacuate a large number of troops from Guadalcanal. Two nights later they evacuated another large contingent, and on the night of 7–8 February the last troops were removed. The American flag now flew over all of Guadalcanal.[38]

But the work of the patrol squadrons was just beginning. Guadalcanal was only the first of many steps as the forces of Nimitz and MacArthur pushed relentlessly northward toward Japan. The Black Cats would be required at every step to cut supply lines and choke off Japanese bases.

As of 27 March, VP-12 had flown 236 missions, mostly at night, flying a total of 1,660 hours. It had carried out bombing raids, torpedo attacks, and gunfire-spotting missions, as well as search, convoy, antisubmarine, and rescue operations. The squadron received a Presidential Unit Citation which read in part, "Outstanding for its indomitable fighting spirit, Patrol Squadron Twelve established a standard for subsequent Catalina squadrons and achieved a gallant record of service which reflects the highest credit upon its pilots and crews in the United States Naval Service."[39]

With the fall of Guadalcanal came a lull in activity while the Americans and the Japanese regrouped. It was fortunate for the patrol squadrons, for the first of several rotations took place in mid-March, with VP-54 moving into the heat, rain, and mud with VP-12 on Guadalcanal. Most of VP-54's pilots and crewmen had no combat experience, the squadron having been in existence only since November. But VP-12's veterans, whom VP-54 would replace in June, were believers in on-the-job training. On the night of 15 March the squadron commander, Lieutenant Commander Carl Schoenweiss and Lieutenant (j.g.) Robert Engemann flew with VP-12 pilots to spot fire for a naval bombardment of Vila airfield, then dropped their own 500-pounders and headed for home. On such orientation flights, pilots and crewmen of VP-54 became proficient in night work: navigation by radar, flying under squalls and avoiding the high volcanic peaks of the islands, and evading enemy fighters. After a few flights, VP-12 left them to their own devices.

The first surface ship contacts were made on 31 March, with Schoenweiss and Lieutenant John Erhard tracking seven Japanese warships off Vella Lavella, which were apparently on a supply mission to Vila airfield. Army B-24s dropped bombs unsuccessfully on the ships, as did the PBY, but the near misses were enough to cause the Japanese commander to take his supplies back to Rabaul in some haste. On 5 April a convoy was located and bombed by Lieutenant (j.g.) James Anderson, but it nonetheless succeeded in unloading troops and supplies for Vila under heavy smoke screen.[40]

There was little doubt that the Japanese intended to hold their remaining positions in the central Solomons and that they would use air power to support their efforts. The enemy-held islands were dotted with airfields: five around the giant bastion at Rabaul; others at Vila on Kolombangara, Munda Point on New Georgia, and Buka Passage; plus a seaplane base at Rekata Bay on Santa Isabel Island. Yamamoto brought the strength up to four hundred aircraft at these bases, and on 7 April hit Guadalcanal with the largest air armada since Pearl Harbor, sinking a destroyer, a tanker, and a New Zealand corvette. Next he aimed his planes at Port Moresby and Milne Bay on Papua New Guinea, but they did relatively little damage; most of the American ships were forewarned and had escaped. It was Yamamoto's last attack: a week later he lay dead in the wreckage of his plane, shot down over Bougainville by an air force P-38.[41]

On 30 June the Allies took the first step in "climbing the ladder" northwestward through the islands, a term coined by Admiral William Halsey, who had been named to head the South Pacific operation on 18 October 1942. In a move officially called Operation Cartwheel, U.S. troops went ashore on New Georgia and Rendova, a small island only a few miles away. By 2 July Rendova was no longer Japanese, but fierce fighting in the dense jungles of New Georgia would continue for more than a month. By mid-August American planes were flying from the Munda airbase.[42]

Schoenweiss extended VP-54's Mike Searches farther north earlier in the month. Six Catalinas patrolled as far as Bougainville each night to intercept Japanese surface craft that headed south to haze the new U.S. positions on Rendova and to build up Japanese strength on New Georgia. A number of small task groups were located, reported, and attacked by the Cats during July. The biggest engagement, the Battle of Kolombangara, came on the twelfth, when Cats flown by Lieutenants William Carter and Harry Sharp called in a U.S. Navy task force to join in battle against a Japanese cruiser and five destroyers. The Cats, flying high above, directed the fire from the American ships. The cruiser *Jintsu* was smashed into scrap metal, then sunk by torpedoes from two destroyers. Carter and Sharp then encouraged the Japanese destroyers to continue their run for Rabaul by dropping their 500-pound bombs on them as they departed the combat arena.[43]

VP-54's Mike Searches continued to produce results. On 17 July Lieutenant Fred Gage bombed, strafed, and sank a "corvette-type" ship off Vella LaVella. On the nineteenth a Cat flown by Lieutenant Harold Johnson reported and then attacked a large force of enemy cruisers and destroyers east of Fauro Island. Johnson flew up the column of ships from behind, dropping his 500-pounders in a stick. The first hit the last ship in the column on the stern, the second missed, and the third hit the fantail of the second ship. The ships scattered and peppered Johnson's Cat with antiaircraft fire as he headed for Henderson Field.[44]

In August the Black Cats undertook an additional activity: that of locating Japanese radar installations. Six enlisted men, who had been trained in electronic countermeasures equipment and techniques in the fall of 1942, began flying first with VP-12 and later with VP-54. Several stations were located from June through August 1943; the information was turned over to the army air force, which put the stations out of action with daylight raids.[45]

By September the Japanese were supplanting their larger transports with barges to resupply and reinforce troops. With a shallow draft, the barges could stay close to island shorelines, and were not as easily spotted on radar as the larger ships were out in the channels. Also, if they were attacked, the loss of men and equipment would not be as great on the smaller craft. Nonetheless, the barges were found by sharp-eyed Black Cat pilots, who, rather than waste bombs on them, settled for strafing. On 23 September Lieutenant (j.g.) Jim Anderson found two barges slipping along the shore of Choiseul Island across The Slot from New Georgia and in twelve strafing runs drove them up on the beach where the survivors ran into the jungle. Later in the month Lieutenant Erhard repeated Anderson's experience with ten barges near Choiseul.

Lieutenant J. T. Casey learned the hard way that some of the barges were armed. On 6 October his Cat was hit several times by machine gun fire from two barges before he drove them ashore. Anderson found twenty-eight barges two weeks later, strafing them and doing considerable damage, then topped off the evening by sinking a freighter with bombs off the coast of Choiseul.[46]

On the night of 31 October–1 November 1943 the Black Cats spotted fire for a surface fleet that pounded the two enemy airfields at Buka Passage. Then they flew antisubmarine and search missions to cover the marine landings made the following morning at Cape Torokina on Bougainville. By mid-month Seabees were at work preparing Torokina airfield for American planes. The Cats extended their Mike Searches well past Buka Island to the northwest of Bougainville and into St. George's Channel between New Britain and New Ireland Islands, not an easy task, as the area was often covered by low clouds. It was not unusual for pilots to spend three-quarters of the flight on radar.

On 1 December 1943 VP-54 was relieved by VP-81. VP-54's pilots and crews, green when they arrived in January, retired as veterans, having flown 376 night missions and having logged 3,024 combat hours. In addition to bombing, strafing, and other missions, they rescued fifty-two downed airmen from the sea.

Patrol Squadron 81 began operations from Henderson Field but in early February moved up to Munda. From there they continued VP-54's work in searching out and destroying barge traffic and, in addition, flew night bombing missions against enemy shore installations and supply points. The Japanese were unending in their attempts to land supplies and additional troops on Bougainville and the islands remaining under their control in the Solomons, but by May 1944 the supply lines had been nearly severed by the Cats and navy PT boats. On 7 May VP-81 began flying from Piva Yoke, a newly built airstrip on Bougainville.[47]

On 15 June, VP-44, under Lieutenant Commander Gerald Bogart,

A VP-44 Catalina delivers supplies to a coast watcher on a South Pacific island. (Gerald Bogart via Richard Knott)

commenced operations from a new airfield on Green Island, which Allied forces had taken in mid-February. VP-44 would be based here until mid-April 1945, harassing the Japanese with attacks on barges, airfields, and other island installations, as well as picking up army, navy, and marine fliers downed in ongoing strikes against Rabaul. VP-44 detachments were stationed at Torokina and northward as the Allies advanced toward the Philippines and at one time had planes scattered from the Fijis to Luzon.

As the war moved north, bases to the rear were closed, and hard-to-get recreational equipment became available as surplus. No place was in more immediate need of such equipment, the VP-44 pilots and crews felt, than Green Island. To wait interminably for delivery through conventional channels was more than they could stand. So they resorted to their own methods and resources, and not too many days passed before a PBY approached for a landing with a piano slung from the bomb racks under one wing and a refrigerator under the other.[48]

If the PBYs had not been proven tough old birds before the Solomons campaign, they were recognized as such during and after. They were shot at and hit by the enemy; they were tossed about by their own bomb blasts; they were hammered and twisted in storms and on rough takeoffs and landings. They suffered from maintenance in salty seas and engine changes under coconut palms on sandy beaches. Their Pratt and Whitneys coughed and sputtered on gasoline contaminated with saltwater and grit.[49] But the engines ran, and the PBYs flew. Undergoing an amazing transformation from docile daytime patrol bombers to nocturnal fighting cats, they took the war to the enemy. They dived through the black of night to deliver lethal punches to enemy bases and shipping. Their pilots no longer talked of how great it would be to fly on a heavily armed B-17 or B-24; the patrol squadrons had developed an esprit de corps around a weapon they created and manned. Lieutenant George Poulos of VP-11 summed up their feelings for the PBY simply and succinctly: "A great, great airplane."

The Southwest Pacific

While U.S. forces under Admiral Nimitz fought for control of the Solomons and other islands of the Central Pacific, General MacArthur's American and Australian troops did the same in New Guinea. On 30 June 1943, the opening day of Operation Cartwheel, an infantry regiment fought high winds and waves to land at Nassau Bay, sixty miles south of Lae. The same day five thousand troops landed on Woodlark Island and Kiriwina Island off the northeastern New Guinea coast, and two weeks later army airfields were operating. On 15 August airborne troops took the airfield at Nazdab, twenty miles west of Lae. Within a few days Australian troops had overrun the city. By October, with the exception of small pockets of resistance, the entire Huon Peninsula was in Allied hands.[1]

VP-101, the surviving squadron from the Philippines, played a part in the action. The unit, which had been flying antisubmarine patrols out of Perth and other bases on Australia's west coast since the pull-back from the Philippines, moved up to Samarai on the southeastern tip of New Guinea in June 1943, where its PBY-5s were based on the tender *San Pablo*. Along with Royal Australian Air Force Catalinas out of Cairns on the mainland, VP-101 flew nightly searches in the Solomon and Bismarck Seas, and twice a week scouted the New Guinea coast as far northwest as Wewak.[2]

VP-11 moved from its bases in the Central Pacific to Perth in August, then to Palm Island, Australia, where a new major PBY repair facility had been built. It then joined VP-101 at Samarai, where the unit stayed until the end of May 1944. In August VP-52 arrived; in September, VP-34; in October, VP-33. All three squadrons had been part of Fleet Air Wing 3 in the Atlantic, flying antisubmarine patrols from Norfolk south through Bermuda, the Canal Zone, and as far as Natal, Brazil.[3]

The patrol squadrons became a part of Fleet Air Wing 17 when it was commissioned in Australia on 15 September 1943. The Wing's commanding officer was Commodore Thomas Combs. He reported to General George Kenney, who was in charge of all land-based aircraft and the tender-based PBYs as well. Perhaps because he was unaware of what the Black Cats could do to shipping in the dark, Kenney ordered them to fly scouting missions only. The Cats were to report any ships they located and then allow the bombers of the 5th Air Force to finish the job. They were not to attack unless there was little chance of retaliation.

The Cat pilots fumed but followed orders, dutifully calling for air force bombers when they found enemy ships, a situation that arose frequently between Rabaul and Buka. More often than not, however, the air force bombers were busy elsewhere, and the targets steamed away unmolested to deliver their troops and supplies. Only barges fit the orders, and these received the Cats' full attention.

On 6 October the tender *Half Moon* sailed into Samarai's Namoia Bay to relieve the *San Pablo*. The *Half Moon*'s commanding officer, Commander William Gallery, understood the frustration of the Cat pilots and crews and decided to go out on a limb. At the end of October he instituted some experimental tactics. In the wee hours of the twenty-fourth VP-11's Lieutenant (j.g.) Lavern Nelson found an opportunity to try out the new tactics. In Jacquinot Bay, New Britain, he sighted three Japanese destroyers and nosed down through a hail of antiaircraft fire to drop his 500-pounders on the lead ship. One hit near the after stack and exploded as Nelson banked away. Circling to check out the damage, he found the destroyer ablaze from stem to stern, dead in the water and sinking. The first Black Cat operation in that area of combat had been carried out against the enemy, and the PBY returned with all hands to the *Half Moon* to tell about it. Nelson was awarded the Distinguished Flying Cross for the action.

Thereafter Black Cat pilots attacked enemy shipping when the opportunity arose, although they were not specifically directed to do so. A standard bomb load of a 1,000-pound bomb under one wing and two 500-pound bombs under the other was adopted, each bomb fused for a five-second delay to allow the Cats time to escape the blast when the bombs were dropped from masthead height.

The effect of explosions on impact was made clear in mid-October, when Lieutenant (j.g.) T. L. Hine of VP-11 dropped depth charges from low altitude on a submarine near an enemy base at Gasmata, New Britain Island, and one detonated on hitting the water. Most of the plane's elevator was blown away, the stabilizer was bent upward, and the hull was damaged. Hine managed a forced landing at sea, but the plane sank shortly afterward. Paddling in rubber life rafts, Hine and crew evaded Japanese searchers for three days and nights. They had covered nearly

The CO and the PBY crew that brought Black Cat operations to the Southwest Pacific. Front row: Lieutenant L. M. Nelson, pilot; Commander W. O. Gallery, commanding officer, the Half Moon; Lieutenant (j.g.) J. E. Sullivan. Second row: Ensign E. B. Morris, Tom Gilliam, Jones, Bill Sinclair. Top row: Melvin Hohnbaum, Bill Summers, Vic Kilgore. (John Sullivan via Richard Knott)

ninety miles toward Kiriwina Island when an OA-10A, the air force version of the PBY, picked them up.[4]

On the night of 26 October two attacks were made on Japanese ships with no results, but on 14 November the unit's luck changed. Lieutenant W. E. Shinn came upon three Japanese ships enroute to Rabaul: a light cruiser, a larger freighter, and a smaller ship. Setting up a low-level run on the cargo vessel, Shinn pulled the release handles for his bombs. Three missed; the fourth, a 1,000-pounder, hung up on the rack. Shinn circled and made a run on the cruiser, and this time the bomb dropped when the release was pulled. It hit aft of the stacks and exploded below decks, damaging the ship, but Shinn was driven off by antiaircraft fire and night fighters before he could ascertain the extent of the damage.

That same night Lieutenant Jack Penfold also found a three-ship convoy and scored a hit on one ship. Two nights later Lieutenant (j.g.) Haas attacked a destroyer and a patrol craft. His bombs missed, but Lieutenant Jack Cruze had heard Haas's contact report and initiated an attack of his own, bombing and sinking the smaller vessel. On the twentieth Penfold intercepted six ships off New Ireland and scored three hits on a merchantman, leaving it burning with an intensity that could be seen for miles.

When Commander Gallery told Commodore Combs of the change in tactics and showed him the results, Combs gave his approval: The unit's mission would now be search and attack rather than search and report. The Black Cats had officially arrived in the Southwest Pacific.[5]

On 16 December Catalinas of VPB-11 (since patrol squadron activities had increased to include bombing, the designation of all squadrons was changed to "Patrol Bomber Squadron" on 1 October 1943) took part in an unusual mission. Three Cats, flown by squadron commander Lieutenant Commander C. M. Campbell, Lieutenant Wesley Van Benshoten, and Lieutenant T. H. Ragsdale flew over high mountains and across the dense New Guinea jungle to the Sepik River, where they began to evacuate Australian troops in danger of being overrun by an advancing Japanese force. Later they were joined in the evacuation by Lieutenant (j.g.) T. L. Hine, and Lieutenants G. S. Clute and G. B. Kennington. For five days the planes took off at 0500 and returned at 1400, bringing out 219 Australian troops, 25,000 pounds of equipment, and a number of friendly natives just before the Japanese closed in.[6]

Working feverishly, crewmen repair a damaged starter on a VPB-11 PBY on the Sepik River during the evacuation of Australian troops, December 1943, in time to avoid capture by advancing Japanese forces. (William Barker)

The South Pacific was a spawning ground for field modifications on aircraft and ordnance. By banding sections of steel reinforcing rod used in concrete construction around 500-pound bombs and adding a section of rod to the contact fuse, the bombs were turned into "daisy cutters" which exploded above ground and shredded anything waist high within a hundred yards. Army B-24s began wearing tail turrets on the nose; A-20s and B-25s sprouted .50 caliber machine guns through their noses and along their fuselages.

Lieutenant W. J. Lahodney of VPB-52 at Palm Island in Australia saw merit in the increased firepower of the attack bombers and took steps to turn his PBY into an attack bomber, too. In place of the bombsight and bombardier's window, four .50-caliber machine guns were mounted in pairs, one pair above the other. The window was replaced with a steel plate fitted with seven-inch blast tubes that covered the gun barrels. A firing trigger was attached to the pilot's yoke, along with a selector switch so that the guns could be fired one at a time or all at once. The .30-caliber gun in the bow turret was left in place. Amid speculation that the Cat's hull would never withstand the bucking of the heavy guns, Lahodney made a test firing run on a smoke light. The light was extinguished, and the geyser of water thrown up by the storm of .50 slugs was satisfyingly impressive. Of equal importance, the PBY's hull remained as tight as ever. In subsequent trials it was found that the bow gunner could add the firepower of his .30-caliber gun to the quad-mounted .50s by straddling them, protected from burns by a burlap pad laid over their tops.

A similar installation was made in three other Cats in the squadron. Thereafter eyebrows must have been raised at navy supply depots because of a sudden increase in orders of condoms for the patrol squadrons. Someone had found they were perfect for slipping over the blast tubes to keep sea water out of the gun barrels.

On 20 November VPB-52 was deployed to Namoia Bay to relieve VPB-11, and two nights later Lahodney got his chance to try out his lethal setup on an enemy target. Finding a barge in St. George's Channel, he dived and poured tracers into it, leaving it afire and sinking.

On the twenty-fifth Lieutenant H. A. Sommer, VP-52's squadron commander, located, bombed, and tracked a large formation of Japanese ships west of Rabaul, then called on Lahodney, who was patrolling nearby, for assistance. Lahodney picked out the largest ship in the formation, a cruiser, as a target. He dived on it and released his bombs by intervalometer, which was set for seventy-five feet spacing between bombs. He banked and, as he returned through increasing antiaircraft fire for a strafing run, an explosion erupted from below the cruiser's decks.

He continued the run and dropped fragmentation bombs, but the gunners below had gotten the range. The tail of the Cat was riddled and the tunnel hatch shot off; all aileron control and partial elevator control was lost; and the plane was losing altitude. Juggling the throttles, Lahodney kept the plane flying. He was heading for home when the area below the Cat suddenly lit up with gunfire: In the confusion he had wandered directly over Rabaul. Slipping away above a broken layer of cloud, Lahodney and crew struggled toward Namoia Bay. Heavy turbulence, which buffeted the plane fifty miles south of New Ireland, added to the anxiety of flying without ailerons and with frayed elevator cables. Two hours later Lahodney set the plane down hot to keep water out of the tunnel hatch and made a high-speed taxi to the ramp, where the plane sank in shallow water. Lahodney later received the Navy Cross for his night's work.[7]

VPB-52 continued to send enemy warships and merchantmen to the bottom through December, compiling a total 76,000 tons in 137 missions. The squadron rotated to Port Moresby the first of January, again replacing VPB-11, which had been flying air-sea rescue missions.[8]

On 1 February 1944, VP-52's Lieutenant Robert Dilworth and crew were sent to Finschafen, New Guinea, to operate from the *San Pablo*.

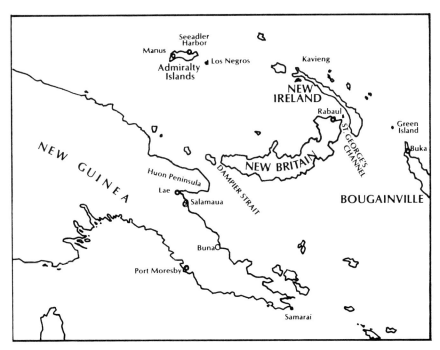

New Guinea and Bismarck Archipelago

Because enemy air attacks were common and Allied forces were not as well trained in aircraft recognition as they might have been, the PBY received friendly fire more than once. Even so, Dilworth and crew found life less exciting than it had been for the past two months. On the night of 11–12 February, he decided to add some interest by reconnoitering the enemy's big base at Wewak farther up the coast. Coming in from the north ahead of rain squalls, he saw lights, an airfield, and a merchantman anchored off shore. He climbed above the overcast, then dropped out again when he thought he was over the field. With some surprise, he found himself in the landing pattern with a flight of Japanese planes.

He had entered a safe distance behind the plane ahead of him but had cut the plane behind him out of the formation. The enemy pilot buzzed up alongside and flashing his lights angrily, apparently thinking the big flying boat was one of theirs. Dilworth continued the charade, flying along as though he belonged there, but rather than turning on final he bored straight ahead toward the merchantman. At the appropriate moment he yelled at his copilot to release all the bombs. The first brought down the Wewak lighthouse; the second and third were direct hits on the ship. Turning steeply, Dilworth and crew watched the merchantman capsize and start to sink, then strafed shore facilities and barges as they headed back to Finschafen. By the time the Japanese pilots in the pattern realized what had happened, the Cat had disappeared into the darkness. Dilworth was presented the Silver Star.[9]

VPB-34 arrived on New Guinea in mid-December 1943, just in time to taste the benefits of the new seaplane base at Samarai. Its members, never having been on Guadalcanal, were unable to fully appreciate the lack of mud and the presence of handball courts and baseball diamonds, a wharf and seaplane ramp.[10] The squadron's greatest dissatisfaction stemmed from the fact that they were a wartime outfit—only a year and a half old—and had no traditions other than the squadron anniversary beer party. So they originated one: On return from a mission, a pilot was permitted one low-level pass over his tender—the closest a PBY could come to a victory roll—to signify a successful mission.[11] Within a few weeks, buzzing the tender became common practice.

VPB-34 pilots received a short but thorough course in Black Cat techniques and then began a period of destruction that was equal to any of their predecessors or successors. On the night of 15 January 1944, for instance, VPB-34 flew one of its largest and most productive missions. Intelligence reported a large Japanese convoy entering the Bismarck Sea, undoubtedly carrying reinforcements for Rabaul. The bombers of the 5th Air Force were unable to mount a daylight attack, and the weather forecast made it clear that by dawn the convoy would be hidden by a weather front extending along the southwest coast of New Ireland. It was an opportunity that could not be allowed to pass. The squadron skipper, Lieutenant Commander Thomas Christopher, readied six PBYs, four of them loaded with two 500-pound bombs and two 1,000-pound bombs, and the remaining two carrying two 500-pound bombs and one Mark XIII torpedo. The pilots were briefed on the battle plan: On a signal from the CO, the two torpedo planes would make their runs quartering on either side of the convoy escorts, causing them to take evasive action, then the other four planes would attack.

Christopher's small air armada took off at 1800 hours in good weather with a quarter-moon and spotty cumulus clouds. At 0108 the convoy was sighted—four merchantmen and two cruisers—and the CO called in his planes, which had been flying a scouting line ten miles apart. A nerve-wracking two hours followed as the planes gathered in: The enemy had air cover, but for some reason the PBYs were never attacked.

At 0230 Lieutenant E. J. Fisher, pilot of one of the two torpedo-carrying planes, attacked the convoy without waiting for Christopher's signal. He made three runs on the lead ship—a cruiser—but the torpedo release malfunctioned each time. On the second run the escorts fanned out, apparently more concerned with dodging torpedoes than protecting the cargo ships, and began firing at the Cat. After the third run Fisher, discovering a serious oil leak in the starboard engine, aborted the mission.

Fisher's attack had produced the desired result, albeit premature, so Christopher gave the attack signal. He was the first to move in. At 0345 he began his run on a freighter-transport, flying through machine gun fire from it and nearby ships. With his own gunners returning fire, he released his bombs by intervalometer at about five hundred feet. There were no immediate results, but as the plane passed beyond the ship a violent concussion rocked the plane, throwing crew members into the bilges, and seconds later a plume of water two hundred feet high shot up from the center of the ship. Christopher put the plane "on the deck" to get beneath the antiaircraft fire, and escaped without a scratch.

The second torpedo plane was flown by Lieutenant Vadm Utgoff, who made a run on the second cruiser, but the torpedo failed to explode. He gained altitude and glide-bombed a freighter, releasing both of his 500-pounders at two hundred feet. His crew reported a blowout parallel to the waterline amidships and then a fiery glow on the port side.

Lieutenant (j.g.) S. B. Bradley picked out the largest blip on the radar scope and nosed his Cat over in a seventy-degree dive. As he broke through the clouds he found his Cat aiming at a freighter. He flattened the dive to about fifty degrees and came in at two hundred knots, leveling off at one hundred-fifty feet to drop a 500-pounder and a 1,000-pounder. Both bombs hit amidships, and within minutes the ship was ablaze from stem to stern, standing out like a beacon for other Cats in the area.

The final run of the night was made by Lieutenant (j.g.) L. M. Bates, who dived at forty-five degrees on another freighter, releasing his bombs at one hundred-fifty feet. The near-misses enveloped the ship in water, blotting it from view.

Christopher headed for Samarai at 0430, his planes having destroyed three of four merchant ships without suffering so much as a single bullet hole.[12]

How the ears must have rung from the buzzing of low-flying PBYs aboard the tender that morning, and on many mornings thereafter. Large ships, small ships, barges, and harbor installations received no mercy from the pilots and crews of VPB-34, who used torpedoes, bombs, and the popular quad-mounted fifties to dispatch the enemy. Proof of the effectiveness of night attacks by the patrol bomber squadrons became evident when the Japanese picketed a line of flak ships across the entrances to the Bismarck Sea at Dampier Strait and St. George's Channel and reinforced the antiaircraft batteries along the shorelines. Flying through a flak barrage became routine for PBYs each night. The Japanese also sent up night fighters, but they had no radar and were ineffective. No PBYs were lost to either defense.

One of the four points in VPB-34's mission statement was air-sea rescue, as was true of all patrol bomber squadrons in Fleet Air Wing 17. At first Cats were sent out only when a distress call was received. The procedure was superseded near the end of 1943 by one that called for three or four PBYs to take off when army strike planes did, follow them to the strike area, then orbit nearby on call. In this way the time downed army pilots and crews spent in the water could be cut, lessening their chances of being captured by the Japanese.[13] Flying such missions, code-named Dumbo, VPB-34 rescued seventy-seven army, navy, and RAAF flight personnel on its first tour, all in open sea landings, and all but one in enemy-contolled waters.

While no Dumbo mission was without its dangers from the enemy and the sea, the one flown by Lieutenant Nathan Gordon on 15 February involved considerably more risk and produced a greater, more unexpected result. Assigned to cover a B-25 raid on Kavieng Harbor, New Ireland, Gordon could see that the strike had been successful, judging from the amount of smoke in the air, and costly to the bombers, judging from the chatter on the radio. He knew he would be needed, and without waiting for a call he eased his PBY, the "Arkansas Traveler," in close to the island to look for survivors.

A formation of B-25s passed overhead. Two broke away, saying by

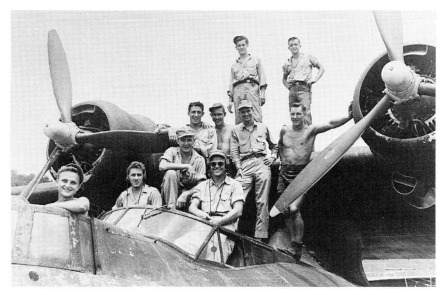

Medal of Honor recipient Lieutenant Nathan Gordon (in sunglasses) and the crew of "The Arkansas Traveler." (National Archives via William Scarborough)

radio they would lead Gordon to six men in the water on a raft near shore. Gordon set the "Traveler" down in swells running eighteen feet from trough to crest. It was a rough landing; the hull seams opened slightly and water trickled into the bilges as he taxied toward the raft. He cut the engines, and with 20-millimeter and 75-millimeter shells throwing up geysers on both sides of the plane, the B-25 crew was hauled in through the blisters. The engines were restarted and Gordon took off.

Then came another call; three men in the water. Gordon landed again, more easily this time, but again under fire, and took the men aboard. Now, counting his own men, he had nineteen aboard. He had not flown far toward home when another B-25 pilot reported six more men in a raft close to shore. Gordon was not one to allow six men to fall into the hands of the enemy, an overloaded and leaky airplane nothwithstanding, and he circled back. This time the Japanese gunners were almost zeroed in; they had been shooting at the raft. It seemed impossible for them to miss the "Traveler's" big wing and hull. But miraculously the PBY took no hits as Gordon approached through a hail of tracer, landed, shut down the engines a third time, and hauled the men aboard. His luck held for a moment longer: Just as the engines were restarted and the plane began to move, a burst of machine gun fire churned the wake into a froth. With twenty-five men and an unknown quantity of water aboard,

Gordon took off after a long, long run, and this time made it all the way back to base.

Admiral Halsey sent his personal congratulations to pilot and crew, but the U.S. Congress went a step further: Gordon was awarded the Medal of Honor, the only PBY pilot in World War II to be so honored.[14]

In mid-February VPB-34's six-week tour as a Black Cat squadron ended and the squadron was rotated to Port Moresby. VPB-33 flew into Samarai to fill the vacancy.

Patrol Bomber Squadron 33, formed in April 1942, was a month older than VPB-34 and, like its counterpart, had been based at Coco Solo in the Canal Zone before deploying to the Pacific.[15] Its pilots arrived eager to make up for lost time, but found few targets around Samarai. The squadron commander, Commander R. C. Bengston, sank two small merchantmen on the nights of 15 February and 9 March, and Lieutenant Commander Fernald "Flip" Anderson destroyed twenty-five barges off the New Guinea coast near Finschafen by strafing.[16]

Enemy shipping in the Bismarck Sea had almost ceased, thanks to the endless hounding of 5th Air Force planes by day and the Cats by night. Rabaul, without supplies, was no longer a consideration for invasion, and was simply bypassed as MacArthur's army troops and Nimitz's marines pushed the Japanese off island after island.[17]

The patrol squadrons of Fleet Air Wing 17 moved northward with the advance. Wing headquarters was moved seven times; from Brisbane, where the wing was organized, to Samarai; then to Lumbrum Point on Manus Island in the Admiralties; Woendi Island near Biak; Morotai Island off the northwestern tip of New Guinea; Leyte Gulf; Lingayen Gulf; and finally to Clark Field on Luzon.[18]

Through the remainder of their tours in the Pacific the PBYs of VPB-11, VPB-33, VPB-52, and VPB-71 rotated through the various bases and detachments, trading off Black Cat operations for air-sea rescue, evacuation, and special support missions.

Some of the squadron activities helped pave the way for invasion forces. On the night of 2 February Lieutenant James Merritt of VPB-34 flew seven Sixth Army rangers to Los Negros Island in the Admiralties, whose mission was to reconnoiter the area in preparation for the assault that would come two days later. Merritt's was the first U.S. plane to land in the Admiralties since the outbreak of war. The next afternoon Lieutenant Walter Pierce landed his PBY in broad daylight, picked up the rangers, and returned them to their base with their valuable intelligence.[19]

On the twenty-ninth the Allied landings took place, and a short time later VPB-34 and VPB-52 were flying missions from Seeadler Harbor, supported by the tenders *Tangier* and *San Pablo*. Los Negros was less than secure, however, for the Japanese sniped at the Cats as they landed and at work crews servicing the planes.

Now the Cats could range as far north as the big Japanese base at Truk in the Caroline Islands. Cats made four raids on the airfield at Woleai in the Carolines during March, with Lieutenant Commander Anderson flying the last, a dive bombing attack, on 31 March. On 5 April he carried out a series of similar attacks on Wakde Island off New Guinea prior to an invasion, setting a series of intense fires.[20]

Numerous air-sea rescues were carried out successfully by VP-34 during 1944, one of them requiring two PBYs. On the morning of 25 April Lieutenant Jules Busker was searching for the crew of a downed B-24 when the crew of his PBY spotted smoke and dye marker in the water about seven miles away. Flying over to investigate, Busker saw another PBY on final, lowering its floats for a landing near two rafts with three men in each. The landing was in rough seas, however, and it became obvious that the plane was sinking. Busker set his Cat down in eight-to-ten-foot swells, took the nine men from the PBY aboard as well as the six-man army crew, jettisoned his waist guns and all but 500 gallons of fuel, then banged across the wave tops, the last one throwing the plane into the air. It almost stalled under the twenty-four-man load but recovered and made the trip home.[21]

In May the Catalina squadrons of Fleet Air Wing 17 were far ahead of the advance westward along the coast of New Guinea. By mid-month Cats were carrying out rescue and attack missions from the tenders *Orca* and *Half Moon* at Hollandia, where Allied troops had landed in late March. Others directed bombardment of enemy positions by U.S. Navy task forces prior to the invasion of Wake Island on 17 May, and did likewise at Biak ten days later.[22]

On 9 July Commodore Combs was relieved as Commander Aircraft 7th Fleet by now-Rear Admiral Frank Wagner, who had commanded Patrol Wing 10 during the dark days of early 1942. About the same time Captain Carroll Jones, who had commanded VP-43 during the Kiska Blitz in the Aleutians in June 1942, took charge of Fleet Air Wing 17. Lieutenant Commander Vadm Utgoff assumed command of VPB-34 in May from Lieutenant Commander Tom Christopher. At that time the squadron was performing rescue missions. Its planes had saved the lives of seventy-seven men by 17 July, when the squadron rotated to search-and-attack duty. Missions were flown from the *Orca* at Woendi Island just off Biak, and ranged westward as far as Celebes Island.

A Cat flown by Lieutenant (j.g.) Richard Ball was lost early in the tour. During the night of 23 July he radioed that he had found a target at Halmahera Island and was beginning his attack. The plane never returned to the tender.

On the thirtieth Lieutenant (j.g.) Joe Ball hit a large transport with all four bombs and sank it. The next night Lieutenant Norman Paxton, the squadron executive officer, set fire to a transport, but in return received a flak burst in the starboard wing which cut the aileron cable and damaged wing panels, struts and the starboard propeller. Despite its wounds, the big Cat brought Paxton and crew safely back to Woendi. The squadron commander, Lieutenant Commander Utgoff, bombed a destroyer on 1 August, and left it circling to port, out of control.

VPB-11 moved into Woendi with VPB-34 on 6 August, and on the twenty-second both squadrons moved up to Middleburg Island near Sansapor to base on the *Orca* and *Half Moon*. The move put their PBYs within striking distance of the Philippines, as VPB-34 was quick to demonstrate. On the night of their arrival, Utgoff and Paxton flew their Cats to Davao Gulf on Mindanao and attacked shipping there but were unable to determine the results because of cloud cover. The Japanese were taken by surprise: Lights burned brightly on the island, and a number of their planes were detected in the air, but none attacked the Cats.

Japanese ships, active in the area around Manado Bay on Celebes Island, attracted the Cats of VPB-34 and VPB-11 like honey does flies. VPB-34 pilots and crews sent several thousand tons of shipping to the bottom by the end of August, with Lieutenant (j.g.) William Garrett closing out the tour on the twenty-ninth with a busy night's work. Flying in clear skies under a half moon, he located a small cluster of ships in Manado Bay and dropped a 500-pounder in the midst of it, then dropped another squarely amidships on a small one-stack cargo vessel, which exploded and sank at once. On the north side of the bay he dropped 100-pounders on a group of barges and two parafrags on a barracks at Cape Pisok, then poured .50-caliber machine gun fire into a two-masted schooner. Next Garrett flew around behind the town of Manado at the back of the bay and circled out over the harbor, releasing a 500-pound bomb from a steep glide on a ship anchored off shore. The bomb, with its delayed action fuse, hit the water and exploded under the ship's keel. The ship disintegrated in a cloud of debris. All ordnance expended, Garrett and crew returned to the *Orca*.

When VPB-34's tour was completed, the squadron returned to Manus in the Admiralties. The Japanese hardly knew they were gone, however, for VPB-11 took over where VPB-34 left off.

Lieutenant Lavern Nelson dove his PBY through intense antiaircraft fire to severely damage a destroyer in Lembeh Strait on the night of 29 August. The squadron commander, Lieutenant Commander Thomas

White, sank a small freighter in Bangka Strait the same night and another in Manado Harbor the following night.

On the night of 3 September in Davao Gulf gunner Howard Kenyon, aboard Lieutenant T. L. Hine's PBY, set fire to an enemy tanker with .50-caliber slugs. As the plane flew away, flames were towering hundreds of feet into the air.

On 4 September Lieutenant Jack Penfold sank three small ships and damaged two others in Sarangani Bay on Mindanao. Four days later Lieutenant (j.g.) James Dyer sent a 10,000-ton tanker to the bottom off Basilan Island, south of Zamboanga.

On 1 September VPB-33 commenced another search-and-attack tour, replacing VPB-34 on the *Orca* at Middleburg. During the first four nights its pilots and crews sank four ships and damaged others. On 5 September the squadron commander, Lieutenant Commander Anderson, took the war back to the Philippines, striking at the Japanese base at Zamboanga on Mindanao. Locating two enemy destroyer escorts anchored alongside each other, he dropped two bombs and both ships exploded, starting fires that could be seen for forty miles as Anderson and crew returned to the *Orca*.

Masthead-high runs were the rule for navy patrol planes on search and attack missions, but Lieutenant James Merritt, who had transferred from VPB-34 to VPB-33 as executive officer, carried the tactic to the extreme. On the night of 16 September he dropped two 500-pound bombs on a freighter in Kendari Harbor on the southeast end of Celebes Island. Unsure of the damage done, he made several strafing passes, then another bomb run, this one so close to the deck that his last 500-pounder could not miss. There was a jolt as the Catalina passed over the ship, and then a blast as the bomb struck home. The ship remained afloat, however, and Merritt made one last run while his crew dumped parafrags out the hatches. One landed in a hold and set the ship afire. With Merritt's gunners holding the would-be firefighters at bay, the ship soon became an inferno. Only then did he turn the Cat for home.

When he inspected his plane back at the tender, Merritt found the cause of the jolt on the next-to-last bomb run; a piece of the ship's king post was imbedded in the leading edge of the wing. Ten days later the squadron commander, Captain Jones, sent Merritt a tongue-in-cheek letter headed, "Ramming Tactics Plane Versus Surface Ship—Disapproval of." The letter detailed the history of ramming, going to great lengths to point out the futility of such an operation in light of differences in construction of air and surface craft at that time. He opined, however, that because of the rapid decimation of enemy shipping, the time might not be far off when Japanese surface ships were built of materials light enough to make such an attack profitable.[23]

General MacArthur sent troops ashore on Morotai, north of Halmahera, on 15 September. He had intended to use the island as a base for army bombers, but he quickly determined that the Japanese airfield there was unsuitable and a new field could not be completed in time for the invasion. PBYs were not bound by such restrictions, however. Four days after the invasion VPB-33 moved up from Middleburg Island and was operating from Morotai, using the *Orca* as a base.[24]

VPB-33 completed its tour with losses for both sides. On 23 September Lieutenant (j.g.) William Sumpter sank two Japanese destroyer escorts and a seaplane carrier from which they were refueling in a single pass, his first bomb hitting a destroyer escort, the next two the carrier, and the fourth the remaining destroyer escort.

That same night Lieutenant (j.g.) Robert Schuetz bombed a transport in Tolitoli Bay on the northwest coast of Celebes Island, but in the attack antiaircraft fire hit the starboard propeller, blew two cylinders off the engine, holed the wing, and killed Schuetz's navigator. Schuetz wrestled the battered Catalina up to 2,000 feet on the remaining engine and flew 550 miles back to the tender.[25]

The squadron closed out its tour on the night of 3–4 October with "Wild Bill" Sumpter and crew turning in a stellar performance. During September, they had sunk thirteen ships and damaged three others. They were hoping to add at least one more to their score on their last search-and-attack mission. Flying in clear weather under a bright moon, they found what they wanted in Tolitoli Bay; two cruisers, a destroyer, and a destroyer escort. Sumpter turned the Cat out to sea and flew for an hour, hoping the Japanese would think they had not been seen. Then he turned back, and upon reaching the island flew low along the shoreline, at the last moment popping up and over the mountains bordering the bay to pounce on the unsuspecting ships. His ploy had worked: he got within a quarter-mile of them before their gunners awoke. Despite the fiery storm of tracers that spewed out at him, Sumpter held his course down the centerline of a cruiser and let go all four bombs in a stick. All four hit the ship. The blast tossed the big plane around like a kite, but Sumpter squared it away, dropped down to the harbor surface, and headed for the entrance, his way lighted by the tracers from the remaining ships. He circled in the blackness outside the bay and watched the cruiser burn for a time, then, with nothing more to drop, he headed for Morotai.[26]

The scythe of Allied armed might was in full swing now, slicing island after island off Japan's Greater East Asia Co-Prosperity Sphere, and swinging ever closer to the Philippines. On 15 September, the same day that MacArthur's troops went ashore on Morotai, three hundred miles

A radar-equipped PBY-5 of VP-52 returns from a mission in daylight. Time, wind, and sea have changed the veteran aircraft into a "Black (and silver) Cat." (U.S. Navy)

south of the islands, Nimitz's marines hit the beaches of Peleliu, three hundred miles due east.[27]

The patrol squadrons were only paces behind the ground troops. The maintenance and repair facilities at Palm Island and Samarai, left far behind, were decommissioned. By September major overhauls were being carried out at Lumbrum Point, with minor repair work taken care of at Woendi. Cat pilots and crews welcomed minor repairs, for Woendi was a veritable tropical paradise. Although rain fell frequently, there was no mud. There were shade trees and an obliging onshore breeze. In addition to the seaplane base, there was a PT boat base, a hospital, a naval operations base, three officers clubs, movies, tennis courts, and baseball diamonds. Fleet Air Wing 17 moved its headquarters there on 7 September.[28]

At MacArthur's and Nimitz's headquarters and in Washington the final draft of the plan for the invasion of the Philippines was being written. Originally, the plan called for an assault on the southernmost island of Mindanao in mid-November, with a subsequent landing in Leyte to the north in mid-December. The Joint Chiefs of Staff, however, approved a change suggested by Admiral Halsey that bypassed Mindanao and struck directly at Leyte.

The Black Cats had an active role in preparing for the invasion. From Morotai they continued their nocturnal forays, mostly to harass and sink Japanese shipping. But on 12 October Lieutenant Walter Shinn of VPB-11 drew a different assignment. He flew Commander Charles Parsons and Colonel Frank Rouelle to a spot south of Tacloban, Leyte's capital, and put them ashore to meet with Filipino guerrilla leaders, so that their efforts could be coordinated with those of the American invasion forces.

In mid-month planes from VPB-33 and VPB-34 began arriving at Woendi, where they were serviced and made ready to support the Philippines campaign with search-and-attack, antisubmarine, rescue, and special missions. Their crews were briefed on survival techniques in case they were forced down on one of the islands.

On 20 October General MacArthur made good his promise: He returned to the Philippines, wading ashore on Leyte with President Osmena. Three days later two detachments of five planes, one each from VPB-33 and VPB-34, arrived in the area to begin operations from the tenders *San Carlos* and *Half Moon.* The planes were moored to buoys in a sheltered area in Hinunangan Bay on the western side of Cabugan Chico Island.[29]

Early the following morning the veteran Cat crews were suddenly reminded what it was like to have the enemy as a close neighbor. The *Half Moon* and its planes were attacked by two Val dive bombers. Hellcats in the area put a quick end to it, shooting down one Val and chasing the other away. That afternoon a pair of twin-engine Sally bombers plummeted from the sky, one diving on the ship, the other on the Cats riding at anchor. Their bombs did no damage, but one navy crewman was wounded by strafing. The *Half Moon*'s gunners sent one Sally away smoking.

When word of a possible Japanese naval counterattack against the Allied invasion forces was received, PBYs were dispatched to patrol the Mindanao Sea. Lieutenant Commander James Merritt, in charge of the VPB-33 detachment, sighted a number of ships shortly after takeoff, but they were so close that he dismissed the possibility that they were Japanese. In all likelihood they were, however, because a short time later a portion of the Japanese fleet attempted to break out of Surigao Strait at the upper end of the Mindanao Sea into Leyte Gulf. The *Half Moon*'s crew and squadron personnel had a ringside seat for the battle that followed; shortly after the search planes departed the ship that morning her captain had taken her north and anchored off Cabugan Grande Island.

Merritt completed a fruitless patrol and returned to find the battle raging. His plane was shot at by both sides before he could find a quiet place to land. Lieutenant (j.g.) Maurice Moskaluk of VPB-33 received the same sort of treatment. His PBY was so badly shot up by American antiaircraft fire that it sank almost at once upon landing. Luckily none of his crew was injured.

The Japanese fleet had fared far worse than the PBYs. Two battleships, one cruiser, and three destroyers were sent to the bottom by the pounding of American PT boats, destroyers, cruisers, and battleships. A single Japanese destroyer escaped.

The enemy tried twice more to destroy the American beachhead at Leyte Gulf, but both times its ships were unsuccessful. After the third engagement Lieutenant Commander Vadm Utgoff, in charge of the VPB-34 detachment, flew north along the coast of Samar to search out the retreating Japanese fleet. Along the route his crew spotted and reported a lone man in a life raft. The patrol proved negative: the fleet had sailed beyond range during the night. On the way home Utgoff sighted the same life raft with its lone occupant and attempted a landing, but the swells were high, the bow hit hard, and a large hole was opened. The plane bounced, a wing tip float dug in, and the Cat did a water loop before it stopped. It sank quickly, but not before the crew put a raft over the side and piled in. A Grumman TBF torpedo bomber came on the scene and flew cover while they paddled for a nearby island, driving off a Japanese plane in the process. Natives paddled out to escort the Americans ashore. That afternoon another VPB-34 Cat picked up the crew and the lone survivor Utgoff had hoped to rescue.

There was still considerable Japanese air activity in the Philippines at that time. Allied ships were subjected to frequent air attacks. PBYs were sometimes mistaken for enemy aircraft by Allied gunners even in daylight. At night they were sure to draw fire. For self-preservation, the Black Cats made it a rule to take off before dusk and not return before dawn.

Lieutenant Lawrence Heron was forced to violate the rule, and his PBY paid for it. Heron was head of a top-secret "Ferret" group that used PBYs equipped with special electronic equipment to locate enemy radar stations. Taking off for a night of specialized searching, an engine on Heron's plane caught fire. He radioed the tender that he was returning for an emergency landing and came down in the darkness on the far side of the Gulf to avoid being fired on by the navy. But Heron had not considered the army, and his plane took several hits before it eventually made the tender.

On 29 October a typhoon hit Leyte. A number of surface ships were lost, but good luck and good thinking saved the PBYs. Only two were driven ashore and damaged. Two others, from VPB-33, were on patrol when the storm hit, and waited on Palau until it passed. The remainder were saved by their crews, who started the engines and used them to maintain the planes' positions until the storm abated.

One of the largest air-sea rescue operations ever carried out by PBYs took place on Ormoc Bay on the west side of Leyte during daylight on 4 December. The bay was then Japanese territory, and the destroyer *Cooper* had been torpedoed and sunk there. Half of its crew had survived and were bobbing in the water, hoping to be picked up by PBYs before the Japanese reached them. Five planes of VPB-34 and an army air force

0A-10A were sent to bring in the survivors, with the army also providing fighter cover. When Lieutenant (j.g.) Joe Ball loaded up and began his takeoff run, he had sixty-three men aboard, counting his crew. The run was three miles long. Melvin Essary brought home forty-five men that day, and Dar Day another twenty-five. The two other PBYs had nine and sixteen aboard respectively. None of the PBY pilots knew how many were brought in by the 0A-10A.

On 10 December Lieutenant Commander Utgoff flew north to Luzon, deep in Japanese territory, to pick up some downed fliers and escaped prisoners of war who were being hidden by Filipino villagers. An escort of eight marine Corsairs went along for protection. Utgoff landed and took the Americans aboard without encountering the enemy, but he was told that a Japanese motor launch was on the way. There was no danger to the PBY, since it had plenty of time to take off before the launch arrived, but Utgoff was concerned over reprisals against the villagers for helping the Americans. He radioed the Corsair leader and told him of the situation, whereupon the Corsairs located the launch, peeled off, and ended the threat to the Filipinos.

On 14–15 December the Black Cats flew advance scouting patrols for an Allied invasion force sailing for Mindoro, just south of Luzon. The landing was made on the fifteenth and almost immediately army engineers went to work on an airfield to support the upcoming landing on Luzon. Troops went ashore there on 9 January 1945, and the next day the Black Cats of VPB-71, which had been flying search-and-attack missions from Moratai since late November, were sent there to base on the tenders *Currituck* and *Barataria* in Lingayen Gulf.[30]

In February VPB-71, based on the tenders *Tangier* and *Mangalden,* roamed the South China Sea northward to Formosa, the Pescadores, and the coast of the Chinese mainland. The squadron's pilots reported sinking eight ships and damaging nine others that month.[31]

The Cats had such an impact on what was left of the Japanese merchant fleet that it began moving again in the daytime and hiding in harbors and hugging shorelines at night. The Cats could no longer find ships in the sealanes after dark. Rather the ships huddled together in protected anchorages for defense, and the Cat crews found it inadvisable to mount more than one attack against their massed firepower. The saying among pilots was: "You get one free pass."

Cooperation with submarines was also instituted to a greater degree than ever before. Each day search planes were given positions of subs and details for making contact. If a worthwhile target was found by a search plane, word was transmitted to a nearby sub, which was then coached into position by the plane. The technique worked with disastrous consequences on the last large Japanese convoys.[32]

The Philippine campaign marked the end of concentrated activity by the Black Cat squadrons in the Pacific. VPB-11 flew to the U.S. mainland in November, and VPB-34 followed a month later. VPB-33 left the Pacific in February 1945. Lieutenant Lawrence Heron's Ferret Group remained in the area until May; only VPB-71 stayed until war's end. All of the other PBY units had been ordered home or had been reassigned, some as early as March 1943.

The Black Cats had done their job well. Fleet Air Wing 17's administrative history claims a tenth of all of the Japanese shipping blasted into oblivion during the forty-four months of fighting in the Pacific. The Japanese corroborated the claim, saying that their 7,000,000-ton merchant fleet had been sent to the bottom and that the wing was responsible for 717,025 tons of that total. The record shows 1,914 ships sunk by the wing's planes.[33]

Oddly enough, it was not newer, more modern flying boats that replaced the aging PBYs. Most of the patrol duties of the Cats were gradually taken over by land-based aircraft—the longer-range, faster PB4Y-1 Liberators, the Lockheed PV-1 Venturas, and the PB4Y-2 Privateers—their operation made possible by the Seabee's polished techniques for quickly building airstrips on newly captured islands.

The Atlantic

When the Wehrmacht invaded Poland in September 1939 and her treaty partners declared war on Germany, Great Britain's need for war matériel exceeded her immediate resources, so she turned to the United States for help. Agreement to obtain the necessary goods was a relatively easy task. Delivery across three thousand miles of the North Atlantic, however, was another story. The ocean itself was inimical. Overcast and dreary much of the time, it was frequently lashed with storms that whipped up fifty-foot waves. Its surface was oftentimes dotted with icebergs and ice floes. Air temperatures turned spray to ice, which coated ships with extra tons; water temperatures took a man's life within minutes. Germany's U-boat fleet was even more vicious. Equipped with modern submarines crewed by men well schooled in the lessons of World War I, the fleet was driven by a single-minded determination to send all Allied aid to the bottom.

The British, too, remembered their lessons from World War I. Only eight days after Poland was attacked they revived their system of delivering goods with large convoys of merchantmen protected by fast, heavily armed escort ships.[1]

The United States had proclaimed its neutrality on 5 September. As soon as U.S. Navy air and sea units could be redeployed, Neutrality Patrols began operating in and over the approaches to U.S. mainland and West Indian harbors.

A year later the "bases for destroyers" agreement between the United States and Great Britain led to the first major expansion of the Neutrality Patrols. On 15 May 1941 the seaplane tender *Albemarle* dropped anchor at Argentia, on the island of Newfoundland, to prepare for the arrival of the PBYs of VP-52, which were to fly the first U.S. Navy patrols over the western end of the North Atlantic convoy routes.[2]

The *Albemarle* quickly laid thirteen heavy plane moorings and began transmitting weather reports, and on 18 May VP-52's planes took off from Quonset. Bad weather forced them back, however. Another attempt on the twentieth was successful, but only because the planes made an instrument landing approach to Argentia. It was a portent of how most patrols would be flown. Pilots and crews quickly learned that the *Albemarle* would be their home, for there was nowhere else to go. The island offered little more than a rugged landscape and generally bad weather. Even in the anchorage, protection was poor under certain wind conditions. Atmospheric conditions created difficulties for radio communications.

During the spring and summer the prevailing winds would be southwesterly, bringing warmer temperatures but also fog much of the time. From October on through winter, pilots and crews found icing conditions, not only in flight but also on the water. Long strings of icy sludge formed across the harbor, which was kept from freezing solid only by the constant passage of ships which broke up the ice. The wind would carry the chunks away. In such conditions, the PBY pilots were happy to see ships in the harbor. In warmer weather, ships offered no such compensation. Taking off and landing in a harbor filled with anchored and moving ships made arrivals and departures exciting, to say the least. The waters were often made so choppy from the criss-crossing wakes of fast-moving boats that PBY hulls were damaged at their moorings. A speed limit had to be imposed to prevent further damage.[3]

VP-52 PBY-5s ride at their moorings on a relatively clear day in Argentia, Newfoundland. In the background is their tender, the *Albemarle*. (U.S. Navy)

On 24 May VP-52's routine patrols were interrupted by an electrifying assignment: Search five hundred miles to the southwest of Cape Farewell, Greenland, for the German battleship *Bismarck*. The terror of the seas had slipped out of harbor in the Baltic a week before, sunk the British battle cruiser *Hood*, eluded a large portion of the remainder of the Royal Navy, and now was at large somewhere in the North Atlantic. Foul weather created dangerous flying conditions and poor visibility, but eleven PBYs took off late in the afternoon. Almost immediately they disappeared into the low ceiling. They tried to climb above the overcast and, with their crews using chest-pack oxygen supplies, several reached as high as 18,000 to 20,000 feet before they broke into the clear.

There was no hope of finding the *Bismarck*. The search was eventually canceled and the planes ordered back to the *Albemarle*. Finding the tender in darkness and cloud proved to be as difficult as finding the German battleship, however. None of the PBYs made it home by direct route. Some came close, landing in the waters off Newfoundland within taxi distance. After twenty-one hours in the air Naval Aviation Pilot First Class William Scarborough set 52-P-9 down in an open area between Argentia and St. Johns. Other pilots ranged farther afield. One landed on the shore of Anticosti Island off Quebec Province. The squadron commander, Lieutenant Commander C. C. McDonald, ended up in Newport, Rhode Island.

The only plane damaged was 52-P-11, which landed in rough seas off the Labrador coast. In trying to reset the anchor during the night the pilot, Naval Aviation Pilot First Class Robert Weber, was swept off the bow and disappeared in the dark, icy waters. The crew beached the plane in desperation, and the rocky shore holed the hull in several places. The incident ended happily when people from a nearby village brought the missing pilot back to the plane uninjured, and a repair crew patched the holes in the PBY's hull. Eventually all of the planes returned to the *Albemarle*.[4]

On 1 July 1941 the air group of the Atlantic Support Force became Patrol Wing 7, under command of Captain H. M. Mullinnix, and Argentia became the Wing's principal base for North Atlantic operations. Headquarters remained there until August 1943 when it was transferred to the United Kingdom. That same day the patrol squadrons were redesignated VP-71, VP-72, VP-73, and VP-74. All were PBY-5 equipped, with the exception of VP-74 which flew Martin PBM-1 Mariners.

By 18 July one PBY in each squadron had been fitted with British-style radar, making Patrol Wing 7 the first U.S. Navy unit to be so equipped.[5] Squadron radiomen were sent to Canada for training in operation and maintenance of the equipment. By September more of the Wing's planes were similarly fitted.[6]

A camouflaged USS *Albemarle* under way in the North Atlantic with a PBY-5 aboard for servicing. (U.S. Navy)

In addition to their regular patrols, the PBYs flew reconnaissance and aerial survey missions to Labrador, Greenland, and Iceland and conducted air-sea rescue operations during the latter part of 1941.

A thousand miles to the northeast of Argentia lay the southern tip of Greenland. Despite periods of sunshine that turned the ice fields and icebergs a glistening white against the dark blue of the sea and despite night skies that were streaked with the red, green, and yellow shafts of the aurora borealis, it was an inhospitable place for flying boats. Temperatures were below freezing five months of the year. Skim ice formed each night on the bays, and farther out drift ice and icebergs lay in wait. Gale force winds of fifty knots or more screamed across the bays and up the fjords once a month, and on the island's west coast "Foehn" winds of eighty to one hundred knots were common. Adding to the difficulties for seaplanes was the narrowness of the fjords. The proximity of the rock cliffs alone made takeoffs and landings hazardous, but the close dimensions created a venturi effect that increased wind velocities even more.

The United States needed weather stations and ice patrol bases on Greenland, inhospitable or not, as well as airfields for transatlantic ferry flights. Also the Danish cryolite mine at Ivigut, the only accessible mine of its kind in the world and vital to the Allied production of aluminum, needed protection. Finally, the U.S. presence in Greenland lessened the danger of German occupation.

In July 1941 the tender *Lapwing* anchored at Narsarssuak to make a home for a detachment of three PBYs led from Argentia by Commander R. S. Clark. Theirs was a survey project, but the weather did not cooperate in the project's completion. On 7 August two planes were sent out to survey Greenland's east coast, but neither was able to return that day because of low surface fog and intermittent rain. They spent the night in separate fjords, making their way back to the *Lapwing* the next day. Weather precluded any more flights until the twelfth. Two planes ventured out and, despite the weather closing in, finished their missions and completed the project.

On 18 August, Wing headquarters ordered the *Lapwing* and the PBYs back to Argentia, but by 1800 wind velocities had reached forty-five knots and the *Lapwing* began to drag anchor. It stopped short of the rocks in the fjord only when a second anchor was dropped. The security crews—each consisting of a pilot, mechanic, and radioman—had returned to their planes after a meal on the tender just as the storm blew in. It was to be their last meal for twenty-four hours: During that period, with winds registering seventy-seven knots on the airspeed indicators, the crews "flew" them on the surface. Even the constant use of rudders and ailerons could not prevent the planes from yawing violently and occasionally dipping their wing tips into the water. But the crews' efforts paid off. When the storm abated the PBYs had suffered only minimal damage.

A decision was reached to build a seaplane ramp at Kungnat Bay so that the PBYs could be pulled up on land at night and during storms. However, when the ramp was completed, the navy found it had gained little: Tides produced by the violent storms rose so high that the parking area was under several feet of water.

Patrol Wing 7 headquarters had intended for the PBY detachment to fly convoy patrols from bases in Greenland throughout the winter, but it became increasingly obvious that the weather would make it impractical. Ice was becoming an ever-greater problem. On 2 October a PBY flew from Kungnat Bay to Narsarssuak to carry two soldiers from an army base to a hospital in Newfoundland. The plane was anchored in the fjord overnight, and the next morning neighboring ships had to break the half-inch-thick ice that had formed before it could be refueled. Later the pilot found a clear spot and took off with no damage to the plane. But the PBY was lucky; the ice-breaking boats were badly cut along the waterline. On 18 October, after an inch of ice was broken from the surface of Kungnat Bay, the detachment returned to Argentia.

In April 1942 the PBY-5As of VP-93 were sent to Greenland, but they operated mostly as land planes from an army base's runways. Occasionally they became seaplanes again, taxiing to a nearby lake for takeoff. Their missions were limited to convoy cover, antisubmarine sweeps, and ice observation flights.

On 6 July a PBY made what was claimed to be the first successful landing on the Greenland ice cap. An army B-17 had been forced down, and a PBY-5A of VP-93 was assigned the rescue mission. The pilot found the downed bomber, and near it a lake formed by melting ice in a dimple on the ice cap. From the color of the water the lake appeared deep enough for landing, and a little over a mile long. The pilot's estimate was correct. He made the landing, brought aboard the B-17 crew, and flew the plane back to base.

Greenland weather not only made flying hazardous but maintenance too. When operating from a tender, the crews performed minor maintenance and sixty-hour checks on the water at the mooring buoys despite rain, snow, and the omnipresent winds. Mechanics were in constant danger of sliding off PBYs whose upper surfaces were coated with snow, ice, and frost. The men of VP-93 discovered that maintenance which took one day in a warm climate required two or three in Greenland.

Three times during the squadron's tour the winds developed to gale force. Each time the crews rode out the blast with their planes moored to 2,000-pound anchors, emerging after a day unharmed and with big appetites, and with their PBYs showing little damage.[7]

A thousand miles east of Greenland's southern tip lay Iceland. The island, less than a thousand miles from the upper coast of Scotland, was the last link in the northern air route between the United States and Great Britain and was an indispensable fueling stop for the warships and merchant ships of both nations. Had Iceland been occupied by Nazi Germany, the northern convoy and air routes would have been closed, the fjords would have become anchorages for the U-boat fleet, and the airbases would have served the deadly long-range Focke-Wulf Fw.200 Condor bombers.

In May 1941 PBYs of VP-72 made a survey of Iceland from which the conclusion was drawn that only airports, as bases for land planes, presented any possibility for large-scale air operations from Iceland. Rocks projected from the bottom of bays and fjords, making flying boat landings at night dangerous and even daylight operations unsafe. In the event of a forced landing at sea by either a land or seaplane it was felt a land plane with flotation gear would have an equal or better chance for survival.

But long-range land planes were in short supply, and although the United States was technically at peace, "Mr. Roosevelt's war" remained to be fought. On 6 August 1941 six PBYs of VP-73 and five PBMs of VP-74 landed at Skerfjordhur, south of the peninsula on which Reykjavik is located. Borrowing moorings from the British, who also had a squadron of Catalinas and Sunderlands tender-based there, the squadrons began operations from the tender *Goldsborough*. Convoys were escorted east as far as five hundred miles—almost to the British Isles—and regular patrols were flown over the Denmark Straits as far west as Greenland.

The squadrons had arrived in Iceland at an ideal time. In August, the Gulf Stream warmed the south coast of the island and made the weather pleasantly cool. Summer ended a month later, however, and the squadrons' troubles began. Pilots and crews called the weather the world's worst—a point open to debate between PBY pilots and crews in Greenland and those in the Aleutians. A five hundred-foot ceiling marked a good day. Much of the time patrols were flown on instruments. Winds were often thirty to fifty knots. Patrols were flown even when the weather was sinking ships at sea. While one PBY was out on a 600-mile sweep, three ships sent SOS signals and sank in a storm.[8]

With the onset of winter the hours of daylight dwindled. This, coupled with low ceilings and poor visibility in the best of times, made the PBY crews' job more difficult. A common complaint lay in not being able to

Ship's masts and submerged rocks made takeoffs and landings hazardous for PBY squadrons based at North Atlantic stations. (National Archives)

find the convoy they were to escort and, if found, in staying with the ships, for radio transmissions as well as lights were blacked out.

As predicted in the May 1941 report, after-dark landings were hazardous for PBYs. In October, after the bottoms were ripped out of two of its Catalinas, the RAF pulled its squadron out, saying the anchorage was too unpredictable and the winds too high for seaplane operations. Thereafter, night landings were ruled out for the U.S. Navy squadrons, but predawn takeoffs were made possible by using seadrome lights strung by the tender.

Patrol Squadron 73 continued to operate despite the weather during the winter of 1941–42. The Gulf Stream held the average wintertime temperatures to thirty degrees during the day, but they seemed much lower because high winds and high humidity drove the chill factor down. When temperatures dropped into the low twenties, the Pratt and Whitneys were hard to start, and sometimes the planes were too heavily iced to fly. One morning two PBYs were late leaving on patrol because of a half-inch of ice inside the cockpit windshields and a quarter-inch on the hulls aft of the blisters.

Maintenance duty was no less nightmarish in Iceland than it had been in Greenland. All routine checks, repair work, and overhauls were done around the clock in the open no matter what the weather, as much of it as possible at the buoys because only one small seaplane ramp was available for beaching. In the worst conditions tools froze to mechanics' gloves, and the men became so cold that they worked in shifts, relieving each other every ten minutes. The situation prevailed until Seabees built a nose hangar late in the war. Servicing a plane with fuel at its moorings

VP-73's morning patrols from Iceland during the winter of 1941–42 were sometimes delayed while ice and snow were cleared from the planes. (National Archives via David Lucabaugh)

was wet and dangerous, and loading one with bombs, never an easy task, was impossible in rough weather.[9]

Electric generators on the PBYs failed frequently because, it was thought, of an overload resulting from the increasing demand of electrical equipment beyond the original design. The solution was to remove all superfluous gadgetry. This cost the PBY crews dearly on long patrols: Among the gadgets removed were the hot plates used to make coffee and to cook flight rations.

Sleeping accommodations and shore-based facilities were practically nonexistent. At the outset as many men as possible were berthed aboard the tenders, with the balance sleeping in the planes, in tents ashore, and in a few huts loaned by the RAF.[10] In order to keep warm ashore, the "Quiet May" came into being. This was a five-gallon oil can fitted with a drip valve and filled with used engine oil, then hung over a coke stove. A little experimentation with the valve allowed the temperature to be regulated so that the men were warm from the knees up, while beer stored under the bunks remained tastefully cold.[11]

The recurrence of gales increased from one per month in October to three per month by January. On 9 December 1941 the winds rose to seventy knots, and seas began breaking over the PBYs at their moorings. The nose of 73-P-1, moored in the most exposed position, began to sink rapidly, then its mooring cleats pulled out and the plane began to drift, partly submerged. The winds blew her into 73-P-8, damaging P-8's bow, port wing, and port wing tip float before an RAF crash boat got a line on P-1's hull fitting and towed the plane to shore, where it grounded in twelve feet of water just off the ramp. Three planes were still serviceable when the wind died.

This was but a prelude to the "big wind" of 15 January 1942. At 1400 that afternoon the wind reached its peak. Gusts of more than one hundred knots were registered at the seaplane base, with 133 knots recorded by an RAF weather station at Kaldadarnes. All eleven planes at Skerfjordhur were sunk at their buoys from shipping water over their bows and from constant rains. One plane was flipped on its back. Several ships in the harbor were sunk and a U.S. Navy heavy cruiser escaped going on the rocks only by using anchors and running its engines at full speed.

Undoubtedly out of concern for their safety, the security crews had been taken ashore and the moored PBYs left untended. Had the crews been aboard to bail and maintain position, said Captain Gallery, commanding officer of the naval air station at Reykjavik, the planes might well have been saved. Lieutenant (j.g.) D. W. Hundley had flown his PBY to a nearby fjord. It was moored there with himself and three crewmen aboard when the winds struck. Hundley started the engines and for nine hours kept the plane headed into the gale, using a single-cylinder bilge pump to bail continuously. Although a wing tip went under on two different occasions, he managed to bring the plane through with no damage.

VP-73 was lucky in one respect: All of its newly received PBY-5A amphibians, tied down at an airfield on shore, were saved. At one time the winds lifted the eleven-ton craft to the limit of their tethers, so that they were flying, unmanned, engines stopped, with their wheels a foot off the runway.[12]

Storms were not the only cause of aircraft losses. Operational accidents took their toll as well. A PBY sank in March 1942 when it attempted a landing beside the USS *Decatur*, where it was to pick up a sailor with appendicitis and fly him to Reykjavik for surgery. The plane bounced on landing and took on a large amount of water. The pilot applied full throttle to regain control, and as he did so a wing tip dug into a wave top. The PBY water-looped and went down in eighteen minutes. The crew was rescued by the USS *Babbitt*.

Convoy escort also had its hazards. In June a VP-73 Catalina was flying cover for a convoy and was fired on by an unseen ship below the clouds. The plane took hits in the instruments, wing, hull, and tail. For the next seventy minutes the pilot flew it in a fifteen-degree bank to compensate for a loss of rudder control, then landed about a mile off the beach at Stokkseyri. The crew, some of them wounded, were sent ashore in rafts, but the pilot and copilot decided to taxi the sinking plane to the beach. They grounded just as water began to break over the windshields.[13]

During the spring and summer of 1942 the pilots and crews of VP-73 sighted submarines almost daily and mounted thirty attacks on U-boats during one two-month period. Captain Gallery was irked because out of all the attacks there had been no confirmed sinkings. Determining the cause to be a lack of sleep resulting from too much time in the officers club, he ordered the institution closed until such time that a sinking could be confirmed. About that time the Navy Department issued new, more rigid rules governing reports of sinkings, saying that positive and irrefutable evidence would be needed to substantiate such claims. Captain Gallery summarized the rules succinctly for the PBY crews: "You gotta bring back the skipper's pants."

On 20 August the long dry spell was broken by Lieutenant Robert Hobgood, who was on escort patrol. "We were flying about 500 feet above the water in a forty-knot gale," his report read, "saw a ship on the surface, dived down, realized it was a sub and dropped our bombs, getting a nice straddle, hitting the sub." Hobgood circled back and made a strafing run, taking return fire as well. Inspection later revealed twenty-four holes in the plane. "We could see the sub beginning to blow compressed air and oil, and realized it was badly damaged," Hobgood continued. "Then the weather got worse and we lost contact, but we radioed the convoy escorts what was happening."

Two hours later they sighted the U-boat again, this time with its bow run up on the deck of an Icelandic fishing boat to keep it afloat. Two messages were sent following the incident. One, to VP-73 headquarters, said, "Sank sub, open club." The other called in the British destroyer HMS *Castleton* to take the fifty-two-member U-boat crew prisoner. Hobgood further requested that as soon as the U-boat skipper was given dry clothes, his pants be forwarded to Captain Gallery. Probably wondering if this was a variation of the American tradition of scalp collecting, the *Castleton*'s commanding officer complied. The salt-encrusted trousers served as a valance over the mirror in VP-73's officers club bar for the remainder of the squadron's tour.

Later it was learned from the imprisoned U-boat crew that Hobgood had received unexpected and unintentional help in making his kill. One of his depth charges had crashed squarely onto the deck of the sub and lay there, cradled by broken planking. While the deck officer's attention was elsewhere, possibly diverted by Hobgood's strafing attack, a seaman ran to the depth charge and, no doubt expecting a medal for heroism, rolled it over the side. When it reached its preset depth it exploded, almost directly under the sub.

In addition to hard-to-get trousers bearing a "Made in Germany" label, Hobgood received the Navy Cross for his action, and the members of his crew were given commendations.[14]

In their zeal to carry out their missions, the PBY crews sometimes erred. A low-lying reef off the Icelandic coast was bombed more than once. The whale population suffered. On one occasion, Lieutenant Bert Benton depth-charged what he took to be a submarine periscope and was astounded at the results. He had attacked a floating mine, one of several in a field. When his depth charge exploded, the waters erupted for some distance around as the mine and its counterparts detonated from the recurring shock waves.

In mid-summer 1942 Lieutenant William Cole flew a special mission to investigate a report of a German weather station transmitting from Little Germania island off the east coast of Greenland. Because of the length of the mission, Cole's plane carried the maximum weight in fuel and therefore no bombs, so when he had located the station, there was little he could do but map and photograph it. Then he radioed a Coast Guard cutter to take the staff prisoner and destroy the station.[15]

On 1 August 1942 a new phase of the Battle of the Atlantic began, one which would last until May 1943. During that period the U-boats exercised their wolf pack tactics, whereby one submarine would locate a convoy and call others into the area so that an attack could be made en masse. From the East Coast of the United States to the Bay of Biscay between France and Spain the wolf packs cost the Allies 3,857,705 tons of shipping. But the cost to Germany was 123 U-boats during the period, and the cost would rise steadily. Increased numbers of Allied sub-hunting planes and ships with improved equipment and techniques gradually turned the German submarine service into a suicide organization. Of the thirty-thousand men who went to sea in U-boats, two-thirds never returned home.[16]

PBY-equipped squadrons and detachments in addition to VP-73 did their part to decimate the wolf packs. VP-84 was based in Argentia from June 1942 until October, moving eastward to Iceland where it stayed until September 1943. The squadron completed its tour with the highest score of the PBY squadrons: five confirmed U-boat kills. Detachments of VP-31 and VP-52 pulled tours in Argentia during the winter of 1942–43. VP-63 worked its way across the North Atlantic after the wolf pack activity had peaked, first pulling duty in Argentia and Iceland in the fall of 1942, then moving on to Pembroke Dock in South Wales.

As the U-boats were gradually herded back toward their own shores, the need for PBYs along the convoy routes moved with them. Headquarters of Fleet Air Wing 7 moved from Argentia to Plymouth, England, in late August 1943, and then to Dunkeswell, England, where it remained for the duration.

By September 1943 all of the PBY squadrons were gone from the North Atlantic. They were replaced for the most part by Consolidated PB4Y Liberator bombers, which stayed with the convoys just as long but were faster and carried more ordnance. The western end of the convoy route was covered by Lockheed PV-1s flying out of Argentia.[17]

Even though U.S. Navy PBYs in Iceland sank few U-boats, they did the next best thing: They stopped them from sinking Allied ships. If left unhindered by the patrol bombers, the submarines would run on the surface during the day, pacing the convoy, then attack under cover of darkness. But when PBYs shepherded the convoys, the U-boats' pattern of attack was broken. The PBYs forced them to spend their daylight hours submerged, where their forward speed was almost a crawl, and their nights on the surface racing to catch up with the convoy again. By dawn they would be in place, but there were the PBYs, and the situation would be repeated.

While the pilots and crews of Fleet Air Wing 7 concerned themselves with ice, frostbite, gale-force winds, U-boats, and the protection of North

Atlantic convoys, five thousand miles south by southwest the pilots and crews of Patrol Wing 3 concerned themselves with heat, sunburn, hurricanes, U-boats, and the protection of the Panama Canal.

Patrol Wing 3 had been headquartered at Coco Solo Naval Air Station since it was formed in 1937, and for the next two years its planes took part in routine pilot and crew training, a few air-sea rescues, searches for lost boats, and fleet exercises. The planes carried mail and played war games, attacking an "enemy carrier," the tender USS *Langley*. On 13 July 1938 the crew of a crashed army bomber was picked up off the beach at Bahia Honda, Panama, by a PBY of VP-2. Five days later the same squadron flew the seriously ill American vice consul from Buenaventura, Colombia, to a hospital in Balboa, Canal Zone.

On 5 September 1939, following President Roosevelt's creation of the Neutrality Patrol, the Wing's mission to defend the Panama Canal took on new emphasis. The seaplane tender *Sandpiper* was anchored in the entrance to Cristobal Harbor as a guard ship. PBYs began flying daily two-plane patrols along the coast of Panama to Caledonia Bay to observe ship movements. Reports of sightings were sent by radio in plain English. This not only informed headquarters, but belligerent and friendly ships as well, so that appropriate action could be taken. Missions were flown to investigate specific ships and activity at various harbors and islands.

By July 1941 twenty-one PBYs and two tenders were carrying out Neutrality Patrols in the Caribbean and the Gulf of Mexico. The following month VP-31 received its first PBY-5s, which replaced its PBY-3s.

When Pearl Harbor was attacked, Patrol Wing 3 faced a unique problem. Most U.S. Navy units had one enemy to deal with; it had two. The Canal could be attacked from either side, or from both sides at once in a coordinated effort. An attempt to destroy the locks was expected, and all forces in the Canal Zone were placed on full alert. There were several scares, warnings, and drills, but the enemy never materialized.

At that time Patrol Wing 3 had twelve PBY-3s and fifteen PBY-5s in VP-31, VP-32, and detachments of VP-52 and VP-81. The planes of VP-31 were stationed at San Juan, Puerto Rico; the remainder were at Coco Solo. Twelve planes flew daily patrols in the Pacific between Salinas, Ecuador, the Galapagos Islands, and the Gulf of Fonseca, Nicaragua, keeping an eye out for Japanese submarines and surface craft.

German U-boats began to slip into the Caribbean in February and March 1942, and PBY patrols increased their vigilance there. VP-32 celebrated the Fourth of July by bombing a U-boat. It claimed a possible sinking but was unable to get positive confirmation.

On 3 August 1942 VP-32 was placed under the 6th Bomber Command of the army air force, releasing a squadron of heavy bombers from patrol duty over the Pacific. VP-31 was rotated to Norfolk at this time. VP-33 and VP-34 were brought in as replacements. VP-33 carried a heavy operational load, with detachments at Coco Solo, Portland Bight, Jamaica, and Cartagena, Colombia. VP-34 flew patrols out of Guantanamo Bay, Cuba, for three months and then was transferred to the South Pacific. VP-33 remained on station for almost a year before following in VP-34's flight path.

Beginning in early 1943 and continuing for the duration, Fleet Air Wing 3 would fight a "holding war" in the Canal Zone. The daily patrols continued, interspersed with occasional air-sea rescues and transport flights. The phase-out of PBY-equipped squadrons began in April 1943 with the arrival of VP-206, which was equipped with Martin PBM-1s. By war's end all flying boat activity would be carried out by PBMs, with short tours by the PBYs of VP-84 and VP-73.[18]

Early in the war several PBY squadrons saw service in Bermuda. VP-51 was there at the outbreak, then relinquished its duties to a detachment of VP-52, which stayed from April 1942 until May 1943. VP-63 sent a

Life for PBY crews assigned to the Bahamas was not always idyllic; they fought their share of hurricanes and high seas. (U.S. Navy)

detachment to the island in the spring of 1943. The planes were based in Port Royal Bay, Granaway Deep, and Darrell's Island. Weather was usually good, but hurricanes could move in during the summer months, and gale-force winds could arise during the winter. High seas made open sea landings risky at any time of year. A PBM went down on 7 June 1942, and a PBY of VP-81 out of Norfolk landed to pick up the nine-man crew. One wing tip float was torn off on landing, the other on takeoff, and the plane sank. Both crews were rescued by the USS *Nemesis* and taken to Key West. A week later the commander, Atlantic Fleet, issued a directive that open-sea landings were to be avoided unless no surface vessel was near enough to prevent loss of life and if the chance of completing the rescue outweighed the chance of partial or complete loss of plane and crew. With rescue work given a high priority in the Bermuda area, the pilots' decision usually favored an attempted landing. As a result many successful rescues were conducted.[19]

The closest U.S. forces came to island warfare in their immediate sphere of influence occurred in the Caribbean and involved a PBY squadron of Fleet Air Wing 9, VP-92. The squadron made the nine-hour flight from Norfolk, where its members had just completed training, to San Juan in mid-March 1942. The arrival of the PBY-5As created a stir, as they were the first to be seen on the island. Because of a breakdown in communications the planes failed to receive instructions to use the small landing strip and instead landed on the bay. The beach crew, used to installing and removing beaching gear from VP-31's flying boats, watched in happy amazement as the amphibians lowered their wheels while taxiing and thundered up the ramp under their own power.

The squadron was broken into detachments, with one group flying patrols from San Juan, another from Guantanamo Bay, and the third from Antigua, British West Indies.

Farther down the island chain at the upper end of the Windward Islands lay Martinique, at that time in the hands of the Vichy French, who became allies of the Germans following the fall of France. On 15 May a VP-92 PBY on patrol near the island reported he had been fired on. This was an open act of war. Immediately, all of the squadron's PBYs were ordered out to bomb and destroy the airfields on the island and the ships in harbor. They had been in the air ten minutes when they were recalled. The reason given for the recall was that the attack order had been based on faulty information: The flashes of light the pilot had seen were flashes of low-static lightning.

Perhaps they were, perhaps not; it became a moot point, anyway. That same day Martinique surrendered to the Allies. It is possible that some islanders continued to collaborate with the Germans and that French surface craft in the Guantanamo Bay passed along information on ship movements to the U-boats, for of all the areas in the Caribbean, shipping losses from submarines were the greatest there.

The PBYs of VP-92 flew armed and ready in case a U-boat was sighted, and on 22 May that readiness paid off. Lieutenant Bettens and crew reported the unit's first probable U-boat kill, this in the Windward Passage between Cuba and Haiti. Three days later Ensign Layton located and depth-charged another in the same area.

Several other probable sinkings were credited to VP-92 planes, but one cooperative venture on the night of 27 August seemed more probable than others. At 2200 hours Lieutenant Gordon Fiss spotted a submarine fully surfaced on the moon path about three miles astern of the convoy he was escorting. Fiss aimed the PBY up the moon path and dropped his depth charges. They landed on either side of the U-boat's hull and exploded. Towering columns of water obscured the U-boat's conning tower. A crewman watching from the PBY's tunnel hatch said the sub's stern was blown out of the sea. "Sub, sub, sub," was flashed by Aldis lamp to a corvette circling nearby, and a flare was dropped to mark the U-boat's position. The corvette closed in and started firing at about two hundred yards, holding a collision course until it finally rammed the sub. The PBY crew could see the flashes of gunfire as the battle continued. The two vessels finally separated, still firing. Then a destroyer moved in and opened up with its 5-inch guns. The U-boat disappeared in the darkness. All that was ever found were two small lifeboats and an oil slick.[20]

The air-sea war in the South Atlantic was hotter, in two senses of the word, than the war in the Caribbean: First, the South Atlantic was closer to the equator; second, the Axis powers had a special interest in South America, having entrenched themselves there long before the conflict began in Europe.

In the early 1930s tacticians on both sides recognized that South America would be important if a European war spread to Africa. The northeast coast of Brazil was of particular importance: The city of Natal lay only about 1,700 miles from Freetown in Sierra Leone on Africa's west coast, the closest point between the two continents.

As early as 1935 the Germans began to court influence in Brazil under the guise of commercial favors, blocked deutsche marks, and government-subsidized corporations and airlines. The United States had a head start, however. A U.S. Navy presence had been established in Brazil in 1914, and the two countries enjoyed good relations in the intervening years. In the late 1920s and early 1930s American commercial aviation interests, particularly Pan American Airways, had pioneered the development of seaplane bases at Belem, Natal, Recife, and Rio de Janeiro, and on south to Buenos Aires.

With the outbreak of war in 1939, the bases took on a quasi-governmental quality. A company called ADP (Airport Development Project) used U.S. government funds to build airfields near the seaplane bases, partly to offset the competition of the German Condor airline and the Italian Lati and Taca airlines then operating in Brazil and throughout South America, and partly to provide western terminals for a potential military aircraft ferry route to Africa. These airfields could also serve as bases for antisubmarine and anti-blockade-runner operations. Finally, the airfields would provide a deterrent to an Axis military push across the South Atlantic should Germany and Italy drive deeply enough into Africa.

The Brazilian government cooperated with the United States in the establishment of the Neutrality Patrol, and in December 1941 Catalinas of VP-52 landed at Natal, where they remained until May 1942. The planes operated from the Pan Am seaplane ramp. The crews lived in town, in tents, and in makeshift quarters near the ramp. Their mission was threefold: to fly patrols; to promote good relations with Brazil; and to prevent seizure of the facilities by enemy groups.

Although Brazil did not declare war on the Axis until August 1942, six PBYs of VP-83 were allowed to operate out of Natal beginning 7 April. The detachment came from Norfolk, where they had flown antisubmarine patrols from January through March. In January, they had made two confirmed U-boat kills. The pilots and crews were surprised to hear the nightly news broadcast from Berlin announce to the world that the six Catalinas had arrived in Natal "in charge of a group of drunken aviators." It was later learned that word of their arrival had been relayed to the Fatherland by Condor Air Lines weather station personnel, who had quarters on a hill behind the Pan Am ramp.

A VP-83 Catalina attacked a U-boat in the South Atlantic off the island of Fernando Noronha on 2 May 1942, less than a month after the squadron had arrived. Individual ship sinkings increased at an alarming rate around Trinidad, so the convoy system was instituted along with air cover, and the U-boats operating there moved on to less dangerous hunting ground.

From their arrival in April 1942 until 15 May 1943 the pilots and crews of VP-83 carried out successful antisubmarine warfare operations in the South Atlantic, despite inadequate communications facilities and outdated ordnance. Depth bombs used at that time were the round-nose type that were subject to erratic underwater travel, and machine guns were largely .30-caliber. In addition, rough weather in the northern portions of VP-83's territory was a problem, not only for the squadron itself but also for the army, which lost an inordinate number of pilots and planes on ferry flights.

Critical shortages of spare parts and fuel persisted until the last year of the war. New tubes were difficult to obtain for radar, as were tubes and parts for radios. Spare parts of all types were obtained by scrounging from every source in the South Atlantic. The army often came to the navy's rescue, lending R-1830 engines, communications equipment, and other supplies, and even providing living space when needed.

Relief was almost in sight on 4 July 1943 when a U-boat sank the supply ship *Pelotasloide* off the Amazon delta. The ship went down with great loss of life and with new engines, radios, and assorted replacement parts.

Aviation fuel was so short that on at least one occasion patrols were halted. On 21 April 1943 Lieutenant Weeks, with a VP-83 detachment at Aratu, sent a note to the squadron commanding officer, saying: "We are out of gas completely here and don't know when we'll get any. We have a couple of PBYs, one with about 600 gallons, the other with 450, and one PBM with 600."

In January 1943 the headaches of maintenance were supposedly transferred from each operating unit to a headquarters squadron. The move was universal in every theater, and so were the complaints about the system. The centralization eliminated the parts shortage problems for the individual units and freed the flight crews from the burdensome chore of performing their own maintenance. But in some cases the parts shortages were simply consolidated, and in others the quality of the maintenance was questionable. Maintenance was only as good as the men performing it, and if the headquarters squadron was staffed with "goof-offs" from the operating units, then the worst men were given the task of carrying out the most important work. Even in situations where the reverse was true, there was always the underlying feeling that a man who did not fly in the airplane would not be as cautious in making sure it was in top condition as the man who did.

Supply and maintenance problems notwithstanding, the war between airplanes and U-boats continued in the South Atlantic. Fleet Air Wing 16 moved its headquarters from Norfolk to Recife in mid-April 1943, from where it could exercise closer control over the activities of its patrol squadrons. Its flying boat squadrons were VP-83, which stayed only another month; VP-74, a PBM squadron which arrived in November 1942 and transferred out in October 1943; VP-94, which operated in the area from 19 January 1943 until mid-December 1944; and VP-45, which arrived at the end of April 1944 and stayed until the end of the European war. Nine squadrons of land planes, mostly Venturas and Liberators, were also under the Wing's command, as well as two more

PBM squadrons later on. At various times the tenders *Humbolt, Barnegat, Sandpiper, Matagorda, Lapwing, Rehoboth,* and *Rockaway* served as bases up and down the Brazilian coast.

The patrol area for Fleet Air Wing 16 ranged down the Brazilian coast and out to sea from Amapa on the north, near the French Guiana border, to Bahia (Salvador) to the south. The Brazilian Air Force provided cover from Bahia south to Rio de Janeiro and beyond.

All squadrons had their work cut out for them. Ship sinkings off the Brazilian coast rose steadily in the latter months of 1942 and continued into 1943. In May a number of U-boat sightings were reported. On 23 June a submarine was spotted by an army plane near Rio de Janeiro, the farthest south one had been reported. Four Catalinas from VP-94 were sent to Santos Dumont airfield from where they were to locate and sink it. On the twenty-fifth Lieutenant Buckwalter lost an engine just after takeoff on a night patrol. Rather than return to base in the darkness and chance slamming into Sugar Loaf or one of the lesser granite monoliths jutting out of the harbor, he circled all night on one engine. A Brazilian Air Force plane was the only one to find the sub, however. A bomb was dropped on it while it ran on the surface, but apparently little damage was done, for it managed to torpedo three ships before it disappeared from the area.

In July 1943 an estimated thirteen submarines were stalking ships off the Brazilian coast, and no fewer than five at any one time. On the ninth VP-94 sunk its first sub and lost its first pilot in combat in two separate incidents.

In the first incident, Lieutenant Stan Auslander was on patrol two hundred miles off Amapa when he sighted a U-boat as it was submerging fifteen miles away. He searched for an hour, and just as he was about to call it off his bow gunner saw the sub below. From 3,700 feet Auslander nosed the PBY over into a screaming dive, leveling off only about ten feet above the waves and dropping his bombs as the plane crossed over the sub at about two hundred knots. Most of the crew of the U-590 probably never knew what hit them, but the PBY crew did: The bomb explosions threw all hands violently into the bilges, and the toppling starboard waist gunner, who had been attempting to get a shot at the sub, hung onto his gun and perforated the PBY's wing with a burst. When the plumes of water from the bombs subsided, only bits of deck planking and other flotsam were left, along with five men floundering in the water. The navigator, Lieutenant (j.g.) Frank McMackin said: "We couldn't hear what they were saying, but we could see their open mouths. We dropped Mae Wests, and they grabbed onto them."

That same day Lieutenant (j.g.) Hare and crew took off in a ready plane to check out a U-boat contact report. From 4,500 feet he located the sub and dived on it, but the PBY had been seen, and the Germans opened up with antiaircraft fire. A 20-millimeter shell exploded in the port wing, tearing a hole in it about four inches from the bombs. A second 20-millimeter round shattered the instrument panel, setting fire to the cockpit and wounding Hare in the head and throat only seconds after he released the bombs, which straddled the U-boat. The radioman extinguished the fire, but Hare was beyond help and died on the return to base.

The attacks by the PBYs were enough to make the U-boats wary from that time on, but they continued to prowl the area singly and in small groups until late December 1944. An all-Wing reported dated 23 October 1943 said: "We have about three submarines operating in our area, but their activities are most obscure. It is evident they are operating with extreme caution. Ships are not being attacked, and we are not attacking subs."

A report from February 1944 said: "For the first time in several months we have a submarine to work on, now plotted 400 miles east of Recife and moving south." Five were reported in April, with the report saying: "Two are being worked on, and one is about to enter the frying pan."

In May 1944 no attacks on or by submarines took place, but there were sightings that confirmed new enemy equipment. One item was a small autogiro that was towed behind the U-boat, and could lift a man as high as 400 feet in the air, permitting a 360-degree visual search at much greater range. Another was a "schnorkel" exhaust and intake pipe that, when run up to periscope height, allowed the U-boat to run submerged on its diesels with little danger of being detected visually or by radar. Later the U-boats were equipped with radar detectors and jamming devices.

The all-Wing report for June 1944 said that twenty-four submarines had patrolled the area or passed through on their way to the Indian Ocean in the past six months. "Of these," the report read, "two were sunk, one was damaged."

The Allied landing in Normandy on 6 June 1944 marked the beginning of the end for the U-boats in the South Atlantic. Their bases on the Bay of Biscay were overrun and they were driven north, where they operated out of the fjords of Norway. The all-Wing report dated 6 December 1944 told the story: "From an operations standpoint the month of November gave us the longest uninterrupted breathing spell from submarines we have had since the fall of 1942. No subs are now estimated in the area."

On 15 December the navy instituted a series of regional supply centers to eliminate once and for all the aviation supply problem. That same date the problem was reduced by the number of PBYs in VP-94: the squadron was relieved of duty and rotated to Quonset Point Naval Air Station. Only the PBYs of VP-45 were left to drone on over a monotonous ocean devoid of any activity other than air-sea rescue missions until June 1945. Fleet Air Wing 16 was decommissioned that same month, and all personnel and equipment were transferred to Fleet Air Wing 5.[21]

Morocco

In the dark of midnight on 7–8 November 1942 the ships of an Allied Expeditionary Force assembled off the coast of Morocco and Algeria in northwest Africa. Operation Torch, a coordinated effort of the United States and Great Britain, began about an hour later in Algeria when invasion forces went ashore at Oran and Algiers on the Mediterranean coast. At 0530 an all-United States team landed at Casablanca on the Atlantic.

One part of the fleet, which numbered 500 warships and 350 transports in total, had sailed from England and another from the U.S. mainland, all somehow evading the wide-ranging German U-boats. At 0630, in an attempt to lock the stable door, the German U-boat command in Paris sent messages to fifteen of its submarines to rendezvous off the coast of Morocco and intercept the invaders. They were of course many hours too late; the ships were well beyond their rallying point.[1] The move did, however, mark the beginning of a period of intense submarine activity and an entirely new phase of antisubmarine operations for the PBYs.

Patrol Squadron 73, badly in need of defrosting after a year in Iceland and experienced in antisubmarine warfare, was transferred to Port Lyautey, eighty miles north of Casablanca, where its PBY-5As were based on the tender USS *Biscayne* until shore facilities were ready. VP-92 arrived at the same time at Casablanca. The two squadrons flew their first patrols on 14 November, less than a week after the invasion forces went ashore.

The previous year British surface ships and aircraft had done a remarkable job of intimidating the U-boat fleet, destroying 60 percent of the submarines in the area. For six months afterward no damage was done by or to U-boats. But the contingent sent in to follow up Operation Torch made up for lost time. During the height of the invasion, these U-boats sank nine ships and two escort vessels and damaged five others.

Of these, four freighters and a destroyer were sunk the night of 11 November alone. The British responded by sinking two U-boats in seven attacks.

The PBYs of VP-73 joined in the fray on 17 and 22 November, attacking a U-boat each day west of Casablanca. No sinkings were reported, but the attacks, plus those of the British, were enough to cause the U-boat commanders to pull back into the Atlantic for a time, out of aircraft range.[2]

When VP-73 moved its PBY-5As ashore at Port Lyautey they found no modern facility. Cattle ranged over open land, and it became common practice for the PBYs to taxi the length of the runway to drive off errant cattle before predawn takeoffs. There was no such opportunity to clear the runway for a night landing, however, and Lieutenant Robert Hobgood, returning from a long patrol in the darkness, struck a cow with a landing gear. The gear was damaged and a crackup was inevitable, so he opened the throttles, retracted the gear, circled, and put the plane down on the nearby Oued Sebon river. Next day the plane was pulled out, repaired, and returned to service.[3]

Shortly after their arrival the patrol squadrons adopted a search technique called the "canned patrol," a series of standard sweeps flown over areas where U-boat activity was heaviest. By the end of December six attacks had been made on submarines, but these caused only light or no damage. Reports cited the slowness of the PBYs, not inefficiency of the crews, for the lack of results. In response, two squadrons of army B-24s whose crews were trained in antisubmarine warfare were assigned to Port Lyautey and placed under the command of Fleet Air Wing 15, which had set up headquarters in Casablanca.

The B-24s took over VP-73's long-range patrols, and a detachment of the squadron's PBYs moved south to Agadir.[4] VP-92, in the meanwhile, moved from Casablanca to Port Lyautey. From there the squadron patrolled stretches from the Canary Islands north to points near Gibraltar and west near the Azores, and provided part of the air coverage for President Roosevelt in February 1943 when he sailed to the Yalta Conference aboard the USS *Quincy*.[5]

From Agadir, two hundred miles south of Casablanca, VP-73 could easily cover the Spanish-controlled Canary Islands, which were thought to be haunts of the U-boats. But while the crews found Agadir's weather to be as favorable for flying as Iceland's had been unfavorable, they found few U-boats. The long boring patrols over hundreds of miles of sparkling water caused pilots to hallucinate. One reported a good humor man pedalling his bicycle across the waves. Another sent recognition signals to a cloud, mistaking it for a cruiser. A third depth-charged a whale, thinking it was a U-boat.[6]

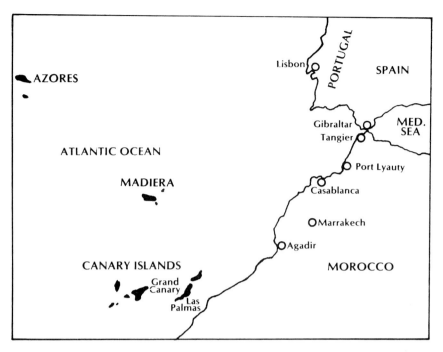

Operations Area: Fleet Air Wing 15, 1942-1945

There were two true U-boat sightings, however. On 8 July 1943 Lieutenant (j.g.) Joe Brummet dived on a sub, but the sub did likewise, and while Brummet's bombs struck directly over it, there was no evidence of a kill.[7] Lieutenant Bert Benton also attacked a sub. "It was coffee time," he reported, "and we had our hands full of java when we saw it. We dived at top speed, well over what was supposed to be our terminal velocity. It was a good attack and we scored two depth charge hits as the Nazis were crash-diving. A heavy oil slick arose." The planes of VP-73 followed the trail for three days and on the third day saw a green flare. Whether it was a distress signal or a rendezvous signal they never knew, but the oil slick disappeared that evening and there was no further contact.[8]

In February the Wing discarded the canned patrols in favor of flights laid out each day on the basis of plotted U-boat positions. VP-73's Agadir patrols ranged south down the coast of Spanish Sahara to the twenty-sixth parallel and as far west as Las Palmas, the westernmost of the Canary Islands. From Port Lyautey the remainder of VP-73, all of VP-92, and the two B-24 squadrons patrolled north to the thirty-fifth parallel and three hundred miles off shore. Above the thirty-fifth the British patrolled with Hudsons and Swordfish.

That same month the Germans instituted a new tactic in that theater. They began to send four-engine Focke Wulf Fw.200 Condor bombers to attack convoys. Up to that time Condors had been used simply as scouts, locating convoys and calling in the U-boats. But in May two violent attacks were made by the Condors themselves against small British convoys, and a month later two Hudsons drove off three Condors attacking a convoy off Cape Espechel.[9]

It was inevitable that the PBYs and Condors would cross swords, however ill-matched, and on 12 July it came to pass. On the eleventh PBYs belatedly arrived on the scene of a Condor attack on a convoy in which two merchant ships were sunk. The following day two PBYs were sent out to fly cover for the freighter *Port Fairey*, which was carrying survivors of the previous day's attack, and an escorting corvette. One PBY stayed low over the water to guard against submarine attack, and the other flew high to watch for Condors.

The high plane, flown by Lieutenant John Drew, had not long to wait. A Condor appeared, heading directly for the ships. The Condor was almost twice as fast as the PBY and carried four machine guns and a cannon, but Drew bravely climbed, turning tightly inside the Condor, keeping the PBY between the enemy plane and the little convoy. Lieutenant (j.g.) E. Bourgeault, the copilot, said:

> The Heinie leveled off to make his run and we set a collision course for him. Both planes were shooting, and he had a cannon in addition to machine guns. At the last minute he turned off to keep from getting rammed. He kept climbing and leveling off to get a pass at the ship, but we kept climbing with him, always inside, and would get in the way every time he made his run. Then we'd chase him away. Imagine a PBY chasing a Focke Wulf. Once we lost him in the clouds and he got in for one drop on the convoy. It was good bombing, for he got a hit, but he didn't try again. We chased him a ways, but couldn't catch him, of course. The ship [the *Port Fairey*], though hit [on the stern], kept going, and we started watching for subs.
>
> Then another Fw appeared and attacked the convoy. We applied the same tactics as before and had climbed to nearly 13,000 feet when the Nazi started a really determined run. We got square in his way. The airplanes were shooting at pretty close range and fire from the Fw was whipping through our plane. Lieutenant Lee Kennedy, our navigator, had a narrow escape. The nose gunner, Carl Adams, got in some good bursts. He said he was working his guns up and down like a pump handle. The Fw started trailing smoke and turned tail and headed for home.

That was the last attack; the little convoy made port. Lieutenant Drew and each man in his crew received the Distinguished Flying Cross.[10]

The first half of July was a period of increased U-boat activity, with consequent repercussions from the patrol squadrons. On 5–6 July two attacks on submarines were carried out by Fleet Air Wing 15 planes without damage to the enemy. A short time after the second attack a PBY flown by Lieutenant (j.g.) George Morris of VP-92 encountered the same U-boat, still on the surface, which responded to his presence with a terrific antiaircraft barrage. Morris dropped his depth charges with no effect on the sub, but his plane and crew took considerable punishment. The second radioman, Seaman Gibson, leaned out of the port blister to take a picture of the sub and was hit by shellfire. Mortally wounded, he died on the catwalk. Four other crewmen were wounded before the U-boat submerged. The PBY was badly shot up and its rudder cables were nearly severed, but Morris brought it back to Casablanca. This engagement marked the beginning of a new U-boat tactic: Stay on the surface and fight back.[11]

The final blow in the eleven-day "battle for the approaches" to the Mediterranean was struck on 15 July by a PBY of VP-92 flown by Lieutenant (j.g.) R. J. Finney. Receiving word of a radar contact from a convoy, he homed in and found a surfaced U-boat locked in a gun battle with three corvettes of the convoy's escort group. Finney dived to the attack, and his bow gunner cleaned the gun crews off the sub's afterdeck. His depth charges were well placed and the explosions blew the foredeck gun crew overboard. No longer endangered by cannon fire, a corvette charged in and rammed the sub, which rolled over and sank. In total, sixteen attacks were carried out by Fleet Air Wing 15 aircraft during those two weeks. Three B-24s and one PBY were slightly damaged by antiaircraft fire and ten crewmen were wounded. But the Germans took the worst beating by far: The Wing reported five U-boats sunk and six more damaged. During the same period the Hudsons and Wellingtons of the British also sank five U-boats and damaged another.

There was little respite for the embattled U-boats. British and American planes blasted them as they made their way past the coast of Portugal on their way home; they were badly mauled by U.S. hunter-killer groups as they prowled south of the Azores. For several months thereafter the patrol squadrons of Fleet Air Wing 15 saw no submarines.[12]

The Germans resorted to increased air attacks in the fall of 1943, but not all of the attacks on PBYs came from enemy forces. For several months VP-73's Catalinas had been flying antisubmarine patrols in and around the Canary Islands. A squadron of Martin Marylands operated by the French Navy flew similar patrols. The Spaniards on the supposedly neutral islands were familiar with the patrols, and if a plane ventured within the three-mile limit a Spanish antiaircraft battery would fire a warning shot, apparently with no intention of scoring a hit. But on the afternoon of 26 October a VP-73 PBY on patrol off Las Palmas was jumped by a Spanish Air Force Fiat CR-42 fighter. The attack lasted well beyond the three-mile limit, and the PBY took numerous hits before the fighter broke off. The pilot, Lieutenant W. G. Hoffman, brought the badly holed PBY back to Agadir with its tires flat, one engine and the radio out, and three crewmen wounded. He made an emergency water landing and saved the plane.[13]

A second attack on a PBY by a Spanish fighter came on 11 November. This brought two countermeasures. One was diplomatic: Pressure was put on the Spanish government in Madrid to end the attacks. The other was tactical: The navy substituted two PV-1s for the PBYs on the Canary Island patrol, and when Spanish fighters pounced on them they were disagreeably surprised to find a much faster, more heavily armed aircraft. The fighters were quickly driven off.

In November navy PB4Ys replaced the army B-24s at Port Lyautey, and in December VP-73 was rotated to the United States for a well deserved rest following thirty straight months of duty in Iceland and Africa. VP-92 returned to the mainland a month later. Their slot was filled by VP-63, which brought along a new weapon to fight the last battle of the U-boat war.[14]

Almost from the time of its commissioning 19 September 1942 at Alameda (California) Naval Air Station, VP-63 was a special outfit. Its formation coincided with three technical breakthroughs. First, the Magnetic Anomaly Detector (MAD) was perfected, an instrument that could sense changes in the earth's magnetic field caused by the presence of a large metallic object such as a submerged submarine. Second, a sonobuoy was developed that could be dropped in the water by a plane in flight and would report by radio submarine-propeller noises and underwater explosions. Third, retro bombs and retro smoke lights were created. These were rocket-powered missiles that could be fired in the direction opposite to the plane's travel, in effect cancelling out the plane's speed, to strike the water at the point where the MAD signal was the strongest: directly over the submarine. At the time these devices were developed, U-boats were sinking ships off the East Coast of the United States at an alarming rate, and the current antisubmarine devices and tactics seemed unable to cope with the situation. The commander in chief, U.S. Fleet, ordered the new equipment installed in a patrol squadron's aircraft for trials.

Patrol Squadron 63 was in the right place at the right time, and it got the job. Alameda was near Goldstone Lake, where scientists from the University of California were testing the retro bombs.[15] Under the command of an enthusiastic Lieutenant Commander Edwin Wagner, the squadron hustled about, installing the MAD equipment and weapons in three planes and setting up a training program. The squadron's PBY-5A amphibians had been traded in for PBY-5 flying boats; the weight of the new equipment plus landing gear made the -5As too heavy for long-range operations. The -5s, on the other hand, could take off easily with MAD gear and 1,600 gallons of fuel. Some redesign was necessary to accommodate the new equipment, the most noticable change being a long probe extending from the tail of each plane out past the rudder. Special rails were built and installed under the wings to carry twenty-four retro bombs, each weighing sixty-five pounds. Warheads were filled with Torpex, an explosive more powerful than TNT. The bombs could be fired automatically or manually by the pilot or MAD operator, all at once or in groups of eight. The bombs exploded only on contact, so that a submarine would not be aware an attack had been made if they missed. Retro smoke lights, used to mark the position of a submerged submarine, were placed to fire through the tunnel hatch. After several smoke lights were fired on successive passes, the submarine's course was evident.

Following the initial successful testing, all twelve planes of the squadron were equipped with MAD gear. Since MAD was the acronym for the equipment, and the PBY was called "Cat," it was only natural that VP-63 came to be known as the MAD CAT squadron.

After a strenuous period of tactical development and training, part of the time using a real submarine for a target, VP-63 left Alameda 13 March 1943 for Elizabeth City, North Carolina, where the squadron's complement was increased from twelve to fifteen MAD-equipped planes. Detachments operated at various times from Elizabeth City; Quonset Point Naval Air Station, Rhode Island; Jacksonville and Key West, Florida; and Bermuda.

During this period some of the shortcomings of the MAD equipment came to light. Although it was extremely accurate, its range was quite short: only 400 feet. Two U-boats were reported and hunted during VP-63's tour, one off Key West and the other off Bermuda. Neither was located by the specially equipped PBYs, and the short range of the MAD gear was thought to be a factor. In the Florida hunt, which began 7 April, four planes flew abreast a quarter-mile apart and one hundred feet off the water, turning in formation at the end of each sweep to start the next. The MAD gear worked, for five shipwrecks were found. But it appeared that a magnetic net was not good for catching submarines; the "mesh" was too big and the subs could slip through.

Shortly afterward it became evident from the reduced number of ship sinkings and submarine sightings that the U-boat menace had ended along the Atlantic seaboard. On 7 June VP-63 was ordered to Iceland, where the targets were more plentiful. For a month they flew patrols, but not a single submarine contact was made, either visually or magnetically.

The squadron took another step closer to the enemy in July, when it was loaned to 19th Group, Royal Air Force Coastal Command, to assist with an all-out offensive against U-boats sailing to and from their bases in France on the Bay of Biscay. The fifteen planes of VP-63 landed on the twenty-fifth at Pembroke Dock, South Wales, and began five months of operations.

Three days after their arrival Lieutenant (j.g.) Sam Parker made the squadron's first sighting: two U-boats running on the surface. As he brought his PBY closer the subs began throwing up a heavy antiaircraft screen, and Parker, following instructions, did not attack, but called more planes to the location. While waiting for their arrival his gunners traded shots with the U-boats, getting hits on the conning tower and crew of one sub. When two RAF flying boats came on the scene the U-boats dived, and Parker along with them, but his bombs apparently scored no hits. Attempts to follow the movements of the submarines with MAD gear were unsuccessful.

German fighters were often seen by VP-63 crews on patrol, but the PBYs exercised their number-one defensive tactic, slipping away into the clouds before any contact was made. On 2 August, however, Lieutenant William Tanner could find no clouds close enough to help his PBY escape. What few clouds there were worked against him, shielding at least eight Junkers Ju.88 fighter-bombers from view until it was too late for Tanner to run. Although he took violent evasive action and turned into each pass, the plane was shot to shreds by machine gun and cannon fire. Lieutenant Robertson, the navigator, was killed by an exploding cannon shell while directing fire from the blisters. Another shell wiped out the radio compartment and killed the operator. A third blew open the bow and killed the gunner. The plane captain died in his tower. The gas tanks were set afire and the blazing fuel spread along the wings. Aileron and rudder controls were shot away, and the starboard engine was knocked out.

Tanner and his copilot, Lieutenant (j.g.) Robert Bedell, were both hit by machine gun bullets but somehow managed to keep the plane level as it settled toward the surface of the bay. Luckily it was headed into the wind, for there was no way to turn it. The wing tip floats could not be lowered, and, when the riddled PBY touched down, it waterlooped and broke in half at the blisters, throwing four men into the water. Tanner and Bedell climbed out of the sinking bow section through the overhead hatches in the cockpit and, along with the seriously wounded starboard gunner, spent twenty hours in the water before they were picked up. These three were the only survivors. The RAF, which had been monitoring German aircraft radio broadcasts, reported that Tanner's gunners had registered hits on two Ju.88s, one of which went down at sea.

After that, complaints by VP-63 pilots and crews concerning the English weather all but stopped. Even though they never knew when taking off on patrol in the morning where they would land on return that evening, the fog and rain gave them protection from the German fighters. Unfortunately, the weather also gave protection to the U-boats. There were no more sightings by VP-63 for the remainder of its tour in England.[16]

During that six-month tour, however, VP-63 flew more hours and missions than any other squadron attached to the 19th Group, and lost only one aircraft, while others lost several. On leaving, the unit was congratulated by the commander, Fleet Air Wing 7; the commander, Naval Forces in Europe; and the commander in chief, Naval Operations. The residents of Pembroke Dock showed their feelings for the squadron by depicting one of its PBYs in a stained glass church window.

In late December 1943 VP-63 was ordered to Port Lyautey to fly antisubmarine patrols near the Strait of Gibraltar. The flight from England to Africa, made in three-plane increments, was not without incident. Lieutenant Commander Curtis Hutchings, who had taken over as squadron commander in September, was flying through rain on Christmas Day, when suddenly flak burst around his PBY. In a preflight briefing he had been warned of six enemy destroyers in the area; apparently he had flown directly over them. He circled on station until the location was confirmed and then headed once again for Port Lyautey. He learned later that British surface craft sank three of the destroyers.[17]

Retro bombs pack the underside of the wings on a VP-63 "Mad Cat" flying "the fence" across the Strait of Gibraltar. (U.S. Navy)

At Port Lyautey VP-63 began flying routine antisubmarine patrols and convoy escort duty in the Atlantic, but made no U-boat contacts. The U-boats were fewer in number and more cautious, but they had far from given up the fight. Rather than face the wrath of the air and surface antisubmarine teams in the Atlantic, however, they slipped into the Mediterranean to do their dirty work, easing through the Strait of Gibraltar just before dawn. They ran submerged, taking advantage of the east-west current, screws turning so slowly that hydrophones would not pick up the sound.[18]

Hutchins felt that, because of its narrow confines, the strait could be sealed off from U-boat penetration by his squadron, even given the short range of their MAD equipment. He devised a plan under which two Catalinas would establish a magnetic barrier across the strait by flying a race track course with straightaways four miles long and three-fourths of a mile apart over the deepest part of the strait, roughly on a line from Point Camarinal in Spain to Point Malaba in Spanish Morocco. The planes would fly at altitudes of fifty to one hundred feet and hold positions directly opposite each other at all times. This meant a plane would be passing any given point on the circuit at one-to-two minute intervals, and no U-boat could pass through the barrier without being detected.[19] To escape the morning fog at Port Lyautey, Hutchins would have his MAD CATs change shifts at noon. The afternoon shift would fly until dusk, then land and spend the night at Gibraltar. The planes would return to the barrier before dawn the next day and fly until noon.

Hutchins's idea was approved by both the Americans and the British. The situation had grown serious. The invasion of Europe was only months away, and any attempt to land U.S. troops in southern France would be disastrous if U-boats could ply their trade among the landing craft.

PBYs began flying "the fence" on 8 February 1944, along with their regular patrols and escort duties. It was an exacting task to stay on the oval course, and trigger-happy antiaircraft gunners in Spanish Morocco did nothing for the nerves, firing on the planes if they came close to the three-mile limit. One PBY was, in fact, hit but damage was minor.[20]

Two weeks later—on 24 February—VP-63 made naval history. A pair of MAD CATs flown by Lieutenants (j.g.) Howard Baker and T. R. Wooley became the first aircraft to use magnetic detection equipment in locating and sinking a fully submerged enemy submarine.

Contact was made at about 1500, after which Baker and Wooley flew a cloverleaf pattern and marked the U-boat's course with retro float lights. At that moment two British destroyers, HMS *Anthony* and HMS *Wishart*, steamed in and scattered the lights, announcing that the PBYs had found no more than a school of fish. The ships were invited to leave in no uncertain terms, but by that time the MAD CATs had temporarily

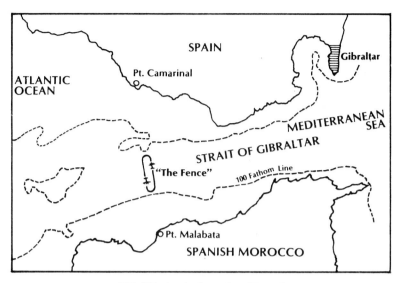

VP-63's Antisubmarine 'Fence'

lost contact with the U-boat. At 1557 they found it again and fired their
retro bombs two minutes later. Some of the bombs struck home, and
the explosions caused the two British warships to return and fire depth
charges. A few seconds later the submarine surfaced and the crew abandoned ship. The destroyers picked up about fifty crewmen, among them
the captain, who confirmed that the first explosions had severely damaged the U-boat, U-761, and he was preparing to surface when the
destroyers joined in the action.[21]

The lesson learned from the incident was that cooperation between
surface craft and aircraft would improve chances for success. Shortly
afterward a procedure was agreed upon between the Americans and the
British: The senior patrol plane commander would be in tactical command of all ships and aircraft when a MAD contact was made. All vessels
would stay clear of the area until the MAD CATs had attacked, then
would move in slowly and carry out their own attack. Also they were to
warn the PBYs when they were about to heave depth charges and hedgehogs into the air, as it was entirely possible to shoot down one of the
low-flying planes with an underwater missile.[22]

On 15 March an opportunity arose to try the new procedures. Periscope sightings and radar blips reported by patrols in the Atlantic alerted
the barrier fliers to the strong possibility that a U-boat might try to slip
through that day. As a safety measure a third PBY was sent out to fly

its own barrier east of the regular one. At 0845 that morning, Lieutenant R. C. Spears and Lieutenant (j.g.) V. A. T. Lingle made contact with a U-boat, tracked it and verified its course, then coached HMS *Vannock* into position. The *Vannock* fired twenty-four hedgehogs. Moments later oil and bubbles came to the surface, along with pieces of wood identified as locker tops. Months later the submarine was identified as the U-392. The two pilots, plus Lieutenant (j.g.) M. J. Vopatek, the pilot of the third plane, received the Distinguished Flying Cross, and their crews received the Air Medal.[23]

To force the U-boats to cross the barrier in daylight hours, Commander Hutchins arranged to have a British searchlight squadron illuminate the strait at night. Any submarine entering the Mediterranean in darkness would have to do so underwater. The theory was that their batteries would have to be charged farther west for a submerged run, and they could not reach the barrier before daybreak.[24]

The tactic apparently worked. On 15 May Lieutenant (j.g.) Vopatek and Lieutenant A. L. Worrell were flying the afternoon shift on the fence when a contact was made with MAD gear and then confirmed through propeller noises picked up by sonobuoy. At 1530 the MAD CATs attacked, firing a total of thirty retro bombs. Splintered wood floated to the surface, but the U-boat continued under way. The planes continued to track, and shortly afterward British ships arrived on the scene. HMS *Kilmarnock,* having been guided into position, fired its hedgehogs ahead of the line of float lights. Two minutes later the plane crews saw shock waves from two underwater explosions, followed by two great air bubbles bursting on the surface. There was no further contact with the submarine.[25]

The submarine, the U-731, was the last to attempt to cross the MAD CAT barrier. Months later it was learned that the German Naval High Command had issued orders that no more U-boats were to be sent to the Mediterranean because losses in the strait were too heavy. After that, the number of U-boats operating in the Mediterranean steadily declined because of the action of submarine-hunting ships and planes and the bombing of their harbors.[26]

In June the barrier became a twenty-four-hour-a-day operation, with MAD-equipped blimps of ZP-14 flying the course at night. ZP-14 had flown from the United States in eighty hours, the first non-rigid airships to make the Atlantic crossing.[27] In August the U.S. troop landings in southern France took place without U-boat opposition. Later a navy press release said: "In the process of turning the Mediterranean into an Allied lake, Patrol Bombing Squadron Sixty-Three's Gibraltar U-boat 'fence' is credited with being a major factor in the successful invasion of Southern France since no allied vessel was sunk by enemy submarine."[28] The capture of Toulon and Marseilles brought U-boat activity in the Mediterranean to a virtual close.[29] Patrol Squadron 63 would register one more U-boat kill, this less than three weeks before the war ended. On 20 April 1945 Lieutenant F. G. Lake, flying a MAD CAT that was part of a detachment sent back to England during the final months, sighted a snorkeling submarine. He nosed the PBY over from 2,000 feet and flew up the snorkel's wake, and when the magnetometer needle pegged he fired all of his retro bombs. Debris that rose to the surface, plus an oil slick 2,700 yards long, seemed to be proof enough of a kill. Lake was awarded the Distinguished Flying Cross for his day's work.

VP-63 continued operations in Morocco until June 1945, and then returned home after two years of continuous antisubmarine activity. The squadron was decommissioned in July, but its personnel were scattered throughout the navy, to exert, in time, considerable influence on current antisubmarine weapons and tactics. It is a just claim that VP-63 is the father of modern antisubmarine warfare.[30]

And so the navy's PBYs came home, middle-aged now, mellowed and approaching retirement, but still tough and proud and ready for a good day's work. They had seen it all, from Pearl Harbor to the Philippines to Australia to the Aleutians to Guadalcanal and a host of islands to the west and north, ever north; from Greenland to the United Kingdom, the Canal Zone, the Caribbean, and Brazil.

Many tributes have been paid concerning the contribution of the PBYs to the war effort, but few are more to the point than the comment made by a Britisher in Iceland: "Everywhere you go in this war you always find three things: DC-3s, Jeeps, and those bloody Catalinas. They're our reliables, our indispensables. It's really amazing how those Cats fly in all sorts of weather on all sorts of missions. You come out in the morning up here, wipe the snow out of your eyes and still can't see a thing, and in the pitch blackness in the heavy weather you hear a roar, and it's those Yanks going out on patrol in those bloody Catalinas."

Take out the snow and the "bloody," and the same could be said for PBYs and PBY crews in hundreds of stations in every hemisphere. Little wonder PBYs seemed to be everywhere: The U.S. Navy accepted more than two thousand from Consolidated prior to and during the war. More than twenty thousand pilots and crewmen flew them on the long, dull patrols and through the brief, frightening moments of combat. And heaven only knows how many nameless, unthanked sailors filled the tanks, serviced the engines, loaded the ordnance, and patched the holes in all kinds of weather to keep them flying.

Too old, too slow, and too vulnerable, some said of the PBY. Yet it

Faded and patched, war-weary PBYs hitch a ride home on the escort carrier USS *Thetis Bay* in July 1944.

was young enough, fast enough, and tough enough to do jobs that no other aircraft could do as well. It earned the love and admiration of the men who flew it, and the fear and respect of the enemy beneath it. Of all the flying boats in the history of aviation, the PBY has earned the honor of standing at the apex.

PBYs with the Coast Guard

The U.S. Coast Guard took delivery of its first PBY in late 1940, some twenty-five years after aircraft had become a part of its array of search and rescue equipment. Coast Guard aviation began in 1915, when Captain B. M. Chiswell, commanding officer of the cutter *Onondaga*, and two of his junior officers, Lieutenants Norman Hall and Elmer Stone, conceived a plan for an air patrol to search for disabled vessels. The plan, presented to the commanding officer at Curtis Field near Hampton Roads, sounded feasible and test results were excellent.

Because of this, in August 1916 ten Coast Guard air stations were authorized by Congress, but little money was made available for their construction until 1924. Then, appropriations were forthcoming only because a considerable need had developed: Enforcement of the 18th Amendment—Prohibition—was proving difficult, and aircraft surveillance was needed to help locate and arrest rum runners.[1]

From its inception until 1926, Coast Guard air activity was limited to "spasmodic flying" in Curtiss HS-2Ls and H-10 flying boats borrowed from the navy. Spasmodic or not, the Coast Guard carried out reconnaissance patrols, located fish schools, transported emergency medical cases, and made general humanitarian flights to an extent great enough to demonstrate the need for its own planes. That year five single-engine Loening OL-5 amphibians were purchased.

During the remainder of the 1920s and through the 1930s the Coast Guard air arm grew. By 1940, from stations on both coasts, it was operating a mixed bag of fifty flying boats, amphibians, and land planes: Hall PH-2s, Sikorskys, Douglases, Fokkers, Vikings, Voughts, Curtisses, Stinsons, Wacos, Northrops, and others. Prior to the delivery of its first PBY, the Coast Guard had only one aircraft built by Consolidated: a two-place, single-engine, Model 21 N4Y-1 biplane trainer, known in the army air corps as a PT-11.

The approach of war attracted flocks of Grummans to Coast Guard fields: J2F and later-model Ducks, JRF Gooses, and J4F Widgeons. The inventory swelled with Douglas R4Ds, Vought Kingfishers, and Curtiss Commandos, as well as an ever-increasing number of Martin Mariners and Consolidated PBYs.

When Neutrality Patrols began in 1939, Coast Guard planes took an active part along the coasts. The area of activity was enlarged in 1941: Following the signing of a treaty between the United States and Denmark for the defense of Greenland, cutter-based Coast Guard planes began operations there.

Shortly before Pearl Harbor the Coast Guard was made a part of the navy by order of President Roosevelt. Afterward many of its routine activities were discontinued; Coast Guard services were needed elsewhere. Rescues of downed fliers increased in direct proportion to expanding army and navy flight training programs, ferry flights, and antisubmarine patrols. As the number of attacks on coastal shipping by enemy submarines rose, there came a similar rise in rescues of survivors of torpedoed ships. During the war more than a thousand sailors were saved through the efforts of Coast Guard fliers. Planes alone rescued ninety-five people.[2]

Coast Guard planes began antisubmarine patrols shortly after war was declared. The first wartime order received from the navy by the Coast Guard station at Elizabeth City, North Carolina, directed its planes to patrol the steamer lanes off the Chesapeake capes and be on the alert for submarines. The patrols were carried out each day, weather per-

The crew of a U.S. Coast Guard Catalina climbs aboard as the engines warm up for an early-morning takeoff on a search-and-rescue mission. (U.S. Coast Guard)

mitting. Even so, Germany's U-boats took an ever-growing toll of coastal shipping. It was a frustrating time for Coast Guard pilots and crews. Their planes were unarmed, and they could only report U-boat sightings and stand by helplessly as ships below them were torpedoed. When the stations began receiving armed aircraft the Coast Guardsmen gave a good account of themselves. They made sixty-one bombing attacks on U-boats. One U-boat was sunk, bombed by a Grumman Widgeon off the mouth of the Mississippi in the Gulf of Mexico.[3]

On 5 October 1943 a U.S. Coast Guard squadron—VP-6—was formed by the navy at Argentia, Newfoundland. It was the only patrol squadron staffed entirely with Coast Guard personnel during World War II. The squadron began operations out of Narsarssuak, Greenland, where ten PBY-5As were land-based at a field code-named Bluie West-One (BW-1). With Commander Donald MacDiarmid in charge, the unit performed ice surveys, delivered mail and supplies to military bases and civilian villages, flew convoy escort and antisubmarine patrols and, because U-boats were still active in the area, performed more than a few air-sea rescue missions involving torpedoed surface ships.

At BW-1, winds were rarely under twenty-five knots. The lone concrete runway sloped downward from the foot of a mountain towards Narsarssuak Fjord; consequently all takeoffs were downhill and all landings were uphill, no matter which way the wind blew. When the ceiling was low, the PBYs flew through the fjord between 4,000-foot mountains to get in or out of the field. At first, incoming pilots depended on radio to warn them of a possible midair collision with a plane outbound from BW-1. The tension eased somewhat after radar was installed. Radar also kept them from colliding with the walls of the fjord in times of near-zero visibility. The pilots flew at 400-foot to 600-foot altitudes and followed the directions of the radar operator. If BW-1 couldn't be seen after the final turn—it was only a mile away—the pilots would pull up, climb out, and go around again.

Some of VP-6's rescue missions were flown over Greenland's ice cap as well as over the North Atlantic. On 28 November 1943 the squadron's PBYs began a three-day search for an army aircraft down on the cap. Lieutenant Alexander Wuerker's PBY found the plane on the cap's edge and marked the location with flag stakes. A second PBY guided a rescue party overland to the site, and a third dropped supplies to the party on its way back to base.

In February 1944 Lieutenant Commander John McCubbin spotted a red flare at sea while on routine ice patrol. Banking in the direction of the flare, he came upon a ship which identified herself by blinker as the British trawler HMS *Strathella*. She had been adrift for five weeks and was out of food and water. With the aid of a second PBY, the Coast Guard cutter *Modoc* was guided to the rescue.

During twenty-seven months of operations in Greenland, VP-6 flew many similar missions, along with routine ice survey, convoy, and anti-submarine patrols, many of them in high winds and near-zero visibility. The hours were often long. During a three-month period in early 1944 Lieutenant Carl Allen flew 100 hours per month on convoy and ice patrols, one flight taking him over the magnetic North Pole.

At the end of hostilities in Europe in May 1945, VP-6 simply dropped its antisubmarine activities and continued to function as a typical Coast Guard unit, performing routine duties and flying special missions to accommodate ships and aircraft in distress. In August 1945 the squadron's headquarters was transferred to Argentia, Newfoundland. Patrol Squadron 6 was decommissioned as a navy squadron in January 1946.[4]

A Coast Guard Catalina simulates an air-sea rescue. In real life, the "Ugly Duck-ling" never looked better. (U.S. Coast Guard)

With the lessening of the U-boat menace along the sea frontiers of the United States, the Coast Guard began once more to concentrate heavily on air-sea rescue. Until 1941 Coast Guard rescues had mostly involved surface craft. Its aircraft would locate ships in distress and would then call in a cutter or, if no cutter was close, a commercial vessel to render aid. But Pearl Harbor changed the scenario. Increasingly, aircraft began to play a more active role in rescues, and rescues themselves began to absorb a greater percentage of Coast Guard effort. The upswing in rescues was due in part to the greater number of flights over water, once war had broken out. Before the war, for example, few army air corps flights were over water. After the outbreak, there were more flights, most of them made by inexperienced pilots.

The first Coast Guard unit entirely devoted to air-sea efforts was established in San Diego in December 1943, where the large number of military and naval flights created an obvious need for a well-organized, highly trained group whose primary function was rescuing fliers forced down at sea or on land. The following year in Washington the Joint Chiefs of Staff requested that the secretary of the navy form a Coast Guard Air-Sea Rescue Agency to develop equipment and techniques and to establish procedures to better coordinate the rescue efforts of the army, navy, and air force, as well as those of the Allies.

The air-sea rescue methods of the Royal Air Force, proved during the Battle of Britain, were studied by the U.S. Coast Guard. Administratively, the result was the establishment of regional air-sea rescue task units, each headed by the commanding officer of the Coast Guard Air Station in each region. When a report of an emergency was received, notice was sent to the nearest air-sea rescue unit regardless of nationality or branch of service. If the situation was grave enough, the entire region's resources were alerted.

Technical advances were made as well. Stripped down versions of the PBY-5A—the Coast Guard's favorite air-sea rescue aircraft—were equipped with life rafts, Gibson Girl transmitters, shipwreck kits, markers, smoke and light buoys, and other emergency equipment. This included a Coast-Guard-designed "provision bomb," a watertight practice bomb filled with canned water, food, and medicine.

For the next two years, while the dramatic events of the war in Europe and the Pacific captured the headlines, the Coast Guard quietly went about its work, with little notice and with little thanks, except by those aided and rescued. In 1943 and 1944 alone Coast Guard planes spent 131,277 hours in the air, logging 42,282 training, administrative, test, and patrol flights, plus 1,295 assistance flights. The planes covered more than twelve million linear miles, and searched almost eighty-six million square miles of land and sea. In total, 207,522 ships and planes were identified, 401 ships and planes—207 of them disabled—were assisted, 659 individuals were assisted, and 175 medical cases were transported.[5]

By the time peace came, the Coast Guard had accumulated 114 PBYs. Most of them were -5As; six were -6As received late in the war. Their retirement began in 1946 but, since the Coast Guard's requirements for airborne search, rescue, and other services were ongoing, some PBYs served on for another eight years.[6]

The Air Force's Navy

When the United States entered World War II the army air force faced a monumental problem created by large numbers of aircraft making over-water flights for the first time. In addition to bomber and fighter missions, air force crews flew antisubmarine patrols and convoy escort duty; they ferried aircraft, carried personnel, and hauled cargo. Many flights were over vast stretches of ocean. It was inevitable that, because of mechanical failure, enemy action, or disorientation, some planes would be forced down at sea. The planes would float long enough for crews to escape in rubber rafts, but the air force, entirely land-based in concept and equipment, had no aircraft that could put down on water to pick them up. In the early days in the Pacific, the air force called on the U. S. Navy patrol squadrons and the Royal Australian Air Force to bring home their airmen; in Europe and the Mediterranean they depended on the Royal Air Force.

While this system saved a number of lives, members of the air force's top echelon were aware that the missions of other branches and other nations came first and that the rescue of air force crews had to come second. They recognized that the air force would be men and money ahead if it had its own rescue units whose primary duty was the retrieval of downed fliers. Such a possibility was discussed by the Joint Chiefs of Staff in December 1942. At first, serious consideration was given to expanding the Coast Guard, to which rescue operations were second nature. But the subcommittee investigating the idea determined that too many obstacles beset an expansion great enough to allow the Coast Guard to cover all types of rescues in all parts of the world. Discussions continued, and eventually a decision was reached: Each branch of service would conduct its own air-sea rescue efforts. General Henry H. "Hap" Arnold, wartime chief of the air force, was quick to order the organization and training of seven air-sea rescue squadrons.

Of the aircraft then available the best suited for plucking men from the sea was a Consolidated PBY-5A. It was considered obsolescent, but it had its advantages: it was amphibious, its slow speed allowed time for careful scrutiny of search areas, its range allowed it to accompany bombers to their targets and back (until the advent of the B-29), and it could take off with a heavy load of waterlogged airmen.

However, Consolidated was working to capacity on wartime contracts, and the prospect of obtaining PBYs direct from the factory within a reasonable period looked grim. The navy came to the rescue, transferring fifty-four PBY-5s and PBY-5As—air force designation OA-10 and OA-10A—to begin filling out the air force table of organization and equipment. The bulk of the air force requirement for amphibians was filled by Canadian Vickers, which found room in its production schedule for an order of 230 OA-10As. Deliveries began in December 1943 and continued until February 1945. Late in the war seventy-five PBY-6As were delivered to the air force by Consolidated as OA-10Bs.[1]

On 11 March 1943 the air force started training its "navy." Special Order 58 transferred thirty-nine newly trained second lieutenant pilots from Advanced Flying School at Stockton Field, California, to Pensacola, Florida, "for the purpose of naval air intermediate training in PBY-5 aircraft." The following day an identical order was given to nine pilots at LaJunta, Colorado. The course included two weeks of advanced navigation training at Selman Field, Louisiana, and then six weeks flight training in PBYs at Pensacola, this conducted by the navy according to the navy training syllabus.[2]

The early training program consisted of cross-country and night flying, water landings, instrument flying, and gunnery practice. Those in charge of the program quickly saw that six weeks' flight training was not enough,

U.S. Air Force OA-10As roll off the assembly line at the Canadian Vickers plant in Cartierville, Ontario. (K. M. Molson)

and the time was increased to ten weeks, with a heavier concentration on rough-water techniques and advanced seamanship. Training was hampered by a lack of serviceable aircraft: Eleven PBYs were assigned for training use, but only four were flyable at any one time.

Many of the concepts on which air force air-sea rescue training was based came from the British and the Germans. Luftwaffe fighters carried inflatable dinghies before British fighters did; these were bright yellow in color, as were pilots' life vests. The Germans pioneered the use of fluorscine dye marker and even anchored rescue floats, stocked with blankets, food, water, and distress signals, in high-traffic areas. In these floats, as many as four men could await pickup by boat.

The British adapted these ideas to their already well-stocked bag of tricks. As early as 1925 their seaplanes were equipped with inflatable dinghies. In the mid-1930s high-speed launches were used for emergency pickups near RAF Coastal Command bases. In 1938 RAF land planes began carrying rubber dinghies. There was, however, no formal air-sea rescue organization. Such efforts were coordinated mission-by-mission between the RAF and the Royal Navy, using whatever equipment and personnel were available.

In 1940, even before the Battle of Britain, the problem of air-sea rescue became acute for the RAF. Two-hundred-twenty aircrewmen crashed, ditched, or parachuted into the English Channel and the North Sea during the last twenty-one days of July. Fighter Command borrowed Lysanders and went hunting its men, dropping inflatable dinghies from the bomb racks when a man was found in the water. In 1941 air-sea rescue operations were formalized under an air commodore. Specific units were organized and assigned. Emergency equipment was refined and designed: balloons, kites, flags, flares, wireless transmitters, and even homing pigeons became a part of the program. High-speed launches were also a part of the system. By 1942, 150 of them were performing rescue service in British waters.

In 1943, while new air force pilots and crews were learning to fly PBYs at Pensacola, old hands in the 8th Air Force were learning air-sea rescue procedures directly from the British. At that time the RAF was using fighter planes to spot downed aircrews, with shore bases fixing the location. The plane dropped emergency equipment and stayed on station until a boat arrived to pick up the aircrew. This was the system the 8th relied on until 1944, when its own squadron of forty-two P-47 spotters took over. The following year the 5th Emergency Rescue Squadron arrived with the first OA-10A rescue aircraft to see service there. The squadron remained for the duration.

Because of the accomplishments of the British air-sea rescue (ASR) system, two British ASR instructors were made a part of the air force flight training program at Pensacola, where they gave lectures and advice. Also following the British lead, crash boats were included in the air-sea rescue system. Boat crews received 144 hours of instruction at Gulfport, Mississippi. Ninety-five crews were trained by the time the school was disbanded in October 1944. Crash boats were no longer needed after that time, having been replaced by B-17s equipped with air-dropped lifeboats.

When the first OA-10 pilots were graduated from Pensacola, two detachments were formed. One was sent to the 5th Air Force Rescue Service in the Southwest Pacific in late summer 1943, the other to the RAF's 12th Fighter Command Rescue Service in the Mediterranean during the summer and fall of 1943. In early 1944 the 1st Emergency Rescue Squadron (ERS) moved to the Mediterranean. The success of these first units brought favorable attention to the program, and in the spring of 1944 an all-air-force air-sea rescue school was opened at Keesler Field, Mississippi. An expanded course was taught by instructors rotated from the two detachments and the 1st ERS. By the time the school was disbanded on 22 April 1945, four squadrons and sixty replacement crews had been trained at Keesler.

Before the air force detachment arrived in the Mediterranean, responsibility for air-sea rescue had rested entirely on the shoulders of the

A native boatman paddles a downed U.S. Air Force pilot out to an OA-10A of the 2nd Emergency Rescue Squadron waiting with engines running just off the enemy-held New Guinea coast while a crewman swims out to meet him. (L. M. Myers)

RAF, which continued to provide the bulk of the service throughout the war. Three OA-10s, arriving at Malta in June 1943, were assigned to the RAF's 12th Fighter Command Air-Sea Rescue Service. The pilots were fresh from school at Pensacola, and the OA-10s were old training planes, ferried to the Mediterranean by way of South America. Five planes had left Pensacola, but one was damaged and had remained in Puerto Rico, and the other had landed in Spanish Morocco, where the crew was interned. There were no other OA-10s on Malta, and maintenance was almost impossible, so the planes were transferred to Bizerte, Tunisia, where maintenance was merely difficult. The planes, abused by the inexpert handling of many inexperienced pilots, were grounded after each open-sea landing to replace rivets, sheet metal, and plexiglass.

Some missions were completed only because the crews were able to make on-the-spot repairs. On 30 July 1943 an OA-10 was guided by a Wellington to a dinghy containing five members of a B-26 crew. The landing and rescue was accomplished, but the plane was so heavily damaged in the landing that eight hours of work by its crew was needed before it could take off again. Other missions were completed only with outside help. On 18 August an OA-10 picked up twenty men, survivors of two ditched B-17s, but this time the damage from landing was so severe that the pilot elected to taxi to port. Launches eventually met the plane, took off the passengers, and towed the plane in.

However difficult it was to keep the three planes in the air, they rescued forty Allied and five Axis airmen during July and August 1943 in eleven open-sea landings and two hundred hours of operation.

The detachment's service ended when one OA-10 was shot down in flames by three Messerschmitts while on a mission, and a second was strafed and destroyed on the water. This plane had landed to pick up an Italian airman who later died on board. On takeoff the port propeller struck a wave, broke off, and slammed through the hull. The plane was a sitting duck for shore batteries, but final destruction came at the hands of a Macchi 200 fighter that made three strafing runs, setting it on fire and killing a gunner. The rest of the crew abandoned the plane and clung to a half-inflated dinghy for four hours until they were picked up by a launch. What remained of the detachment returned to the United States in December 1943.

For the next three months air-sea rescue was again the sole province of the RAF. Then on 11 March the air force's 1st Emergency Rescue Squadron, under the command of Lieutenant Colonel Littleton Pardue, began arriving by plane and ship at Casablanca. The unit was typical of all air force emergency rescue squadrons, staffed with fifty-two officers and 147 enlisted men, and equipped with nine OA-10s and six other planes. The squadron was broken into three flights, which were stationed first at Sidi Ahmid Air Base near Bizerte, at Port Lyautey, and at Ajaccio, Corsica. As the war progressed they moved to Grottaglie, Foggia, and Falconara in Italy, and Cuers, France.[3]

Six weeks after their arrival, a Corsica-based OA-10 set the pace for succeeding missions. On 29 April all crews at Ajaccio were standing by to pick up survivors of bombers shot down on a 640-plane raid on Toulon. At 1230 the OA-10s were ordered in the air. At 1300 a B-24 radioed it was ditching; at 1400 two dinghies containing ten men were sighted by an OA-10 flown by Second Lieutenant John Mork. Permission to land was given, and Mork set the plane down at 1500 in a sea corrugated by moderate swells. The B-24 crewmen were taken aboard, and Mork sent the plane pounding across the swells and into the air at 1530, taxiing up the ramp at Ajaccio at 1645.

On 6 June 1944, while General Dwight Eisenhower's troops were keeping the Germans busy in France, air force B-24s were occupying them in Romania. A 350-plane raid had been carried out against a favorite target, the oil refineries in Ploesti. Many B-24s were hit, and Lieutenant Mork found one of them limping along on two engines and about to ditch. When the bomber hit the water it exploded and broke in half. Mork made a landing in rough seas, popping a minimum number of rivets. His crew found three survivors and four bodies floating in their Mae Wests; four others had gone down with the bomber. While the OA-10A rolled in the swells, the three survivors were taken aboard

Operations Area: U. S. Air Force 1st Emergency Rescue Squadron

through the port blister. One had a hip injury and was strapped to a basket litter; with one survivor pushing from below and the crew pulling from above, he was lifted inside. A flight surgeon riding with Mork that day became seasick, much to the amusement of the crew and the rescued. Mork made a beautiful takeoff, but it was to be expected. He had had a lot of practice. It was his sixteenth rescue.

Some of the 1st's customers were regulars. One fighter pilot was shot down three times, each time landing in a mine field, each time having a lifeboat dropped to him by a B-17, and each time being picked up by an OA-10 or a launch.[4]

The OA-10s of the 1st ERS were under continual danger of attack from enemy fighters and from shore-based antiaircraft fire as well. On 16 November an OA-10 was hit by coastal guns while on a search mission in the Adriatic and was forced to ditch. The plane sank at dusk and the crew bobbed about in rubber rafts until the next morning, when one of their own effected the rescue. On 21 March 1945 Lieutenant Dunn landed to pick up a P-40 pilot after making sure there were no floating mines in the area. As the plane taxied up to the pilot, German 88s on shore opened up. The weakened pilot was hauled aboard with a boat hook, and the plane took off, but not before two crewmen had been wounded and the plane damaged in the wing, tail, and right blister from shell fire.

Not all of those rescued were Allies. On 8 June 1944, Lieutenant Walker and crew, on standby at Grottaglie, were awakened at 0500 and told of a ditching fourteen miles south of the Italian boot heel. During the night a British Beaufighter had shot down a German Ju.88 which had established a regular pattern of reconnaissance flights over convoy routes and harbors during the evenings. With two Spitfires for protection, the OA-10A was directed to the area, where Walker found two Germans in life vests floating near a red flare. Walker landed and his men tossed a rope to the Germans, who were pulled aboard. They said a third crewman was nearby, and about 500 yards away his body was found floating. Since there was room in the plane, the body was hauled aboard and Walker took off in moderate swells, landing back at Grottaglie at 0745.

A second rescue of German fliers, this by a Corsica-based OA-10A, took place a week later. The pilot's report said the Germans showed no hostility and considerable gratitude for their lives being saved.

In January 1945 two flights of the 1st Emergency Rescue Squadron were ordered to India, leaving only one flight in the Mediterranean. Although the full unit had operated there for less than a year, its records showed a total of 244 airmen rescued.[5]

In Europe, land bases for air-sea rescue activity were plentiful. In the Pacific it was another story. Small islands made land basing difficult, and bases were constantly moving as the Allies smashed their way north. Many Japanese-held islands were bypassed in the island-hopping war, creating situations where rescues were carried out under the noses of the enemy, and under direct threat of death: The Japanese had said they would execute any Allied flier who fell into their hands. This fact made rescue services a powerful morale builder among air force fliers.

During the first year of the war no army air force rescue units operated in the Pacific. Navy PBYs carried out air-sea rescues for both branches of service and for all of the Allies. In early 1943 the 5th Air Force Rescue Service was established on New Guinea, headed by Major John Small, Jr. With no equipment of his own, no precedent to guide him, and only one assistant, he directed search and rescue missions for more than six months, using the planes of operational units for search, often calling on the Catalinas of the Royal Australian Air Force as well as the RAAF's small-boat unit. In August 1943 Small got his first airplanes: two OA-10s with crews fresh from Pensacola. Using these plus his catch-as-catch-can methods, Major Small accounted for 455 lives saved by April 1944.

Three months later, in July 1944, the first complete squadron was assigned to the 5th Air Force: the 2nd Emergency Rescue Squadron. It did not stay long with the 5th, however. The 13th Air Force had watched the 5th's air-sea rescue efforts with interest and had formed a rescue service of its own. Then, when the 3rd Emergency Rescue Squadron arrived in the Pacific in September, the 2nd ERS was transferred to the 13th Air Force, and the 3rd assigned to the 5th Air Force. Major Small was instrumental in seeing that in each case the rescue squadrons were assigned to air force headquarters.

The 2nd ERS, nicknamed the "Snafu (air force code for a downed aircraft) Snatchers," began operations in the Pacific with a dozen OA-10As, four C-45s, and four L-5s. Later three life-raft-carrying B-17s, three C-47s, a B-25, a P-38, and a P-47 were added to the squadron's equipment list, and the L-5s were mounted on floats. On 14 July the squadron was broken into flights and assigned to Biak, Hollandia, and Nazdab, all on New Guinea. On 8 September Flight C from Nazdab and Flight B from Biak were consolidated and transferred to Middleburg Island off the northern New Guinea coast to give better coverage to bombardment groups striking at Japanese positions on the islands of Borneo, Celebes, Halmahera, and Morotai.[6]

The 2nd's services were in great demand from the start. Most flights were long, and combat hours mounted by leaps and bounds. The planes were gone all day, so ground crews worked all night.

On 16 September a "Daylight Special" (air force code for OA-10s on

An injured airman is offloaded from an OA-10A at the 2nd Emergency Rescue
Squadron base at Biak. Difficulty in getting injured men in and out of the blisters
was one of the drawbacks of the PBY in rescue service. (L. M. Myers)

rescue missions) piloted by Lieutenant John Dennison rescued survivors
of a B-24 down at sea, and the same day a second Daylight Special flown
by Lieutenant Yagla picked up a navy Hellcat pilot.

On 1–2 October the 2nd ERS had its first OA-10 fail to come home
from a flight. Daylight Number Thirteen, flown by Second Lieutenant
John Dickinson, took off from Middleburg Island at 1615 to locate a
snafu off Cape Momfafa, Waigeo Island. At 1715 hours the snafu, a P-
38 pilot, was spotted in a life raft about one-and-one-half miles off shore.
It was then 1730; the light was poor and Dickinson was not sure how
rough the seas were, but it was now or never, for the pilot was drifting
toward breakers and a rocky cliff. Dickinson elected to land. When he
did he found out how rough the seas were. The OA-10 banged down
in six-to-ten-foot swells which made it impossible to see the snafu pilot
at first, but within ten minutes he was located and brought aboard. The
plane had been dented and bent in landing, however. A number of rivets
had popped, allowing the plane to take on water.

Dickinson decided not to try a takeoff in the gathering darkness and
heavy swells. He and his crew put out the sea anchor at 1810 and tried
to settle down for the night in the rolling, pitching plane. Then the bilge
pump gave out, and a seasick crew took over the bailing operation by
hand. An hour later the sea anchor line parted, and maintaining position
also became a hand operation. Dickinson would fire up one engine, taxi
out near the reefs, shut the engine down, allow the wind to blow the

plane back near shore, then repeat the operation. When the batteries were exhausted, the crew hand-cranked the engine.

At 2300 a PT boat took station outside the reef, maintaining a vigil throughout the night. At 0630 a line was passed from the boat to the plane in an attempt to tow the plane back to base, but the OA-10 was too far gone. Seams had opened during the night and, despite the crew's desperate bailing, it had settled below the waterline. Towing pulled the nose under. The plane was beached, the radar and IFF gear—a new device that identified the plane to its base—were destroyed, and the rescuers and the rescued came home by PT-boat. The plane was not forever lost, though. An air force repair crew from Middleburg bummed a bulldozer and a ride in an LST and went to Waigeo Island. They towed the OA-10 up on the beach where emergency repairs were made. It was flown back to base, where it was fully repaired and returned to service.

The 2nd flew 1,127 hours and 184 successful missions during October. The number of rescued during the month was 51, three of them Japanese who were mistaken for Australians.[7]

On 10 October two flights moved up to Morotai to cover strikes on Palau and the Philippines. This put them much nearer the fighting; Morotai was still being bombed by the Japanese, and flight crews sometimes spent the night in foxholes. One plane was destroyed in a bombing raid; others were damaged by flying bomb fragments. The following month two officers were killed when a bomb exploded in the officers' area. The planes returned from Daylight missions with bullet holes and flak scars inflicted by island defenders to the north.[8]

After the invasion of the Philippines, the 2nd ERS added guerrilla supply to its workload. On one such mission Lieutenant Schandelmeir pulled double duty. Landing at Naburos Island to pick up five airmen from the 5th Bomb Group, he distributed pamphlets, fifteen machine guns and ammunition to the natives and, going strictly by the book, got a signed receipt for the weapons and munition.[9]

Rescues made in cooperation with Filipino guerrillas became so common that specific stations were set up where survivors would be harbored until the next OA-10 came by on its way to or from a scheduled mission.

Now that many of the 2nd's flights were over large islands, the rescue crews were given training in jungle survival in January 1945 by five members of the Australian ground forces. By March four detachments were stationed in the Philippines. In February the base at Middleburg Island had been closed and the flight there moved up to Morotai.

Most missions were carried out in relative safety, with the greatest danger coming from landings in seas rough enough to hinder takeoff. However, occasional direct contact was made with the enemy. On 4 March "Playmate 42"—the name had replaced "Daylight"—piloted by

Lieutenant Frank Rauschkolb took off at 0515 and was orbiting over Malanipa Island to cover B-25 strikes on Zamboanga. Three B-25s went down, and at 0940 Rauschkolb located one crew a mile off the target. A string of Japanese barges opened fire on the plane as it taxied up to the life raft, then they, too, headed for it, still firing machine guns and possibly 20-millimeter cannon, judging from the shell bursts in the water behind the plane.

Rauschkolb called for help from four B-25s circling overhead and got it. The barges came no closer, and five of the six-man crew were taken aboard. A second downed B-25 was located ten minutes later. It had crashed on a reef and was being shelled by shore batteries as its crew paddled away in a raft. The shore batteries sent a few rounds toward the OA-10A, but the best they could do was a few near misses.

A third downed B-25 was spotted about fifteen miles away by a pair of B-25s which guided Rauschkolb to the site. With nineteen men aboard and a heavy load of fuel, he opted to taxi from the second downed B-25 to the third. The crew bailed furiously to offset water coming in through the flare tubes in the tunnel hatch. At 1130 the six-man B-25 crew was picked up and, after dumping 400 gallons of fuel, Rauschkolb made a perfect takeoff. He landed at Morotai at 1615 with twenty-five men aboard.[10]

On 31 March Playmate 41, which had taken off from Morotai to locate the crew of a Beaufighter, diverted to pick up two men in a dinghy in Haroekoe Strait about 300 yards offshore from Waal village. Flying at zero altitude, the plane was subjected to heavy fire from at least eight antiaircraft positions on both sides of the strait. The survivors were swimming beside their dinghy, taking rifle fire from the village. The OA-10A landed, receiving no more fire from the heavy guns but also subjected to rifle fire, which was returned by the gunners in the blisters. One gunner was hit in the back by a rifle bullet and the plane was holed in many places. The takeoff was made in rough water, which caused structural damage, despite which the plane was able to fly back to the base at Morotai.

In April a detachment of the 2nd was sent to Palawan and another to Zamboanga. An OA-10A was destroyed and another damaged on the Palawan air strip by a Japanese air strike shortly after the detachment's arrival. Two men were wounded by antiaircraft fire on a rescue mission.

On 8 April Playmate 37, piloted by Lieutenant Robert Davis, was directed by a P-38 pilot to a dinghy containing the crew of a B-25 near Japanese-held Tarakan Island. Aware of the danger, Davis nevertheless set up his approach. As the plane neared the water, the Japanese opened up on it with 40-millimeter shells and machine gun fire. A four-foot hole was blown in the starboard wing, a gas tank was punctured, and the stabilizer trim tab was shot away. A shell exploded in the port blister, wounding the two gunners. Sergeant August Rosnovsky was hit in the face, and Sergeant Fred Bernard was badly injured in the chest and one leg.

Davis set the plane down despite the beating it and its crew were taking. The bleeding Rosnovsky did what he could for Bernard's wounds, then helped Lieutenant Craig, the navigator, pull the B-25 crewmen in through a shattered blister. When all were aboard, Davis opened the throttles and the OA-10A took to the air in disregard of its own damage. The two injured sergeants remained on duty as long as they could. Bernard stayed with his gun until he could no longer stand, and Rosnovsky finally collapsed from loss of blood. Davis headed for the nearest friendly base, Zamboanga, to unload his cargo of survivors and heroes.[11]

On 12 April the 2nd provided ambulance service to Jolo Island. Lieutenant Hutchings, pilot of Playmate 47, made two trips, each time bringing sixteen wounded soldiers back to the hospital at Zamboanga.[12]

The sea took its toll in many ways. On 23 June Playmate 42, with Lieutenant Guess at the controls, took off from Morotai at 0300 to cover a bomber strike on a target in the southern part of Celebes Island. Receiving a message that a B-24 was down, he flew to the position, and found Playmate 41 already on the water, taxiing toward six men on an island beach. The stranded men climbed into two life rafts and paddled out to the plane, and Guess watched them climb aboard. But as Playmate 41 started its takeoff run, it nosed into a swell, and the hull in the navigator's section broke open. Eleven men escaped as the plane sank, but two went with it: the OA-10 navigator and a B-24 crewman. Guess sat Playmate 42 down beside the survivors and took them aboard but, learning from someone else's experience, rode out the heavy seas until they subsided enough for a safe takeoff and a return to base.

Number 82, a favorite aircraft of Flight C, 2nd Emergency Rescue Squadron, warms up for a mission at its base on Middleburg Island in 1944. (L. M. Meyers)

On 2 August Lieutenant Hayes put Playmate 61 down in heavy swells to pick up survivors of a B-24 raid. A lone flier was taken aboard at 1515, then Hayes taxied two miles northeast through rough water to find seven more in five one-man rafts which were tied together. At 1630 he began taxiing farther north, hoping to find water smooth enough for a takeoff. At 1800, smooth water or no, he made the first of four attempts to lift the plane off, but it had taken on too much water while taxiing, and the weight in the bilges was overwhelming. Hayes put his crew to bailing, but the high waves made it futile. He tried a fifth takeoff, however, and this time the plane broke free, but with the bombardier's window smashed, and the radio, radar, and flight instruments damaged and of no use. Nonetheless he found Morotai, landing there at 0145.

The 2nd Emergency Rescue Squadron war diary entry dated 31 August 1945 read: "The war is over. No more sweating out air raids in foxholes, no more missions where enemy fire is probable or expected." It went on to say that only ten rescues had been carried out that month. But those ten brought the squadron's total to 548 men rescued from the time it began operations eleven months before.[13]

The 3rd Emergency Rescue Squadron began operations with the 5th Air Force on 17 September 1944, flying off Biak's Sorido airstrip in New Guinea. The unit's first rescue was the pickup of two navy fliers. "Beginner's luck," the pilot's report read. "Everything went right."

On 13 October Lieutenant Griffith and his OA-10 crew carried out a mission that was fraught with danger from the beginning. Griffith stalled the plane into the sea among jagged coral reefs off the northeast coast of Ceram Island and picked his way close to a shore known to be infested with Japanese. There he waited while four crewmen of a ditched B-24 paddled out to the plane in a life raft. A fifth man tried to swim the distance but was too weak. As he started to drown, Griffith dived off the port wing, swam to the man, and towed him to safety. With all five survivors aboard, Griffith attempted a takeoff, but reefs blocked every stretch of water long enough for a straight run. So he tried the next best thing. Once again picking a course through the reefs, he built up speed and performed one of the most perilous of seaplane maneuvers: a circular takeoff. The thirteenth had been a lucky day for Griffith, his crew, and the B-24 survivors.[14]

That same day the 3rd lost its only crew in a combat operation. An OA-10A pilot, Captain Lew Carnegie, radioed that he was about to attempt a rescue landing. No more messages came through; the plane and crew disappeared.[15]

Biak was home to the 3rd for only a month and a half, during which time a number of rescues were effected. Then on 30 October the ground echelon moved to Dulag, Leyte, to set up a base. A detachment of four OA-10As worked off the tender *Orca* until the shore installation was completed.

It was from this base that a rescue was carried out in a style worthy of the Old West: a shootout between opposing sides. On 12 November Lieutenant Edward Garich set out to retrieve a B-25 crew that had been brought down by enemy fire on Panson Island two days before. The area was known to be a hotbed of Japanese activity, but when Garich saw a signal from shore he put the OA-10A down on the water near the island's northeast tip. Then, as he taxied up the coast to pick up the survivors, three boats containing about sixty Japanese soldiers put out from shore a mile away, squarely between the OA-10A and the B-25 crew. Garich never varied his course. He taxied straight at the boats and, when the OA-10 came within range, the navigator, Lieutenant Marcus Kaufman, opened up on the boats with the twin .30-caliber machine guns in the bow. He blazed away until no enemy soldiers were left alive on the boats; most of them were either blown overboard or jumped to escape the murderous fire. The report of the incident concluded: "(The B-25 crew) came home: the Japs didn't."

On 4 December an OA-10A piloted by Captain George Helmick joined five navy PBYs in saving the crew of the destroyer USS *Cooper*, which had been torpedoed and sunk in Japanese-held Ormoc Bay. He and his men searched all that day but picked up only one man. Although the chances of finding more men seemed hopeless, the next day they returned and continued the search, and about noon were rewarded when Filipino guerrillas signaled that they were protecting several men. Helmick landed, and for four hours the OA-10A rocked in the waves offshore, in constant danger of enemy air attack, until the guerrillas brought the sailors out, thirteen in all. The navy recommended Helmick for the Distinguished Flying Cross; his crew received navy commendations.

Helmick and an all-volunteer crew risked their lives again on 2 January 1945 to lift a P-51 pilot out of Lingayan Gulf, Luzon, then an area of great enemy strength. The rescue had to be undertaken immediately to prevent the pilot's capture, and Helmick planned to fly to the Gulf in predawn darkness, land at first light, and pick up the pilot before the Japanese could see what was happening. But an enemy air attack on his base that night prevented the 0300 takeoff, and he got away at 0700 instead.

The P-51 pilot was found on the beach at 1330, but a landing was suicidal—waves were fourteen-feet high and an unfavorable wind was blowing. About four miles away a sheltered cove offered only ten-foot waves, but anchored there were three Japanese freighters and two barges, all of which opened fire when the plane touched down only 250 yards away. Helmick's gunners returned the fire as the OA-10A taxied toward the P-51 pilot. Helmick moved to within 100 yards of the beach so the pilot could easily reach the plane, running the risk of it striking submerged rocks. Then danger of another sort arose: Small arms fire from the shore began thumping holes in the wings and hull; the radio was shot out, as was the IFF gear. The starboard fuel tank was pierced and gasoline streamed into the fuselage center compartment. The danger of explosion prevented any defensive fire.

As Helmick taxied out to takeoff position, the starboard engine cut out. After some coaxing, it restarted and operated on reduced manifold pressure. The takeoff was made in heavy rolling seas which broke over the wing tip floats and the tail surfaces. Helmick kept the plane mushing through the air at only fifty feet for the entire return trip. He landed at 1630 hours, and learned he had almost been brought down by his own people: with no IFF to identify the plane, he had caused a Red Alert.

During the invasions of Mindoro on 14–16 December 1944 and Luzon on 3–22 January 1945, the 3rd's OA-10As became the first air force planes to land in those areas since 1942. Rescues were only part of their duties: They shuttled messages and supplies to the guerrillas and evacuated escaped prisoners and wounded men; they dropped intelligence men in enemy-held territory, flew Japanese prisoners to headquarters for interrogation and carried out photographic and reconnaissance missions. On one occasion the big amphibians played mother hen, acting as lead navigators for a flight of artillery-spotting L-4s and L-5s enroute to a new base.

At 0800 on 11 February Lieutenant Garbe and crew took off to cover air strikes on Corregidor and the coast of Bataan, orbiting near Limbones Cove with two P-38s for fighter protection. Throughout the morning P-47s and A-20s hammered away, ignoring enemy fire and getting away with it until near noon, when a P-47 pilot's luck ran out. The plane's engine sputtered to a halt, the pilot ditched about two miles off Bataan, and he waited in his rubber raft for either capture or rescue. Capture looked the most likely, for a dozen Japanese Q-boats—small, fast patrol craft—darted out from shore. By this time Garbe had reached the scene and made his landing while the two P-38s blasted the Q-boats. The enemy boat captains made brave runs at the lone pilot, but each time the P-38s drove them off, holing one boat so badly that it sank. Garbe taxied in, his crewmen hauled the pilot aboard, and the OA-10A got away without being hit.

In April one of the 3rd's planes had a run-in with Japanese fighters. Lieutenant Frazer's OA-10A was jumped by two Oscars while covering air strikes on Indo-China. The fight lasted for four minutes. Frazer not only got away, but one of his gunners registered a probable Oscar kill.

On 20 June the 3rd moved to Okinawa and covered 5th Air Force antishipping sweeps between Japan, Korea, and China coast installations. After the war ended, the squadron was one of the first units to occupy Japan, landing at Atsugi air strip outside Yokohama in September along with other elements of the 5th.[16]

As in the Mediterranean, the British were the sole purveyors of air-sea rescue service in the Indian Ocean until the summer of 1944, when a U.S. Air Force detachment was sent to cover 20th Air Force bombing strikes. Two OA-10As arrived in June at 10th Air Force headquarters in Calcutta and were immediately assigned to the RAF's 231 Group, British Primary Command. In a short time, however, the air force operation became a one-man band, conducted by Lieutenant C. J. Graham.

"It was planned that we would have three PBYs and three pilots," Graham wrote in an end-of-tour report. "One fellow, already in India, was to join us, but before we arrived he was placed on B-24s and had finished his missions, so he was no longer available. After we arrived in India, we found that our Canadian-built PBYs had to be beefed up before they could be used. This required a period of about four months, during which time the kid who went over with me turned the one flyable PBY over, killing himself and ten others, and left me with the responsibility of doing the rescue work."

After that Graham flew one OA-10A while the other was being serviced. In two-and-one-half months, he piled up 250 hours. "One Thursday night I took off for an 18-hour mission," Graham said. "When I returned I was on the ground for only an hour when it became necessary to fly a nine-hour mission. I returned from this and was on the ground for five hours before I had to go out on a fourteen-hour flight. When I came back it was Sunday."

Graham worked entirely with B-29s, timing his takeoffs so that he met the big bombers about twenty minutes into their return from the target and then followed them home. For some reason the bombers and the Catalina were not allowed to use the same radio frequency. "Mayday" calls were radioed from the bombers to 231 Group headquarters, then relayed back to the rescue plane. "All this time was wasted when we were only twenty minutes away from the bombers. I know of three crews I could have saved if they had communicated directly with us."

Graham said the B-29 life rafts weren't provided with enough flares and that the men in the rafts didn't know how to use what they had. Air crews especially needed training in signaling techniques and equipment. A man in a dinghy "will fire a Very pistol right square at you

every time, rather than at ninety degrees as he should," he said. "By
doing this [firing at ninety degrees], your attention is attracted to the
trail of smoke. If he shoots it right at you, all you see is a tiny red dot."
Those in a life raft needed all the help they could get. "From 500 feet
a dinghy looks like a spool of thread. There are so many reflections on
the water that it's difficult to distinguish a raft from them. I've seen
sharks and big turtles the same color as a raft; I've circled some for
hours. Even after you see a dinghy on the water it's hard to hold it,
unless it's a perfect day. When we'd find a raft I'd keep my eye on it
while the copilot flew the plane.

"I rescued thirteen men one time because one man out of the thirteen
knew how to use the signal mirror with the little cross on it. That was
the only thing that saved them."

Despite the deficiencies in equipment and the lack of survival training,
a number of airmen were saved by Graham before he returned home.
"I landed one night about one o'clock contrary to orders and was almost
court martialled for doing it to pick up the crew of a B-29 snooper plane.
It had come up from Singapore, run out of gas, and floated for four
days. A B-24 was circling him, as well as two RAF Cats. They told me
not to land on the water at night, but I did, and we pulled twelve living
men and one dead one on board. We had a tough time getting off. The
first try the ship yawed to the right; the wing tip float hit the water and
I had to try again. After a run of about three miles, she picked up, then
hit five times before we got off."

Maintenance on the OA-10As was a nightmare, according to Graham.
"I had to fly 900 miles to get parts," he said. The hydraulic systems went
bad, and the fuel transfer systems were a source of trouble. They were
replaced with ones from a B-25. "We had to tear out every bit of radio
equipment, beef up the bottoms, and put in new equipment. This took
about three months in one plane and two months on another. When we
arrived overseas we found there wasn't one bolt we could replace. It cost
the Army the initial cost of the airplane to modify it."

One source of irritation was even greater than aircraft maintenance:
"We couldn't get our enlisted men promotions because we were a detached outfit," Graham said. "I was a Second Lieutenant for twenty-one
months."

Just before a war-weary and now First Lieutenant Graham was rotated
home—in January 1945—two detachments of the 1st Emergency Squad-
ron arrived in India to become the nucleus of the newly activated 7th
Emergency Rescue Squadron. Equipped with OA-10As, B-17s, L-5s, and
PT-19s, they took over the job Graham had been doing alone in two
Catalinas. "[They] arrived just a year too late," Graham concluded, "for

the CBI had just about folded up as far as air-sea rescue was concerned."[17]

Throughout their tours in the Pacific, the Emergency Rescue Squadrons registered many of the same complaints as Graham. They were frustrated by the weakness in the bottoms of the Canadian-Vickers-built OA-10As (which the company rectified by supplying field modification kits), the unavailability of mechanical and electronic parts for Canadian-built radio and radar equipment, and the time-consuming job of replacing Canadian equipment with American-made gear.

The navy was a continuing source of help. Parts often came from navy stores, and maintenance problems were solved with the aid of navy personnel. Air Force boat crews also took advantage of the navy's generosity to obtain parts, fuel, and oil when they were unavailable through regular channels.

The help was appreciated, but intraservice pride did nothing to ease the pain of asking for it: "Engineering and supply officers had to go to Australia and beg the navy for help," a situation, the 3rd ERS war diarist pointed out, "that was laborious, humiliating, and used needed personnel to effect it." He went on to commend the ground crews "for doing a wonderful job when they had no material to work with."

Although not perfect, the OA-10 continued to be the most commonly used air force rescue aircraft in the Pacific. Small numbers of B-17s came into use in the spring of 1945, these carrying parachute-dropped, twenty-seven-foot boats that could support twelve people for five weeks and had a range of five hundred miles at eight knots. Helicopters, used mainly for overland rescues and evacuations, were shipped in during the last months of the war.

And the OA-10s continued to come. In the Central Pacific the navy handled all air-sea rescue services until 6 February 1945, when the air force's 4th Emergency Rescue Squadron landed at Peleliu in the Palau Group with fourteen OA-10As and eleven B-17s to cover strikes against Japan. In July detachments of the 3rd and 4th Emergency Rescue Squadrons were sent to Saipan and Iwo Jima to extend the coverage even farther. The 6th Emergency Rescue Squadron also began operations in the Central Pacific in 1945.

During the last few months of the war air-sea rescue procedures in the Pacific were honed to a keen edge, as a result of better coordination between the air force and navy. One of the earliest and best examples of interservice cooperation followed a strike on Balikpapan, Borneo, on 10 October 1944, in which a large number of planes of the 5th and 13th

Air Forces were involved. To cover an operation of such magnitude, a central rescue control was established to assemble intelligence on enemy fighter strength, weather conditions, and other factors. From this data decisions were reached concerning the number of planes needed for rescue and fighter cover, where they should be stationed, and what the duties would be for air force and navy rescue units.

A method called a "rescue line" was originated for the operation. The rescue line consisted of seven OA-10As of the 2nd ERS, several navy PBYs, and one submarine from the 7th Fleet. Two OA-10As were assigned to the forward area, two to the rear, and three were held on call as ready planes. The submarine was stationed fifteen miles off Balik-papan. OA-10A and PBY pilots received detailed instructions regarding coded radio contact with the sub so as not to give away its location to the enemy.

The system worked: All of the airmen who reached water beyond the target area alive were rescued, as were most of those near it. In total, forty men were rescued, twenty-four by plane and sixteen by submarine.

The central control center concept worked so well for the Balikpapan mission that a similar center was set up on Iwo Jima to coordinate rescue efforts for raids on Japan. While ostensibly a navy responsibility, the center was manned and equipped almost entirely by the air force.

Submarines were used in rescue service until the end of the war. A great effort was always made to keep a sub's location a secret, so that enemy fighters and coastal artillery could not hit it. When the potential loss of a sub was weighed against the loss of an air crew, the balance always tipped in favor of the sub. One technique, however, minimized the possibility of giving away a sub's position while maximizing its life-saving potential. If an airman was found close to shore but still at a submersible depth, the submarine would ease in and raise its periscope. The airman would tie his life raft to it. Then the submarine would tow him out to sea where it could safely surface and take him aboard.

Another cooperative effort between the air force and navy followed the raids on Truk in April 1944. A "lifeguard" sub was part of the equipment, and was credited with saving twenty-two men.

Sometimes the presence of a submarine benefited the rescuers as well as the rescued. On 29 May 1945 an OA-10A of the 4th ERS was on station directly over a lifeguard sub, both providing cover for a B-29 bombing raid on Japan. A B-29 was reported ditching, and the OA-10A flew to the location, landed, and picked up the crew. But on takeoff the OA-10A slammed into three huge swells. The port engine was wrenched from its mount and crashed into the cockpit, severely injuring the pilot. The copilot called in the sub, which took the survivors of both planes aboard. The pilot, who died during the night, was buried at sea, but the remaining survivors were put ashore on Iwo Jima the next morning.

From November 1944 until 14 August 1945 the 21st Bomber Command lost 361 B-29s and 3,125 crewmen in attacks against Japan. Of the crewmen, 1,424 were known to have gone down at sea. Of these, air force and navy units rescued 687 men, only 22.1 percent of the total number lost, but 48.2 percent—almost half—of those who ditched.

Air Force rescue teams operated OA-10As in areas of the world other than the major battle areas. Two planes flew search missions for the Air Transport Command's Caribbean Division at Morrison Field, West Palm Beach, Florida. By the end of the war OA-10As were stationed at widely scattered points in the South Atlantic: at Belem, Brazil; Fernando De Noronha Island off the Brazilian coast; Ascencion Island, halfway between South America and Africa. Two OA-10As were assigned to the Alaska Wing Search and Rescue Squadron of the Air Transport Command in December 1944. OA-10As were also a part of rescue efforts in Greenland, where some open-sea landings were made. Many of the searches in Greenland, however, were over the icecap, where melt-water lakes provided landing areas for rescue planes.

The records of some of the air force's emergency rescue squadrons are no longer available, making it impossible to compile a complete count of the lives saved by all squadrons in all theaters. The count would at least run to several thousand; the 5th Air Force's ERS squadrons alone accounted for more than sixteen hundred men. Many men lived and fought again only because of the efforts of ERS pilots and crews. The job might not have been glamorous, but no wartime task was more immediately gratifying than that of pulling cold, wet, dehydrated, sunburned, and sometimes injured men in through the blisters to safety. These sentences from the mission statement of the 1st Emergency Rescue Squadron say it well:

> The purpose of this organization is to accompany fighter and bomber squadrons, effecting immediate rescues of their crews whose misfortune may lie in being set adrift on the open sea. It is no small comfort to be assured that hovering on the edge of the battle is a friendly formation waiting expectantly to pull one out of the drink should one be so ill fated in combat. Once the ship has been abandoned, the location accurately plotted, and a PBY launched on its mission, the hope of survival is made almost a certainty. This gives the airman an additional measure of confidence so vital to mental composure, for no man is unafraid.

And while the rescued felt gratitude toward the rescuers, they also were grateful for the machine that carried them to safety. One airman, plucked from the Mediterranean, spoke for every downed airman in any body of water when he said, through chattering teeth, "Thank God for the PBY."[18]

16

Catalinas and Cansos
with the Allies

GREAT BRITAIN

Early in 1939 it became apparent that Great Britain's deep-chested Saro Lerwick, a twin-engine flying boat that looked remarkably like a cutdown version of the four-engine Short Sunderland, had a number of problems and would not be ready for patrol service on the appointed date. With the Nazi menace looming ever larger across the Channel, the Air Ministry thought it best to buy some insurance. A purchasing commission journeyed to the United States to obtain patrol aircraft to fill the Lerwick void. For training and medium-range reconnaissance work, the commission selected a land-based aircraft, the Lockheed Hudson. Commission members were invited to visit Consolidated's plant in San Diego where they might consider the PBY for the same role. They were told that a landing gear was being incorporated which would allow the big flying boat to become a dual purpose aircraft.

The commission was not impressed, however. Its members saw little merit in amphibians. Neither did they feel that the PBY's flight characteristics were up to Royal Air Force standards, nor did its limited armament and archaic gun positions indicate a long life in combat. They much preferred the multiple guns and power turrets of the Sunderlands, whose long-range patrols brought them into frequent contact with the enemy. But a long-range flying boat was needed to stand in for the Lerwick until it became operational, and range was a PBY strong point. Despite its other deficiencies, a Consolidated Model 28-5, the civilian version of a PBY-4, was ordered. In July it proved its range by flying across the Atlantic to Felixstowe, England, for evaluation. Unarmed but painted in British prewar Coastal Command colors and markings, the Model 28-5 was the first of many to make the transatlantic flight. For flight testing and the ferry flight across the Atlantic, the CAA licensed the plane as N P9630. The British dropped the "N" and retained the "P9630," a designation that was kept throughout its service life.

The test pilots at Felixstowe, in contrast to the members of the purchasing commission, were enthusiastic about P9630. Apparently other evaluators there felt the same way: An order for thirty-seven flying boats was placed with Consolidated in November 1940. The British, with their penchant for alliterative names (Short Sunderland; Supermarine Spitfire; Hawker Hurricane), accepted a suggestion made by Reuben Fleet: The plane was called the Consolidated Catalina. The name was adopted by the U.S. Navy and Air Force and all of the Allies except Canada.[1]

Counting planes ordered in 1941 and those delivered under Lend Lease, 578 Catalinas of various marks were delivered to Great Britain by the end of the war. Twenty RAF squadrons were equipped with Catalinas, some for short periods until the supply of Sunderlands could catch up, others for the duration. Two of the squadrons were manned by Canadians, two by Norwegians, and one by Dutchmen.

The British never accepted the idea that a flying boat should carry its own beaching gear: Only twelve Catalinas delivered were amphibians, these used mostly in ferry service between Canada and the United Kingdom.[2] Neither did they improve the armament. A single Vickers .303-caliber machine gun was mounted in the bow and another in the tunnel hatch, but in the blisters they were mounted in pairs.[3] The most that was done to offset the light armament was to assign the Catalinas long-range patrols far out at sea where there was little chance of confrontation with the enemy. As a result the sun rarely set on the British Catalinas: The squadrons operated from the Atlantic to the Indian Oceans; from northern Russia to the Cape of Good Hope. Patrols where combat was likely were given to the Sunderlands and Hudsons.[4]

The first Catalinas were delivered to No. 240 Squadron at Stranraer, on Scotland's southwest coast, on 5 March 1941. Others in the aircraft order were delivered to Manila where they were picked up by No. 205 Squadron, then based in Singapore.

The first Catalina to be fired on in anger was WQ-Z of No. 209 Squadron. Pilot Officer Dennis Briggs was in charge, but his copilot was an American naval officer, Ensign Leonard Smith, one of seventeen U.S. Navy pilots sent to England in secret to give British pilots on-the-job training in handling the aircraft. The date was 26 May 1941; they had been in the air over seven hours searching for the German battleship *Bismarck,* which had sunk the British battle cruiser HMS *Hood* and heavily damaged the new battleship HMS *Prince of Wales* two days before, then slipped away from its pursuers in the fog. WQ-Z was one of five Catalinas that had been a part of the search at various times in the past twenty-

An RAF Coastal Command Catalina I flies over the North Atlantic on a rare sunshiny day. (United Technologies Archives via William Scarborough)

four hours and was one of two sent to patrol some five hundred miles out in the Atlantic almost due west of Land's End.

At 1030 that morning, flying through clouds and haze at 500 feet on autopilot, Smith, who was in the left-hand seat, suddenly asked, "What the devil's that?" Briggs stared down at a huge black shape below and answered, "It looks like a battleship."

Briggs scrambled out of the right seat and into the radio compartment to get off a position report; Smith disengaged the automatic pilot and circled through the clouds, taking the plane up to 1,500 feet. He had hoped to come in astern for another look, but he misjudged the battleship's speed or the Catalina's drift, and he broke out of the clouds directly over the ship.

The *Bismarck* erupted in countless winking flames, and black puffs thunderclapped around the flying boat. Shell fragments popped holes and dented the aluminum skin. The pilots threw the Catalina into a series of violent evasive maneuvers. Below the battleship did likewise, its captain apparently thinking it was about to be bombed. No one aboard the Catalina was hit in the brief encounter, but a shell fragment ripped through the floor between Briggs and Smith while they were changing seats. The only casualties were in the galley, where a crewman dropped two china plates and broke them.

By the time the Catalina was out of antiaircraft range, contact with the battleship was lost, but planes from the carrier HMS *Ark Royal* found it again an hour later. Swordfish torpedo planes attacked at 1950 that evening, damaging the *Bismarck*'s steering gear and slowing the ship considerably. Just before midnight a Catalina of No. 210 Squadron, piloted by Flight Lieutenant Hatfield, found the ship and shadowed it until 0300, when dwindling fuel forced him to break off and return to base. Another Catalina, flown by Pilot Officer Goolden of No. 240 Squadron, also found the ship that morning and shadowed it for four hours.

During the night the British Home Fleet moved into position, and at 0847 on 27 May its battleships and cruisers opened up with their heavy guns on the *Bismarck*. By 1010 she was reduced to a burning silent hulk. At 1015 the cruiser HMS *Dorsetshire* fired torpedoes into the wreck. Then scuttling charges planted by her crew exploded. At 1040 the pride of the German navy capsized and sank, taking all but four officers and 110 enlisted men of her 2,300-man crew with her.[5]

At one time or another during the war, eight Catalina-equipped RAF squadrons plied the northern convoy and ferry routes from the North Atlantic west of Iceland through the North Sea, the Norwegian Sea, the Barents Sea, and the White Sea to Archangel in the Soviet Union.

No. 209 Squadron was one of the first to do so, equipped with biplane Stranraer flying boats and flying from Stranraer. That same year, 1939, the squadron was both blessed and cursed with a change of aircraft. It was given P9630, the Model 28-5, following its evaluation at Felixstowe, and the plane was put into courier service. In December No. 209 Squadron became the first squadron to receive the Saro Lerwick. Despite groundings and various mishaps with the Lerwicks, the squadron managed to fly a number of antisubmarine missions during most of 1940, but in November began converting to Catalinas. In August 1941 the squadron moved to Iceland, and by the end of the month had made two attacks on U-boats, one resulting in a confirmed sinking. Two more attacks were made before the squadron returned to the United Kingdom in October.[6]

No. 210 Squadron began flying convoy patrols in Sunderlands, but in April 1941 it converted to Catalinas for long-range operations. In June the squadron instituted antisubmarine patrols out of Iceland. Although several attacks were made, no sinkings were reported. In early 1942 the squadron moved to Sullom Voe in the Shetland Islands northwest of Scotland to escort convoys bound for Russia. The area was a beehive of U-boat activity, and many attacks were mounted. One U-boat was sunk by Flight Sergeant Simmons.

In January 1944 No. 190 Squadron was renumbered 210, the original squadron having been deactivated after service in the Bay of Biscay in

1943. U-boat hunting and convoy escorting resumed from Sullom Voe. On 25 February Squadron Leader French began a convoy-escort mission but was never able to find the ships. Instead he found the U-601 and sank it. In May 1944 two more U-boats were sent to the bottom.

In July another pair of submarines was sunk, the squadron's sixth and seventh kills. The sinking of U-347 by Flight Officer Cruickshank earned him the Victoria Cross, Britain's highest award for valor. On his first run over the U-boat his depth charges would not release. Braving heavy antiaircraft fire, he made a second pass, this time getting a perfect straddle, and U-347 was finished. It was a costly effort: Cruickshank was badly wounded and his navigator killed. Despite periods of unconsciousness, Cruickshank remained in control of the Catalina on the five-and-one-half-hour flight back to base and helped his inexperienced copilot land and moor the plane. At the hospital doctors treated him for seventy-two wounds.

Pilots of No. 240 Squadron at Stranraer began operations in March 1941 with Catalinas. One of the first missions was an unsuccessful search for the German battle cruiser *Scharnhorst*. The squadron mounted attacks on U-boats while flying convoy escorts across the North Atlantic, and one Catalina fought off a Focke-Wulf Fw.200 patrol bomber before the squadron transferred to India.

The first of the Norwegian-manned squadrons, No. 330, operated out of Reykjavik in Iceland, its Northrop seaplanes supplemented in June 1942 with a pair of Catalina IIIs. Both were involved in shootouts with Fw.200s and U-boat attacks. No. 333 Squadron, also manned by Norwegians, was equipped with Mosquitos and Catalinas and flew antisubmarine patrols over the North Sea and the Norwegian coastline. The Catalinas were used to maintain contact with the underground in Norway. Later they were stationed in the Shetlands, where they flew special missions to Grasnaya in northern Russia.

No. 202 Squadron, which had been stationed at Gibraltar and had patrolled the Mediterranean since the Spanish Civil War, began collecting its Catalinas in England in April 1941. The planes arrived at Gibraltar in May and the following month began to see action, attacking three U-boats. One of these was sunk by a destroyer which had been called to the scene. In May 1942 Flight Lieutenant Bradley's Catalina was attacked by Dewoitine D.520 fighters of the Vichy French forces and was shot down in the Mediterranean. Bradley and crew were rescued by a destroyer.

The squadron flew cover for the Allied fleets during the invasion of North Africa in November 1942, joined by a large detachment of Catalinas from No. 210 Squadron, then based at Pembroke Dock, South

A Catalina I of No. 202 Squadron, stationed at Gibraltar, flies past the rock. (Courtesy the Trustees of the Imperial War Museum)

Wales. Three of No. 202's Catalinas were lost, one of them shot down by a "friendly" convoy. No. 210 lost one.

U-boat action picked up in February 1943. No. 202 Squadron pilots made six attacks during the month, with Flight Lieutenant Sheardown scoring a kill. The squadron reported few sightings the next year, but in February 1944 Flight Lieutenant Finch spotted a U-boat and mounted an attack with no discernable results. Later in the month he found another and, sharing the attack with a U.S. Navy PBY, sent it to the bottom. The squadron squeezed in one more attack before returning to the United Kingdom in September 1944.

In the meantime, No. 210 Squadron experimented with Leigh Lights mounted on their Catalinas, conducting night submarine searches from their base at Pembroke Dock. Flight Lieutenant Martin made an unsuccessful lighted U-boat attack on 10 March 1943. The squadron's main activity was daylight antisubmarine patrols over the Bay of Biscay. Seven submarines were sighted during the squadron's tour, two of which were attacked and severely damaged. The cost: one Catalina shot down and another lost in a fatal crash.

In the Far East, No. 205 Squadron picked up its Catalinas at Manila in March 1941 and returned them to base at Singapore, where they replaced four-engined, biplane Short Singapore IIIs. A detachment of

Catalinas was sent to Koggala at the southern tip of Ceylon. Bases were set up between there and Singapore. On 6 December the squadron lost its first aircraft to enemy action. It was shot down by a Zero while searching for a Japanese fleet in the Gulf of Siam. Undaunted, the squadron flew daily antishipping patrols, these bringing frequent contact with the enemy and costing more Catalinas.

By 1 January 1942 No. 205 Squadron had five Catalinas remaining. These were not safe on land or water. Their base at Singapore was subject to frequent bombing attacks. By mid-month it was no longer safe for the planes to return directly from their reconnaissance and bombing missions. Instead they landed at waiting areas, being called in for servicing when the all-clear sounded. Another Catalina was lost that month, and the remaining four flew to Sumatra and then to Java in the Dutch East Indies. From there they flew patrols over Sunda Strait and West Borneo, where they lost two more planes. On 3 March the last two Catalinas escaped to Broome, on Australia's northwest coast, only to be destroyed in an air raid later that month.

The squadron was revived again in July 1942 at Koggala and equipped with planes pulled from other squadrons. For the remainder of the war No. 205 flew antishipping patrols, air-sea rescue, and anti-invasion missions, and carried mail.

One of the first full squadrons assigned to the Indian subcontinent was No. 240 Squadron, which had previously flown missions in the North Atlantic. The flight to India saw action: Flight Officer Godber dropped depth charges on a U-boat as he crossed the Mediterranean. The squadron commenced flying antishipping and antisubmarine patrols over the Indian Ocean from its base at Red Hills Lake on 1 August 1942.

In October 1942 No. 212 Squadron was formed at Korangi Creek on India's west coast and equipped with Catalinas. No. 191 Squadron formed there in May 1943. Late in the war No. 357 Squadron, a special-duties unit equipped with Liberators, Hudsons, and Catalinas, operated out of Red Hills Lake, flying mainly to Burma and Malaya where they picked up and dropped off subversive agents. The Catalina section became a squadron in its own right near the end of the war—No. 628 Squadron—and flew meteorological and air-sea rescue missions.

For the most part, duty for the Indian Ocean squadrons was a series of long, dull, hot, unrewarding antishipping and antisubmarine patrols, with the monotony broken only by an occasional attack on an enemy ship or submarine or by an air-sea rescue mission. On 23 January 1944 Flight Lieutenant Groves of No. 240 Squadron found a submarine lurking near a convoy he was escorting and depth-charged it, producing a large oil slick. On 16 August Squadron Leader Robinson attacked a Japanese tanker, taking hits on his Catalina in return. Also in 1944 two

Ground crewmen and native helpers strain at the tow rope as they haul a No. 240 Squadron Catalina onto the beach at Red Hills Lake. (Courtesy the Trustees of the Imperial War Museum)

submarines were sighted by crews of No. 212 Squadron. The first crash-dived and escaped; the second was depth-charged but left no evidence of a hit.

In 1945 No. 240 Squadron joined No. 628 in flying agents in and out of Burma and Malaya and making weather and survey flights. No. 212 freighted supplies to guerrillas in enemy-held territories and provided air-sea rescue service for U.S. 20th Air Force B-29s returning from bombing missions over Singapore.

The squadrons in India had no corner on long, dull patrols; those stationed along the African coasts could claim only slightly more activity. No. 270 Squadron, based at Jui in Sierra Leone, covered the west coast south from the Canary Islands. Nos. 209, 259, 262, and 265 covered the east coast from the Cape of Good Hope north to the Gulf of Aden. No.

209 Squadron was the first to begin operations. The others arrived from late 1942 to early 1943.

No. 209 established a base at Kipevu, Kenya, in July 1942, afterward setting up a series of stations along the coast, with its pilots flying anti-submarine patrols enroute to and from the bases. Later the squadron became a conversion unit for new Catalina squadrons forming in Africa.

No. 270 broke the monotony of convoy-escort duty and antisubmarine searches with air-sea rescues and hunts for blockade runners heading for Vichy French ports. In its nearly two-year stay, it attacked only two submarines, with no reported sinkings.

The east coast squadrons fared somewhat better in dispatching submarines. On 20 August 1943 Flight Lieutenant Barnett, flying with No. 259 Squadron out of St. Lucia northwest of Durban, South Africa, found a U-boat on the surface and dropped depth charges, damaging it to the point where it could not submerge. Barnett continued to circle, harassing it with sporadic strafing attacks, until a No. 265 Squadron Catalina flown by Flight Officer Robin moved in, dropped more depth charges on the U-boat, and sank it.

The U-boats did not take such attacks lightly. On 19 May Flight Lieutenant Grant from No. 262 Squadron bore down on a U-boat and released his depth charges, but the U-boat's guns sent him home on one engine.

As the war wound down, the Catalina squadrons saw no more submarines. No. 262 Squadron was given over to the Union of South Africa, becoming in February 1945 No. 35 Squadron of the SAAF. No. 265 Squadron added freight hauling to its list of duties, then disbanded in April 1945. No. 270 disbanded in July. No. 259 Squadron converted to Sunderlands in early 1945, as did No. 209.

CANADA

In the fall of 1939 the Royal Canadian Air Force began to look for a successor to its Supermarine Stranraer flying boats. In December the RCAF announced the successor: the Consolidated PBY. The name "Convoy" was selected for the aircraft, but, as it was easily confused with ship convoys, it was discarded in favor of "Canso," after the Strait of Canso between Cape Breton Island and the mainland of Nova Scotia. No PBYs by any name could be obtained, however, because the U.S. Navy and the RAF had contracted for all the flying boats Consolidated could produce. In May 1940 negotiations were begun that would allow Canada to build its own PBYs.

In September 1940 the Boeing Canada Company in Vancouver, British Columbia, received the first contract, this for fifty-five PBY-5As assembled from parts made by Consolidated. In early 1941 the Canadian

Vickers plant at Montreal began tooling up for PBY production. Boeing produced its first Canso A (PBY-5A) on 27 July 1942; Canadian Vickers's first roll-out came on 3 April 1943. When the last Canso was completed— on 19 May 1945 at a new Canadian Vickers plant built in 1943 in Cartierville, Quebec—the two plants had built 731 planes, 362 by Boeing of Canada, 369 by Canadian Vickers. Boeing's Cansos were manufactured under the designation PB2B-1, the equivalent of a PBY-5 flying boat, and PB2B-2, a nonamphibious version of the high-tailed PBY-6A.

Most were built for Lend Lease, many going to the RAF, others to the Royal Australian Air Force and the Royal New Zealand Air Force. Two-hundred-thirty planes produced by Canadian Vickers went to the U.S. Air Force as OA-10s and OA-10As; the remainder went to the RCAF as Cansos and Canso As.[7]

The RCAF received its first new patrol bombers when U-boats began attacking ships in the western North Atlantic in the spring of 1941. The RAF then thought it expedient to release nine Catalinas from Bermuda for service with No. 116 Squadron at Dartmouth, Nova Scotia. Others would follow in large and small batches from U.S. and Canadian plants. By war's end, 274 would see service with thirteen squadrons of the RCAF, five on the West Coast, five on the East, and three with the RAF Coastal Command.

Employees mate the wing to the hull of a Canso A in the Canadian Vickers plant at Cartierville, Ontario. (K. M. Molson)

West Coast squadrons No. 4, 6, 7, 9, and 120, equipped with Cansos during the last two years of the war, flew antisubmarine patrols and carried out search and rescue work. One enemy submarine was attacked.

On the East Coast, squadrons No. 116, 5, 162, 117, and 161 received Cansos during the first two years. Their antisubmarine patrols accounted for twenty-five of the eighty-four attacks on U-boats made by Eastern Air Command planes of all types, the eighty-four attacks resulting in seventeen kills.[8]

Of the three RCAF squadrons attached to the RAF, No. 422 was shortlived as a Canso-equipped unit. First based at Lough Erne, Ireland, in April 1941, it was equipped with Saro Lerwicks, which were quickly replaced by Cansos. Its pilots flew convoy patrols to Soviet ports and delivered Hawker Hurricane parts into Grasnaya. In September the squadron changed planes once more, this time into Sunderlands.

No. 413 Squadron flew Cansos its entire service life. The squadron began existence in 1941 at Stranraer, Scotland, coincidentally on Canada's Dominion Day, 1 July. After three months of training, the unit transferred to Sullom Voe and for five months flew northeast Atlantic convoy and antisubmarine patrols.

When Japan entered the war and the British Empire crumbled in the Far East, No. 413 was sent to India to shore up its defenses. On 2 April 1942 operations began out of Koggala with a reconnaissance mission flown over the Bay of Bengal and the Indian Ocean, the first of several searches for a Japanese fleet believed to be preparing a strike on the island. Two days later, Squadron Leader L. J. Birchall found what they had been looking for. Radio operators at Koggala heard the Canso's operator tap out the position, course, and speed of a large enemy force, then in mid-transmission the signal stopped.

Birchall was hailed as "the Savior of Ceylon." Thanks to his warning, the defenses were ready and the Japanese attack was beaten off. He was awarded the Distinguished Flying Cross, it was thought posthumously, but many months later it was learned that his plane had been shot down near the ships he was reporting. He and his entire crew had been captured and were held prisoner for the next three years.

Four days after Birchall's disappearance, Flight Lieutenant R. Thomas, holder of a Distinguished Flying Cross awarded for action with the RAF, reported a Japanese naval force heading for Colombo on Ceylon. Like Birchall, his radio message ended in mid-sentence, but he and his crew were never heard from again. Nonetheless his warning came in time, and the enemy attack on the naval base at Trincomalee the following day was thwarted by British fighter planes and coastal artillery. After two resounding defeats the Japanese backed off. For the

Working under a blazing sun, ground crewmen of No. 413 "Tusker" Squadron pull maintenance on the empennage of a Canso at the squadron's base at Koggala, Ceylon, in 1942. (Canadian Forces Photographic Unit)

next several days No. 413 Cansos searched but found no trace of the fleet.

From that time on life for No. 413 settled into a routine of convoy escorts and antisubmarine patrols, broken only by a 2,000-mile bombing and reconnaissance mission to investigate Japanese activities in Northern Sumatra. Freight service was begun between Ceylon and Australia, a twenty-three-and-one-half-hour flight outbound, two hours longer on the return.

As the war progressed, the squadron became fragmented, with detachments at Addu Atoll five hundred miles south of Ceylon, Diego Garcia in the middle of the Indian Ocean, the Seychelles off the African coast, Aden, the Persian Gulf, Kenya, Natal, and South Africa. Some crews were five thousand miles from home base in Koggala, and the squadron boasted that it was the most widely dispersed unit in the world.

In 1944, its third year in Ceylon, No. 413 received its official badge from King George VI. It was an elephant's head on a maple leaf background and from it came the nickname, "Tusker Squadron." Patrols and rescue work continued until December of that year, when the squadron was placed on nonoperational status, and its Cansos and some of its crews transferred to RAF squadrons.

No. 162 Squadron came into existence quietly enough in April 1942 at Yarmouth, Nova Scotia, and the uneventful antisubmarine sweeps that began the following month gave no hint of the whirlwind it would reap two years hence. In November 1943, because of an absence of U-boats along the East Coast, Eastern Air Command recommended that No. 162 be offered to RAF Coastal Command for operations out of Iceland. The recommendation was approved on 7 December 1943.

The squadron was hardly bedded down when the action began to break. On 22 February Flight Officer C. C. Cunningham and his crew attacked and scored two hits on a U-boat. On 17 April Flight Officer T. C. Cooke, on a weather reconnaissance flight, saw a submarine wake about six miles ahead of his Canso. He homed in out of the sun, but the U-boat crew spotted him and sent up a barrage. Cooke veered away, then bored in for a beam attack, the new twin-mount Vickers guns in the bow chipping paint off the U-boat's conning tower. As the Canso passed over the submarine Cooke released his depth charges, getting a good straddle. The U-boat emerged from the plumes, but seemed to be settling in the water. Nine minutes after the attack the U-boat was about to submerge when a violent explosion forward of the conning tower blew it apart, and it sank almost at once. Both Cunningham and Cooke were awarded the Distinguished Flying Cross.

The month of June would be the greatest in the squadron's history. At 0211 hours on 3 June Flight Lieutenant R. E. McBride, operating out of Wick, Scotland, dropped four depth charges on a submarine, blowing it out of the water and swinging it to port. All forward movement ceased, and it sank on an even keel, leaving five survivors in the water.

On 11 June Flight Officer L. Sherman sighted a surfaced U-boat at 1550 hours. The four depth charges he dropped buried the submarine under the plumes, but it emerged, circling slowly and trailing oil. A few minutes later it sank, leaving thirty-five survivors adrift.

Two days later Wing Commander G.W.C. Chapman located a U-boat and carried out a standard four-depth-charge attack. After the explosions the U-boat travelled about four hundred yards, then went down by the bow, her stern high in the air. Many of her crew were seen in the water. The story was not over, however. Somehow the conning tower resurfaced; a crewman ran to the antiaircraft guns and scored several hits on the Canso as it made a photo pass overhead. Oil and black smoke belched from the Canso's port engine; it was shut down but the propeller refused to feather. Despite full boost to the starboard engine, altitude could not be maintained, and the plane hit the sea hard and sank. The

Last moments of a U-boat: Flight Officer T. C. Cooke's depth charges straddle a submarine on 17 April 1944. Nine minutes later the submarine exploded forward of the conning tower and sank. (Canadian Forces Photographic Unit)

crew, having escaped into two dinghies, was rescued by surface craft after two unsuccessful attempts to air-drop lifeboats and life rafts to them.

That same day Flight Officer Sherman reported the location of a U-boat, but no more messages were received and the Canso failed to return to base.

On 24 June Flight Lieutenant David Hornell began a mission that would end in heroic tragedy and for which he would posthumously be awarded the Victoria Cross. The citation tells the story:

Flight Lieutenant Hornell was captain and first pilot of a twin-engine amphibian aircraft engaged on anti-submarine patrol in northern waters.

Flight Lieutenant David Hornell and the crew of his Canso before their Nissan hut in Iceland. Front row: Fernand St. Laurent, Donald Scott, Flying Officer Graham Campbell, I. J. Bodnoff. Back row: Flying Officer F. W. Lawrence, Flying Officer S. E. Matheson, Hornell, Squadron Leader W. F. Poag. (Canadian Forces Photographic Unit)

The patrol had lasted for some hours when a fully surfaced U-boat was sighted travelling at high speed on the port beam. Flight Lieutenant Hornell at once turned into the attack.

The U-boat altered course. The aircraft had been seen and there could be no surprise. The U-boat opened up with antiaircraft fire which became increasingly fierce and accurate. At a range of 1,200 yards the front guns of the aircraft replied. Then its starboard gun jammed, leaving only one gun effective. Hits were obtained on and around the conning tower of the U-boat but then the aircraft itself was hit, two large holes appearing in the starboard wing.

Ignoring the enemy fire, Hornell carefully maneuvered for the attack. Oil was pouring from his starboard engine which was by this time on fire as was the starboard wing, and the petrol tanks were in danger. Meanwhile the aircraft was hit again and again by the U-boat guns. Holed in many places, it was vibrating violently and was very difficult to control. Nevertheless the captain decided to press home his attack, knowing that every moment the chances for escape for him and his gallant crew would grow more slender.

He brought his aircraft down very low and released his depth charges in a perfect straddle. The bow of the U-boat lifted out of the water. It sank and its crew were seen in the sea. Flight Lieutenant Hornell contrived by superhuman effort at the controls to gain a little height. The fire in the starboard wing had grown more intense and the vibration increased. Then the burning engine fell off.

The plight of the aircraft and crew was now desperate. With utmost coolness the captain took his aircraft into the wind and despite the manifold dangers brought it safely down in a heavy squall. Badly damaged and blazing furiously, the aircraft rapidly settled. After the ordeal by fire came the ordeal by water. There was only one serviceable dinghy and this could not hold all the crew. They took turns in the water holding onto the sides.

Once the dinghy capsized in the rough seas and was righted only with great difficulty. Two of the crew succumbed from exposure. An airborne lifeboat was dropped to them but fell some 500 yards downwind. The men struggled vainly to reach it and Hornell, who throughout had encouraged them with his cheerfulness and inspiring leadership proposed to swim to it though he was nearly exhausted. He was, with difficulty, restrained.

The survivors were finally rescued after they had been in the water for

Canso crews of No. 162 Squadron in Iceland found little use for the bombardier's window as originally conceived. They found it served a much better purpose in clearing U-boat decks of crewmen when fitted with four additional Vickers .303-caliber machine guns. (Canadian Forces Photographic Unit)

twenty-one hours. By this time Flight Lieutenant Hornell was blinded and completely exhausted. He died shortly after being picked up.

On 30 June another U-boat was attacked and sunk with the help of a Liberator. The month's work prompted a letter from Sir Sholto Douglas of the RAF Coastal Command: "I would like to express to you my appreciation of the fine work that No. 162 squadron has been doing since the beginning of June. In 750 flying hours they have attacked and sunk no less than four U-boats out of a total of five sighted. This is really a magnificent effort and shows a very fine standard of efficiency."

Another U-boat was attacked by a No. 162 Canso in August, but it escaped, damaged, into a fog bank. The last U-boat sighting was on 11 May 1945. The U-boat was flying the black flag of surrender, and Flight Officer R. L. Clarke called in surface units to accept it.

No. 162 Squadron was disbanded on 7 August 1945, after compiling an outstanding record in antisubmarine warfare.[9]

17

More Catalinas with the Allies

AUSTRALIA

On 8 December 1941 the Catalinas of the Royal Australian Air Force faced a situation similar to that faced by the PBYs of the U.S. Navy's Patrol Wing 10. They were few in number, had vast areas of the Pacific to patrol without benefit of fighter escort, and were pressed into all sorts of service beyond their original reconnaissance mission. They became day and night bombers; they ferried intelligence personnel and supplies; they carried out air-sea rescues and evacuations. Many were lost in action against the advancing Japanese, but they persevered, performing invaluable service to the Allies in stemming the enemy tide. As the number of planes increased, RAAF Catalina crews undertook a series of operations not flown by PBYs in any other theater: About mid-war they began mining enemy harbors from the air, bottling in ships while keeping others out, sinking many, all of which disrupted the flow of oil and other vital raw materials to Japan.[1]

Until the outbreak of war in Europe Australia had no patrol squadrons. Its first, No. 11 Squadron, was organized in 1939 and sent to Port Moresby on New Guinea for reconnaissance duty. The squadron was equipped with two four-engine Empire-Class flying boats and two single-engine Seagull amphibians. The big boats were taken over from Qantas Empire Airways by the RAAF; almost half of No. 11's crews came from the same source.

Great Britain was to supply Sunderlands to fill out the complement, but not enough were available even for the RAF's needs. The Australians then looked to the United States as a source of supply, where a year earlier they had obtained fifty Lockheed Hudsons. The search was successful: In June 1940 the Australian War Cabinet ordered seven PBY-5s, and in September ordered eleven more. The United States was not yet at war, and in order to avoid a further strain on relations with Japan, Consolidated crews flew the planes to Honolulu, where civilian Qantas crews took over and ferried them the rest of the way to Australia. The first ferry flight, in January 1941, was only the third flight ever made across the South Pacific from the United States to Australia.

After a training course at Rathmines in New South Wales, the first Catalina crews and planes were sent to Port Moresby on 30 April 1941. A second squadron, No. 20, was spun off from No. 11 in August. The two units flew shipping searches and base-reinforcing missions from Port Moresby to Vila in the New Hebrides, Noumea on New Caledonia, Kavieng on New Ireland, Tulagi in the Solomons, Rabaul on New Britain, and Buka off the northern tip of Bougainville.

When Japan attacked Pearl Harbor and the Philippines and began to roll south down the Asian mainland and through the islands, the RAAF patrol squadrons increased their surveillance flights. On 16 January 1942 they flew their first bombing mission, this to destroy enemy ships in Truk lagoon. The mission was reminiscent of the U.S. Navy's PBY bombing raid on Jolo. Six Catalinas took off from Port Moresby. One crashed on takeoff after a refueling stop at Kavieng, and a second stayed behind to render aid. Three of the remaining four failed to find the target, but the fourth delivered sixteen 250-pound bombs as scheduled. Results, however, could not be seen because of poor visibility.

Less than a week later the Catalinas had their first disastrous encounters with Japanese fighters. One Catalina was shot down near Salamaua, New Guinea, and another near Gizo in the Solomons while on a search for enemy carriers that had launched a devastating raid against the RAAF base at Rabaul. The carriers were part of an invasion force that eluded searching RAAF Catalinas in foul weather and sent troops ashore to capture Rabaul and Kavieng on 21 January. These were the first of many such landings, ones which would carry the enemy to within striking distance of Australia's north coast in a matter of months.

During the remaining days of January, Catalinas leveled three attacks at Japanese shipping in Rabaul's Simpson Harbor. On each mission, they encountered increasingly heavy antiaircraft fire. Two ships burned as a result of the missions. And as the Japanese pushed southward, crushing the lightly manned Australian defenses on each island, the Catalinas were assigned still another mission: evacuating personnel from the doomed outposts.

Soon Port Moresby was within range of Japanese aircraft. It was bombed for the first time on 3 February by Mavis flying boats. That same date five Catalinas on night missions over Rabaul were attacked by Zeros. RAAF crews had quickly learned the Catalina's first line of defense—ducking into clouds—but at the time none were available, so Pilot Officer

Home from a rescue mission on which seven persons were taken off New Britain, crewmen of RAAF Catalina A24-17 enjoy the breeze as their plane taxis toward its buoy at Port Moresby, 24 March 1943. (Australian War Museum)

B. G. Higgins escaped the fighters by diving into the smoke of a volcano. That night the Catalinas chalked up their first Zero score: Sergeant Douglas Dick, aboard Flight Lieutenant G. E. Hemsworth's Catalina, sent a fighter spinning into the sea with fire from the port blister's twin Vickers .303-caliber machine guns. Other fighters knocked out the Catalina's port engine, however, and on the return to base Hemsworth flew the plane for more than ten hours on the starboard engine. On landing, 157 holes were counted in the plane.

With the Japanese steadily adding victory upon victory, it was apparent that a landing on New Guinea was not far distant. To forestall that as long as possible, the United States ordered twelve B-17 bombers to attack Rabaul on 23 February. In hope of increasing the chances of success, men who knew the tactics and the territory were sent along. Riding with the leaders of each of the two six-plane flights were No. 11 Squadron Leader Dick Cohen and Pilot Officer Norm Robertson. This was the first of many such cooperative missions throughout the war on which experienced Catalina pilots of the RAAF and the U.S. Navy rode with U.S. Air Force B-17, B-25, and B-26 crews. A number died on such missions.

Apparently to put an end to the aggravating raids on Rabaul and other targets by RAAF Catalinas, the Japanese struck back at Port Moresby on 28 February, destroying three flying boats at their moorings and damaging a fourth. This left the defense of the base to two Catalinas and one Hudson.

The anticipated landing on New Guinea began on 8 March at Lae and Salamaua. An RAAF Catalina watching the action called in Hudsons to make two strikes on the invaders. Manning the turrets were gunners from No. 11 Squadron, who had been without Catalinas since the Port Moresby raid.

In March and April Japanese convoys moved invasion forces about almost at will, each movement observed and some bombed, but with little effect, by RAAF Catalinas. The enemy easily took islands and bases in the Admiralties, the Bismarck Archipelago, the Solomons, and on New Guinea. Port Moresby was next on the list. On 4 May, at a cost of two planes and crews, RAAF Catalinas located and reported the Japanese invasion fleet heading south from Rabaul toward Port Moresby. The reports enabled U.S. Navy Task Force 17 to home in on the enemy ships. Contact between carrier planes of both sides erupted into the Battle of the Coral Sea on 7–8 May 1942. The battle turned back the invasion fleet, ended the threat of seaborne invasion to Port Moresby, and put an end to the enemy's relentless march toward Australia. The event is remembered there each year during Coral Sea Week.

Although the Japanese invasion fleet had been sent packing, Australia was by no means secure. For the remainder of 1942, Nos. 11 and 20 Squadrons spent much of their time in night bombing attacks on the newly conquered Japanese positions on the islands to the north and northeast of the mainland, harassing and destroying shipping and installations in an attempt to keep the wolf from the door. The missions were flown from Bowens on the Australian mainland, the squadrons having moved their headquarters there from Port Moresby in early May.

Three Catalinas bombed Tulagi in the Solomons on 29 May, starting fires and inflicting heavy damage. Cooperation between the RAAF and U.S. Navy made subsequent raids on the island possible, with the Catalinas refueling at the navy base at Havannah Harbor on Efate in the New Hebrides Islands. This was not without its excitement: Following a raid on 26 June an RAAF Catalina was reported as an unidentified aircraft and was shot up by a Marine Corps Wildcat. None of the crew was injured, however, and the plane was patched on the water so that it could fly back to the mainland for permanent repairs.

Also that month Rabaul, Lae, and Salamaua received nuisance visits from the Catalinas. Planes were over Lae and Salamaua for four hours, dropping 500-pound high-explosive bombs, 20-pound fragmentation bombs, and a liberal supply of beer bottles filled with old razor blades which produced a demoralizing high pitched whistle on the way down. When the Japanese conquered Buna and Gona on New Guinea's north shore in July, the Catalinas pressed home similar attacks on the enemy there. That same month they bombed supply dumps on Guadalcanal. During August the RAAF Catalinas joined B-25s, B-26s, and B-17s in pounding Lae, Salamaua, and Rabaul, the latter attack in support of the U.S. Marine Corps landings on Guadalcanal on 7 August.

The determined bombing attacks carried out by the Catalinas during September against enemy bases on Buka and Bougainville, often during bad weather, gained the attention of Major General George Kennedy, then head of the Allied Air Forces in the Southwest Pacific. "Your squadrons compiled an enviable record by completing missions on twenty-nine days," he wrote. "The attacks resulted in heavy damage to enemy airdromes and installations. . . . The courage and determination with which the numerous operations were carried out . . . were a contributing factor to the success of our combined Allied forces."

While U.S. Navy PBYs were beginning Black Cat "Mike Search" pattern operations against enemy shipping in the Solomons, the RAAF began a similar pattern called Run "M"—the "Milk Run"—which formed an aerial shipping blockade along the northern New Guinea coast. The first was flown on 5 November; the runs continued for nine months. The success of the missions was due in large part to the RAAF's first airborne radar, copied from a British design and built in Australia. During the month two destroyers were attacked, as well as a submarine, and eight Japanese aircraft were destroyed on the ground. Although few vessels were sunk on the Milk Runs, the danger of attacks by RAAF planes discouraged the enemy from sending ships beyond Lae after 1942. The greatest success came on 6 January 1943 when a Catalina bombed and sank a Japanese cruiser. Two days later another cruiser was bombed, and a merchantman, part of a convoy, was hit.

Flying supplies to coast watchers was an ongoing activity for the Catalina squadrons during 1942. Coast watchers were highly regarded by squadron personnel because of their reports on Japanese ship movements and especially bomber flights; these often allowed enough time for Catalinas to become safely airborne before their bases were hit. Operating deep in Japanese territory, the lives of the coast watchers were in constant danger, and some paid the ultimate price.

Information concerning Japanese activity on New Guinea was given a high priority by the Australians, and many hours were spent by Catalina crews flying intelligence units and supplies to the Sepik and Yellow Rivers, where the planes were under constant threat of enemy attack.

On 1 March 1943 a Catalina from a base at Cairns on Australia's northeast coast flown by Flying Officer Terry Duigan reported and shadowed a large Japanese convoy approaching Vitiaz Strait between New Guinea and New Britain. The following morning U.S. Air Force bombers and RAAF Beaufighters attacked the convoy, sinking or crippling seven transports in fifteen minutes and sinking or damaging the

A radar-equipped RAAF "Black Cat" returns from a "Milk Run" and blasts up a wooden ramp on its beaching gear. (Australian War Museum)

escorting destroyers. The action, known as the Battle of the Bismarck Sea, ended Japanese attempts to resupply troops in the area by surface fleet.

April 1943 saw the inauguration of the RAAF's top secret aerial mine-laying operation, one which was carried out solely by Catalinas. U.S. Navy PBYs had sown mines by air the month before, but the effort was halted by General MacArthur, who felt more direct action was needed against ships. Lieutenant Commander P. E. Carr of the Royal Australian Navy headed the Australian operation. It was his suggestion that Cat-alinas be used and, despite fears in RAAF command circles that casualties would be high, the idea was adopted.

Working in cooperation with the U.S. Navy for training, supplies, and equipment, the planes and crews were ready for their first mission on the night of 23 April. Eight Catalinas laid sixteen magnetic mines in Silver Sound, near Kavieng on New Ireland. Light antiaircraft fire was encountered, but all eight planes returned safely to their base at Cairns.

Two nights later eight Catalinas performed the same feat in Ysabel

Passage, an approach to Silver Sound. By monitoring Japanese radio, the RAAF got firsthand information on the success of the operation: Messages between Kavieng and Singapore told of a convoy being delayed while minesweeping equipment was brought in to clear the passage. Before mining was stopped at Kavieng in June, at least six ships were damaged or sunk by the Catalinas' airborne mines.

After the apparent success of the first missions, the scope of the mining operation was expanded from a few select targets to any major harbor or passage in the Netherlands East Indies within range of the mine-laden Catalinas.

The harbor at Surabaja on the island of Java was one of these. On 25 August four Catalinas flew to Darwin where they were refueled and loaded with two mines each. The following morning the four began the ten-hour flight to the target. Encountering no more than small arms fire on their arrival, they laid their mines and headed for home with a few bullet holes and a gunner wounded in both thighs. Refueled on the return trip by the USS *William B. Preston,* the four planes made the circuit again on the twenty-ninth, this time encountering heavier opposition but again leaving behind eight mines in the harbor. Japanese radio reported that fifteen Catalinas had attacked Surabaja without reaching their objective.

In May a campaign was launched to free the Bismarck Archipelago of Japanese domination, and the Catalina squadrons were called on for more bombing raids. The Milk Run was expanded to the north; Run "O" being added to Run "M," mainly to hunt enemy submarines that were operating in increased numbers. Three were bombed in the next several weeks, but none were sunk. Two were Japanese. One was American: The USS *Tuna* failed to identify herself quickly enough. No. 20 squadron personnel saw the error as an opportunity to check the effectiveness of their depth charges. A message was sent to the *Tuna*'s captain requesting information, but for some reason no reply was received.

During July the Japanese made valiant attempts to resupply their troops on New Guinea by means of barges, but these made excellent targets for RAAF and U.S. Navy patrol planes. Nearly two hundred were sunk or damaged that month.

At the end of August a third Catalina-equipped squadron, No. 43, began operations out of Karumba, on the Gulf of Carpentaria on Australia's north coast. On 7 September the new unit carried out its first mission, a four-plane attack on the former Allied base at Ambon, where it started two large fires. After that, Ambon became a regular target for bombing missions by the Catalinas of all three squadrons, along with enemy bases at Kavieng, Gasmata, Babo, Langgoer, Sorong, Boela, and Kaimana.

On 3 September nine Catalinas of Nos. 11 and 20 Squadrons bombed Rabaul to lessen the effect of enemy attacks on Allied forces gathering off Buna for the invasion of Lae. Whether the Catalinas deserved full credit is unknown, but less than half of the two hundred enemy planes known to be at Rabaul attempted to strafe the landing barges, and these did little damage. The landings, carried off on schedule, resulted in the retaking of Lae and Salamaua.

Aerial mining of harbors was resumed in early September 1943. Two Catalinas were lost that month. One, on a mission to complete the mining of Sorong in Dutch New Guinea, was thought to have struck a mountain.

Armorers bomb up a No. 43 Squadron Catalina from a scow at Darwin in preparation for a mission. (Gordon De'Lisle via David Vincent)

The other, on a passenger flight, hit a freak wave on landing, which knocked loose the two depth charges the plane was carrying. They exploded, destroying the plane and killing all but three of the crew and passengers.

Late in September two new East Indian targets were struck, Batu Kilat and Pomellaa. At Pomellaa a large merchant ship was trapped in the harbor by the mines. A torpedo-equipped Catalina was sent out to dispatch the sitting duck. Antiaircraft fire from shore turned the tables, however, and the plane was shot down. The only survivor was Lieutenant Commander Carr, head of the RAAF mining operation, who had ridden along as an observer. He was taken prisoner and held for the duration.

Other harbors in the Dutch East Indies were mined during the fall months. A few Catalinas carried a mixed load of mines and torpedoes, and often strafed docks and warehouses on shore as they left a target area. The torpedoes, however, were not productive. By the end of the period all planes were carrying only one type of ordnance.

The softening up for landings in western Dutch New Guinea commenced at the end of 1943. While U.S. Navy and Air Force fighters and fighter-bombers tackled the nearest airstrips, the Catalinas and other long-range bombers took on the more distant targets. The three RAAF squadrons hammered away at Kavieng for seventeen straight nights, starting fires and causing secondary explosions. Intense antiaircraft fire damaged several planes but none were lost.

Mining operations picked up in January 1944, with Catalinas flying four sorties from Darwin to Kaoe Bay in the Halmaheras, trapping fifteen motor vessels and two warships inside the harbor.

The tender *William B. Preston* became home for six Catalinas from Darwin at Cygnet Bay on 19 February. The planes flew the first mine-laying sorties against the former Dutch oil port of Balikpapan on the twenty-fifth, a successful operation that mined in at least two tankers. Two days later a second mining mission was carried out there. Opposition in both cases was light, with the exception of an eighteen-minute attack on one of the planes by two Rufe float plane fighters, but the Catalina escaped with only fourteen holes.

At the end of February, Fleet Admiral Ernest King wrote Vice Admiral Thomas Kincaid: "The energy and skill displayed in the planning and execution of mining operations by the forces under your command and the resultant losses and damage inflicted upon the enemy reflect credit upon all concerned." These forces were largely Nos. 11 and 20 Squadrons, and from that time on the crews felt they were more a part of Kincaid's 7th Fleet than of their own RAAF command.

In March the squadrons were directed to close as many of the remaining enemy ports on New Guinea as possible with mines in preparation for Allied landings in April at Aitape and Hollandia. These landings would bypass and neutralize Japanese forces at Madang, Hansa Bay, and Wewak.

On 8 April Admiral Nimitz requested the RAAF to mine Woleai Atoll in the Carolines, this also in support of the Hollandia invasion. Nos. 11 and 20 Squadrons reponded, sending eight Catalinas to base on the tenders *Tangier*, *Heron*, and *San Pablo* in Seeadler Harbor on Manus Island in the Admiralties. The mining was carried out on three successive nights, and by the third night the Japanese gunners were waiting for them. With illumination from a prematurely igniting photo flare as an aid, they put a shell through the hull of Flight Lieutenant Eddie Ham's plane between the blisters, killing both of his gunners and severely wounding an observer. Emergency repairs were made to the hull, and Ham flew the plane back to the *Tangier* where it was hoisted out of the water and permanent repairs were effected by the U.S. Navy crew.

Balikpapan came in for more mining in mid-April when a half-dozen Catalinas from No. 43 Squadron based themselves on the tender *Childs* in Yampi Sound on Australia's northwest coast. Antiaircraft fire from the ships in Balikpapan harbor brought Flight Sergeant Don Abbey's plane down in flames as the operation began on 2 April, and a three-by-four-foot hole was blown in the bow of Flight Lieutenant Robin Gray's. Gray and his copilot were injured in the blast but managed to keep the plane airborne all the way to the tender. Landing it nose high, they ran it up on the beach before it could sink. After repairs, it returned to service.

Two more sorties were flown before the mining operation at Balikpapan was complete. After the war it was learned that the harbor had been closed for an indefinite period following the mining, and the Japanese destroyer *Amagari* was sunk while sweeping the harbor.

On 9 June Admiral Nimitz again asked for help from RAAF Catalinas in mining the harbors at Kaoe Bay and Palau. The operation, carried out a week later by Nos. 11 and 20 Squadron planes, rendered the harbors inoperable for Japanese forces when U.S. Marines invaded Saipan.

During the spring and summer of 1944, No. 11 Squadron was sent south to Rathmines to assume training and patrol duties. Nos. 20 and 43 Squadrons, along with newly formed 42 Squadron, were consolidated in the Darwin area and assigned to full-time mining operations. From there the three squadrons conducted an average 100 sorties a month as far west as Surabaja on Java, north to Tarakan on Borneo, and east to Makassar on Celebes Island. Although the war was winding down for the Japanese forces in the fall of 1944, they were far from out. Ship-

and shore-based antiaircraft fire and fighter opposition cost the squadrons several aircraft, either shot down or damaged and lost.

After Morotai was retaken from the Japanese, detachments of Nos. 20, 42, and 43 Squadrons were sent there in October to base on the USS *Tangier*, from where they could easily reach a new series of mining targets: the harbors of North Borneo. Thanks to their actions, twelve enemy warships were penned in Brunei Bay. At Balikpapan two merchantmen were sunk.

On 7 December the RAAF began its largest mining operation of the war, in terms of numbers of planes and crews participating and miles flown: the mining of Manila Bay. Twenty-five planes drawn from all four Catalina squadrons flew to San Pedro Bay on Leyte, which only recently had been wrested from the Japanese. The Australians were displeased at being based on the USS *Heron*, a small tender never intended to handle the needs of twenty-five Catalinas. Also they were displeased with the limited amount of intelligence available to them from the U.S. Navy and Air Force regarding the Japanese defenses around the harbor and the amount of shipping located there. Otherwise both American services did all they could to help out. Two B-24s were provided by the U.S. Air Force to bomb and strafe enemy air bases in the area at the time set for the mining. In addition, an electronics countermeasures officer from the tender *Currituck* flew a specially equipped navy PBY with the RAAF Catalinas to jam Japanese radar.

The mission was carried out on the night of 14 December. Fifty mines were released on target with only sporadic small-arms fire directed at the planes. The operation completed, the Catalinas flew back to their bases in Australia, with No. 11 Squadron planes covering nine thousand miles since their departure.

At year's end the RAAF had received 116 Catalinas, including the first of the PB2B-1 and PB2B-2 flying boats from Boeing of Canada, the latter with tall tails and improved radar. In total the RAAF received 168 of all Catalina models, with all but three delivered directly from the North American continent. During the summer of 1944 the first PBY-5As were flown in but, as range was more important than wheels, many had their landing gear removed and the hull faired over on the outside. Inside, the port wheel well became a compartment for the auxiliary power unit; the starboard well became a food locker. The conversion received an official designation: PBY-5A(M). The -5s and -5A(M)s were flown on long-range missions, the heavier amphibians being used for communications and air-sea rescue work.

At the end of the year the RAAF set up an Air-Sea Rescue Branch, with three flights—Nos. 111, 112, and 113—equipped with Catalinas.

Up to this time air-sea rescue had been handled on a catch-as-catch-can basis by the operating squadrons, and despite the press of other duties, a number of American and Australian airmen had been saved during the three years of war. The new ASR flights were patterned after the U.S. Air Force's Emergency Rescue Squadrons that had begun operating early in 1944 with great success. In fact, No. 113 ASR Flight was sent to Morotai and attached to the 2nd Emergency Rescue Squadron until March 1945. Material assistance and valuable experience was gained from this union, for by that time the 2nd had rescued more than three hundred men.

By late February 1945 the Philippines were secure enough for an advanced base to be set up on Jinomoc Island, from where detachments of Nos. 20, 42, and 43 Squadrons could carry their mining efforts to enemy ports in the South China Sea. Operations began on 3 March with the mining of Hainan Strait and Yulinkan Bay on Hainan Island on the Gulf of Tonkin. Next came minelaying in the harbors at Hong Kong, Amoy, Swatow, and Wenchow, the northernmost port mined by the RAAF. During this period the RAAF began a new technique, that of dropping different types of mines on a single mission, which made mine-sweeping extremely difficult and increased the danger to shipping. Minelaying in the South China Sea ended on 1 June, and all RAAF minelaying operations came to an end on 30 July with a sortie to Bangka Strait.

Following the formal capitulation of Japan in Tokyo Bay on 2 September, the surrender of bases in the Australian area of operations began. The first was Rabaul, followed by Bougainville, Dutch and British Borneo, the Netherlands East Indies, and the Natoena Islands. In the last instance, preliminary surrender talks between Australian and Japanese officials were conducted aboard an RAAF Catalina of 113 ASR Flight. On 9 September the same plane was the first RAAF aircraft to land at Singapore since its fall in 1942, bringing observers to witness the surrender of the Japanese garrison there.

That same day four Catalinas took off for Singapore, taking with them medical supplies and bringing home the first prisoners of war. The planes were involved in repatriation work through October, returning more than twelve hundred former prisoners of the nearly fourteen thousand total to Australia.

Once the prisoners were home, it was the turn of the long-serving personnel in forward areas. Food supplies were flown out, and military personnel were brought back, as many as twenty at a time.

By the end of November the services of the Catalina squadrons were no longer needed. On the thirtieth No. 42 Squadron was disbanded. No. 11 Squadron was disbanded in February. When 20 and 43 Squadrons disbanded in March 1946, the minelaying Catalinas of the RAAF became history.

NEW ZEALAND

The Royal New Zealand Air Force was scheduled to receive a delivery of Catalinas from Great Britain in early 1942 when Japan began its march southward. With U-boats wreaking havoc on its supply convoys in the Atlantic, however, Great Britain decided to keep its patrol bombers at home. The RNZAF continued to fly its few aging Short Singapores for another year—until April 1943—when the first Catalinas (PBY-5s) in an order of twenty-five on Lend Lease from the United States began to arrive at Hobsonville, which was to be their main base. The following year the complement swelled with the delivery of thirty-four PB2B-2s built by Boeing of Canada.[2]

The first Catalinas were used to equip No. 3 OTU, a training unit, and No. 6 Squadron at Lauthala Bay, Fiji. Later a third squadron, No. 5, was formed as aircraft deliveries continued. By this time the war had moved north, and the two operational RNZAF squadrons did likewise. No. 6 Squadron was stationed at Halavo Bay on Florida Island near Guadalcanal, No. 5 Squadron at the U.S. Navy base at Segond Channel on Espiritu Santo. A detachment also operated out of Funafuti in the Ellice Islands. Both squadrons flew long-range antisubmarine sweeps and convoy escort and performed transport and air-sea rescue operations. Many Allied fighter and bomber pilots and crews rode home in RNZAF Catalinas. One squadron recorded seventy-nine rescues, many of them in rough weather, some under the noses of the Japanese. On one such mission, Flying Officer D. S. Beauchamp brought home five members of a downed U. S. Air Force B-24. He was awarded the Distinguished Flying Cross for his efforts.[3]

Seven Catalinas were lost in wartime service but only two on operational flights. One spectacular loss occurred in Segond Channel in October 1943 when a Catalina waterlooped on landing and struck a liberty ship. The crew survived. Another Catalina was lost a year later, on 5 October 1944, when Warrant Officer Donaldson and crew landed in heavy swells west of Espiritu Santo to retrieve the two-man crew of a Grumman J2F Duck. On takeoff the Catalina waterlooped, which damaged the starboard wing tip float and made another takeoff try impossible. An attempt was made to tow the plane back to harbor, but the float collapsed and the plane rolled over and sank. The Catalina crew and survivors of the Duck returned to the island on the tow ship.

At the signing of the Japanese surrender RNZAF Catalinas were in attendance with the British fleet. Then they returned to New Zealand, where most were placed in storage. Eight were kept on flight-ready status.[4]

SOUTH AFRICA

With the Mediterranean Sea closed to British shipping following the onset of war in Europe in September 1939, the sea route around Cape Town took on new importance. The Germans were as aware of it as the Allies: During the first four months of the war 28,296 tons of shipping were sent to the bottom by U-boats off the South African coast. The War Office and the South African General Staff began a campaign for long-range patrol bombers in 1940, but it was not until 29 May 1941 that the British high commissioner advised the South African prime minister, Field Marshall Jan Christian Smuts, of Britain's intention to establish four squadrons of flying boats to end the threat to shipping in the Indian Ocean. Two squadrons would operate out of Colombo, Ceylon, one from Mombasa, Kenya, and the last from Durban on the east South African coast.[5]

The base at Durban was an important one, as the Mozambique Channel between the African mainland and the island of Madagascar had become one of the U-boats' favorite hunting grounds. Extensive patrolling would be needed in that region.

Catalinas of No. 209 Squadron (RAF) began flying from Langebaan, an inlet on the west coast of South Africa, on 19 October 1941, but much of the time the waters were too rough for refueling and rearming. This, coupled with an escalation in U-boat and surface raider activity on the east coast, led to a change of station to Durban in mid-November.

Congella, the base at Durban, also left something to be desired. The landing and takeoff area was much too small, and Catalinas with a full load of ordnance and fuel barely had room to become airborne. Group Captain R. F. Shenton solved the problem by establishing another base on Lake St. Lucia, to the north. Catalinas would take off from Durban with only a partial fuel load, then top off at St. Lucia before beginning a long patrol.

No. 209 Squadron then moved to Mombasa, and No. 262 Squadron took over the base at Congella. Eventually the squadron grew to fifteen Catalinas. Although it was an RAF squadron, many of the squadron's 121 officers and 497 other ranks were South Africans. Depots similar to the one at St. Lucia were set up at Langebaan and Bots River, so that if the Catalina's services were required in the southern areas, they could fly there and be refueled and armed before undertaking a patrol.

Eventually Nos. 259 and 265 Squadrons (RAF) joined the Catalina air umbrella over the African east coast, and U-boats found operations

With antiaircraft fire splashing below it, a No. 262 Squadron Catalina piloted by Flight Lieutenant E.S.S. Nash begins a bombing run on U.I.T. 22 on 11 March 1944 off the South African coast. The U-boat was sunk. (South African Defence Force)

there more and more hazardous. On 12 July 1943 a Catalina from No. 262 Squadron surprised U-197 on the surface and depth-charged it, but the vessel escaped unharmed. A month later the same U-boat was sunk through the efforts of a pair of Catalinas, one each from Nos. 259 and 265 Squadrons. On 11 March 1944 three Catalinas from No. 262 Squadron sank U.I.T. 22, with Flight Lieutenants F. Roddick, E.S.S. Nash, and A. H. Surridge commended for bravery. On 4 July another No. 262 Catalina damaged U-859 in the last recorded attack by Catalinas on submarines off the South African coast. A Catalina brought about the demise of the German U-boat supply ship *Charlotte Schlierman* by reporting her position 950 miles east of Mauritius. She was sunk on 12 February 1944 by HMS *Relentless.*

Three Catalinas were lost in wartime operations in South Africa. The first loss occured on 25 June 1943 when Flight Officer White's plane crashed and exploded on takeoff, killing all on board. On 7 June 1943 a No. 259 Squadron Catalina crashed on landing, killing all eight of the crew. The last two fatalities occured on 30 January 1945, when a Catalina overshot a lake landing area and smashed into trees.

So many South Africans had become a part of No. 262 Squadron by 15 February 1945 that it was renumbered No. 35 Squadron, South African Air Force, on that date. Lieutenant Colonel E.S.S. Nash became its first commanding officer.

As the submarine menace subsided near the end of the war, the Catalinas were relegated more and more to convoy escort, survey work, air-sea rescue missions, and training activities. At war's end they played a part in bringing back South African soldiers from Europe. After that the planes were quickly phased from the active list.

THE NETHERLANDS

Flying boats were found to be ideal for rapid transport among the islands of the Dutch East Indies in the late 1930s. As a result seventy-two Dornier Do.24Ks were ordered by the authorities. On 10 May 1940 the twenty-fifth of these was delivered, but that was also the day Germany invaded Holland, and no more Dorniers were forthcoming. A year earlier, the Dutch had looked into the possibility of buying a dozen PBYs, so now, at least to partially fill the forty-seven-plane deficit, Consolidated was given an order for thirty-six Model 28-5NMEs.[6]

Because of a backlog of orders from the U.S. Navy and Great Britain, Consolidated was unable to deliver any planes until August 1941. Two were delivered that month, and through the fall more aircraft followed. Three were enroute on 7 December 1941. Two were caught at Pearl Harbor, one of which was destroyed. The other, damaged, was flown back to San Diego for repairs. The third, in the air on the way to Wake Island, escaped harm.

Three Catalinas were signed over to the British in early 1942 to replenish the decimated No. 205 squadron on the Malay Peninsula. They were only the first planes to go. The remainder of the Dutch Catalina fleet was whittled away in a war of attrition with the Japanese that in a few months eroded all Dutch possessions in the Southwest Pacific: real estate, ships, and aircraft.

On 10 January a Japanese invasion fleet heading for Tarakan on northern Borneo was sighted by Catalinas, but they could do little more than report it. The airfield and oil fields fell on the thirteenth. Manado on Celebes Island was assaulted on 11 January, and one Catalina was shot down in an air attack on the invasion fleet.

Catalinas from the overrun outposts withdrew to the island of Ambon, which was becoming thickly populated with remnants of the U.S. Navy's Patrol Wing 10 and stray Australian Catalinas. The island did not remain overcrowded for long; the Dutch planes left for Surabaja after a Japanese bombing raid on the sixteenth.

Invasion of the main East Indian islands was imminent, and the Dutch Catalinas were continually on patrol, watching for the enemy fleet. During this time, six planes were lost, four caught by strafing Japanese raiders on the water and two shot down on patrols. Air-sea rescue activity was included along with surveillance, and on 17 February a Dutch Catalina undoubtedly set a record for the number of survivors picked up on a single rescue mission. A Dutch freighter had been hit by Japanese bombers and left to sink. Somehow, the Catalina crew managed to cram the ship's entire complement of eighty-seven sailors on board and flew them to safety.

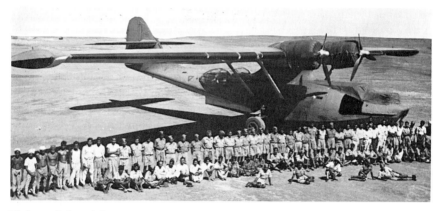

Eighty of the eighty-seven sailors rescued from a torpedoed ship on a single mission by a Royal Netherlands Navy Catalina on 17 February 1942. (Courtesy of the Trustees of the Imperial War Museum)

On 25 February a Catalina located the Japanese Eastern Fleet heading for Java. The Allies, under command of Dutch Rear Admiral Karel Doorman, threw most of what they had into the Battle of the Java Sea but, outnumbered, outgunned, and outclassed, nearly all of the attacking Allied warships and two more Catalinas were lost.

On 1 March a Japanese air attack on the base at Morokrembangan destroyed two Catalinas at their moorings. On 3 March eight more were lost. Three were on the water at Morokrembangan and one at Tandjong Priok on Java. Four were moored at Broome, Australia, where the Japanese also destroyed several Catalinas of the RAAF and PBYs of the U.S. Navy, along with a number of Dorniers and two Short Empire flying boats.

The Dutch government surrendered the East Indies to the Japanese a week later, on 8 March. One of the last planes to leave Java was a worn out and unflyable PBY that had been abandoned by the U.S. Navy. Dutch ground crews patched it up, however, and flew it to Australia, where it was once again placed in U.S. Navy charge.

At the time of the surrender only nine of the original thirty-six Catalinas were still in service, and these were flown to Ceylon to form the Dutch Naval Air Squadron. In July 1942 the squadron became a part of Britain's Royal Air Force. On 15 August it began operations as No. 321 Squadron. The unit, which had been formed in England in June 1940 around Dutch crews who had escaped the Germans in Holland, had flown convoy escort in Avro Ansons over the Irish Sea. It was disbanded in January 1941 and its crews assigned to No. 320 Squadron.

Reformed at Kogalla around the Dutch East Indies pilots, crews, and planes, No. 321 Squadron immediately began antisubmarine patrols. In October the unit moved to China Bay, with a detachment sent to Mombasa to patrol the west side of the Indian Ocean. By 1943 the squadron's planes were scattered from Ceylon to Cape Town, flying shipping searches and photo reconnaissance missions, dropping off and picking up agents in enemy territory, and continuing antisubmarine activities.

For the most part the submarine hunts were exercises in futility. On 24 May 1943, however, Lieutenant Vonk sighted a U-boat, but it dived before he could get in position for an attack. Forty minutes later he saw the wake of the U-boat's periscope and dropped depth charges, damaging it. Another attack took place on 22 January 1944, when Lieutenant Haman claimed a probable kill. On the thirtieth a third submarine was depth-charged, the last to be attacked by planes from No. 321 Squadron.

The squadron's patrol activities were supplemented by Liberators beginning in December 1944, but the Dutch crews preferred their Catalinas. When the war ended the big bombers were withdrawn, to be replaced with more Catalinas.

On 12 December the first Dutch Catalinas returned to their old base at Tandjong Priok on Java, and on 19 December the RAF relinquished control of No. 321 Squadron to the Dutch government. Two of its Catalinas had gone full cycle: they were the last survivors of the original thirty-six and the nine that had left the East Indies three years before.

Postwar PBYs

With the signing of the surrender documents by Japanese and Allied representatives aboard the battleship USS *Missouri* in Tokyo Bay on 2 September 1945, World War II formally ended. The massive fleet of patrol bombers that had served so admirably found itself nearly out of work. Only the air-sea rescue phase of patrol operations remained, but even this was drastically cut back with the end of combat, convoy escort, and ferry missions, as well as reductions in pilot training. The PBYs that had been forced into retirement late in the war by land-based patrol planes and later-model flying boats were now joined by hundreds of others on the back lots of naval air stations and military airfields along the coasts.

The Navy's VP-73 was one of the few patrol squadrons to continue operating PBYs after the war. It had nine aircraft: seven PBY-5As and two PBY-6As. Broken into two detachments, the squadron carried out air-sea rescue missions from Port Lyautey in Morocco and from Trinidad Naval Air Station in the West Indies. On 1 May 1946 the squadron was ordered back to Norfolk, where its pilots conducted familiarization flights for midshipmen at the U.S. Naval Academy. By year's end, VP-73 was down to seven PBYs, these engaged in training.[1]

Other PBYs remained active for a time. Almost every naval air station had a utility unit with one or two PBY-6As on standby for rescue, photo, ship gunfire observation, and other missions as assigned, but by 1948 the navy had only five PBYs remaining anywhere in the fleet. A number still flew with reserve units, but even these were gradually written off. On 3 January 1957 the last operational U.S. Navy Catalina, a PBY-6A, was stricken from the records of the Atlanta, Georgia, reserve unit.[2]

With its air-sea rescue workload greatly reduced, the Coast Guard began divesting itself of its 114 PBYs in 1946. A number remained operational, however, and continued to serve in various capacities and

The last-known PBY-5 in existence was restored by the Smithsonian Institution Air and Space Museum and is on display in the Naval Aviation Museum in Pensacola, Florida. (Roscoe Creed)

at widely scattered stations. Beginning in March 1941 and continuing for the next thirteen years, Coast Guard PBYs served an entire hemisphere, from stations as far east as Greenland to stations as far west as Sangley Point in the Philippines. Only eight were lost during that period. In April 1954 the PBY-6As, the last PBYs delivered to the Coast Guard, were taken off the rolls. Their work was taken over by newer Martin Mariners and Marlins, by Grumman Albatrosses, and, in increasing numbers, by Bell and Sikorsky helicopters. Nineteen of the retired PBYs went to South and Central American nations under the Mutual Defense Assistance Program, one was assigned to the air force, and the last were turned over to the navy.[3]

The air force kept its OA-10As in service for eight more years after the war, although they were not generally considered an ideal airplane for air-sea rescue work. They continued to be criticized by some because of hulls too weak for open-sea landings, and because of the difficulty in getting an injured person out of a raft and into the blisters.

The air force's answer to its problems was the Grumman SA-16 Albatross, a plane designed specifically for air-sea rescue work, one which incorporated all the features that grew out of the lessons learned from the OA-10As. Its hull was sturdy enough to satisfy the critics. It carried a crew of four and had room for twelve stretcher cases or ten passengers.

A Coast Guard PBY gets a JATO assist as it takes off from the Miami, Florida, air station. All Coast Guard PBYs were decommissioned by 1954. (U.S. Coast Guard via William Scarborough)

A U.S. Air Force OA-10A on a rescue mission in June 1948. The last three OA-10As were taken off Air Force rolls in 1953. (William Larkins via William Scarborough)

Its twin 1,475-horsepower Wright R-1820 Cyclone engines could pull it along for 2,700 miles at 225 miles per hour. Its stalling speed was 79 miles per hour, which made it relatively easy to land at sea and aided in making low-speed searches. Designed as an amphibian, it could become triphibious by adding skis for landings on snow or ice.

The OA-10As continued to be used in effecting air-sea rescues as well as in testing new procedures and training crews, but as the SA-16s moved in, the OA-10As moved out.[4] The last three OA-10As were removed from the air force inventory in January 1953.[5]

The phase-out of Catalinas from Allied air forces was swift or delayed, depending on a particular nation's needs. In Great Britain the Catalinas were rapidly removed from service at war's end. According to the Lend Lease agreement, any aircraft surviving the war were to be returned to the United States but, with the country already sated with surplus planes, most were disposed of locally by U.S. field commissioners. Nearly all of the RAF's Catalinas were reduced to scrap by March 1947.[6]

In Canada, Canso As enjoyed a long service life. They continued to fly with Royal Canadian Air Force Squadrons Nos. 13, 408, 413, and 123, as well as Rescue Flights 102, 103, 111, and 121. Thirteen RCAF Canso As were converted from patrol bombers to freight carriers, with a crane mounted on board for handling cargo. These were used to haul freight and supplies to outlying communities in northern Canada.

RCAF Canso As also saw considerable service in mapping northern Canada. One expedition relocated the Spicer Islands in the Arctic, whose exact position had been lost for fifty years. In the twilight of their military life the planes were used almost entirely for air-sea rescue work. The last Canso As were retired by the RCAF in November 1962.[7]

After its combat squadrons were disbanded in early 1946, the Royal Australian Air Force was left with five Catalina-equipped air-sea rescue flights. One of these, No. 113, flew cover for the movement of the eighty-four Mustangs of No. 81 Wing from Labuan to Japan in February of that year. Wintertime weather was too much for some of the Mustangs; three were lost. Catalinas of No. 113 found the wreckage of each, but no survivors. When the transfer was complete, No. 113 stayed on in

An RCAF Canso, its nose and blisters modified for peacetime use, is beached at Golden Lake, Ontario, in May 1953. (Canadian Forces Photographic Unit)

Japan, based at a former Japanese navy field at Iwakuni where there were seaplane facilities. It was the only RAAF rescue flight to serve in Japan, but only for a short time, and it was No. 113's final tour. The unit was called back to Australia in April 1946 and disbanded.

In January 1947 No. 111 Flight was disbanded. In October Nos. 112 and 114 followed suit, after a number of air-sea rescue and search missions.

A Catalina formerly of No. 113 Flight served as a guinea pig in 1948 for JATO testing by the Australian Aircraft Research and Development Unit at Point Cook, but time off was granted for plane and crew to fly an engineer to the Australian Antarctic Research Expeditions base on Macquarie Island. After several landing attempts were foiled by bad weather, the delivery was finally completed in winds so strong that the anchors dragged; engines were run to hold positions. The takeoff run was made in only 900 feet by using the additional 4,000 pounds of thrust produced by the experimental JATO units.

In July 1948 the equipment and personnel of the former 112 and 114 Flights were combined. The unit, redesignated No. 11 General Reconnaissance Squadron, performed the same sort of missions as did the rescue flights. The end of the unit's and the Catalinas' active-duty days was in sight, however. By 1949 No. 11 had only two Catalinas operational, and in April 1950 the squadron was disbanded.

No. 11's two Catalinas joined the others in outdoor storage at Rathmines. In 1952 the planes were declared surplus, and in September twenty-three were offered for sale. Six were turned over to the Dutch government.[8]

At war's end New Zealand's Catalinas returned to the base at Hobsonville, where all but the eight best were placed in storage. These eight were fitted with new radar, after which some were placed in service with No. 5 Squadron at Lauthala Bay in the Fijis. Others went to No. 6 Squadron when it was reformed at Hobsonville. While No. 5 Squadron's primary mission was maritime reconnaissance with a secondary role in air-sea rescue, it provided a great deal of emergency medical service to ships at sea and to residents of the remote islands in the Fiji group. The longest mercy mission carried a surgeon to Penhryn in the Cook Islands, a distance of 4,600 miles. The surgeon arrived in time to operate and save the life of a woman who had suffered complications following childbirth.

In 1953 the arrival of the first of sixteen ex-RAF Short Sunderland flying boats in New Zealand sounded the death knell for the Catalinas. As the Sunderlands gradually took over their duties, most of the Catalinas were sold for scrap.[9]

In the East Indies, No. 321 Squadron, which the British had turned over to the Dutch on 19 December 1945, was renamed the Eastern Reconnaissance and Transport Squadron. For the next three years it operated more or less on a wartime footing: On 17 August 1945 independence movement leaders declared the islands to be the State of Indonesia. The squadron was first based on Java, where it searched for ships running guns to the independence movement. The squadron suffered from aircraft fires, crashes, and retirements but, thanks to the infusion of the six Catalinas from Australia and another six Cansos from Canada, its strength was maintained. Two more Catalinas were captured, one owned by the Republic of Indonesia, the other by a gun runner from the Philippines, but neither was placed in active service with the squadron.

Although their job was mainly to patrol and control the sea lanes to prevent arms smuggling to the insurgents, Dutch Navy Catalinas also found time to carry out scheduled transport flights all over the archipelago.

In December 1949 the Dutch granted independence to the Netherlands East Indies. The Catalinas of the Eastern Reconnaissance and Transport Squadron were transferred to Biak on New Guinea where they took up their transport role across that vast, jungle-covered, thinly

A Royal Netherlands Navy Catalina is surrounded by native canoes on a regularly scheduled stop at a remote Indonesian island. RNN Catalinas remained in service until 1955. (Netherlands Ministrie van Defensie)

populated territory. More PBYs arrived at Biak in February 1951 from Valkenburg, Holland, where they had been overhauled after being flown from the United States.

The PBYs remained in active service in New Guinea until 1955, when the first Martin Mariners arrived to take over. By the following year all the PBYs were retired, most being scrapped at Biak. Two PBYs continued to be based in Holland, where they served as trainers and air-sea rescue planes. One was scrapped in May 1958, but the other spent many years of its retirement in a children's playground in Hoven, its young "pilots and crews" blissfully unaware of the part it had played in the history of their country and of the world.[10]

Although the end of military service for PBYs and Catalinas with U.S. and Allied forces meant a trip to the smelters for many, for others it marked the beginning of a new life of military service with other nations, some in Europe, others in South and Central America.

France had ordered thirty PBYs in 1940, but the country fell to the Germans before the planes were delivered. After the war, however, the French Navy picked up three PBY-5As. These were based at Papeete, Tahiti, and flown by the Section du Liason du Pacifique until 1968. At one time the quasi-military French Protection Civile in Europe had six PBYs, all used to fight forest fires.

Norway received the same benevolence from the British as had the government of The Netherlands: The Catalina-equipped No. 333 Squadron was turned over to the Norwegians on 21 November 1945. The planes remained in service only two years, however. By mid-1947 all had been retired and scrapped.

Sweden acquired three PBYs following the war, employing them extensively until the mid-1960s. One had the dubious distinction of being the only PBY to be shot down by a Russian MiG, the event occurring over the Baltic Sea in June 1952. Another PBY was retired in 1960. The last was taken out of service in August 1966 and placed on display by the Swedish Air Museum.[11]

The Danish Air Force was the largest user of PBYs in postwar Europe. The Danes received six ex-RCAF Cansos in mid-1947 and two ex-U.S. Navy PBY-5As in 1951. These flew maritime patrols and rescue missions. Two were lost in service. In 1957 eight more PBYs—former U.S. Navy PBY-6As—became Danish property. These saw service with No. 721 Squadron at Vaeggerlose on the Baltic, with detachments at Aalborg, Skrydstrip, and Sondestrom on Greenland. Attrition gradually reduced the size of the squadron: two PBYs were destroyed in a hangar fire; one crashed into a mountain. Another landed safely at sea after an engine quit but was lost when it became frozen in the ice. By the end of 1970

One of six navy surplus PBY-6As bought by Denmark in 1957, this Catalina saw service in the Baltic and North Atlantic for fifteen years. In 1982 it was acquired and restored by the Confederate Air Force, only to crash off the Texas coast in October 1984 with the loss of five crewmen. (William Barker)

only three PBYs remained. Two were sold in the United States in June 1972, and the last was given to the Cosford Aerospace Museum.[12]

In Brazil PBYs first saw military service in 1942 when the United States provided six for antisubmarine patrols. These were turned back to VP-74 when it began operations there. More were forthcoming, however, and between 1942 and 1944 the Force Aerea Brasileira received thirty PBY-5As. Six of these hold the record for longevity among military PBYs: five remained in regular service until late 1981; one was still in operation in 1982.

The big boats were modified in the 1950s to provide freight, passenger, and communications service to jungle-locked settlements along the Amazon River, a region that constitutes nearly half of Brazil's total area. Modifications included removal of the bow turret and its replacement with a semi-clipper bow. Blisters also were removed and a large hatch was cut in the hull's port side just forward of the old blister position to facilitate loading and unloading of freight. With elimination of the engineer's station in the tower, his controls were situated in the cockpit for two-man operation.

The planes were based at Belem at the lower end of the Amazon, and Tabatinga, at the upper end, near the confluence of the Brazilian-Peruvian-Colombian borders. Besides freight and supplies, the PBYs delivered medical and educational materials to the settlements along the river. When necessary, the PBYs acted as aerial ambulances for the native population, flying individuals hundreds of miles to hospitals at no charge.

The 1970s and 1980s saw the jungles pushed back to make room for airstrips near the Amazon settlements. These were made necessary, in the eyes of the Brazilian government, because there were no seaplanes in existence that could replace the aging PBYs. Land planes were the only possibility. With the completion of the airstrips, the PBYs were retired, the last in June 1982, and stored at Belem.[13] One of the six planes went to a museum in Rio de Janeiro; another was to be displayed on a pylon at Val de Caes International Airport near there. Four, sold to David Tallichet, a Los Angeles businessman and warbird collector, were flown from Belem to Orlando, Florida, in early 1984.[14]

Argentina also kept PBYs in the air for many years. The country's first PBY-5A was bought from a private citizen in the United States in 1946. After a year of service, it had proved itself far superior to the half-dozen elderly Consolidated P2Y-3 Rangers then in operation with the Escuadrilla de Patrulleros at Puerto Belgrano Naval Air Station. As a result, the Argentine Navy bought sixteen surplus Canso As from Canada and, after overhaul, flew them in small contingents and with several refueling stops to Base Aeronaval Comandante Espora (BACE) in Argentina. The delivery flights, begun in 1947, continued through 1949. On one flight a Canso grossing 35,000 pounds crossed the Andes at 13,000 feet.

New pilots trained in the Cansos at Argentina's naval air school, developing skill in bombing and torpedo-launching techniques, in anti-submarine warfare, and in reconnaissance work. Some Cansos were fitted with 7.62-millimeter machine guns and others with four 12.7-millimeter machine guns. Four Fairchild cameras could be mounted for photo-reconnaissance work. The Cansos could carry a variety of high-explosive and depth bombs. These could be exchanged for two Bliss torpedoes but, when the planes were so armed, they required JATO to take off.

Accidents were few with the Cansos, and in every case damage to the planes was repairable. In an early accident, an engine failed, and the pilot was forced to land on a farm. The accident report said there were no injuries and damage to the plane was slight, but the landing destroyed eighty dollars worth of the farmer's cabbage crop.

The Cansos saw service in patrolling the Beagle Canal at the southern tip of South America, a channel claimed by Chile as well as Argentina. They also made several flights to Antarctica and aided in mapping the continent. Numerous searches for ships in distress were carried out, as well as many air-sea rescue missions.

In September 1955 the Cansos returned to wartime status, taking part in the revolution that overthrew the government of Juan Peron. The Cansos took to the air on missions against army and air force factions loyal to the dictator. On one such mission 2-P-7 made reconnoitering runs over troop concentrations at Rio Colorado, then dropped its bombs on the railway station, destroying the installation and several feet of railroad track. The PBY took ninety-two hits from antiaircraft fire, but returned safely to BACE with no injury to the crew. After Peron's defeat, the erstwhile dictator was spirited away from Argentina in a PBY provided by the president of Paraguay.

When Martin Mariners and Lockheed Neptunes began arriving on the Argentinian scene in the late 1950s, the Cansos were taken out of service in ones and twos. One of the last Canso operations took place in January 1960 when the planes participated in a search for two unidentified submarines.

In April that year the Canso squadrons were disbanded, but some of the planes continued to serve as general-purpose aircraft for several more years. The last Canso was retired from military service in 1971.[15]

The government of Chile received six PBYs from the U.S. Navy and six OA-10As from the U.S. Air Force. Beginning in February 1948, they flew search and rescue flights from Quintero, about midway down Chile's long coast. In the mid-1960s they were replaced by Grumman Albatrosses.

Several other South and Central American nations received PBYs from the United States after the signing of the Inter-American Treaty for Reciprocal Assistance in 1947. The planes were supplied along with other war surplus equipment in exchange for defense concessions in each country.

Colombia was sent thirteen former U.S. Air Force OA-10As. Stationed at the Colombian Navy's main base into Cartagena, they served into the early 1960s. Three PBYs went to Ecuador, where the Transportes Aeros Militares Ecuatorianis flew supply and communications missions to the Galapagos Islands. Peru received three PBYs and three OA-10As. These were stationed at Callao and put to use by the Servicio de Reconocimiento Maritimo y Busqueda y Rescate on maritime patrols and search-and-rescue operations. Albatrosses took their place in the mid-1960s.

Paraguay received one plane, a PBY-5A which became Paraguayan "Air Force One" after its conversion into a luxury land-sea-air transport for use by the nation's president. This was the plane that carried ex-dictator Juan Peron on the first leg of his journey into exile following the Argentinian revolution.

In the Caribbean, Cuba received six PBYs, those being the halcyon days when good relations were enjoyed with the Batista regime. Four PBYs were delivered to the Dominican Republic in the mid-1960s. Five PBY-5As went to Mexico in 1947, where the Mexican Navy made use of them in offshore patrols and search and rescue work.[16]

Paralleling the importance of the postwar military redistribution of surplus PBYs, Catalinas, and Cansos was the regeneration of the big flying boats and amphibians for commercial and private use.

In Australia, the best-known operator of Catalinas was Qantas, whose crews were no strangers to the planes. Airline personnel had ferried in the RAAF's Catalinas before the war and during hostilities had pioneered a twenty-seven hour, 3,000-mile route from Perth to Colombo, Ceylon, using five Catalinas leased from the Australian government. The planes carried vital dispatches and sometimes as many as three passengers, the number limited by extra fuel tanks in the hull which left room for only two bunks and three chairs. During the early part of each flight, passengers became ballast: They were required to stand in the forward compartment for takeoff and remain there until enough fuel had been burned off so they could be seated aft without adversely affecting the aircraft's trim.[17]

In the first four years after the war Qantas purchased fifteen Catalinas, all of them PB2B-2 models. Seven were modified for passenger carrying by adding soundproofing, upholstery, and luxury seats taken from prewar Short Class "C" flying boats. The other eight were retained for spares.

The first flights were made to Lord Howe Island in December 1947, and to Espiritu Santo via Noumea in October 1948. The flights continued without incident for two years, then one of the two Catalinas broke its moorings in heavy seas at Lord Howe and was wrecked on the rocky shore. Two months later the second plane exploded and burned at anchor. Evidence of arson was found, but no one was ever convicted of the crime.

In May 1949 three Qantas Catalinas began operating out of Port

Beginning in 1948 Australia's Qantas airlines utilized seven Boeing PB2B-2 Cansos to provide passenger service to islands in the South Pacific. The last two planes were retired in 1958. (Qantas via David Vincent)

Moresby from the former RAAF facilities. Providing regular airline service to sixteen stations, from Daru in the west to Tonelei Harbor in the east, the Catalinas made emergency flights and air-supply drops as well.

One Catalina was taken out of service in 1953. The remaining two were retired in 1958, after having flown 12,427 hours while carrying 54,259 passengers and 7,367 short tons of cargo. Both planes were broken up for scrap.

One of the more notable Australian civil endeavors was the flight of "Frigate Bird II," a Catalina turned over to Captain P. G. Taylor by the Australian government in 1950 for a record-setting survey flight from Australia to South America. Taylor was renowned for such work, having been in charge of the airline survey flight from Australia to Africa aboard Richard Archbold's Guba II in 1939. Also he had made the first flight from Mexico to Australia in the first Frigate Bird, an RAAF Catalina, in 1944.

Despite rough weather and a difficult refueling stop at Easter Island, Taylor and Frigate Bird II proved that an airline route between Australia and Chile was feasible. No serious negotiations took place between the two nations, however, until 1970, four years after Taylor's death.

Taylor donated Frigate Bird II to the New South Wales Museum of Applied Arts and Sciences in 1961. Later it was put on display at the Camden Museum, Camden Airport, New South Wales.[18]

The New Zealand government loaned TEAL—Tasman Empire Airways, Ltd., owned by New Zealand, Australia, and Great Britain—two Catalinas for a short time after the war. One was used as a trainer, the other to survey a flying boat route to Tahiti. For passenger service, however, TEAL used British Short Sandringham flying boats.[19]

Farther north, Cathay Pacific Airlines was formed in Hong Kong in 1946. Its main carriers were surplus C-47s, which flew freight from Shanghai to Sydney. When a need was recognized for passenger service between Hong Kong and Macao, a distance of only sixty miles but a time-consuming trip by boat, two Catalinas were purchased and put in daily service. They plied the short route until July 1948 when one became involved in one of the earliest aerial hijackings on record. Fishermen in a junk who saw the incident said the plane made a violent maneuver to the left, then right, and then plunged into the sea. They rescued a single survivor who, as it turned out, was one of the four hijackers.

He said he and his companions had attempted to force the pilot, an American, to fly the Catalina to the Chinese mainland, where they planned to hold the passengers for ransom. When the pilot refused to cooperate he was shot through the head. The authorities believed, however, that the hijackers were after the gold that was frequently shipped aboard the plane.

Cathay Pacific sold the remaining Catalina to Macao Air Transport the following year. It continued to fly the Hong Kong–Macao route until 1961 and later saw service with Trans Australia Airlines in New Guinea. It was finally scrapped in 1968.[20]

In the East Indies, flying boats and amphibious aircraft played an important role in rebuilding shipping and transport services, which had become virtually nonexistent in the last months of the war. In the immediate postwar years KLM/KNILM Airlines flew four converted PBY-5As owned by the Netherlands Indies Government. In 1949 the airline acquired three PBY-5As of its own, these fitted with square windows and seating for eighteen passengers. After Indonesia's independence, Garunda Indonesian Airways purchased and operated two PBY-5As.[21]

The seven Catalinas operated by New Guinea Petroleum Company, a subsidiary of Shell Oil Company, took part in oil prospecting and exploration in the "Bird's Head," the northwest section of New Guinea. The planes transported seismographic parties and equipment into and out of jungle areas and kept the parties supplied while searching for oil. From 1946 until 1948 the Catalinas maintained a regular schedule between Shell refineries at Balikpapan on Borneo, Pladju on Sumatra, and the main island of Java, flying in food, special equipment, and tools, as well as ferrying employees to and from vacations in the highlands of Java. The last two PBYs in the fleet were retired in 1960.[22]

In Chile, Aeroservicios Parrague (As.Par.) was formed by General Roberto Parrague Singer with two PBYs bought in 1959 and 1960 from TRANSA, an airline that had failed. The planes had been purchased originally as U.S. Navy surplus in 1957. Parrague had flown PBYs in the Chilean Air Force and had set a nonstop long-distance record for his country by flying 2,047 miles to Isla de Pascua (Easter Island) in 1951. As soon as his planes were overhauled and converted to carry passengers and freight, he set up a regular flight schedule to the island and maintained it for the next three years.

In 1965 Parrague made another pioneering flight, this one to Tahiti, afterward setting up a regular schedule that was flown until 1969. During this period General Parrague offered to buy one of the three French Catalinas that had been taken out of service at Papeete. Instead of selling him a plane, the French donated all three to his airline as a tribute to the initial flight between the island and South America. The planes were shipped to Valparaiso and then taken to Quintero Air Base for overhaul and repair.

When the Tahitian run was discontinued for lack of business, one of As.Par.'s Catalinas was flown to Canada, where it underwent a second conversion, this time to a water bomber. Returning to Chile, it fought forest fires from 1970 to 1973, augmenting aerial fire fighting services that had previously been provided entirely by American and Canadian firms.

During 1968 As.Par. made weekly flights from Santiago to San Fernandez Island, where the PBYs were forced to anchor at sea because of the steep cliffs rising from the water on all sides. It was not uncommon for the planes to break their moorings in rough weather. Return flights to the mainland carried a mixed load of passengers and lobsters, the latter being the island's main export crop. Up to 2,000 lobsters were carried on a single flight, with the number reduced according to how many humans were seeking passage.

Regularly scheduled flights ended in 1970 when one of the As.Par. PBYs was cannibalized for parts. The airline continued to make charter flights, however, many of them to the southern lakes region of Chile.[23]

As the United States and Canada were the major producers of naval and military PBYs during World War II, it should be no surpise that the two countries were the major converters of PBYs when peace returned. The conversion of wartime PBYs into private and corporate luxury air yachts, airliners, cargo carriers, geological survey aircraft, insecticide sprayers, and water bombers became an industry unto itself in the late 1940s and the 1950s.

Large and small firms prospered. In Canada the de Havilland facility at Toronto Island began overhauling and modifying surplus Cansos in 1946, with work continuing steadily for ten years. The six Cansos acquired by the Danish Air Force were refitted at de Havilland; eleven were modified into cargo carriers for the Royal Canadian Air Force; a number were redone for passenger service for Canadian Pacific Airlines; special configurations were prepared for exploration and mining companies. In all, de Havilland modified and overhauled seventy-four of the big planes.[24] In the United States, Steward-Davis, of Long Beach, California, was perhaps the largest producer of PBY conversions. In both countries small, fixed-base operators modified PBYs in ones and twos in their hangars.

The first item to go in almost every modification was the bow turret. This was replaced by either a semi-clipper bow that faired over the turret opening and covered the bombardier's window with a flat aluminum plate, or by a full clipper bow that rounded out the lines of the nose. Both types featured some sort of forward hatch to aid in docking.

Some PBYs and Cansos, generally those used to haul cargo, had their blisters removed and replaced by large hatches. However, many private and corporate aircraft, as well as airliners, retained their blisters as bay windows for viewing the land or seascape. Most had additional windows cut in the hull to reduce passenger claustrophobia. Some had enlarged hatches cut into the radio compartment. A few passenger carriers and luxury amphibians had retractable stairways installed as replacements for the tunnel hatches.[25]

Airline PBYs and Cansos were soundproofed as much as possible, decks were laid, and a variety of seating arrangements was installed, but usually they were configured for twenty to twenty-eight passengers. If the plane was to carry cargo or a combination of cargo and passengers, tie-down rings were bolted in. The luxury air yachts were fitted with sofa seats, reclining chairs, tables, sleeping accommodations, and personal comforts to suit individual tastes. Fitted with electric kitchens, the big amphibians became flying lodges for hunters and fishermen who wanted and could afford quick access to game and comfortable quarters in the wilderness.

In nearly all civil PBYs the engineer's controls in the tower were removed to the cockpit so a pilot and copilot could fly the plane without need of a third person. Most PBYs retained their faithful Pratt and Whitney engines, but others became "Super Cats," their R-1830s replaced by North American B-25 medium bomber engines and cowlings. These Wright R-2600 Cyclone engines boosted horsepower from 1,200 to 1,700 per engine, increased the cruising speed from 110 miles per hour to 145, and increased the gross weight from 34,000 pounds to 40,000.[26]

Many PBY-5As had their rudders replaced by ones with balance horns to ease the load on the rudder pedals. PBY-6As, particularly Super Cat conversions, received squared off fins and rudders, the additional area aiding in stability and control.

Some PBYs were modified for special purposes. One made by the Bird Corporation of Palm Springs, California, fell into this category. The PBY had long been considered a four-engine airplane with only two engines, and Bird set out to rectify this oversight. The corporation, at that time the world's largest developer and manufacturer of medical respirators, used a PBY-5A conversion called the "The Wandering Albatross" as a flying classroom, office, hotel, and transport for medical teaching teams. The company was concerned because their extensively and expensively equipped plane could not long remain in the air if one of the two engines failed. One solution was to increase performance with R-2600 engines, but these also increased vibration, noise, maintenance, and operating costs. Bird considered turboprops, but this was rejected for a number of reasons. The ultimate answer was two more engines, supercharged 340-horsepower Lycomings mounted on the outboard wing panels.

The Lycoming engines achieved Bird's goal. The PBY could fly with one of its R-1830s out and still maintain a 142 mile-per-hour cruising speed. With all four engines in operation, it was a 200 mile-per-hour airplane. The corporation was so pleased with the improvement in the plane's performance that its executives renamed it the "Innovator" and offered to so modify the PBYs of others, claiming that the plane offered the highest performance and the greatest safety of any large amphibian available. For whatever reason, there were no takers, and the Innovator remained a one-of-kind airplane.[27]

Other special purpose PBYs were the "Mad Cats" of geological survey companies. These ranged throughout the world prospecting for ferrous metals with hulls crammed full of magnetic detection gear and with giant antenna loops draped from noses to wing tips to stingered tails.

In the late 1950s Ace Flying Service, then of Salem, Oregon, converted several of its PBYs into insecticide sprayers. On each, one of its fuel cells was made into a chemical tank. Ten-horsepower auxiliary engines pumped the chemicals from the tank into two-and-one-half-inch diameter pipes inside the wings and out through spray nozzles mounted below. The company contracted for forest spraying in the northwestern United States for five years, ridding a million and a half acres of damaging pests in 1958 alone. The Ace PBYs ventured into the Midwest and Southwest at times, spraying large areas of Colorado and New Mexico for grasshoppers.[28]

Most North Americans who remember the PBYs of the early postwar

The Bird "Innovator" was the only four-engine PBY conversion. Two 340-horsepower Lycoming engines boosted the plane's cruising speed to 200 miles per hour. Even with one of the Pratt and Whitneys out, the plane could still cruise at 142 miles per hour. (William Larkins via William Scarborough)

A Canadian Aero Service "Mad Cat" Canso rigged for ferrous metal prospecting. Similarly equipped PBYs continue to perform this service for firms around the world. (Larry Milberry)

A Canso converted for airline use by Queen Charlotte Airlines stands for passenger boarding at a lumbering center in British Columbia. (K. M. Molson)

years probably lived in Alaska, Canada, or the Caribbean. Alaska had its Ellis Airlines; Canada its Canadian Pacific, Queen Charlotte, and Pacific Western Airlines; the Caribbean its Antilles Airboats, to name a few of the larger ones. As airliners, the PBYs and Cansos served on land and water for ten to fifteen years, but in the 1960s most of the brightly painted amphibians gave way to land-based, jet-powered aircraft with greater seating capacity, increased passenger comfort, reduced operating costs, and more profitability. In the 1980s Antilles Airboats still operated amphibians, but its three PBYs were replaced by Grumman

Gooses whose smaller size gave them the ability to taxi up the narrow ramps in the hearts of the island cities, something the big PBYs could never do.[29]

In the 1970s, television brought the millions who had never seen or heard a PBY "Flying Calypso," a PBY-6A owned and operated by the Cousteau Society on a number of its oceanic expeditions. The plane had been a passenger transport, flying between the United States and Costa Rica, and still later it had been a water bomber. Jacques Cousteau's son, Phillippe, who was the plane's pilot, masterminded the Calypso conversion, which included installation of camera platforms in the blisters, scuba equipment storage, sophisticated radio and weather reporting equipment, sleeping accommodations, and a complete kitchen, from which ten men were fed three meals a day when the plane was in the field.[30]

Phillippe logged more than a thousand hours in the PBY, flying to remote Pacific islands and to Alaska, to the Caribbean to study sharks, and up the Nile in a study of pollution in the Mediterranean. The Flying Calypso crashed in Portugal on 28 June 1979 during a landing attempt. Others in the plane survived, but Phillippe Cousteau was killed by a broken propeller.[31]

Currently another PBY commands the attention of thousands of enthusiasts each year who attend the air shows of the Confederate Air Force's (CAF's) World War II "Ghost Squadron."

The CAF's PBY-5A flew patrols in the Atlantic and Pacific for the U.S. Navy and Coast Guard during and after the war. In 1954 the plane was retired and mothballed, to be resurrected four years later and turned into a flying yacht with an interior similar to that of Jules Verne's *Nautilus* submarine for television personality Herb Shriner. In August 1979 the

The ill-fated "Flying Calypso" was a flying camera platform and home base for ten men during the filming of the Cousteau Society's televised environmental programs. (Courtesy The Costeau Society)

PBY was purchased by CAF Colonel Michael Wansey of New South Wales, Australia, and donated to the CAF. In January 1981 the plane began a 25,000-mile tour of Australia and the Pacific to commemorate the sixtieth anniversary of the Royal Australian Air Force. The PBY returned to the United States in September and was based with the Pacific Wing of the CAF at the Oakland, California, airport.[32]

Of all the services performed by PBYs in the postwar era, forest-fire fighting undoubtedly has been the most beneficial.

Aerial fire fighting began in 1930 when barrels of water were kicked out the door of a Ford Trimotor onto a fire near Spokane, Washington, but little more was done with water bombing until after World War II. By 1950 the Canadians were experimenting with dropping large water-filled paper bags onto forest fires from a conveyor belt aimed out the door of a de Havilland Beaver. Later, they dumped water from tanks mounted on its pontoons. In the United States, former military and naval trainers—Stearman and N3N biplanes—were being equipped for fire fighting with front-seat tanks and dump gates.[33]

By 1960 the tools of the trade had progressed from single engine to multiengine aircraft. In Quebec five Cansos were equipped with external tanks and water-pickup probes to fill them on the move, but the effort was only marginally successful because of the limited size of the tanks and the inability to control the depth of the probes. The provincial authorities sought professional help from J. Knox Hawkshaw of Field Aviation in Toronto. They asked him to design an internal tank for the PBYs that could be filled on the go. He first told them it couldn't be done. But a year later he successfully tested the "impossible" project at Lake Marion, South Carolina, an event that added still another dimension to the careers of the venerable Catalinas and changed the course of forest fire fighting around the world.

Hawkshaw's design features a divided 1,000-gallon (U.S.) tank that occupies the lower half of a PBY's center compartment and replaces the bottom of the hull in that section. The tank is filled by means of a four-and-one-half inch diameter electrically operated probe behind the step that the pilot lowers and raises from the cockpit. The load is released when the pilot presses solenoid-actuating buttons on the control column and a door in the bottom of each half of the tank drops open.[34]

Once installed and proven in Quebec's Cansos, the race was on to convert other Cansos and PBYs to Hawkshaw's design. Field Aviation made forty such conversions during the 1960s. Other conversions, some identical to Hawkshaw's, some with different design features, were done by Fairey Aviation of Canada and by firms in the United States. By the

J. Knox Hawkshaw's water-bomber design features a pilot-operated probe behind the step that puts 1,000 U.S. gallons of water in a Canso's center-com-
partment tank in fourteen seconds. Drop is made through reinforced doors in
the bottom of the hull. (Roscoe Creed)

early 1970s the market was sated, and few conversions have been done
since then.

So equipped, the PBYs have become aerial fire trucks under contract
to provinces, states, and nations of North and South America and Europe. They stand waiting and ready at airports near the points of greatest
danger should fire break out. When a fire is reported, the procedure
becomes one of takeoffs and landings, as many as 125 per day, depending
on the distance between the fire and the water. The pilot goes through
the normal checklist for landing the plane on the water, but rather than
cutting the throttles on touch down, he maintains flying speed, lowers
the probe, and in fourteen seconds sends 8,000 pounds of water surging
into the tanks. Then the pilot makes a normal takeoff, flies to the fire,
and, after receiving directions from a fire-control officer hovering near
the scene, wrestles the plane down through unbelievable heat and turbulence to about 25 to 50 feet above the treetops and releases his load.
Then he pulls up and goes through the procedure all over again.[35]

In a short time some of the first PBY water bombers made more water
landings than they had made in their entire previous existence. At first,
the original airframes showed no ill effects from the increased activity,
but after a few hundred hours some door warping and bottom wrinkling
showed up in the hulls of the early Field Aviation conversions. Reinforcing the tank doors and doubling the number of Zed sections and
rivets in the hull bottoms solved the problem.[36]

The toughness of the reinforced hull was demonstrated one day by a tired pilot who landed wheels up on a sod strip. The Canso banged off the hard ground and richochetted into the air; the pilot, now fully awake, hit the throttles and went around, landing this time wheels down. The only damage was a small piece of aluminum peeled off the step.[37]

The incident showed more than a tough airplane: It showed how a grueling day of aerial fire fighting could cause both pilot and copilot to miss the red landing-gear warning lights on approach. Indeed, exhaustion proved to be the greatest danger to water bomber pilots. Another tired Canadian landed to fill his tanks at an airport and found they were already full. A water bomber—not a PBY—crashed when its crew apparently forgot to watch the fuel gauge: When investigators examined the wreckage they found the tanks dry. Despite the dangers only two PBYs have been lost in aerial fire fighting in Canada. These collided head-on in smoke over a forest fire while searching for a downed helicopter.[38]

In Canada the water-scooping technique proved ideal because of the many lakes and rivers in or near the forests, but in the United States the technique failed to flourish because of the lack of natural reservoirs. Tank filling at airports was much more common, and any aircraft capable of lifting heavy loads could become a water bomber. As a result, only one fire fighting firm—Schlaeco, Inc., of Moses Lake, Washington— was still flying PBY water bombers in the United States in the 1980s. The firm's four Super Cats and one standard model constituted a fifth of the operational PBYs in the United States in 1983.[39] The nation's other aerial fire fighters sold off their PBYs to Canadian firms, no doubt in part because of the $650,000 to $750,000 price the planes commanded there. While the number of PBYs licensed in the United States shrank over the years, the Canadian registry showed a steady increase. Forty-one PBYs were licensed there in 1983.[40]

The ideal situation for a water bombing firm is to fight fires in the northern hemisphere in the summer and in the southern hemisphere in the winter, since the summers and falls—the fire-danger seasons— are opposed and year-round income can be derived from the planes. Taking advantage of this, American and Canadian firms contracted with Chile to supply PBYs and crews for forest-fire control in the mid-1960s. The next-best arrangement is to contract the planes out whenever and wherever they are needed. Avalon Aviation of Parry Sound, Ontario, Canada, whose eight Cansos constitute one of the two largest fleets of PBYs now active anywhere in the world (Flying Firemen of Sidney, British Columbia, also has eight), has had one of its planes under contract to Norway for some time. Negotiations are under way to supply water bombers to Finland and China.[41]

How much future can there be for a forty-year old airplane? Quite

This "Super Cat" water-bomber conversion, operated in 1972 by Hemet Valley Flying Service in California, features Wright R-2600 engines that could lift a gross weight of 40,000 pounds. (R. L. Lawson via William Scarborough)

The eight water-bomber Cansos of Avalon Aviation, Parry Sound, Ontario, were one of the two largest fleets of PBYs anywhere in the world in 1984. C-FCRR (No. 1 on rudder) is probably the only PBY remaining with a kill to its credit: It was flown by T. C. Cooke when he sank a U-boat off Iceland in 1944. (Roscoe Creed)

a bit, according to the Canadians. J. Knox Hawkshaw foresees another possible thirty years of life for Canso water bombers, based on his study of hours flown per year. He compared the condition of a few high-time Cansos—ones with 12,000 to 15,000 hours on the airframe—with the average, which is about 5,000 to 6,000 hours. His assessment is based on the dual facts that the high-time aircraft are still in good condition and that water bombers fly about 200 hours annually. At that rate, it would take thirty years for the low-time planes to reach the status of the lowest of today's current high-time planes.[42]

For some Cansos the future may hold a different look and a different sound. Avalon Aviation is considering plans to replace the reciprocating engines of its Cansos with Rolls Royce Dart turboprop engines, creating a "Turbo Cat" that would outperform even the Super Cats. Because the planes are based on land and scoop their loads from fresh water lakes and rivers, none of the corrosion problems attendant on turbine-powered seaplanes which operated on salt water after the war would be likely.

A dearth of parts will not contribute to the PBY's demise. Most owners and operators are packrats out of necessity. R-1830 engines exist in large numbers. And if the owner's own storeroom doesn't yield a needed airframe part, a phone call or two nearly always does. If none can be located, parts are custom manufactured from drawings.[43]

It will be attrition that writes the final chapter of the PBY story. Not often, but every two or three years, one of the last ninety or so PBYs goes down, never to rise again. The effect on the PBY community is about the same as when a well-known, elderly-but-hale war veteran departs this world. Owners, pilots, mechanics, former pilots and crewmen, and afficionados express wonder, shock, and sorrow, and go on about their business feeling somewhat diminished. And out on the tarmac the last few of history's greatest flying boat stand, engines silent, shifting and creaking on their landing gear as the wind sighs through their struts and cowlings, gently rocking their great wings as though in final salute.

Painting shows a proposed turboprop conversion being considered for its water bombers by Avalon Aviation. So equipped, a Canso would out-perform even a Super Cat. (Avalon Aviation)

Appendixes

A

Museums Displaying PBYs and Cansos

National Air and Space Museum, Smithsonian Institution, Washington, D.C. 20560, (on loan to Naval Air Museum, Pensacola, Florida). (Museum code 700)

New England Air Museum, Bradley International Airport, Windsor Locks, Connecticut 06096. (Museum code 690)

Victory Air Museum, Polidori Airfield, P.O. Box 340, Rte. 2, Mundelein, Illinois 60060. (Museum code 733)

Confederate Air Force Museum, P.O. Box CAF, Rebel Field, Harlingen, Texas 75550. (Museum code 900)

Yesterday's Air Force, Hangar 4, Chino Airport, Chino, California 91710. (Museum code 680)

National Aviation Museum, Rockcliffe Airport, Ottawa, Ontario K1A OM8, Canada. (Museum code 185)

Royal Air Force Museum, Hendon, London NW9 5LL, England. (Museum code 610)

Warbirds Aviation Museum, Mildura Airport, P.O. Box 288, Mildura, Victoria 3500, Australia. (Museum code 139)

Museum of Applied Arts and Science, 659–695 Harris Street, Utlimo, New South Wales 2007, Australia. (Museum code 132)

Museum of Transport and Technology of New Zealand, Great North Road, Western Springs, Auckland 2, New Zealand. (Museum code 425)

Royal Netherlands Air Force Museum, Luchtmacht Museum, Soesterberg Air Force Base, The Netherlands. (Museum code 415)

Museu Aerospacial, Av. Mal. Fontnelle 2000, Campo Dos Afonsos 21740, Rio de Janeiro, RJ Brazil. (Museum code 176)

Flygvapenmuseum Malmen, Box 13300, 580 13, Linkoping, Sweden. (Museum code 542)

(Data courtesy K. M. Molson)

PBY Technical Data

PBY Performance

Model	Gross Wt. Pounds	Max. Speed MPH/Altitude	Service Ceiling	Patrol Range (Mi)	Climb Ft/Min	T/O Time Calm-Sec.
XP3Y-1	19793	169/SL	18600	2070	5000/4.1	22
XPBY-1	20226	184/8000	24000	2110	5000/4.6	21
PBY-1	22336	175/8000	20900	2115	840/1	31
PBY-2	22490	178/8000	21100	2131	860/1	32
PBY-3	22713	191/12000	24400	2175	930/1	28
PBY-4	24813	198/12000	24100	2070	870/1	25
PBY-5 (Early)	26200	200/5700	21600	1965	990/1	25
PBY-5 (Late)	31813	195/7000	17700	2860	660/1	45
PBY-5A	33975	180/7000	14700	2545	880/1	30
PBN-1	36353	186/6700	15100	2590	970/1	23
PBY-6A	34550	178/7000	16200	2535	630/1	?
PB2B-1	33133	187/7000	15800	2690	660/1	?

Fuel capacity, all PBY models: Integral tanks, unprotected—1750 U.S. gallons
with self-sealing liner—1495 U.S. gallons
PBN Nomad: Integral tanks, unprotected—2350 U.S. gallons
with self-sealing liner—2095 U.S. gallons
(Data courtesy Captain W. E. Scarborough, USN [Ret.])

U.S. Navy Production and Serial Numbers

Type	Number Built	Serial Numbers	Date Ord.	First Del.	Last Del.	Contract Number	Remarks
XP3Y-1	1	9459	28/10/33	3/35		31792	Prototype
XPBY-1	1	9459	28/10/33	5/36		48710	Rebuilt prototype
PBY-1	60	0102-0161	29/6/35	9/36	6/37	43087	VP-3,6,8, 11,12
PBY-2	50	0454-0503	25/7/36	5/37	2/38	49653	VP-2,10, 11,17
PBY-3	66	0842-0907	27/11/36	11/37	8/38	51701	VP-4,5,9,16
PBY-4	32	1213-1244	18/12/37	5/38	6/39	58101	VP-1,18
XPBY-5A	1	1245	7/3/39	11/39		58101	First amphibian

U.S. Navy Production and Serial Numbers (continued)

Type	Number Built	Serial Numbers	Date Ord.	First Del.	Last Del.	Contract Number	Remarks
PBY-5	167	2289-2455	20/12/39	9/40	9/41	70496	2290 to USCG
PBY-5A	33	2456-2488	20/12/39	10/41	12/41	70496	3 to USAAF
PBY-5A	134	7243-7302; 04972-05045	25/11/40	12/41	3/42	77713	2 to USAAF
	30	02948-02977	30/6/41	3/42		88476	
	22	04399-04420	27/10/41	4/42		88476	1 to USAAF
PBY-5	90	04425-04514	15/9/41	4/42	5/42	91876	
PBY-5A	94	08030-08123	25/4/42	8/42	9/42	88476	12 to USAAF; 11 to RAF
PBY-5	426	08124-08549	20/4/42	11/42	7/43	91876Ext.	14 to RNZAF
PBY-5A	100	33960-34059	11/10/42	7/43	10/43	NXa 13595	
	130	46450-46579	12/8/43	10/43	12/43	NOa-464	36 to RAAF; 30 to France
	200	48252-48451		12/43	3/44	NOa-464	31 to USAAF
San Diego Total	1,636						
PBY-5	1	63992	8/7/43	4/44		NOa-259	449 cc start New Orleans
PBY-5A	59	46580-46638	12/8/43	6/44	1/45	NOa-464	
PBY-6A	61	46639-46698, 46724	12/8/43	1/45	5/45	NOa-464	30 to USSR
	114	63993-64106	19/6/45	5/45	9/45	NOa-259	64100 cc
New Orleans Total	235						
PBN-1	155	02791-02946	16/7/41	2/43	3/45	P.O.3-42	NAF 02802 cc

PBYs Built on Non-Navy Contracts

Type	Number Built	Identity Numbers	Date Ordered	First Del.	Last Del.	Contract	Remarks
28-1	2	NC777,AGBJ	1/37	6/37	4/38	Museum	Guba
28-2	3		3/37	12/37	1938	USSR	GST
28-4	1	NC18997	9/38	6/39		A.E.A.	To USN 99080
28-5	1	N P9630		7/39		RAF	Lost 10/2/40
Catalina I (28-5ME)	30	W8405-8434		11/40	5/41	A37 (SO-2)	28-5ME to Britain; W8430-32 to Canada
Catalina II	7	AM264-270		11/40	12/40	A2587 (SO-71)	Britain

PBYs Built on Non-Navy Contracts (continued)

Type	Number Built	Identity Numbers	Date Ordered	First Del.	Last Del.	Contract	Remarks
Catalina I	40	AH530-569		12/40	5/41	F-210	Britain; AH534 to Australia
Catalina I	20	Z2134-2153		5/41	7/41	A37 (SO-2)	Britain; 6 to Canada
Catalina I	9	AJ154-162		10/41	11/41	A37 (SO-2)	Britain
28-5NME	18	A24-1 to -18		2/41	10/41	AUS58 (SO-4)	Australia
Cat. IIA	50	9701-9750		8/41	1/42	Can 78	VA9701-36 to Britain; 9737-50 to Canada
28-5NME	36	Y-37 to -72	7/40	8/41	10/41	N36 (SO-5)	Netherlands
28-5NME	12	Y-74 to -85		9/42		N36 (SO-5)	Netherlands
Catalina IB (PBY-5B)	225	FP100-324	30/6/41	5/42	11/42	88477-DA	60 to USN; 9 to Canada; 2 to BOAC
Cat. III	(11)	FP525-536				(USN)	PBY-5A minus FP534 to USN
Cat. IVA	(11)	JV925-935		9/43	10/43	(USN)	ExPBY-5A
	70	JX200-269	30/6/42	1/43	7/43	91876-DA	PBY-5; 8 to Canada, 8 to New Zealand
	(16)	JX570-585				(USN)	PBY-5; 4 to Canada, 33965 to BOAC
San Diego Total	524	(Plus 38 transferred to Lend Lease from USN contracts)					
Canso A	55	9751-9805		10/42	7/43	Canada	To RCAF
PB2B-1	240	72992-73116* 44188-44227	31/12/42	7/43	10/44	NOa-782	Cat. IVB JX270-617; 34 to New Zealand, 7 to Australia
PB2B-2	53	44228-44280*		9/44	2/45	NOa-782	Cat. IV, JX618-662; 47 to Australia; 6 to U.S. Army
PB2B-2	14	JZ828-841		3/45	5/45		
Boeing of Canada Total	362	*USN numbers, but some for RAF also assigned JX numbers					
Canso A	139	9806-9844 11001-11100		4/43	7/44	Canada	To RCAF, 9 to Australia
OA-10A	230	44-33868-34097	25/1/44	12/44	2/45	NOa(a)-296	To USAAF
Canadian Vickers Total	369						
Canadian Total	731						

Serial Numbers Assigned to USAAF OA-10As

Type	Number Built	Identity Numbers
OA-10	5	42-107401-107405
OA-10	6	42-109020-109025
OA-10	12	43-3259-3270
OA-10	25	43-43839-43863
OA-10	6	43-47956-47961
Total		
OA-10	54	
OA-10A	230	44-33868-34097
OA-10B	75	45-57833-57907
Total	359	

PBY Line Drawings

CATALINA LINEAGE

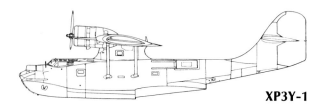

XP3Y-1

XP3Y-1 (Modified Tail)

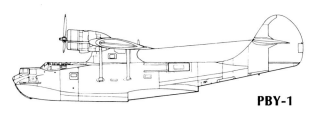

PBY-1

Anchor box and tunnel hatch added.

PBY-2 and PBY-3

PBY-1 had solid rudder and cut-out elevator; PBY-2 and later had solid elevator and cut-out rudder. Note fuselage armor for ice thrown by propellers on PBY-2 and later models.

CATALINA LINEAGE

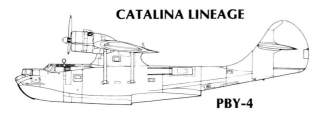

PBY-4

Spinners fitted to PBY-4s only.

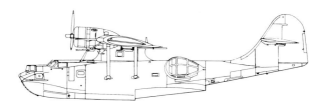

PBY-5

PBY-5A

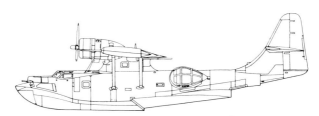

PBN-1 Nomad

Note differences in length, nose and hull steps from PBY-6A.

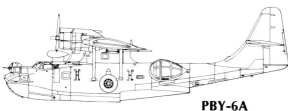

PBY-6A

Eyeball nose turret also fitted to late-model PBY-5A s.

CATALINA SPECIFICATIONS: PBY-5A

Wingspan	104 feet
Length	63 feet 10 inches
Height	20 feet 2 inches
Wing area	14,000 square feet
Gross Weight	34,000 pounds
Power Plant	R-1830-92
Horsepower	1,200
Maximum speed	180 miles per hour
Cruising speed	117 miles per hour
Ceiling	15,000 feet
Range	2,550 miles

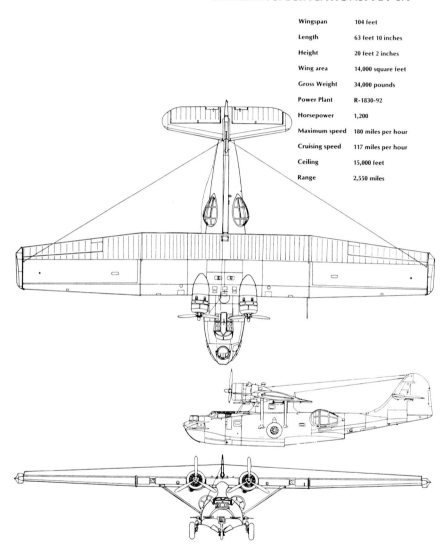

PBY-5A INTERIOR

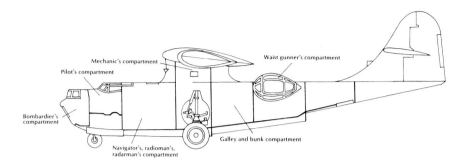

Notes

Chapter 1

[1]All information in this chapter, except as otherwise noted, is drawn from W. Wagner, *Reuben Fleet*, books one through four, 1–172.

[2]Niven, *The Pathfinders*, 51–54.

Chapter 2

[1]Data on General Billy Mitchell's campaign for a single U.S. Air Force, the flight of the PN-9, and its repercussions are drawn from Messimer, *No Margin for Error.*

[2]Toland, *Infamy*, 262–63.

[3]W. Wagner, *Reuben Fleet*, book four, 107–72.

Chapter 3

[1]Lippincott, "The Parallel Development of the Pratt and Whitney R-1830 Twin Wasp Engine."

[2]Except as otherwise noted, all data regarding design and development of the XP3Y-1 are extracted from navy contract file no. 31972, Old Army & Navy Branch, National Archives.

[3]G. Garner Green, letter to author, 12 May 1983.

[4]National Archives, XP3Y-1 contract file.

[5]San Diego Aero-Space Museum, Jackman, "The Wreckers."

[6]W. Wagner, *Reuben Fleet*, 178.

[7]Newspaper clipping courtesy William Wagner.

[8]National Archives, navy contract file no. 31792 (XP3Y-1), Secretary of the Navy Claude Swanson, letter to Chief, Bureau of Aeronautics, 21 June 1935.

[9]W. Wagner, *Reuben Fleet*, 185.

[10]Knott, *The American Flying Boat*, 106.

[11]W. Wagner, *Reuben Fleet*, 185.

Chapter 4

[1]W. Wagner, *Reuben Fleet*, 186.

[2]R. Wagner, *The Story of the PBY Catalina*, 4.

[3]Scarborough, "P-Boat, Consolidated Catalina Design, Development, and Production."

[4]R. Wagner, *The Story of the PBY Catalina*, 4.

[5]Scarborough, "Flying the PBY."

[6]San Diego Aero-Space Museum, Chourre, "Big Boats Can Take It."

[7]W. Wagner, *Reuben Fleet*, 187–88.

[8]San Diego Aero-Space Museum, R. Fleet, "The President's Column."

[9]W. Wagner, *Reuben Fleet*, 188.

[10]San Diego Aero-Space Museum, letter from Kinney to Wheatley.

[11]W. Wagner, *Reuben Fleet*, 189–90.

[12]San Diego Aero-Space Museum, Hemphill, "A Proven Flying Boat."

[13]R. Wagner, *The Story of the PBY Catalina*, 5.

[14]W. Wagner, *Reuben Fleet*, 197.

[15]Scarborough, "Flying the PBY."

[16]W. Wagner, *Reuben Fleet*, 189.

[17]Ibid., 190.

[18]Scoles, "The PBY Story."

[19]W. Wagner, *Reuben Fleet*, 216.

[20]San Diego Aero-Space Museum, "World's Largest [Amphibian]."

[21]San Diego Aero-Space Museum, "Current Designs in Production."

[22]San Diego Aero-Space Museum, "World's Largest [Amphibian]."

[23]R. Wagner, *The Story of the PBY Catalina*, back cover.

[24]W. Wagner, *Reuben Fleet*, 205–06.

[25]Van Vleet and Armstrong, *United States Naval Aviation 1910–1980*, 93.

[26]Ibid., 93.

[27]Scarborough, "Flying the PBY."

[28]Van Vleet and Armstrong, *United States Naval Aviation 1910–1980*, 93.

[29]W. Wagner, *Reuben Fleet*, 214.

[30]Van Vleet and Armstrong, *United States Naval Aviation 1910–1980*, 105.

[31]Scarborough, "'Cause a PBY Don't Fly That High."

[32]Van Vleet and Armstrong, *United States Naval Aviation 1910–1980*, 104.

[33]San Diego Aero-Space Museum, Towers, "The Naval Aviation Expansion Program."

[34]Van Vleet and Armstrong, *United States Naval Aviation 1910–1980*, 105.

[35]W. Green, *War Planes of the Second World War*.

[36]Casagneres, *The Consolidated PBY Catalina*.

[37]Van Vleet and Armstrong, *United States Naval Aviation 1910–1980*, 110.

[38]R. Wagner, *The Story of the PBY Catalina*, back cover.

[39]Van Vleet and Armstrong, *United States Naval Aviation 1910–1980*, 109.

[40]R. Wagner, *The Story of the PBY Catalina*, 14.

Chapter 5

[1]Guba data compiled from W. Wagner, *Reuben Fleet*, 190–94; Scarborough, "P-Boat, The Consolidated PBY Catalina Design"; San Diego Aero-Space Museum, *Consolidator*, December 1937, February, May, June, and September 1938, and December 1940.

[2]W. Wagner, *Reuben Fleet*, 194–95; R. Wagner, *The Story of the PBY Catalina*, 5.

[3]W. Wagner, *Reuben Fleet*, 195–96; San Diego Aero-Space Museum, *Consolidator*, May 1938.

[4]Scarborough, letter to author, 10 March 1984.

[5]San Diego Aero-Space Museum, Hemphill, "Nature Prefers Flying Boats."

[6]San Diego Aero-Space Museum, "PBY and a Mud Puddle."

[7]W. Wagner, *Reuben Fleet*, 196.

[8]Scarborough, letter to author, 10 March 1984.
[9]Ibid.
[10]San Diego Aero-Space Museum, *Consolidator*, November 1939, back cover.
[11]R. Wagner, *The Story of the PBY Catalina*, back cover.

Chapter 6

[1]A. J. Barker, *Pearl Harbor*, 125.
[2]Toland, *Infamy*, 32.
[3]W. A. Barker collection, Bellinger report.
[4]Captain H. C. Smathers, USN (Ret.), telephone interview with author, 19 April 1984.
[5]W. A. Barker collection, Bellinger report.
[6]Poulos, letter to author, 1 June 1984.
[7]W. A. Barker collection, Historical Resume, Kaneohe Bay Naval Air Station, 7 December 1941.
[8]Poulos, letter to author, 1 June 1984.
[9]W. A. Barker collection, Bellinger report.
[10]Sulzberger, *American Heritage Picture History*, 147.
[11]Naval Operational Archives, VP-22 Squadron History.
[12]W. A. Barker collection, Bellinger report.
[13]Naval Operational Archives, VP-24 Action Report, Serial 061, 15 December 1941.
[14]Naval Operational Archives, VP-22 Squadron History.
[15]Naval Operational Archives, VP-24 Action Report.
[16]Zich, *Rising Sun*, 55.
[17]Jablonski, *Airwar*, 19.
[18]Ibid., 21.
[19]Tillman, *Dauntless Dive Bomber of World War II*, 20–21.
[20]W. A. Barker collection, Bellinger report.
[21]W. Wagner, *Reuben Fleet*, 248–49.
[22]Smathers interview.
[23]Naval Operational Archives, VP-24 Action Report.
[24]Ibid.
[25]A. J. Barker, *Pearl Harbor*, 120.
[26]Naval Operational Archives, VP-22 Squadron History.
[27]Naval Operational Archives, VP-24 Action Report.
[28]W. A. Barker collection, Bellinger report.
[29]Poulos, letter to author, 1 June 1984.
[30]Scarborough collection, Johnson, letter to Rosenthal, 25 April 1973.
[31]W. A. Barker collection, Bellinger report.
[32]Knott, *Black Cat Raiders*, 15.
[33]Smathers interview.
[34]W. A. Barker collection, Historical Resume, Kaneohe Bay NAS.
[35]W. A. Barker collection, Martin report.
[36]W. A. Barker collection, Historical Resume, Kaneohe Bay NAS.
[37]W. A. Barker collection, Martin report.
[38]W. A. Barker collection, Historical Resume, Kaneohe Bay NAS.
[39]Jablonski, *Airwar*, 25.
[40]Naval Operational Archives, VP-24 Action Report.
[41]Naval Operational Archives, VP-22 Squadron History.
[42]Hanson, "The Forgotten Warriors."

[43]A. J. Barker, *Pearl Harbor*, 145.
[44]Ibid., 22.
[45]Zich, *The Rising Sun*, 72.
[46]Ibid.
[47]A. J. Barker, *Pearl Harbor*, 9.
[48]Nimitz State Park, Nimitz letter.
[49]Toland, *Infamy*, 263–66.
[50]A. J. Barker, *Pearl Harbor*, 17–18.
[51]Ibid., Introduction.
[52]Knott, *American Flying Boat*, 162–63.
[53]Zich, *Rising Sun*, 51.
[54]A. J. Barker, *Pearl Harbor*, 59.
[55]Knott, *American Flying Boat*, 159.
[56]A. J. Barker, *Pearl Harbor*, 24.
[57]Ibid., 81.
[58]Knott, *American Flying Boat*, 160.
[59]Zich, *Rising Sun*, 53–54.
[60]A. J. Barker, *Pearl Harbor*, 144.
[61]Ibid., 45.
[62]Ibid., 124.

Chapter 7

[1]Knott, *Black Cat Raiders*, 18–19.
[2]Zich, *Rising Sun,* 87.
[3]*American Heritage World War II Chronology,* December 1941.
[4]Zich, *Rising Sun,* 87.
[5]*American Heritage World War II Chronology*, December 1941.
[6]Knott, *Black Cat Raiders*, 21–22.
[7]Ibid.
[8]Messimer, *In the Hands of Fate,* chapter 2.
[9]Knott, *Black Cat Raiders,* 22
[10]Zich, *Rising Sun,* 89–90.
[11]Knott, *Black Cat Raiders,* 24.
[12]Naval Operational Archives, Payne, "The Story of VP-101."
[13]Naval Operational Archives, Christman Action Report, Serial 25, VP-101.
[14]Knott, *Black Cat Raiders,* 30.
[15]Naval Operational Archives, Christman Action Report.
[16]Knott, *Black Cat Raiders,* 31.
[17]Van Vleet and Armstrong, *United States Naval Aviation 1910–1980,* 111.
[18]*American Heritage World War II Chronology,* January 1942.
[19]Knott, *Black Cat Raiders,* 32–34.
[20]*American Heritage World War II Chronology,* January 1942.
[21]Knott, *Black Cat Raiders,* 36.
[22]Ibid., 35.
[23]Messimer, *In the Hands of Fate,* chapter 7.
[24]Van Vleet and Armstrong, *United States Naval Aviation 1910–1980,* 112.
[25]Knott, *Black Cat Raiders,* 36.
[26]Ibid., 38.
[27]Author's collection, Moorer Action Report, 23 February 1942.
[28]Sulzberger, *American Heritage Picture History,* 147.
[29]Knott, *Black Cat Raiders,* 40–42.

[30]Van Vleet and Armstrong, *United States Naval Aviation 1910–1980*, 112.

[31]Salmaggi and Pallavisini, *2194 Days of War*, 221.

[32]Knott, *Black Cat Raiders*, 42.

[33]Sulzberger, *American Heritage Picture History*, 148.

[34]Zich, *Rising Sun*, 94.

[35]*American Heritage World War II Chronology*, March 1942.

[36]Zich, *Rising Sun*, 95.

[37]*American Heritage World War II Chronology*, April 1942.

[38]Zich, *Rising Sun*, 97.

[39]Naval Operational Archives, VP-101 file, Action Report, Operation Flight Gridiron.

[40]Knott, *Black Cat Raiders*, 48.

[41]Zich, *Rising Sun*, 97.

Chapter 8

[1]Prange, Goldstein, and Dillon, *Miracle at Midway*, 13–30.

[2]Ibid., 370–73

[3]Ibid., 24–25.

[4]Ibid., 40–46.

[5]Ibid., 38.

[6]Ibid., 65.

[7]Reid, letter to author, 15 May 1984.

[8]Naval Operational Archives, VP-24 Squadron History.

[9]Prange, Goldstein, and Dillon, *Miracle at Midway*, 60–61.

[10]Ibid., 77.

[11]Ibid., 121.

[12]Ibid., 117–18.

[13]Reid, letter to author, 15 May 1984.

[14]Prange, Goldstein, and Dillon, *Miracle at Midway*, 133, 138–39.

[15]Ibid., 60–61.

[16]Ibid., 49–50.

[17]Ibid., 122.

[18]Ibid., 81.

[19]Ibid.,128–29.

[20]Reid, letter to author, 15 May 1984.

[21]Prange, Goldstein, and Dillon, *Miracle at Midway*, 170–72.

[22]Commander Alan Rothenberg, USN (Ret.), telephone interview with author, 19 April 1984.

[23]Captain H. C. Smathers, USN (Ret.), telephone interview with author, 19 April 1984.

[24]Rothenberg interview.

[25]Smathers interview.

[26]Knott, *Black Cat Raiders*, 55–56.

[27]Naval Operational Archives, VP-24 Squadron History.

[28]Smathers interview.

[29]Knott, *Black Cat Raiders*, 56–57.

[30]Naval Operational Archives, VP-24 Squadron History.

[31]Rothenberg interview.

[32]Smathers interview.

[33]Knott, *Black Cat Raiders*, 58.

[34]Reid, letter to author, 15 May 1984.

[35]Naval Operational Archives, VP-23 file, Ady Action Report.

[36]Naval Operational Archives, VP-23 file, Barthes Action Report.

[37]Naval Operational Archives, VP-23 file, Chase Action Report.

[38]Prange, Goldstein, and Dillon, *Miracle at Midway*, 187–98.

[39]Ibid.,199–206.

[40]Ibid.,207–13.

[41]Haber, letter to author, 25 August 1984.

[42]Prange, Goldstein, and Dillon, *Miracle at Midway*, 212.

[43]Ibid., 224–30.

[44]Ibid., 223–35.

[45]Ibid., 231–36.

[46]Ibid., 261–66.

[47]Ibid., 276–90.

[48]Ibid., 292–300.

[49]Ibid., 308–14.

[50]Ibid., 322.

[51]Naval Operational Archives, VP-23 file, Brady Action Report.

[52]Naval Operational Archives, VP-23 File, Theusen Action Report.

[53]Reid, letter to author, 15 May 1984.

[54]Prange, Goldstein, and Dillon, *Miracle at Midway*, 329.

[55]Ibid., 320.

[56]Ibid., 303–04.

[57]Ibid., 336–42.

[58]Ibid., 349–53.

[59]Ibid., 357.

[60]Ibid., 355.

[61]Gay, *Sole Survivor,* 141–42; 147–48.

[62]Scarborough collection, Mayabb, letter to Scarborough, 7 August 1973.

[63]Prange, Goldstein, and Dillon, *Miracle at Midway,* 273.

[64]Frieze, letter to author, 19 November 1984.

[65]Naval Operational Archives, VP-24 Squadron History.

[66]Smathers, letter to author, 15 August 1984.

[67]Prange, Goldstein, and Dillon, *Miracle at Midway,* 361.

[68]Ibid., 396.

Chapter 9

[1]Prange, Goldstein, and Dillon, *Miracle at Midway,* 23, 337.

[2]Garfield, *Thousand Mile War,* 16.

[3]Ibid., 17–18, 23.

[4]Prange, Goldstein, and Dillon, *Miracle at Midway,* 20.

[5]Ibid., 158.

[6]Garfield, *Thousand Mile War,* 20–21.

[7]Ibid., 117–18.

[8]Ibid., 79.

[9]U.S. Navy Library, Administrative History, Fleet Air Wing 4.

[10]Ibid.

[11]Louis Peterson, former VP-61 pilot, telephone interview with author, 24 May 1984.

[12]Amme, letter to author, 17 April 1984.

[13]Peterson interview.

[14]Garfield, *Thousand Mile War,* 21–23, 135–37.

[15]Prange, Goldstein, and Dillon, *Miracle at Midway*, 152–53.
[16]Garfield, *Thousand Mile War*, 29.
[17]Ibid., 11.
[18]U.S. Navy Library, Administrative History, Fleet Air Wing 4.
[19]Garfield, *Thousand Mile War*, 25.
[20]U.S. Navy Library, Administrative History, Fleet Air Wing 4.
[21]Ibid.
[22]Garfield, *Thousand Mile War*, 32.
[23]U.S. Navy Library, Administrative History, Fleet Air Wing 4.
[24]Naval Operational Archives, VP-42 War Diary.
[25]Garfield, *Thousand Mile War*, 36.
[26]Ibid., 38–39.
[27]Ibid., 40.
[28]Naval Operational Archives, VP-42 War Diary.
[29]Garfield, *Thousand Mile War*, 40–43.
[30]U.S. Navy Library, Administrative History, Fleet Air Wing 4.
[31]Ibid.
[32]Prange, Goldstein, and Dillon, *Miracle at Midway*, 154–55.
[33]Garfield, *Thousand Mile War*, 45.
[34]Ibid., 86–87.
[35]U.S. Navy Library, Administrative History, Fleet Air Wing 4.
[36]Ibid.
[37]Garfield, *Thousand Mile War*, 91–94.
[38]U.S. Navy Library, Administrative History, Fleet Air Wing 4.
[39]Ibid.
[40]Ibid.
[41]Garfield, *Thousand Mile War*, 110–12.
[42]Ibid., 117–18.
[43]Naval Operational Archives, VP-42 War Diary.
[44]Garfield, *Thousand Mile War*, 127–31.
[45]U.S. Navy Library, Administrative History, Fleet Air Wing 4.
[46]Garfield, *Thousand Mile War*, 140–45.
[47]Amme, letter to author, 17 April 1984.
[48]Garfield, *Thousand Mile War*, 145.
[49]Ibid., 146.
[50]Ibid., 139–40.
[51]U.S. Navy Library, Administrative History, Fleet Air Wing 4.
[52]Van Vleet and Armstrong, *United States Naval Aviation 1910–1980*, 119.
[53]U.S. Navy Library, Administrative History, Fleet Air Wing 4.
[54]Garfield, *Thousand Mile War*, 169.
[55]Ibid., 156.
[56]U.S. Navy Library, Administrative History, Fleet Air Wing 4.
[57]Garfield, *Thousand Mile War*, 173–86.
[58]Ibid., 203–68.
[59]U.S. Navy Library, Administrative History, Fleet Air Wing 4.
[60]Garfield, *Thousand Mile War*, 266.
[61]Ibid., 269–74.
[62]Amme, letter to author, 17 April 1984.
[63]Garfield, *Thousand Mile War*, 280–306.
[64]U.S. Navy Library, Administrative History, Fleet Air Wing 4.
[65]Naval Operational Archives, VP-43 War Diary.

⁶⁶Garfield, *Thousand Mile War*, 304.
⁶⁷Naval Operational Archives, Fleet Air Wing Historical Data.
⁶⁸Garfield, *Thousand Mile War*, 301.

Chapter 10

¹*American Heritage World War II Chronology*, May 1942.
²Steinberg, *Island Fighting*, 21–22.
³Knott, *Black Cat Raiders*, 62.
⁴Steinberg, *Island Fighting*, 20.
⁵Ibid., 22–23.
⁶Naval Operational Archives, Fleet Air Wing Historical Data.
⁷Coley, letter to author, 2 May 1984.
⁸Knott, *Black Cat Raiders*, 64.
⁹Scarborough collection, Attrition Report on PBY Patrol Planes.
¹⁰Knott, *Black Cat Raiders*, 64.
¹¹Steinberg, *Island Fighting*, 23–24, 29.
¹²Ibid., 28–29.
¹³Scarborough collection, Clark Action Report.
¹⁴Knott, *Black Cat Raiders*, 66.
¹⁵Ibid.
¹⁶Hoyt, *Guadalcanal*, 142–44, 153–57.
¹⁷Knott, *Black Cat Raiders*, 68.
¹⁸Ibid.
¹⁹Coley, letter to author, 2 May 1984.
²⁰Commander Alan Rothenberg, USN (Ret.), telephone interview with author, 8 April 1984.
²¹Ibid.
²²Coley, letter to author, 2 May 1984.
²³Knott, *Black Cat Raiders*, 72.
²⁴Rothenberg interview.
²⁵Knott, *Black Cat Raiders*, 84.
²⁶U.S. Navy Library, Administrative History, Fleet Air Wing 17.
²⁷Coley, letter to author, 2 May 1984.
²⁸U.S. Navy Library, Administrative History, Fleet Air Wing 17.
²⁹Coley, letter to author, 2 May 1984.
³⁰Knott, *Black Cat Raiders*, 78.
³¹Ibid., 73–74.
³²Hoyt, *Guadalcanal*, 183–200.
³³Scarborough collection, Atwell Action Report.
³⁴Hoyt, *Guadalcanal*, 212–22.
³⁵Ibid., 246–52.
³⁶Knott, *Black Cat Raiders*, 100.
³⁷Ibid., 84–101.
³⁸Hoyt, *Guadalcanal*, 267–69.
³⁹Knott, *Black Cat Raiders*, 101.
⁴⁰Ibid., 103.
⁴¹Steinberg, *Island Fighting*, 73–74.
⁴²Ibid., 75
⁴³Knott, *Black Cat Raiders*, 109.
⁴⁴Ibid., 112.
⁴⁵Ibid., 114.

[46]Ibid., 116.
[47]Ibid., 117
[48]Bogart, "Black Cats of Green Island."
[49]Poulos, letter to author, June 1984.

Chapter 11

[1]Steinberg, *Island Fighting*, 75–87.
[2]Knott, *Black Cat Raiders*, 120–21.
[3]Naval Operational Archives, Fleet Air Wing Historical Data.
[4]Naval Operational Archives, VP-11 file, Hine Action Report.
[5]Knott, *Black Cat Raiders*, 121–29.
[6]Naval Operational Archives, VP-11 Action Report.
[7]Knott, *Black Cat Raiders*, 131–33, 135–37.
[8]Ibid., 139.
[9]Ibid., 139–40.
[10]U.S. Navy Library, Administrative History, Fleet Air Wing 17.
[11]Naval Operational Archives, VP-34 Squadron History.
[12]Knott, *Black Cat Raiders*, 143–44; Naval Operational Archives, VP-34 Squadron History.
[13]U.S. Navy Library, Administrative History, Fleet Air Wing 17.
[14]Rawlings, "I Heard the Black Cats Singing."
[15]Naval Operational Archives, VP-33 Squadron History.
[16]Knott, *Black Cat Raiders*, 157.
[17]Steinberg, *Island Fighting*, 91.
[18]U.S. Navy Library, Administrative History, Fleet Air Wing 17.
[19]Naval Operational Archives, VP-34 Squadron History.
[20]Knott, *Black Cat Raiders*, 158.
[21]Naval Operational Archives, VP-34 Squadron History.
[22]U.S. Navy Library, Administrative History, Fleet Air Wing 17.
[23]Knott, *Black Cat Raiders*, 160–70.
[24]Naval Operational Archives, VP-33 Action Report.
[25]Ibid.
[26]Knott, *Black Cat Raiders*, 170–73.
[27]Ibid., 174.
[28]U.S. Navy Library, Administrative History, Fleet Air Wing 17.
[29]Ibid.
[30]Knott, *Black Cat Raiders*, 175–82.
[31]U.S. Navy Library, Administrative History, Fleet Air Wing 17.
[32]Ibid.
[33]Ibid.

Chapter 12

[1]Salmaggi and Pallavisini, *2194 Days of War*, 26.
[2]Van Vleet and Armstrong, *United States Naval Aviation 1910–1980*, 107.
[3]U.S. Navy Library, Kammen, Operational History of the Flying Boat.
[4]Ibid.; Scarborough, letter to author, 24 June 1984.
[5]Van Vleet and Armstrong, *United States Naval Aviation 1910–1980*, 108.
[6]Scarborough, letter to author, 24 June 1984.
[7]U.S. Navy Library, Kammen, Operational History of the Flying Boat.
[8]Naval Operational Archives, VP-73 War Diary.
[9]U.S. Navy Library, Kammen, Operational History of the Flying Boat; Naval Operational Archives, VP-73 War Diary.

[10]U.S. Navy Library, Kammen, Operational History of the Flying Boat.
[11]Naval Operational Archives, VP-73 War Diary.
[12]Ibid.
[13]U.S. Navy Library, Kammen, Operational History of the Flying Boat.
[14]Naval Operational Archives, VP-73 War Diary.
[15]Ibid.
[16]Salmaggi and Pallavisini, *2194 Days of War,* 278.
[17]Naval Operational Archives, Fleet Air Wing Historical Data.
[18]U.S. Navy Library, Administrative History, Fleet Air Wing 3.
[19]U.S. Navy Library, Kammen, Operational History of the Flying Boat.
[20]Naval Operational Archives, VP-92 Squadron History.
[21]U.S. Navy Library, Administrative History, Fleet Air Wing 16.

Chapter 13

[1]Salmaggi and Pallavisini, *2194 Days of War,* 312–13.
[2]U.S. Navy Library, Administrative History, Fleet Air Wing 15.
[3]Naval Operational Archives, VP-73 War Diary.
[4]U.S. Navy Library, Administrative History, Fleet Air Wing 15.
[5]Naval Operational Archives, VP-92 Squadron History.
[6]Naval Operational Archives, VP-73 War Diary.
[7]U.S. Navy Library, Administrative History, Fleet Air Wing 15.
[8]Naval Operational Archives, VP-73 War Diary.
[9]U.S. Navy Library, Administrative History, Fleet Air Wing 15.
[10]Naval Operational Archives, VP-73 War Diary.
[11]U.S. Navy Library, Administrative History, Fleet Air Wing 15.
[12]Ibid.
[13]Ibid.; Naval Operational Archives, VP-73 War Diary.
[14]U.S. Navy Library, Administrative History, Fleet Air Wing 15.
[15]Hutchings, "The MAD CATS of Patrol Squadron Sixty-Three."
[16]Naval Operational Archives, VP-63 Action Report.
[17]Hutchings, "The MAD CATS of Patrol Squadron Sixty-Three."
[18]U.S. Navy Library, Administrative History, Fleet Air Wing 15.
[19]Ibid.
[20]Hutchings, "The MAD CATS of Patrol Squadron Sixty-Three."
[21]Ibid.; U.S. Navy Library, Administrative History, Fleet Air Wing 15; Naval
Operational Archives, VP-63 Action Report.
[22]Hutchings, "The MAD CATS of Patrol Squadron Sixty-Three."
[23]Ibid.; Naval Operational Archives, VP-63 Action Report.
[24]Hutchings, "The MAD CATS of Patrol Squadron Sixty-Three."
[25]Ibid.; U.S. Navy Library, Administrative History, Fleet Air Wing 15.
[26]Hutchings, "The MAD CATS of Patrol Squadron Sixty-Three."
[27]Naval Operational Archives, VP-63 Action Report.
[28]Hutchings, "The MAD CATS of Patrol Squadron Sixty-Three."
[29]Naval Operational Archives, VP-63 Action Report.
[30]Hutchings, "The MAD CATS of Patrol Squadron Sixty-Three."

Chapter 14

[1]Willoughby, *U.S. Coast Guard in World War II,* chapter three.
[2]Department of Transportation, U.S. Coast Guard, *Air Search and Rescue.*
[3]Willoughby, *U.S. Coast Guard in World War II.*
[4]Barrow, "VP Coast Guard Style."
[5]Willoughby, *U.S. Coast Guard in World War II.*

[6]Department of Transportation, U.S. Coast Guard, *Air Search and Rescue.*

Chapter 15

[1]Simpson Historical Research Center, Air-Sea Rescue 1941–1945, United States Air Force Historical Study No. 95.

[2]Simpson Historical Research Center, 1st Emergency Rescue Squadron War Diary.

[3]Simpson Historical Research Center, Air-Sea Rescue 1941–1945.

[4]Simpson Historical Research Center, 1st Emergency Rescue Squadron War Diary.

[5]Simpson Historical Research Center, Air-Sea Rescue 1941–1945.

[6]Ibid.; Myers, letter to author, 11 July 1983.

[7]Simpson Historical Research Center, 2nd Emergency Rescue Squadron War Diary.

[8]Simpson Historical Research Center, Air-Sea Rescue 1941–1945.

[9]Simpson Historical Research Center, 2nd Emergency Rescue Squadron War Diary.

[10]Simpson Historical Research Center, Air-Sea Rescue 1941–1945.

[11]Simpson Historical Research Center, 2nd Emergency Rescue Squadron War Diary.

[12]Simpson Historical Research Center, Air-Sea Rescue 1941–1945.

[13]Simpson Historical Research Center, 2nd Emergency Rescue Squadron War Diary.

[14]Simpson Historical Research Center, 3rd Emergency Rescue Squadron War Diary.

[15]Simpson Historical Research Center, Air-Sea Rescue 1941–1945.

[16]Simpson Historical Research Center, 3rd Emergency Rescue Squadron War Diary.

[17]Simpson Historical Research Center, Air-Sea Rescue 1941–1945.

[18]Ibid.

Chapter 16

[1]Author's collection, Air Ministry paper AM.3/77, "The Consolidated Catalina in Royal Air Force Service."

[2]Ibid.

[3]Casagneres, *The Consolidated PBY Catalina*

[4]Author's collection, Air Ministry paper AM.3/77, "The Consolidated Catalina in Royal Air Force Service."

[5]Ryan, "*Parade* Helps Two Foes"; "The Sighting of the Bismarck," AAHS Journal.

[6]Data on Catalina-equipped RAF squadrons compiled from Rawlings, *Coastal, Support and Special Squadrons of the RAF and Their Aircraft;* Halley, *The Squadrons of the Royal Air Force;* author's collection, Air Ministry paper AM.3/77, "The Consolidated Catalina in Royal Air Force Service."

[7]Author's collection, Air Ministry paper AM.3/77, "The Consolidated Catalina in Royal Air Force Service."

[8]Molson and Taylor, *Canadian Aircraft Since 1909*, 203–09.

[9]Author's collection, National Museum of Science and Technology, Aviation and Science Division, "Military History."

Chapter 17

[1]Vincent, *Catalina Chronicle*, 8–92.

[2]Ewing et al., *New Zealand Military Aircraft 1913–1977*, 17.

[3]Author's collection, Museum of Transport and Technology of New Zealand Inc., "Catalina Flying Boats."

[4]Darby, *The First Decade 1937–46*, 85.

[5]Author's collection, Military Information Bureau, Office of the Chief of the South African Defense Force, "The Role Played by the Catalina Flying Boat."

[6]Jackson, "East Indies Catalinas"; Geldhof, letter to author, 26 June 1984.

Chapter 18

[1]Naval Operational Archives, VP-73 War Diary.

[2]Scarborough, *PBY in Action*, 48.

[3]Department of Transportation, U.S. Coast Guard, *Air Search and Rescue.*

[4]Simpson Historical Research Center, Air-Sea Rescue 1941–1945, United States Air Force Historical Study No. 95.

[5]Endicott, letter to author, 11 July 1983.

[6]Author's collection, Air Ministry paper AM.3/77, "The Consolidated Catalina in Royal Air Force Service."

[7]Molson and Taylor, *Canadian Aircraft Since 1909*, 203–09.

[8]Vincent, *Catalina Chronicle*, 93–96.

[9]Author's collection, Museum of Transport and Technology of New Zealand Inc., "Catalina Flying Boats."

[10]Geldhof, letter to author, 17 September 1984.

[11]Bushnell, "Consolidated PBY Catalina."

[12]Hall, "Modelling Danish Cats."

[13]Turner, "Last Cat Up The Amazon?"

[14]Smith, "Adventure of the Amazon Cats."

[15]Nunez, "Argentine Navy PBY Cansos."

[16]Bushnell, "Consolidated PBY Catalina."

[17]Bovelt, "Catalinas in the South Pacific."

[18]Vincent, *Catalina Chronicle*, 97–100.

[19]Rendel, *Civil Aviation in New Zealand*, 59.

[20]Callaghan, "The Strange Fate of Miss Macau."

[21]Jackson, "East Indies Catalinas."

[22]Geldhof, letter to author, 17 September 1984.

[23]Fortner, "Catalinas in Chile."

[24]Hotson, *The de Havilland Canada Story.*

[25]Scarborough, "The Consolidated PBY—Catalina to Canso."

[26]Linkewich, *Air Attack on Forest Fires.*

[27]Scarborough collection, Bird Corporation, "Bird Innovator."

[28]Ace Deemers, Madras Air Service, Madras, Washington, telephone interview with author, 18 September 1984.

[29]Robinson, "Antilles Air Boats of the Virgin Islands."

[30]Rozell, "On the Nile with Cousteau and the Flying Calypso."

[31]Schiefelbein, "The Cousteau Clan."

[32]Author's collection, Confederate Air Force Headquarters, "The Confederate Air Force PBY-5A Catalina."

[33]Linkewich, *Air Attack on Forest Fires.*

[34]J. Knox Hawkshaw, vice president, Field Aviation, Toronto, Canada, interview with author, 2 May 1984.

[35]Jim Pengelly, former water bomber pilot, Avalon Aviation, Parry Sound, Ontario, Canada, interview with author, 29 April 1984.

[36]Hawkshaw interview.

[37]Pengelly and Hawkshaw interviews.

[38]Pengelly interview.

[39]Bob Schlaefli, Schlafco, Inc., Moses Lake, Washington, telephone interview with author, 17 September 1984.

[40]Canadian civil aircraft registry, 1983, 294–95.

[41]Bruce Powell, managing director, Powell Corporation, interview with author, 30 April 1984.

[42]Hawkshaw interview.

[43]Powell interview.

Bibliography

Printed Sources

American Heritage World War II Chronology. New York: American Heritage Publishing Co., 1978.

Angelucci, Enzo. *The Rand McNally Encyclopedia of Military Aircraft 1914–1980.* New York: The Military Press, 1983.

Barker, A. J. *Pearl Harbor.* Ballantine's Illustrated Battle Book Number 10. New York: Ballantine Books, 1969.

Barrow, Jess, Commander USCG (Ret.). "VP Coast Guard Style." *Naval Aviation News* (May 1983).

Bogart, Gerald, Captain USN (Ret.). "The Black Cats of Green Island." *Foundation* (Naval Aviation Museum Foundation) (March 1982).

Bovelt, Allan. "Catalinas in the South Pacific." *Journal* (American Aviation Historical Society) Vol. 16, no. 4 (Winter 1971).

Bushnell, Bill and Sue. "Consolidated PBY Catalina." *Scale Aircraft Modelling* (May 1983).

Callaghan, Leon. "The Strange Fate of Miss Macau." *Air Pictorial* (December 1983).

Casagneres, Everett. *The Consolidated PBY Catalina.* Surrey, England: Profile Publications, no. 183.

Chorley, Desmond. "Recast Cansos." *Canadian Aviation* (October 1982).

Cohen, Stan. *The Forgotten War.* Altona, Manitoba, Canada: D. W. Friesen and Sons, 1981.

Committee on Veterans Affairs, U.S. Senate. *Medal of Honor Recipients 1863–1978.* Washington, D.C.: Government Printing Office, no. 6-489 0.

Darby, Charles. *RNZAF: The First Decade 1937–1946.* Melbourne, Australia: Kookaburra Technical Publications, 1978.

Department of Transportation, U.S. Coast Guard. *Air Search and Rescue: Sixty-Three Years of Aerial Search and Lifesaving.* Washington, D.C.: Government Printing Office, 1978.

Ewing, Ross, Ross Dunlop, David Duxbury, and Ross Macpherson. *New Zealand Military Aircraft 1913–1977.* Aeronautical Press, 1977.

Fortner, Alberto P. "Catalinas in Chile." *Air Pictorial* (July 1983).

Fushida, Mitsuo, and Masatoke Okumiya. *Midway: The Battle That Doomed Japan.* Annapolis, Md.: Naval Institute Press, 1955.

Garfield, Brian. *The Thousand Mile War*. New York: Bantam Books, 1982.

Gay, George. *Sole Survivor*. Naples, Fla.: Midway Publishers, 1980.

Green, William, and Gordon Swanborough. *Royal Air Force Yearbook 1980*. Ducimus Books.

Green, William. *Warplanes of the Second World War: Flying Boats*. Vol. 5. Garden City, N.Y.: Doubleday and Company, 1962.

Hall, Allan. "Modelling Danish Cats." *Scale Aircraft Modelling* (June 1969).

Halley, James J. *The Squadrons of the Royal Air Force*. Kent, England: Air-Britain, 1980.

Hanson, Murray, Captain USN (Ret.). "Kaneohe: The Forgotten Warriors." *The Retired Officer* (Retired Officers Association) (December 1979).

Heape, A. G. "Cathay Pacific Airways." *Air Britain Digest* (March–April 1982).

Hotson, Fred W. *The de Havilland Canada Story*. Toronto: Canav Books.

Hoyt, Edwin P. *Guadalcanal*. New York: Stein and Day, 1981.

Hutchings, Curtiss, RADM USN (Ret.). "The MAD CATS of Patrol Squadron Sixty-Three." *Foundation* (Naval Aviation Museum Foundation) (1984).

Jablonski, Edward. *Airwar*. Vol. 1, book 1. Garden City, N.Y.: Doubleday and Company, 1971.

Jackson, Paul. "East Indies Catalinas." *Aviation News*.

Knott, Richard C., Captain, USN. *The American Flying Boat*. Annapolis, Md.: Naval Institute Press, 1979.

———. *Black Cat Raiders of World War II*. Annapolis, Md.: Nautical and Aviation Publishing, 1981.

Linkewich, Alexander. *Air Attack on Forest Fires*. Calgary, Alberta, Canada: D. W. Friesen and Sons, 1972.

Lippincott, Harvey. "The Parallel Development of the Pratt and Whitney R-1830 Twin Wasp Engine." *Journal* (American Aviation Historical Society), Vol. 16, no. 1 (Spring 1971).

Messimer, Dwight. *No Margin for Error*. Annapolis, Md.: Naval Institute Press, 1981.

———. *In the Hands of Fate: The Story of Patrol Wing 10*. Annapolis, Md.: Naval Institute Press, 1984.

Molson, K. M., and H. A. Taylor. *Canadian Aircraft Since 1909*. Stittsville, Ontario, Canada: Canada's Wings, 1982.

Niven, David. *The Pathfinders*. Chicago: Time-Life Books, 1980.

Nunez, Jorge Felix. "Argentine Navy PBY Cansos." *Propliner* (July–September 1980).

Poulos, George F. "Recollections of a PBY Pilot." *Naval Aviation News* (August 1982).

Prange, Gordon, Donald Goldstein, and Kathryn Dillon. *At Dawn We Slept: The Untold Story of Pearl Harbor*. New York: McGraw-Hill, 1981.

———. *Miracle at Midway*. New York: McGraw-Hill, 1982

Rawlings, Charles. "I Heard the Black Cats Singing." *The Saturday Evening Post* (2 December 1944).

Rawlings, John D. R. *Coastal, Support, and Special Squadrons of the RAF and Their Aircraft*. London: Jane's Publishing Company, 1982.

Rendel, David. *Civil Aviation in New Zealand: An Illustrated History*. Wellington: A. H. and A. W. Reed, 1975.

Robinson, Dr. Douglas. "Antilles Air Boats of the Virgin Islands." *Journal* (American Aviation Historical Society), Vol. 18, no. 2 (Summer 1973).

Rozelle, Roger. "On the Nile with Cousteau and the Flying Calypso." *AOPA Pilot* (February 1979).

Ryan, Bill. "Parade Helps Two Foes Remember The Way They Were." *Parade* (4 January 1981).

Salmaggi, Cesare, and Alfred Pallavisini. *2194 Days of War*. New York: Gallery Books, 1977.

Scarborough, William E., Captain USN (Ret.). "The Consolidated PBY—Catalina to Canso." *Journal* (American Aviation Historical Society), Vol. 16, nos. 1,2,3 (1971).

————. "Flying the PBY." *Airpower* (May 1975).

————. "P-Boat, the Consolidated PBY Catalina Design, Development, and Production." *Wings* (April 1975) and *Airpower* (May 1975).

————. "'Cause a PBY Don't Fly That High." *Naval Institute Proceedings* (April 1978).

————. *PBY in Action*. Carrollton, Tex.: Squadron Signal Publications, 1983.

Schiefelbein, Susan. "The Cousteau Clan." *The Dial* (WNET/Thirteen) (July 1982).

Scoles, Albert, RADM USN (Ret.). "The PBY Story." *Shipmate* (United States Naval Academy Alumni Association) (March 1981).

Smith, Gene. "Adventure of the Amazon Cats." *Air Progress* (April 1984).

Steinberg, Rafael. *Island Fighting*. Chicago: Time-Life Books, 1978.

Sulzberger, C. L. *The American Heritage Picture History of World War II*. New York: American Heritage, 1966.

"The Sighting of the Bismarck." *Journal* (American Aviation Historical Society), Vol. 16, no. 2 (Summer 1971).

Thornburn, Lois and Don. *No Tumult, No Shouting*. New York: Henry Holt and Company, 1945.

Tillman, Barrett. *The Dauntless Dive Bomber of World War II*. Annapolis, Md.: Naval Institute Press, 1977.

Toland, John. *Infamy*. Garden City, N.Y.: Doubleday, 1982.

Turner, Michael. "Last Cat Up the Amazon?" *Aeroplane Monthly* (July 1982).

Van Vleet, Clarke, and William J. Armstrong. *United States Naval Aviation 1910–1980*. NAVAIR 00-80P-1. Washington, D.C.: U.S. Government Printing Office, 1981.

Vincent, David. *Catalina Chronicle: A History of RAAF Operations*. Adelaide, South Australia: LPH, 1978.

Wagner, Ray. *American Combat Planes*. 3d ed. Garden City, N.Y.: Doubleday, 1982.

Wagner, Ray. *The Story of the PBY Catalina*. San Diego: Flight Classics, 1972.

Wagner, William. *Reuben Fleet and the Story of Consolidated Aircraft*. Fallbrook, Calif: Aero Publishers, 1976.

Willoughby, Malcolm F. Lieutenant, USCG. *The U.S. Coast Guard in World War II*. Annapolis, Md.: United States Naval Institute.

Zich, Arthur. *The Rising Sun*. Chicago: Time-Life Books, 1977.

Archival Depositories

Admiral Nimitz State Park, P.O. Box 777, Fredericksburg, Texas 78624.
Letter, Ensign Chester Nimitz to father, 11 December 1907.

National Archives, Washington, D.C. 20408.
Navy Contract file no. 31972 (XP3Y-1), Old Army and Navy Branch.

Naval Operational Archives, Washington Navy Yard, Washington, D.C. 20374
Squadron Histories and War Diaries:

        VP-22
        VP-24
        VP-33
        VP-34
        VP-42
        VP-43
        VP-73
        VP-92

    Squadron Action Report files:
        VP-11
        VP-23
        VP-24
        VP-63
        VP-101

    Miscellaneous:
    Fleet Air Wing and Fleet Airship Wing Historical Data, World War II (bound
        statistics).
    Payne, Earl D., Lieutenant (j.g.). "The VP-101 Story." (manuscript).

San Diego Aero-Space Museum, 2001 Pan American Plaza, Balboa Park, San
    Diego, California 92101.
    Bound issues of the *Consolidator*, employee publication of Consolidated Aircraft
        Corporation 1936 through 1941, containing:
        Chourre, Lieutenant Commander, USN, inspector of naval aircraft. "Big
            Boats Can Take It." (September 1936).
        "Current Designs in Production." (December 1940).
        Fleet, Reuben. "The President's Column." (January 1938).
        Guba (series) (December 1937, February, May, June, September 1938, De-
            cember 1940.
        Hemphill, T. M. "A Proven Flying Boat." (May 1938).
        Hemphill, T. M. "Nature Prefers Flying Boats." (June 1938).
        Jackman, Ken. "The Wreckers." (December 1936). Engineer in charge of
            physical testing.
        Letter, Charles Kinney to Bill Wheatley, 25 June 1938, August 1938.
        "PBY and a Mud Puddle." February 1941.
        Statistics. back cover. (November 1939).
        Towers, John H., RADM. "The Naval Aviation Expansion Program." (De-
            cember 1940).
        "World's Largest [Amphibian]." (January 1940).

Albert H. Simpson Historical Research Center, Maxwell Air Force Base, Ala-
    bama, 36112.
    Air-Sea Rescue 1941–1945; U.S. Air Force Historical Study Number 95 (man-
        uscript).
    Squadron histories:
        1st Emergency Rescue Squadron
        2nd Emergency Rescue Squadron
        3rd Emergency Rescue Squadron

United States Navy Library, Washington Navy Yard, Washington, D.C. 20374.

    Administrative Histories:
        Fleet Air Wing 3

Fleet Air Wing 4
Fleet Air Wing 15
Fleet Air Wing 16
Fleet Air Wing 17
Kammen, Michael G. "Operational History of the Flying Boat, Open Sea and Seadrome Aspects, Atlantic Theatre, World War II, July 1960." (manuscript).

Private Collections

The Author's Collection

Letters:
Amme, Carl, Captain, USN (Ret.). 17 April 1984. Former executive officer, VP-43.
Coley, Jack, Captain, USN (Ret.). 2 May 1984. Former VP-11 pilot.
Endicott, Judy. 11 July 1983. Chief of circulation, Simpson Historical Research Center.
Frieze, Conrad. 19 November 1984. Former VP-11 crewman.
Geldhof, Nico. 26 June 1984, 17 September 1984. Naval historian, The Netherlands.
Green, G. Garner. 12 May 1983. Stress analyst for Consolidated at time of XP3Y-1 development, later chief structures engineer.
Haber, Norman, M.D. 25 August 1984. Former VP-24 pilot.
Myers, L. M. 11 July 1983. Former sergeant, 2nd Emergency Rescue Squadron.
Poulos, George F. 1 June 1984. Former VP-11 pilot.
Reid, Jewell (Jack), Captain, USN (Ret.). 15 May 1984.
Scarborough, W. E., Captain, USN (Ret.). 10 March 1984, 24 June 1984.
Smathers, H. C., Captain, USN (Ret.). 15 August 1984.

Miscellaneous:
Action Report, Lieutenant Thomas Moorer, VP-101, 23 February 1942.
Air Ministry paper AM. 3/77, "The Consolidated Catalina in Royal Air Force Service" (leaflet).
Military Information Bureau, Office of the Chief of the South African Defence Force, Pretoria. "The Role Played by the Catalina Flying Boat in the Southern African and Indian Ocean Areas 1942–1946." (manuscript).
Museum of Transport and Technology of New Zealand, Inc., Auckland. "Catalina PBY Flying Boats." (pamphlet).
National Museum of Science and Technology, Aviation and Space Division, Ottawa, Canada. "Military History: Introduction of the PBY into the RCAF, Operational Histories of PBY Squadrons in the RCAF Commands and Those Attached to the RAF." (manuscript).
Confederate Air Force Headquarters, P.O. Box CAF, Harlingen, Texas, 78551. "The Confederate Air Force PBY-5A Catalina." (pamphlet).

W. A. Barker Collection
Report of Admiral Patrick Bellinger to Commander in Chief, United States Pacific Fleet, 20 December 1941, PW2/A16-3/0850.
Historical Resume, Kaneohe Naval Air Station, 7 December 1941.
Report of H. M. Martin, commanding officer, Naval Air Station, Kaneohe Bay, 8 December 1941.

Scarborough Collection.

Action Reports:
Clark, R.B., Lieutenant (j.g.), VP-14, 26 August 1942.
Atwell, M.K., Lieutenant, VP-91, 27 October 1942.
Attrition Report, PBY-5 Patrol Planes, Lieutenant C.C. Colt, Naval Combat Air Intelligence, September 1942.
Bird Corporation, "Bird Innovator," Palm Springs, California (advertising brochure).

Letters:
Johnson, Norris A., Captain, USN (Ret.), to Vice Admiral C. E. Rosenthal. 25 April 1973.
Mayabb, Virgil, Commander, USN (Ret.), to Scarborough, 7 August, 1973.

Index